The Legacy of North Dakota's Country Schools

The Legacy of North Dakota's Country Schools

Warren A. Henke and Everett C. Albers, Editors

**The North Dakota
Humanities Council, Inc.
Bismarck, North Dakota 58501
*1998***

This book is dedicated to the tens of thousands of teachers who enriched the lives of the hundreds of thousands who attended North Dakota Country schools.

Editors: *Warren A. Henke and Everett C. Albers*

Designer: *Otto Design of Bismarck, ND*

Published by The North Dakota Humanities Council, Inc.
Printed in the United States of America

First Edition

International Standard Book Number: 0-9654579-1-5

Library of Congress Catalog Card Number: 97-75977

This book is printed on acid-free paper which meets the minimum requirements of the American National Standard for Information Sciences—Permanence of Paper for Printed Library Materials, ANSI Z39.48-1992.

To our wives, Rose Marie Fiechtner Henke and Leslie Kubik Albers
you teach us something every day. You found all the errors
and gave us good advice. Any mistakes still here are those
we failed to correct, and any other shortcomings well may
be our failure to follow your counsel. We give you an A+.

Acknowledgements

Thank you . . .

The Legacy of North Dakota's Country Schools came about after the completion of a 1980-82 project of the Mountain Plains Library Association funded by the National Endowment for the Humanities. Participating scholars collected photographs, artifacts, and essays by former teachers and students of country schools in the Dakotas, Colorado, Wyoming, Nevada, Nebraska and Kansas.

William Sherman, P.V. Thorson, Robert and Mary Carlson, and Warren A. Henke of North Dakota were among those who took part in that program; their essays for that project are major chapters in this book.

The North Dakota Centennial Commission made a major award in 1989 to help bring this book about. We thank the people of North Dakota for that grant. We also thank Corliss Mushik and her organization of North Dakota women legislators for helping to meet part of the cost of preparing this book for printing.

The editors thank John Bye and the North Dakota Institute for Regional Studies and Todd Strand at the State Historical Society of North Dakota for their help in gathering photographs.

Nearly one hundred country school teachers and former students have contributed to this book, which is much more theirs than ours. We thank them for the privilege of putting their stories on the pages which follow.

Illustrations

An early unknown school in North Dakota —
croquet mallets and balls lie next to the building; an American flag flies above the small garden lower-right. *(SHSND)*

Contents

Preface

Warren A. Henke

HISTORY IS FOR EVERYONE. In very simplified terms, historians attempt to explain life to the multitude. Among the scores of definitions of history is Frederic W. Maitland's. He says that history is "not what happened but what people thought or said about it." In the essays that follow, scholars share their thoughts and conclusions, and teachers and pupils share their memories about the country school experience in North Dakota. Elias Lieberman says that memory is "all we really own." The reader, then, is fortunate to share in some of the unique and priceless possessions of the contributors. For those who were part of the country school experience, it is reminiscing; for those who were not, it is revealing.

For hundreds of years Native Americans who occupied what is now North Dakota taught their children survival skills and instructed them in tribal religion, history, and customs. Ancestral knowledge, origin traditions, major historic events, particular narratives for teaching certain concepts, along with humorous stories were passed on orally, generation to generation. Native American men often took their sons on hunts to demonstrate techniques and explain its purpose. Likewise, daughters were introduced by tribal women to their distinctive role in the daily activities of the tribe.

Northern Dakota was remote, little known, and all but uninhabited by white settlers when Dakota Territory was created on March 2, 1861. Only one had been organized the previous summer at Bon Homme, South Dakota, where Emma Bradford taught nine students in a log cabin.[1] A plan for classroom-directed education, familiar to modern readers, began in the territory when its first legislative assembly, meeting in 1862, enacted laws establishing a school system. Legislators decided that territorial schools would "at all times be equally free and accessible to all white children over five and under twenty-one years."[2] Two years later a board of education was established, and in 1868 legislation deleted the word "white."[3] There is some controversy over the location of the state's first public school. Some credit Linda Slaughter for establishing it in the summer of 1873 in Bismarck. Teaching a three-month term, Aidee Warfel conducted classes in the Congregational Church at Sixth Street and Thayer. Two years later 105 students were enrolled in the one-teacher school.[4] In 1875 Pembina citizens built the first officially recorded public school building in present day North Dakota.[5]

Two waves of immigrants completed the settlement of North Dakota. During the Great Dakota Boom, 1878-1886, thousands of settlers poured into northern Dakota, increasing its population from 16,000 in 1878 to 191,000 in 1890. Beginning in 1898 and continuing to World War I, a Second Boom brought an additional 250,000 settlers to the state, many of whom settled in the Missouri Plateau region. Railroad mileage almost doubled and homesteading peaked.

Unable to contribute immediately to the development of central schools, the scattered homesteaders created a rural society dotted with one of the state's most ubiquitous and certainly one of its most important artifacts: the one-room country school. That institution lingered on and dominated elementary education in many communities well into the twentieth century.

By 1883 territorial Dakota boasted of 385 public schools employing 426 teachers that were, on the average, attended by 6,927 students each year. Almost all, 98.9 percent, were one-room; each had an average attendance of 15.2 students.[6] The notion that states should establish funds to finance schools can be traced back to the colonial period. Connecticut created a "literary" or school fund as early as 1750; and New York followed suit in 1782, the same year that talks produced a preliminary treaty between the British and Americans to end the American Revolution. Under the Articles of Confederation the congress enacted legislation, between 1784 and 1787, that established a land policy for the future development of the West. One act, the Land Ordinance of 1785, would play an important role in developing public schools in states that would be carved out of the new national domain. It specified that land in the Northwest be surveyed into townships six miles square and that each township to be divided into 36 sections one mile square or 640 acres. Income from section sixteen was reserved for the support of schools. During the next two decades the public endorsed the concept, and by 1803 when Ohio was admitted to the union, it was granted section sixteen of each township for educational purposes. Given discretion to distribute funds obtained from the grant, it gave aid to public or private schools at first.[7]

Acquiring millions of acres of land from the federal government for educational and other public purposes was one of the greatest advantages of moving from territorial status to statehood. Under the Enabling Act of February 22, 1889, North Dakota was granted a total of 3,191,770.28 acres of land; 2,523,385 acres "for the support of common schools"; and additional grants totaling approximately 668,000 acres to support particular institutions.[8]Unfortunately, under Territorial government, there was no legal provision for deriving revenue from "school lands."

> The school section had come to be regarded as common plunder, subject only to the right of possession. Many lands had been cultivated, others fenced and pastured, and a still larger quantity used for herding and hay purposes. This prescriptive right had almost come to be considered, in some instances, a legal one. . . . This erroneous idea . . . was, in some cases, allowed to be kept in mind and to govern in the leasing of these lands as provided this present year. Bidders were naturally governed by self interest, and desirous of renting land at as low a price as possible. They often obtained lands at a ridiculously low figure; many lands being leased for $1 a quarter section, and for even less. People and officers seemed to forget that the intent and true purpose of this grant of land is not as in the homestead and preemption acts, to furnish lands to the intending settler at a nominal price, but to sell or lease these lands at a fair price to raise funds to increase the efficiency of schools and reduce taxation.[9]

Once statehood was achieved squatters could be dealt with, and one of the notions that gained wide acceptance in both Dakotas was the belief that a properly managed "school lands" fund would produce enough revenue to keep general taxation for schools at a minimum. By 1896 in South Dakota, "It was quite generally believed at this date that the time was not far distant when the proceeds from the school lands would be so large that taxation for school purposes would be reduced to a comparatively small sum."[10] In his children's history of North Dakota, *The Story Of The Flickertail State,* William Marks Wemett agrees, and he tells of the significance of the land grants in a section entitled "Its Meaning to Us." Wemett says: "This fund will amount to many millions of dollars, and the interest and income from it will be sufficient to support a splendid system of public schools. The people of this state in the future will not be obliged to raise by taxation the money necessary for the education of their children."[11]

While it is true that the common school funds in the two states have grown, both expectations were fantasy. In 1890 the North Dakota legislature authorized the Board of University and School Lands to select and lease school lands in twenty-nine counties. The lands chosen would provide an annual rental of $60,644.27 that would support education in the several districts of the state. It was ". . . an income of which a new State may well be proud."[12] By 1910 the Common School Fund had grown to $15,285,000; by June 30, 1995 it had increased to $327,805,926.[13] In the school year, 1995-1996, however, the Common School Fund contributed only 4.9 percent of the cost of operating the state's common schools.[14]

Throughout their history North Dakota's one-room schools had to rely, for the most part, on local financial resources. For example, the sources and amounts of revenue for the support of the public schools of North Dakota for the school year ending June 30, 1925 are as follows:[15]

District	$12,627,594.60	84.71%
County: School Poll [Tax]	252,093.00	1.70%
½ mill levy	496,179.86	3.32%
State: Interest & Income From Public School Lands	1,71,413.05	7.86%
Fines & Penalties	17,057.91	.11%
State Aid	341,900.00	2.30%

When statehood was granted, North Dakota had 1,401 schools, 1,366 ungraded and 35 graded and high schools.[16] By 1890 it had 1,583 district schools (mostly country schools) and 1,480 schoolhouses. Most of the 103 schools that were held in privately owned buildings were located in newly organized counties. Of 37,472 individuals between 7 and 20 years of age, 30,821 or 82 percent were enrolled in district schools. But average daily attendance was only 17,546 or 57 percent. The district schools employed 1,894 teachers, 557 or 29 percent were males, and 1,337 or 71 percent were females. Their average salary was $38.97 and $34.42, respectively. School terms were limited. The state superintendent's *First Biennial Report* reveals that 50 districts had no school, 506 had between four and six months of school, and 893 had six months or more. Split terms were not uncommon.[17]

The average value of all district schoolhouses, sites, and furniture in 1890 was $775. Only 43 of the schools had libraries, the number of volumes totaled 2,056; a small number, 16, had no blackboards. Some districts, for whatever reason, failed to comply with one state law. Every district was to furnish each school with *Webster's Unabridged Dictionary*; 314 failed to do so. Concerned with the health and sanitation facilities of the school population, the state counted the number of outhouses, and found that 50 schools had none, 253 had one, and 1,187 had two or a double one.[18]

In North Dakota, as elsewhere, there were few "little red schoolhouses" of folklore. While early records indicate a variety of materials used in building schoolhouses (sod, log, stone, and brick) most were of wood construction, painted white. Of the number of schoolhouses reported in 1890, 2 were sod, 40 were log, 2 were stone, 20 were brick, and 1,392 were wood frame.[19]

From 1898 to 1915 the state's population increased about 135 percent, from 270,000 to 637,000. . . . The number of foreign-born children enrolled would place an additional burden on many country school teachers who had to teach them English.

One-room country schools increased in number during early statehood. Settling on the open prairies many immigrants built small sod houses; but they built few sod schoolhouses. In 1894, the state superintendent's biennial report indicates that of 273 schools constructed, 263 were frame, 5 were stone, 1 was sod, and 4 were log.[20] By 1907 North Dakota had a total of 3,969 schoolhouses: 30 were log, 16 were sod, 115 were brick or stone, and 3,808 were frame. McHenry County had the most sod schoolhouses, five, followed by Mercer County with four, and McIntosh County with three.[21] After 1914-1915 such statistics were no longer compiled. In 1915 North Dakota had a total of 5,421 schoolhouses: 5,150 were frame, 252 were stone or brick, and 19 were log or sod.[22]

From 1898 to 1915 the state's population increased about 135 percent, from 270,000 to 637,000. The foreign-born, eager for land, came in droves. By 1910 they made up about half of the state's farmers.[23] The following year, of the 136,668 pupils enrolled in North Dakota's schools, 117,000, or 86 percent, attended a one-room school.[24] The number of foreign-born children enrolled would place an additional burden on many country school teachers who had to teach them English.

One immigrant group, the German-Russians, posed a peculiar problem for Edwin J. Taylor (R) who served as superintendent of public instruction from 1911-1917.

Unfortunately, their schools too frequently were conducted in a German-Russian dialect into which a certain amount of English was absorbed — an almost impossible dialect developed. The situation was delicate but had to be met head on. E. J. Taylor was not the man to shrink from the task. He found a good ally in Rt. Rev. Vincent Wehrle, a pioneer missionary priest. . . . Superintendent Taylor's insistence that only teachers qualified to teach standard English be employed met with some resistance but with ultimate success. The popular TV star and band leader Lawrence Welk is a product of one of the schools in which English superseded the German-Russian dialect.[25]

To hundreds of children living in rural communities with limited resources and poor transportation, the small one-room school was the only educational facility available. The total number of public one-room schools and one-room schools actually in session in North Dakota in selected years from 1917 to 1997 is shown in the following table.[26]

YEAR	NUMBER	ACTUAL NUMBER IN SESSION	YEAR	NUMBER	ACTUAL NUMBER IN SESSION
1917	4722		1961	1963	817
1924	4730		1965		316
1926	4735		1970		107
1930	4577		1975		66
1935	4732	4121	1980		34
1940	4658	3392	1985		14
1945	4553	3043	1990		12
1950	4251	2641	1995		9
1955	3795	2355	1997		10

Between 1935 and 1960 both the physical number and the actual number of one-room schools in session decreased dramatically. From 1961 to 1997 another striking decline took place. In 1936, of 152,554 students enrolled, 54,900 or 36 percent were enrolled in one-room schools; a decade later, of 114,591 registered pupils, 33,007 or 29 percent attended a one-room school. By 1956 enrollment in one-room schools had decreased to 20 percent, (24,735 of 124,608). During the next decade one-room schools closed by the hundreds. In 1966, of 154,854 pupils enrolled in school, only 3,368 or 2 percent were attending one-room schools.[27]

The statistics illustrate two of the six themes that North Dakota's pre-eminent historian Elwyn B. Robinson says dominated the state's past development. The "Two Much Mistake" is his name "for too many farms, too many miles of railroads and roads, too many towns, banks, schools, colleges, churches, and governmental institutions, and more people than opportunities. . . ." The other theme, "adjustment" or "adaptability to environment," means "both the painful cutting back of the oversupply of the 'Too-Much Mistake' and the slow forging of more suitable ways of living in a subhumid grassland."[28] From 1926 to 1997 thousands (4725) of one-room schools closed their doors. Most likely many closings were "painful" and controversial; numerous decisions to shut down were surely made with regret. Certainly, to many in the community, the loss of their school was disheartening.

Most likely many [country school] closings were "painful" and controversial; numerous decisions to shut down were surely made with regret. Certainly, to many in the community, the loss of their school was disheartening.

Particular ideas and activities present throughout North Dakota's history restructured its school system and helped bring about the decline of the country school: early and continual efforts at consolidation; the arrival of the automobile and the building of better roads, particularly in the post World War II period; ideas of equalization and reorganization; the Great Depression; and the inauguration of the Foundation Program.

Construction of better rural roads beginning in 1920s would ultimately bring improved educational facilities to rural children.

North Dakotans, like other Americans, fell in love with the automobile. To the educational community, particularly those who believed that the way to improve rural education was by consolidation, the coming of the automobile to the prairies hinted at the possibility of transporting students farther, faster, and more freely. Moreover, rural isolation could be alleviated and differences between rural and urban dwellers could be broken down. Because roads were poor, and in some cases nonexistent, and because communities lacked either resources or the will, early efforts at consolidation were limited. There were only 114 consolidated schools in 1911 (the first was in 1901).[29]

Farmers, like their city cousins, embraced the automobile. Fifty-seven percent of them owned automobiles by 1920. And a decade later, 87 percent of them boasted of owning a car. The fact that North Dakotans owned 183,000 automobiles by 1930 (one for every 3.7 persons versus one for every 5.3 persons in the United States) did not escape the notice of the legislature. Construction of better rural roads beginning in 1920s would ultimately bring improved educational facilities to rural children.[30]

Along with building more and better roads during the ensuing decades the legislature enacted other laws that would hasten the passing of the country school. Besides providing an inferior education (mediocre teaching, poor attendance, and a short school term), the one-room school was considered by many to be too costly and inefficient. Politicians and educational reformers believed many of them should be abolished. In an effort to force school districts to realign the legislature created a special Committee on School District Reorganization in 1947. The committee's actions did produce some results; by 1951 reorganization had taken place in 220 districts. However, opposition to the law developed, especially in rural areas. A great number of people believed their community would lose its identity if their school was closed. Many believed as well that reorganization and school closures meant higher taxes and possibly bond issues. Those attitudes convinced the 1951 legislature to abolish the committee and give the state superintendent responsibility for school district reorganization. As a result reorganization slowed. By 1957, under new guidelines, only twenty reorganization plans had been approved.[31]

Certainly, the concept of equalization, promoted and fought for by Arthur E. Thompson, state superintendent from 1933 to 1946, was another milestone in the history of education in North Dakota. Along with future legislation affecting it, the idea of equalization would ultimately reduce the number of one-room schools. Thompson's idea was to establish a fund that would provide state aid for distressed school districts. (From 1899 to 1933 state aid was given to schools that met certain standards.) His concept evolved into one that would not only provide state aid, but also one that would try to equalize aid to local districts. To finance his plan, Thompson, with the aid of the Parent Teachers Association and the North Dakota Education Association, was able to convince the 1933 legislature to pass a 2 percent sales tax. However, voters in a referendum rejected the plan. Undaunted, Thompson and the education lobby continued to promote his ideas. Two years later, the legislature did create a state-equalization fund; appropriated almost $4 million for it; and, to raise money for education and welfare, instituted a 2 percent sales tax. This time voters approved the legislation. In 1929 only 8 percent of the revenue supporting public schools came from the state; by 1937 its contribution had increased to 27 percent. After a county equalization-fund was created in 1949 the state and county share of the cost of public education increased to 41 percent. Two years later a county high school equalization fund was established.[32]

Another turning point in the state's educational history occurred when the legislature established the Foundation Program in 1959. The brain-child of Howard J. Snortland, the director of the state equalization fund, it had mixed results in its early efforts to foster reorganization. By creating a new county equalization fund and supplementing it with a state appropriation, the program was designed to provide that 60 percent of the average cost of operating district schools came from non-local sources. (Its expectation was raised to 70 percent in the early 1980s.) It seemed to encourage reorganization. But the program cost the state equalization fund nearly $20 million in the first two years. It failed to reach its 60 percent goal, and to some extent slowed school reorganization. For example, basic payments per pupil varied; one-room schools were to receive $225 per pupil, larger elementary schools received less, only $150 per pupil. On the other hand, another part of the program encouraged reorganization. For many years local districts bore the full cost of transporting students. Now, they could receive half a cent per pupil-mile for transportation. To protect pupils on buses the state established school bus standards in 1947.[33]

Almost four decades later one of the core ideas of the Foundation Program, to raise significantly the state's share of educating its children, K-12, is still far from being realized. Legislators were unwilling to appropriate sufficient funds to consistently realize the target goal of 60 or 70 percent, established years before. During the school year, 1973-1974, the per pupil payment from state funds reached a high of 69 percent. Thereafter, it steadily declined to 55 percent in 1980-1981. The following year, however, the state's percentage of per pupil expenditure rose to 64 percent. From then on, the state's share of the cost of operating district schools has declined. In the 1994-1995 school year its share was 45.98 percent, only about 6 percent above the state and county level in 1949.[34] Another contributing factor to the decline of the country school was the Great Depression; it forced thousands of farmers off the land and spurred consolidation. From 1930 to 1940 the state lost over 121,000 persons by outmigration. A special census, 1935-1940, revealed that most of the loss was from farms; farm population was reduced by 17 percent. Peaking at 84,606, in 1935, the number of farms decreased to 61,943 in 1954 and to 48,836 a decade later. There were only 30,500 farms in the state in 1997. Between 1935 and 1950 the actual number of one-room schools in session was reduced by 36 percent.[35]

The continuing rural flight to urban population centers in the state also contributed to the decline of the one-room country school. North Dakota was 92.7 percent rural in 1900. By mid-century the state was still 73.4 percent rural. It took over a century for North Dakota to become an urban state. The 1990 census revealed that 46.7 percent of the state's population was rural; 53.3 percent was urban.[36]

The continuing rural flight to urban population centers in the state also contributed to the decline of the one-room country school.

Where did early America's teachers come from? One historian has observed that Colonial education was greatly indebted to the "upper stratum of transported convicts, for even teachers with a cloud on them were better than none." He notes that Benjamin Franklin, while promoting his Pennsylvania Academy, said his school would qualify "a Number of the poorer sort . . . to act as Schoolmasters. . . . The Country suffering very much at present for want of good Schoolmasters, and oblig'd frequently to employ . . . vicious imported Servants, or concealed Papists, who by their bad Examples . . . often deprave the Morals . . . of the Children. . . ." And according to Reverend Jonathon Bourcher "INDENTURED SERVANTS or TRANSPORTED FELONS" provided two-thirds of the schooling in Virginia. "Not a ship arrives . . . with . . . convicts," he said, "in which schoolmasters are not as regularly advertised for sale as weavers, tailors, or any other trade. . . ."[37]

North Dakota did depend, however, on eastern states and other countries for its supply of teachers.

North Dakota, of course, did not have to rely on indentured servants, transported felons, or concealed Papists to educate its youth during the first decades of its history. It did depend, however, on eastern states and other countries for its supply of teachers.

In her comparative examination of *The Country School,* in selected European countries and the United States, Iman Elsie Schatzmann concludes that

> While the rural child has a richer background than the urban child for understanding the physical and biological aspects of life, he has fewer opportunities for various social contacts to stimulate his reactions and to develop his personality and his understanding of human relationships. For this reason the rural child is highly dependent on the character of his school and the qualifications of his teacher for the knowledge and experience which are essential if he is to understand and accept his responsibilities and privileges in a democratic society.[38]

First, what were some of the characteristics of the rural student's school in early North Dakota?

In 1910, according to Superintendent of Public Instruction Walter L. Stockwell, rural schoolhouses were small and unattractive, school grounds were unimproved, attendance was irregular during short terms, there was little or no supervision of teachers, and the *Course of Study* was ill-adapted to the needs of country children.[39]

State school laws were completely revised by the 1911 legislature. One improvement, under the new laws, was to establish a seven-month school term. To receive aid from the county apportionment fund, each school in every district had to hold at least a seven-month school term. However, the *Napoleon Homestead* observed that "many schoolboards throughout the state are asking county superintendents to send them five and six month teachers." The paper said that although "many of the school boards are trying to evade the new law regarding the schools . . . ," it was no longer possible for " . . . one school in the district [to] run three months and another four months, making a total of seven months for the two schools, and be able to get any of the funds." According to some county superintendents, rural school boards did not understand the new provisions when asking for short term teachers. The paper hoped school boards would " . . . make it their business to grasp the meaning of the code." Despite the fact that the minimum term in 1914 was seven months, considerable numbers of school boards continued to ignore the law. To illustrate: 174 schools had no school; 108 had less than 4 months; 85 had 4 months, but less than 5; 172 had 5 months but less than 6; and 429 had 6 months but less than 7.[40]

One promising feature, however, of the country school experience was the state department's successful 1898 experiment in traveling libraries. Building several cases, each holding fifty volumes (history, biography, travel, literature, fiction, science, pedagogy) it circulated them to various schools. School districts had to pay the freight, both ways. So successful was the experiment that the next year the legislature appropriated $750 per year to the department for that purpose; 35 libraries were assembled. By 1906 there were 175 libraries in circulation[41]

Another positive feature of the one-room school experience was that many rural school boards across the state were worried about the safety of their students, especially during the prairie fire season. In 1910 there were 3,124 fire breaks protecting some 4,800 schools. On the other hand, by 1914 the number of schoolhouses had increased to 5,365, but only 600 had wells, and just 143 had cisterns. Individual drinking cups for their pupils were provided by 2,548 schools. Distressing to some country school teachers was the fact that in some cases school boards failed to provide blackboards: 22 schools had none in 1890; 35 teachers struggled without one in 1900; and 21 in 1910. By 1920 all school boards had recognized that blackboards were a basic tool in the learning process.[42]

What sort of teachers were hired to staff rural schools in North Dakota during the early decades of its history? In 1890 W. J. Clapp, the state superintendent, noted that his office and many county superintendents and school boards were "overrun with applications from non-resident teachers who are desirous of gaining more lucrative positions than they can obtain in their own States." Newcomers were heartily welcomed, but he warned them that " . . . this is no place for teachers of doubtful scholarship . . ." and that "mediocrity finds poor encouragement here." Furthermore, teaching in North Dakota was recognized as a profession. However, in scoring teachers' exams for certification the superintendent was forced to admit that:

> Owing to a scarcity of teachers, liberal marking in a few counties is yet necessary. So far as it can be done, I believed that the number of certificates valid in a county should not much exceed the number of schools in the county; and then by gradually raising the standard, the average grade will be raised, and the schools made correspondingly better. When such a corps of teachers is once established, the resident teachers of the county should be given every preference over migratory ones.[43]

Teachers, however, did not remain residents in a particular county for very long. Two decades later State Superintendent Walter L. Stockwell complained that the educational system was dependent on the transient for the bulk of its teachers. Teacher turnover, he said, was excessive and caused problems. Noting that almost all of the teaching force of a county had to be replaced every three years he said it was well-nigh impossible to create an *esprit de corps*, an essential element in effective schooling. Another problem facing education during his tenure was the fact that most teachers were female; marriage proved a greater attraction than the school room to a large proportion of them. Stockwell thought one solution to that difficult circumstance would be to get the general public to embrace the Old World idea of equating the teaching profession with that of law, medicine, or theology. Adopting it would attract able men who would be ready and willing to make teaching their life's work. In Morton County, W. F. Lorin, county superintendent, reported that about half of his teachers, quite well prepared, came from other states. Rarely considering applicants from larger cities; he favored those coming from rural districts and small towns. "They seem best suited to our schools," he said. Inter-

Teachers, however, did not remain residents in a particular county for very long.

estingly, Lorin preferred, for whatever reason, to hire products of the very system he was supervising and perpetuating.[44]

The public, however, was unwilling to subscribe to such a revolutionary principle as proposed by Stockwell. What most school boards did was to include anti-marriage provisions in most female teaching contracts, and some male contracts. Men did not flock to the teaching profession.

After a quarter century of statehood, only 33 percent, of the state's 4,981 teachers were born in North Dakota.

After a quarter century of statehood, only 1,635, or 33 percent, of the state's 4,981 teachers were born in North Dakota. Most of the state's 3,068 rural teachers, were female, 85 percent; were born in rural communities, 71 percent; had only a high school or eighth grade education, 92 percent; had little experience, an average of 2 years; were young, average age was 23 years; and received an average salary of $56.39. Less than 1 percent of the rural teachers had gone to college and almost 8 percent had attended Normal school. Only 8 percent taught with a Professional Certificate; 71 percent taught with a Second Grade Certificate.

The following table, published in 1916, provides a short, but vivid, outline of the most outstanding characteristics of the state's teacher corps.

Summary of the Educational Survey of the Rural, Graded and High Schools of the State of North Dakota.[45]							
PLACE OF ORIGIN	**NUMBER**	**OCCUPATION OF FATHER**	**NUMBER**	**RURAL TEACHERS**	**NUMBER**	**CITY TEACHERS**	**NUMBER**
North Dakota	1635	Farmer	3078	Average age	23	Average age	28
Minnesota	1107	Merchant	306	Average salary	$56.39	Average salary	$82.58
Iowa	412	Contractor	177	Were born — rural	2191	Were born — rural	979
Wisconsin	575	Lawyer	40	Were born — city	877	Were born — city	934
Indiana	221	Clergyman	118	TRAINING — 8th grade	121	TRAINING	
Illinois	154	Teacher	51	H.S. — 1 year	339	H.S. — 1 year	7
South Dakota	169	Laborer	272	H.S. — 2 year	449	H.S. — 2 year	16
Michigan	90	R.R. Man	118	H.S. — 3 year	403	H.S. — 3 year	38
Ohio	78	Salesman	79	H.S. — 4 year	1501	H.S. — 4 year	220
Kansas	41	Lumberman	34	Normal Degree	241	Normal Degree	1070
Nebraska	57	Grain Buyer	51	College Degree	14	College Degree	560
Other States	234	Sea Captain	4	Certificate — 2nd Grade	2190	Certificate — 2nd Grade	23
Canada	87	Dairyman	3	Certificate — 1st Grade	621	Certificate — 1st Grade	248
Norway	43	Baker	7	Certificate — Professional	257	Certificate — Professional	1640
Sweden	17	Banker	32	Average Years Experience	2	Average Years Experience	5.6
Germany	20	Physician	35	Male Teachers	462	Male Teachers	413
Russia	6	Blacksmith	54	Female Teachers	2606	Female Teachers	1500
England	7	Other Occupations	521	Average Enrollment	16	Average Enrollment	34
Austria	2						
Ireland	2						
Iceland	2						
Other Countries	22						
TOTAL	**4981**			**4981**			

By modern standards and for many years, the supply of well-educated teachers in North Dakota was meager. It took the state almost seven decades, in 1957, to require teachers to complete two years of college training to qualify for a Second Grade Professional Certificate. Some two decades later, beginning July 1, 1976, only holders of four-year degrees could qualify for full-time teaching positions in North Dakota's school system.

Like other institutions in American society the one-room school was not immune from controversy, violence, or sordid actions. In 1909 conflict erupted over moving a schoolhouse. A majority of Taft School District patrons, in western Stutsman County, had voted to move their schoolhouse. But they were frustrated in their efforts because under current law a two-thirds vote was needed to change its location. The losing faction had in fact forewarned the community that the building would be moved. They made good their threat, when, in the dead of night, parties unknown, moved it three miles to a new location.[46] The next year a different issue developed in the western part of the state, in Williams County. Someone had discovered that the Stony Creek school was not located in Stony Creek Township, its correct location was in the Nessen School District. Conflict developed between the two districts. The issue was money. Since the building was constructed in 1904 the Stony Creek school board had financed its operation. Now they wanted their money back.[47]

One habit numbers of teachers had developed, that angered many school boards, eventually came under legislative scrutiny. Apparently enough instructors during their careers had engaged in the practice of "jumping a contract" to force the 1923 legislature to take note of the problem. Several members of the House of Representatives portrayed "the pretty young school teacher" as irresponsible, a contract breaker, and a spendthrift. Interested in changing her character, Representative George W. Morton (R-Mercer, Oliver, Dunn), introduced legislation that enabled school boards to retain 10 percent of a teacher's salary every month, until the end of the school year. If the teacher "willfully" violated the contract the board retained the money. The debate on the bill that followed was in part serious, in part fun. In the end the house passed it, 74 ayes, 33 nays. The senate, on the other hand, recommended indefinite postponement. The issue was dead for the time being. Local school boards, however, did include such provisions in many of their contracts. In fact, many one-room school teachers were indeed transients. In the five year period, 1930-1934, pupils attending 55 percent of the state's one-room schools had a new teacher every year.[48]

Apparently enough instructors during their careers had engaged in the practice of "jumping a contract" to force the 1923 legislature to take note of the problem.

Transient or not, one-room school teachers were not guaranteed against personal assault. The Turtle Lake community was shocked in October 1926 when it learned that Ida Nelson, a well known country school teacher, was attacked in her schoolhouse, located about three miles north of Turtle Lake. Shortly after school was dismissed, one H. G. Murbach, who was in the area buying cattle, entered the building and made the assault. Fleeing the community, he was arrested by the sheriff of Williams County, accused of rape, and returned to McLean County for trial. He was found guilty of the charge. After being sentenced to two years in the state penitentiary he was given an extension to appeal his case, it was heard by the state Supreme Court in June 1927. Murbach lost his appeal; the court affirmed the order and judgment of the McLean County Court and remanded him to the state prison to begin his 2-year term in January 1928.[49]

The most horrifying act of violence witnessed by country school children in North Dakota occurred in Billings County in March 1935, in the Manion school, located 15 miles northwest of Gorham. Seven pupils witnessed the murder of their teacher, Miss Emily Hartl, and then the suicide of her killer, Harry McGill. Horror-

Critics point out that for the most part country school teachers were ill-prepared, unskilled, underpaid, and inexperienced. School facilities were inadequate, poorly designed, unattractive, and small. . . .

Others insist attending country schools had certain advantages. . . . Most one-room school teachers insist that one of the greatest advantages of rural schooling was the constant review/preview process to which pupils were subjected.

stricken students at first gave various versions of the incident. But after subsequent investigations authorities were able to reconstruct the tragedy. The two had had a short argument after which McGill struck Hartl over the head with his rifle, fracturing her skull. After he fired two shots into her body, McGill lay down beside her and took his own life. The murder/suicide was apparently a case of unrequited love. After the slaying the victim's sister and a fellow teacher revealed that McGill had sent threatening letters to Hartl in which he indicated he would kill her, as revenge for her spurning his advances. She had not revealed the contents of the letters because she didn't want her parents to worry.[50]

It is impossible to give North Dakota's one-room country schools either a numerical score or a letter grade for their performance. Critics point out that for the most part country school teachers were ill-prepared, unskilled, underpaid, and inexperienced. School facilities were inadequate, poorly designed, unattractive, and small. And the whole country school effort was underfunded. With small classes, competition was limited. Many students don't necessarily challenge themselves. Besides, students were, for the most part, socially isolated; their opportunities to form peer relationships were limited. Some students suffered transfer problems, even though most country school teachers insisted that their students "held their own" when moving to city schools. Furthermore, housing was always a critical problem for the teacher. Living close to school meant having little privacy from their students and having few colleagues available for advice. And the country schoolmarm was plagued with sex-role stereotyping.

Others insist attending country schools had certain advantages. Students didn't try to impress other students or try to copy them. The age differential in the classroom taught students to learn from each other, and how to cooperate and work with younger pupils. Most one-room school teachers insist that one of the greatest advantages of rural schooling was the constant *review/preview* process to which pupils were subjected. Second and third graders were exposed to what was in store for them in the coming grades. And a sixth grader may have learned something he missed while he was in the lower grades. Teachers also insist that there was closer contact with parents in country schools and that students developed more independence and resourcefulness. Moreover, there were closer relationships between students and teachers in country schools than in urban schools. Like today, the key factor in determining the success or failure of any school is the teacher. A French proverb, *"Tel maitre tel serviteur,"* suggests that "As is the teacher, so is the school."

Iman Elsie Schatzmann said that "If the teacher is friendly, courteous, cheerful, and hard working, if he is co-operative, broad-minded, and constructive, he transmits these qualities to the children who catch his spirit."[51] While many schoolmarms and schoolmasters may have been mediocre teachers, or worse, as many were endowed with the qualities Schatzmann lists. Surely, thousands of country school pupils caught the "spirit " of those teachers.

Endnotes

1. E. J. Taylor, Jr., "North Dakota Department of Public Instruction" in *Education in the States: Historical Development and Outlook* (National Education association of the United States, 1969), p. 929.

2. Curt Eriksmoen, "A Brief History of the Elementary/Secondary Education in North Dakota," p. 1, (unpublished, n.d.) North Dakota, Department of Public Instruction.

3. *Ibid.*

4. *Ibid., p.2.* Eriksmoen says there is no documentation to support Walter Loomer's contention that there were two schools in Grand Forks in 1872.

5. *Ibid.*

6. *Ibid.*, p. 3.

7. George Brown Tindall, *America A Narrative History* (New York: W. W. Norton & Company, 1984), p. 489.

8. Harold A. Hagan, "The North Dakota Land Grants," *North Dakota History*, Vol. 18, Nos. 2&3, April & July, 1951, p. 126; Ibid., No. 1, January 1951, p. 24.

9. North Dakota, Department of Public Instruction (DPI), *First Biennial Report*, 1890, pp. 20-21.

10. South Dakota, Department of History, *Report and Historical Collections*, Vol. 36, p. 255.

11. William Marks Wemett, *The Story Of The Flickertail State*, Second Edition (Valley City: W. M. Wemett, 1923), pp. 301-302.

12. DPI, *First Biennial Report*, 1890, p. 21.

13. *Ibid., Eleventh Biennial Report*, 1910, p. 22; North Dakota, Board of University and School Lands, *Fifty-first Biennial Report*, July 1, 1993 to June 30, 1995, p. 16.

14. *Ibid.*, Handout, Table 3, *Proportion of Total Revenue (Excluding Federal Restricted Revenue) by Major Source for North Dakota School Districts in 1984-85, 1990-91, and 1995-96.*

15. DPI, *Biennial Report*, 1926, pp. 12-13.

16. DPI, *First Biennial Report*, 1890, p. 11. It is assumed that the ungraded schools were one-room country schools and the graded were in towns and villages.

17. *Ibid.*, pp. 11-19. The *First Biennial Report* gives statistics for district schools, statistics for special school districts, and statistics for cities.

18. *Ibid.*, If statistics for special school districts and cities are included, 35,543 of a possible 43,153, or 82 percent of individuals between 7 and 20 years of age were enrolled in the state's 1,680 schools, taught by 1,982 teachers.

19. J. C. Furnas, *The Americans: A Social History Of The United States*, 1587-1914, Capricorn Edition, Vol. 1 (New York: Capricorn Books, 1971), p. 546. Furnas says the first mention of the little red schoolhouse that he knows of is in "Artemus Ward, 'The Showman's Courtship' (c.1860): "blushin as red as the Baldinsville skool house when it was fust painted." *First Biennial Report*, 1890, pp. 11-19.

20. DPI, *Fourth Biennial Report*, 1894-1896, p. 194.

21. *Ibid., Tenth Biennial Report*, 1906-1908, p. 299.

22. *Ibid., Fourteenth Biennial Report*, 1916, pp. 63.

23. Elwyn B. Robinson, *History of North Dakota* (Lincoln: University of Nebraska Press, 1966), pp. 235-254.

24. Eriksmoen, p. 5.

25. Taylor, Jr., p. 935.

26. The statistics are taken from the Department of Public Instruction's *Biennial Reports* (BR) and the *North Dakota Educational Directory* (NDED). *Fifteenth BR*, 1918, p. 122; *Nineteenth BR*, 1926, p. 13; *Twenty-First BR*, 1930, p. 126; *Twenty-Fourth BR*, 1936, p. 47-48; *Twenty-Sixth BR*, 1940, pp. 89-90; *Twenty-Ninth BR*, 1946, p. 79; *Thirty-First BR*, 1950, p. 163; *Thirty-Fourth BR*, 1956, p. 137; *Thirty-Seventh BR*, 1962, pp. 152-153; *Thirty-ninth BR*, 1966, p. 155; *Forty-First BR*, 1970, p. 194; *NDED*,1975-1976, p. 74; *NDED*, 1980-1981, p. B-3; *NDED*, 1985-1986, p. B-3; *NDED*, 1990-1991, p. B-3; *NDED*, 1995-1996, p. B-3; *Bismarck Tribune*, September 7, 1997, p. 5A. In the 1980s the Department of Public Instruction changed its categorization of one-room schools. For example in 1988-1989 there were 13 one-room schools in rural districts and 19 one-teacher schools in all public school districts. In 1994-1995 there were 9 one-teacher schools in rural districts and 13 one-teacher schools in all public districts.

27. Taylor, Jr., p. 940.

28. Robinson, p. vii; Elwyn B. Robinson, "The Themes of North Dakota History," *North Dakota History* 26-1 (Winter 1959), pp. 5-24. The other four themes are remoteness, dependence, economic disadvantage, and agrarian radicalism.

29. Eriksmoen, p. 6.

30. Robinson, pp. 379-380.

31. Eriksmoen, p. 8. According to Eriksmoen the first reorganization law "was a timid law . . . with little incentive and no big stick. . . . [It] gave no aid for the transportation of pupils, set no minimum standards for new districts, and withheld no state equalization money from districts which failed to reorganize."

32. *Ibid.*, pp. 7-9; Robinson, pp. 480-481; Taylor, Jr., pp. 936-937; North Dakota, *Centennial Bluebook, 1889-1989*, p. 440.

33. Eriksmoen, p. 9; Robinson, pp. 486-487.

34. DPI, *School Finance Facts*, January, 1996, p. 2; *Ibid.*, Handout, *Historical Per Pupil Expenditure and Pupil Payment Data Including Projected Values.*

35. Robinson, p. 401; North Dakota State Data Center, Facsimile Transmittal Sheet, *Number of Farms and Average Acres Per Farm in North Dakota, 1900-1992,* October 30, 1997.

36. North Dakota State Data Center, Facsimile Transmittal Sheet, *Urban and Rural Population Distribution in North Dakota, 1900-1990,* November 3, 1997.

37. Furnas., p. 107.

38. Iman Elsie Schatzmann, *The Country School* (Chicago: The University of Chicago Press, 1942), p. xii.

39. DPI, *Eleventh Biennial Report*, 1910, p. 23. In 1890, common schools were to be in session not less than 4 months; if attendance was 15 or more, not less than 6 months; school could be discontinued if average attendance dropped below 4 for 10 consecutive days, North Dakota, *Laws of North Dakota,* 1890 c. 62, sec. 84; in 1903 the school term was increased to not less than 6 months, *Ibid.*, 1903, c. 83, sec. 704; in 1911, not less than 7 months, *Ibid.*, 1911, c. 266, sec. 83; in 1939 school could be closed if average attendance for 10 consecutive days fell below 6, *Ibid.*, 1939, c. 206, sec. 2; in 1947, the school term was increased to 8 months, *Ibid.*, 1947, c. 143, sec.15-25-09; in 1959, it increased to 175 days, *Ibid.*, 1959, c. 175, sec 1; and in 1963 the school term increased to 180 days of classroom instruction, *Ibid.*, 1963, c. 169, sec. 1.

40. *The Gackle Republican*, September 1, 1911, p. 1; DPI, *Fourteenth Biennial Report,* 1916, p. 44.

41. DPI, *Fifth Biennial Report*, 1898, p. 31; *Ninth Biennial Report*, 1906, p. 31.

42. *Ibid., Eleventh Biennial Report,* 1910, pp. 152-165; *Fourteenth Biennial Report,* 1916, p. 44; *Sixteenth Biennial Report,* 1920, p. 17.

43. *Ibid., First Biennial Report*, 1889-1890, pp. 24-25.

44. *Ibid., Eleventh Biennial Report*, pp. 19-20, 205.

45. *North Dakota Educational School Bulletin,* Vol. 1, No. 2, May 1916, p. 10.

46. *Gackle Republican*, October 22, 1909, p. 2. It is unknown at this time if the culprits were ever identified and brought to justice.

47. *Ibid.*, December 9, 1910, p. 2. The editors have not as yet researched the outcome of the conflict.

48. North Dakota, Eighteenth Session, Legislative Assembly, 1923, *Billbook*, House Bill No. 159; *Ibid., House Journal,* 1923, pp. 289, 325, 361, 388, 398-399, 403, 750; *Senate Journal,* 1923, pp. 390, 435, 674; *Bismarck Tribune*, February 5, 1923, p. 3; *Ibid.*, May 4, 1934, p. 2.

49. State of North Dakota vs. H. G. Murback, North Dakota, McLean County, District Court, Case No. 654, *Register Criminal Actions, Book C*, p. 455; Appeal File No. 5371; *Washburn Leader*, October 29, 1926, p. 1; November 19, 1926, p. 1; November 26, 1926, p. 1.

50. *Dickinson Press*, March 28, 1935, p. 1; April 4, 1935, p. 1. Gorham was located about 16 miles north of Belfield.

51. Schatzmann, p. 151.

"As is the teacher, so is the school."

Chapter 1

The Country School and the Americanization of Immigrants to North Dakota

Mary C. and Robert L. Carlson

VARIOUS FORCES PUSHED AND PULLED IMMIGRANTS from their native homeland to the northern plains. Whatever their reasons were — the desire for a new home in a new country, the promise of wealth, dissatisfaction with conditions in the old country or personal considerations — the immigrants moved into North Dakota rapidly in astonishing numbers.

In 1890, one year after statehood, the foreign-born comprised 43 percent of the state's 191,000 people. The largest immigrant groups at that time included

- the Norwegians with 25,700 people;
- Canadians numbered 23,000;
- Germans numbered 9,000;
- English and Irish totaled 8,000;
- and 4,100 had come from Russia.[1]

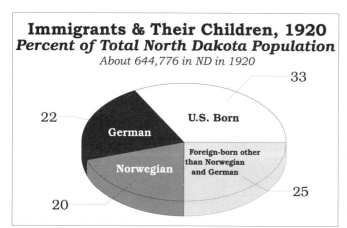

Immigrants & Their Children, 1920
Percent of Total North Dakota Population
About 644,776 in ND in 1920

33 — U.S. Born

22 — German

20 — Norwegian

25 — Foreign-born other than Norwegian and German

By 1910 the foreign-born and their children made up 77 percent of the population, of which the largest groups were the Norwegians with 125,000 closely followed by Germans with 117,000, about half of whom were Germans from Russia. At the end of the decade, during which settlement of the state was completed, the immigrants and their children numbered 432,000, or 67 percent of the population. By this time, 1920, the Germans and the Germans from Russia were the most numerous ethnic group with 22 percent of the population, compared to the Norwegians with 20 percent.[2]

The immigrants tended to cluster in nationality groups in geographic areas of the state, giving communities distinct ethnic identities. The Norwegians, the first large group of immigrants to arrive in the state, settled in the rich eastern counties and along the Great Northern Railway line across northern North Dakota. There was a large concentration of Germans from Germany in Richland County in southeastern North Dakota. Scottish and French settlers, most of whom came from Canada, settled in the northeast counties. Austrians occupied the rangeland in the southwestern counties.

Students and teacher pose in front of a sod school identified as District 37, School No. 3. The boys, obviously younger, stand apart from the girls. Few of the young men have shoes. (*Masonic Grand Lodge of North Dakota Collection, NDIRS, NDSU*)

Smaller groups of immigrants settled in pockets within the broad areas inhabited by the large immigrant groups. Bohemians developed a strong ethnic community in the Lidgerwood area. Jewish farming communities were established near Washburn, Regan, Wing, Devils Lake, and Dickinson. A strong Dutch community of about eighty families developed near Strasburg in Emmons County. Icelanders settled in Pembina County. Poles built communities in Walsh and Kidder counties. Ukrainians homesteaded in substantial numbers in Billings, Dunn and McLean counties. German-Hungarians settled in Stark and Hettinger counties. Russians claimed the area around Butte in southern McHenry County.

If the areas that various nationalities settled in North Dakota were coded on a map, the final product would resemble a mosaic, but the mosaic would require subtle shading and detail. Swedes, Finns, a small colony of Syrians who erected near Ross the first Moslem mosque in the United States, Swiss, Estonians and others scattered themselves throughout the state.

In the midst of a settlement predominantly Norwegian, for example, would appear a family or more of Swiss, Germans, or Irish. These original ethnic settlements have, for the most part, persisted. Traveling north from Minot for twenty miles one will still find a grouping of Norwegians, then Bohemians, Swedes, and Norwegians again. Interspersed are Germans, Germans from Russia, Finns, Danes and Latvians as well as older American stock. The whole made for a rich diversity of ethnic groups who were searching for a living and an identity in their new land.

To make a living farming or in the new towns was one challenge for the immigrant; to acquire American culture was perhaps no less demanding. As a newly arrived Norwegian settler wrote in 1881:

> On the whole it seems to be a good deal easier to make a living; but there are many hardships connected with the life of a pioneer, especially at first. I should like to see you and the others come over, yet consider the matter twice before you leave the Fatherland and the place where your cradle stood. It is not a small matter.[3]

As the children adopted American manners, their parents gradually abandoned their ancestral loyalties. Where the child went, the adult followed.

Spiritedly independent and materialistic, the immigrants arrived possessing traits that suited their new homeland and provided the basis for their move into the stream of American life. Although living and working in America made them part of the new country in a physical sense, years of observation, of informal and formal education were required before the immigrant would feel a part of the country in a cultural sense. The speed with which the immigrants did this varied among nationalities, families and individuals.

The school was the institution that played the major role, directly or indirectly, in imparting American culture to immigrants in North Dakota.

Students and teacher from a rural school near Osnabrook in a flag-draped schoolroom which features maps students have drawn of North Dakota (*Fred Hultstrand History in Pictures Collection, NDIRS, NDSU*)

In the company of fellow nationals, the immigrant observed the customs of the old country and spoke his native tongue at social gatherings and in church. Business and legal transactions required an interpreter if one's knowledge of the English language was insufficient, but such actions were not everyday affairs. The immigrants could cling to their traditions and language in North Dakota, but their children were required to attend school. The school placed the children in contact with other nationalities and with a teacher who instructed them in the English language and attempted to foster patriotism. As the children adopted American manners, their parents gradually abandoned their ancestral loyalties. Where the child went, the adult followed.

Although the rural school was the primary Americanizing agent to immigrant farm families, it was not ideally suited to the task. Modeled on the "Little Red Schoolhouse" of New England, the rural school in North Dakota operated under very different conditions. Harsh winter weather and inadequate facilities forced short school terms, sometimes as little as sixty days or less in the early 1900s. The distance to

Mary C. and Robert L. Carlson

A Country School Teacher Remembers — Gladys Ganser

I signed my first contract at age eighteen, just out of high school, to teach in Jackson Township in Sargent County. I had twenty-nine pupils enrolled, five eighth graders, seven beginners, plus all grades in between. In the winter months a young man from Norway came to school to learn English. I spoke no Norwegian, but one of my pupils did. She did some translation for me. I cut illustrations from a Sears Roebuck catalog and a Guerney seed catalog to make a set of flashcards of common things in American culture. I used these to develop his vocabulary. We had language lessons before and after school. On stormy days the children helped by playing "store" with him. He went shopping for various items, butter and a hammer for example, which were illustrated on flashcards. The game also helped him learn our money system. He did learn to read, to recognize commonly used words, and to speak in such a manner that could be comprehended.

I remember one experience that was quite frightening. I came to school early one morning to build a fire. I went to the coal shed to get a scuttle of coal and found the door open. That was unusual. I also noticed that a large chunk of coal that had an imprint of a leaf on its crust had been moved. We had been studying fossils and I wanted to exhibit it. Then, from behind a partition where storm windows were stored, I saw a pair of big boots showing. I quietly peeked over the partition and saw a huge black man sleeping on hay bales he had taken from the barn. I quietly closed the door, fastened it, and ran as fast as I could to the closest neighbor. No schools had telephones then. They called the sheriff and called other neighbors to go to the school. The large number that gathered then went to the coal shed and awakened the black man. He was a very surprised, bewildered, blurry-eyed individual when he awakened to such a welcoming crowd. The sheriff asked him what he was doing there. He replied he had come in on a train from Minneapolis, where he had met a fellow, Tom Pendray, at a cattle sale. Pendray had invited him to visit his home in the community. He walked to get there, became lost after dark and found the school coal shed un-

continued on next page

school and the practice of some parents of keeping their children home to work produced irregular attendance. Teachers, who often had no knowledge of the language or culture of their pupils, added to the immigrant's difficulties.

Contemporary educational theorists such as John Dewey advocated using the cultural heritage of the community as the basis for education, but few rural schools did so. School curriculum gave slight attention to Scandinavian and German history and culture and none at all to the Germans from Russia. County school superintendents, generally Anglo-Americans, routinely referred to the Germans from Russia as "Russians" in their reports and decried the difficulties imposed upon education by the "foreign element" in their county. With a few exceptions, there was scant sympathy for the immigrants' attempts at cultural adaptation and little effort to relate education to their background.

The inability of teacher and immigrant student to communicate led to humorous, and occasionally traumatic incidents. Guri Sand, who came to the Hatton area in 1892 with her Norwegian parents, began school with a male teacher who was convinced that the Norwegians' inability to pronounce "j's" and "y's" correctly was simple disobedience. When he threatened to whip Guri's younger sister, the little girl became hysterical, behavior that the teacher assumed was meant to mock him. Guri restrained him from striking the child; the teacher "came to his senses, and things were better after that." Ms. Sand recalls that the young man's poor teaching example filled her with determination to find a better method to instruct children. She received a teaching certificate upon graduation from eighth grade and subsequently continued her education at the University of North Dakota.[4]

Coming from a Danish home in Renville County, Mathilda Staael Smith entered school with three other children from her family, all unable to speak English. Her rural school had thirty pupils under one teacher, who was unable to give the Staael children the individual attention they required. Pupils who could speak and read English well were classed as "smart," the others were virtually ignored. The Staaels attended school regularly but had little comprehension of what they were being taught for three years.[5]

4

Icelandic students discovered that teachers frequently found their customs disturbing. Icelandic women retained their original family name after marriage, a practice some thought indecent. The Icelanders' patronymic system, meaning that a brother and sister had different surnames, annoyed some teachers who did not appreciate their ethnic traditions. Icelandic customs celebrating Ash Wednesday included one day similar to Halloween when children would collect sweets from adults. On Ash Wednesday it was customary to play practical jokes, the favorite being to pin a small bag of ashes to the back of a man's coat or trousers, the victim being unaware of his adornment. Once done to a dignified teacher in a predominantly Icelandic school, the pupils were severely punished for a prank that, in their culture, was acceptable humor.[6]

locked, made a bed, and went to sleep. All this was true, but the invitation had been made years before. Our visitor was elderly, had become confused and thought the invitation had been given recently. The person he had known had been dead for some years, so the sheriff put him back on a train to Minneapolis. It was a most exciting and frightening experience for all concerned including the teacher.

If the newcomers' cultures and traditions were not valued or appreciated, if the color and diversity they could have offered to the school were ignored, the oversight was probably the fault of the local teacher. Professional educators encouraged ethnic celebrations and community involvement in the school. Laura Bassett and Alice Smith, two rural North Dakota teachers, published an attractive volume entitled *Helpful Hints for the Rural Teacher* in which they advised:

> If your district is a foreign one, be sure to have one of your very earliest programs, "A Program Of All Nations." Encourage the children to have parents bring pieces of all kinds of their native handwork, lovely Hardanger embroidery, Russian needlework, Italian hand carving. Put on folk dances in costume, encourage old folks to put on costumes, singsongs, play instruments. Let this night belong to the foreign patrons. Show your appreciation of their efforts and your admiration of their ability. Be sincere in this. The Old World has much to give to us that is really worth while and infinitely better than much of the tawdry jazz and bunkum we accept from each other these days.[7]

At the Brenna School District No. 13, Grand Forks County, ca. 1895-1896, school board members pose with the teacher and her students before the doorway draped with American flags. (*Elwyn B. Robinson Collection, UND*)

Mary Gallagher, superintendent of schools in Mercer County in 1896, reported that, "the population of Mercer County is almost entirely composed of the foreign element. Nevertheless," she added, "they have taken advantage of the opportunities afforded in the free schools and have made rapid progress considering the difficulties under which they labor, the first and principal one being their unacquaintance with the English language."[8]

Conscientious country school teachers struggled to overcome handicaps to teach English to the immigrant children. When the teacher could not speak the native tongue of the young pupils, an older student would sometimes serve as an interpreter.

A Country School Teacher Remembers — Alma M. Herman

It was in the fierce winter of 1936. I was teaching my home school in Pomona View Township, LaMoure County, five miles east of Kulm, North Dakota.

The schoolhouse, of modern design for that era, had an artistic bell tower over the entrance. A flag pole rose gracefully about ten feet above the tower. Passers-by on the Schoolhouse Road saw Old Glory waving on any day that school was in session, but never after sundown at Pomona View No. 2.

In opening exercises one morning, my fifteen pupils in grades one through eight discussed the American flag. Herbie called attention to the fact that our outdoor flag was faded and frayed. An appeal to the school board was answered with a beautiful new flag.

One morning we held a serious session. A ceremony was held that fostered patriotism in the heart of even my littlest first grader who watched wide-eyed as we respectfully retired our old frayed flag. Carefully folded, it was laid on the red, live coals of the school stove. Through the open stove door, we all respectfully watched as the red, white and blue colors turned to glowing ashes that mingled with the red coals. At noon that day our new flag was unfurled.

A few weeks later on the afternoon of a day that dawned calmly over beautiful fresh white snow, a northwest wind arose and faintly moaned in the fresh air register—our warning of a coming storm. School was dismissed early. The children were hustled into their overshoes and overcoats to hurry homeward, swinging their empty lunch buckets.

I hurriedly completed my schoolroom chores, locked the outer door behind me, and without looking back, started my two-mile trek homeward with the strengthening northwest wind at my back. Had I looked back, I would have seen the flag still out on the pole, whipping in the wind.

The typical North Dakota blizzard raged for three days. On Saturday the digging out began everywhere. On Sunday morning I was met at the church door by a parent. "Your school flag is packed in the snow on the School Road. I had to drive over it," he said. My mind was not on the sermon during the service. After Sunday dinner, with a team of sorrels hitched to a small runner sleigh, I drove to the schoolhouse. Before I shoveled the snow from the barn door, or

continued on next page

Still, the lack of a common language between teacher and pupil was the major problem regarding the child's educational progress. As one former student recalls:

> In those pioneer days, we did not need any fancy Normal School methods. Our trouble was that we did not understand the language of the textbooks. Frequently, when we asked the teacher to explain the meaning of words to us, he referred us to the dictionary and there we found ourselves entangled in a maze of words that had no meaning to us.[9]

When the teacher could speak the language of the students, English lessons and reading comprehension advanced more smoothly. The teacher in a rural school near the Icelandic settlement at Mountain was able to translate the lessons in *Appleton's First Reader* into Icelandic and then slowly repeat the lesson in English. In this manner the students learned to read and comprehend English quite rapidly.[10]

Though children struggled to use English in school lessons, they happily reverted to their familiar language when out of school. This persisted for many years. As late as World War II, one teacher remembers that her students used more German language than English when not in school and that when in school, "they thought in German and spoke in English."[11]

Some county superintendents, recognizing that students would learn English more rapidly if they were forced to give it practical application on the playground, instructed teachers to forbid the speaking of any foreign language on the school grounds during noon hour and recess. This requirement placed a considerable burden on teachers in some localities. "In one German community," wrote rural teacher Mary Brophy, "I was expected to keep the pupils speaking English at recess, while at home they didn't dare speak English."[12] Many pupils learned more English at recess than in class, however, because the teacher's schedule was too crowded to permit giving much attention to non-English speaking children.[13]

The English-only rule also helped curb ethnic snobbery on the playground because cliques based upon nationality were discouraged. In a McHenry County school, one former pupil remembers that when she started school, "the Norwegians chose to play on the east side of the school and the German-Russians on the west side, speaking our own language. But the teacher soon put a stop to that. We had to play together, and no fighting was allowed."[14] In a Burke County school where the rule was not enforced, Danish children segregated themselves. A non-Danish fellow student recalls childish anger because the Danes "spoke Danish in front of us, but we understood our names and assumed they were making fun of us."[15]

cleared the schoolhouse doorway, I ran to the drifted road. There, partially covered by sleigh tracks, was our new flag of red, white, and blue packed in the driven snow. With a lump in my throat, I fell to my knees to retrieve it.

It was several weeks before the torn, raveled rope could be replaced through the bell tower. Then one bright morning another new flag proudly waved over Pomona View School No. 2.

Teaching a group of students who spoke a foreign tongue made large demands upon young, inexperienced teachers. "I had thirteen French speaking pupils, all grades but the first and seventh," wrote one teacher. "I was very shy and did most of my teaching from the back of the room. The children spoke French at school to one another. Their comprehension of English was very poor; school was difficult for pupils and teacher."[16]

Beginning teacher Clara Jacobs worked with extraordinary patience to instruct a Norwegian boy who refused to speak a word of English. She kept him after school to work on the language — requiring his uncooperative older sister to act as interpreter; she visited the parents and insisted that they encourage him to learn English. A shy grin, but no words, was his only response to weeks of effort. Finally, in the midst of another unproductive session, she grasped the boy by the shoulders and shook him vigorously. The incident troubled her so greatly that she had nightmares about it, until, two days later, the child began to respond and soon began speaking English.[17]

Young student stands on top of school beside flag as his fellow pupils arrive. (*Fred Hultstrand History in Pictures Collection, NDIRS, NDSU*)

Memorization and frequent repetition were the methods commonly used to teach English. In Frances Hitz's childhood home, only Czech was spoken. The little English she knew upon starting school came from her older sisters and brothers who attended school before her and occasionally used an English word. Her first grade teacher, who had come from a Norwegian immigrant family, knew no Czech at all. "How I managed to learn to read, write, and think in English that first year," she wrote, "I do not know. I memorized the *Rose Primer* until I knew each page by heart, and to this day I can close my eyes and see each page, the word or words, and pictures that were above the words."[18]

Teacher Bertha Essler used an innovative method to induce her German-Russian pupils to take an interest in English lessons. Through a student interpreter she would discover what the children discussed at recess; then she would ask the children to discuss the same topic in English. By sketching objects, writing simple sentences and phrases on the blackboard, and requiring the children to participate in the lessons, her pupils were able to speak passable English by the term's end.[19]

A Country School Teacher Remembers — Elenora C. Larson

When I finished high school in 1927 at Bucyrus there was little choice in what kind of a career one could follow. It seems the reasonable choices I was aware of were teaching, nursing, or secretary work, none of which I had money to pursue.

For several months I had no satisfying job. Then, because of the kindness and help of my high school teacher, Joseph Rosenthal, I was able to go to Dickinson State Teachers College. I received a teacher's permit after only two quarters of study. I can't remember taking any courses in methods. I shudder when I think of how ill-prepared I was.

My first school was in the New Castle District in Dunn County. It was in an ethnic community of Bohemians. Children in first grade came without speaking English, parents could not speak the language either. I had fourteen pupils and taught most of the grades. It was very frustrating trying to teach the two first graders who could not speak English. We just kept on trying. Students were to speak only English on the school grounds.

I stayed with a family about a half mile from school. Two of my pupils acted as my interpreter when I spoke with the mother. The family never left me home alone. They were very clannish, going from one home to another, visiting relatives and friends. The men would congregate in one room playing cards, the women in another with their talk, all in Bohemian. I was left to entertain the children.

In winter the cars were put up for two or three months, traveling was done by sleigh and horses. I was sixty miles from home so I did not get home until Christmas, and then not again until Easter. Weekends a neighboring teacher and I would often walk the five miles separating us to be together. We often had dates with the local boys who took us to dances that were held in the homes.

Delores Bertsch Pfeifer asked her German speaking pupils to draw an object on the blackboard. "One wanted to draw a *gutch* (duck), the other wanted to draw a *kraut* (cabbage head). I then had them learn what it was called in English. They were quick to learn, even on the playground because it was not allowed to speak a foreign language on the school ground."[20]

Students who did learn English well and rapidly, like Ida Romsos, daughter of Norwegian immigrants who settled near Crosby, were motivated by a desire to be progressive and blend into their new country as quickly as possible. "I was determined that I wasn't going to be one of those who couldn't speak the American language. I decided that no way can I let that happen. It didn't take long until I learned it."[21] Alida Siverson, the eldest child in a Norwegian farm family in Williams County, was eager to learn English in her school. She in turn taught the language to her younger siblings during evenings.[22]

Other immigrant children found the first days of school frightening. Julia Rindel, from a Belgian family near Crosby, resisted going to school, but was persuaded to enter the first grade at age fourteen. Three weeks later she was advanced to the third grade, but still had no comprehension of the lessons. To ease the boredom of lessons she could not understand, she brought needlepoint work with her to school. The teacher soon banned the needlepoint and began spending extra time with Julia, taking her to the school window and pointing to objects outside and naming them in English. Under that kind of pressure, and with her French language background to aid her learning English, she obtained her eighth grade diploma in two years and went on to attend college and teach in rural schools. Her pronunciation was improved by a neighboring farm wife with pedagogic inclinations.[23]

The school also spread a knowledge of the English language among adult immigrants. Mary Barr Wilson, who homesteaded with her husband and children near Larimore in 1883, used a corner of a large granary on the farm to tutor her children. A German neighbor brought his little daughters to join in the lessons and often remained to listen. Soon both he and his daughters learned English.[24]

Some adults attended the schools expressly to learn English. Teaching at a rural school near Granville in 1910, Maude Youngs Carlson enrolled a nineteen-year-old Norwegian woman who walked to school to learn English. At another school a young

Norwegian man attended the primary reading classes. He was polite but caused Ms. Youngs some consternation by leaving the school during periods between reading lessons to stand outside and smoke.[25] Several teachers recall that the adult students were occasionally disrespectful to demonstrate that they were not to be ordered about by a young teacher simply because she happened to know English.[26]

Some accommodating teachers held special evening sessions for adults who wished to learn to speak and read English. Delrey Webster instructed a forty-year-old Swede in English during recess and often held spelling bees in the evening for adults who wished to sharpen their language skills.[27]

Motives of adult students were sometimes more than purely academic. Some of the young male homesteaders who attended school hoped to improve their social life as well as their English by dating the teacher. A number were successful on both counts. Many so called "schoolmarms" became "farm wives," making marriage a prolific source of Americanization.

Pupils who learned English would impart some of it to their parents. In an age before radio and television, conversation dominated the evening hours, and children related their experiences at school and spoke of what they had learned about their new country. Teacher Winifred Erdman boarded in a rural home and saw the effects of her teaching being passed on. "Little Elsie Buchholz would come home every night with her book, sit on her Dad's lap in the evening and read to him. Oh, that was the nicest thing. He was so proud that little girl could read. He was learning right there too."[28]

The Icelanders, whose cultural heritage placed great emphasis upon teaching children to read and write in their homes, took a lively interest in education and often probed their children as to what they had learned each day. Particular attention was given to American history, which sometimes occasioned controversy. In one family an argument developed over the wisdom of the Boston Tea Party, with one faction holding that the colonists' bold action was correct, another maintaining that it would have been more sensible to take the tea home and drink it rather than waste it. The grandfather took a more lofty view, claiming that if the colonists really wanted to disturb authorities, they would have thrown the coffee overboard.[29]

Rural schools helped Americanize the immigrant settlers because they brought a teacher into the community who usually boarded with one of the families. The teacher was expected to be active in community life, including social and church activities. Millie Morse boarded with a German-Russian family in 1926 and felt segregated at first, her meals being served to her in a separate room. A friendship soon developed, however, and when a daughter of the family married, Millie was given the honor of waiting on the bride's table.[30] Julia Noraker, boarding in a German home, was called downstairs on her first night in her new lodging to discover a group of neighbors, none of whom spoke English, on hand to inspect her, an experience that disturbed her. She, too, developed a warm relationship with her hosts in time.[31]

C. L. Robertson, teaching in a French community, was frequently called upon to help French adults fill out catalog orders. Serena Strand, who taught in a German community near Jamestown, attended the local church and participated in the German language service. She learned considerable German and developed mutual respect between the teacher and area residents.[32]

In one family an argument developed over the wisdom of the Boston Tea Party, with one faction holding that the colonists' bold action was correct, another maintaining that it would have been more sensible to take the tea home and drink it rather than waste it. The grandfather took a more lofty view, claiming that if the colonists really wanted to disturb authorities, they would have thrown the coffee overboard.

A Country School Student Remembers — Iris Hanlon Kline Traynor

I came to North Dakota as a young child in 1903. My parents, James and Mary Ann Hanlon were homesteaders on a claim at the foot of the Blue Hills, on the east side, about fifty miles southwest of Minot. My parents were concerned about their children's education. We had a room in our home called the boys' room. The youngest of my brothers had not finished eighth grade before we left Osakis, Minnesota. So arrangements were made with a neighbor, A.A. Farr, to come into our home and teach classes for John and some neighboring boys who had the same problem. I was not too much aware as to what went on in that school room. The door was closed and we two younger children were not allowed in there.

By the time I was of school age this same A.A. Farr was conducting school in a vacant sod shack three-fourths of a mile east of our home. A long table with benches on each side had been constructed. The furniture was quite primitive as was the teacher's table desk. There was a blackboard of sorts, a few books that had to be shared, and I believe there was a globe. The school term consisted of two months in the spring and two months in the fall. After two terms there, for some reason, the school was moved across the road to another abandoned homesteader's sod shack. This one was built from a thin wooden material called shiplap with sod all around it. The furniture and equipment were the same as in the earlier building. The problem of heating these houses was not very important because we had only spring and fall terms. There was a heating stove and coal was stored in a sodded up area at the back of the shack. We children played on these sod walls until we had them nearly worn down.

Two young women by the name of Romsass lived with their parents on the west side of the Blue Hills. Each taught in this school. Sometimes Ellen Romsaas drove to school in a buggy but sometimes she rode her bicycle. I would watch for her, run out to the road, place my hand on her bicycle and trot along beside her to school.

About 1908 the township was organized and a small school house was built. In the beginning we had only fall and spring terms but then some fall terms became four-month terms. Each year we were promoted to the next grade regardless of the length of the school term. This "real"

continued on next page

Women teachers were always in demand at social functions in rural areas with bachelor homesteaders, regardless of their nationality. Belle Berg, teaching in a Scandinavian community near Ross in 1911, had many suitors and attended a few square dancing parties where the small number of women, including herself, were "whirled hither and yon until dizzy." She boarded with a Norwegian family where neither parent spoke English and all communication was through the children.[33]

Settlers on the prairie had built their social groups and churches around nationalities, but at school functions the ethnic groups had an opportunity to mingle. Despite the tendency for nationalities to settle land in blocks, schools were rarely made up of only one nationality. At the rural schools they met and learned about each other as well as acquiring American culture. Oscar Oium, who attended a rural school near Towner, often exchanged his lunch with a German boy. He recalls enjoying the sausage and the heavy German cake, while the German youth was fond of Oium's Norwegian lefse and rulla pulsa.[34] Mrs. Frank Hitz remembers that even though she could not speak English well, she would entertain the teacher and younger pupils with Czechoslovakian folk tales she had learned from her mother.[35] Gladys Webster asserts that twenty-six different nationalities or combinations thereof attended school with her in Dunn County. She believes the children were motivated to learn English so that they could communicate with each other.[36]

Learning English was merely the first step in the Americanization of immigrant children in the rural schools. The state constitution charged the public schools with "the teaching of patriotism, integrity, and morality."[37] In reading and social studies lessons the pupils were exposed to America's heroes and were presumably inspired to develop a feeling of loyalty and protectiveness toward their adopted country.

Efforts to inspire patriotism were not limited to school classes. "Yankee Doodle," "The Star Spangled Banner," and "America the Beautiful," as well as the "Marine Hymn" were favorite songs in school-centered gatherings. In 1896, Superintendent of Public Instruction Emma Bates informed the governor and legislature that flags should be flown "from every schoolhouse in this state where we have so large a proportion of foreign population. It is a sad sight to an American heart," she continued, "to see audiences called upon to sing the National Air sit indifferently and perhaps only now and then one knowing the words or joining in the melody."[38]

On Columbus Day in 1892 patriotic school exercises were planned for every school in the state, whether the school was currently in session or not. The state superintendent urged county superintendents and teachers to get local residents to lay aside ordinary labor and "give exclusive attention to this grand holiday of the nation." The flag was to be raised accompanied by ringing bells at every school across the state and nation. The celebration, the state superintendent asserted, "will afford the long coveted opportunity for impressing upon the minds and hearts of our children and youth, both native American and those of foreign birth or parentage, those lessons of patriotism and sacred regard for the laws and institutions of our common country, that shall constitute a stronger protection than fleets of war or standing armies."[39]

school house was about two miles from my home but we cut across a school section and had to walk only about one and one-half miles. Unfortunately, some homesteaders began proving up their claims and moving away. Attendance dropped off and the school had to be closed. Those of us who were left were sent to what was called the Moffet School about six miles north of our place.

In this school we numbered about twenty and some were quite grown up. It was rather exciting; ages ranged from six to eighteen. The older boys and some of the girls had to stay out from school to help with the farming and so got far behind in their classes.

One important cultural service that was really great, not only for the school but also for the whole community, was the Traveling Library. After we found out about it our teacher would order out from Bismarck a large box of books. These we could check out, read at home, send them back, and then get another shipment of different books. I am sure that was the origin of my interest in libraries and in later life made me enthusiastic about rural library services and bookmobiles.

American Evenings, a lecture series sponsored by the state department of public instruction, featured popular lectures on patriotic themes in small towns across the state. Rural schools were also urged to connect their Memorial Day exercises with those of veterans groups. Books that would engender a love of country, such as *Morgan's Patriotic Citizenship*, said to foster the "most unselfish patriotism and noblest citizenship," were available to country schools through the county superintendent of school's office.[40]

Added pressure to inculcate patriotism and aid the nation faced the rural school during war time. Leila Ewen recalled how World War I affected her school:

> World War I kind of shook the school, shook the curriculum, shook the teaching, shook everything because the interest of the people was all on the war. We sold Liberty Bonds, we sold stamps, we did everything we possibly could for the soldiers. We put on all kinds of programs. The kiddies made their own programs. . . . The school was the social gathering place. They asked us teachers to put on plays to raise money. Raising money for the war effort besides teaching was a hard job.[41]

In one Wells County school the children adopted a soldier overseas, usually a local boy, and wrote to him faithfully. The children were rewarded for their attention with souvenirs from their adopted soldiers.[42]

World War I had ugly ramifications for the German and German from Russia immigrants in some communities. German speaking immigrants were accused of being sympathetic to the Central Powers and disloyal to America. Some school children taunted their peers who had a German background, leading to hostility on the playground. In McIntosh County prominent businessman John Wishek, a friend of the German-Russian settlers and a man proud of his German heritage, was indicted under the Espionage Act. During a three

The flag was to be raised accompanied by ringing bells at every school across the state and nation on Columbus Day, 1892.

A Country School Student Remembers —
Naomi Hagstrom Frasch

I attended country school through the eighth grade. At the age of four I came to the open plains of North Dakota from Sweden with my parents and a younger brother and sister. When I was seven and one-half years old I went to the first school we had in our community. Since the community was Scandinavian we had learned no English before entering school. It was a three-month summer term, held in an abandoned farmhouse. We were the only young students; the others were good-sized teenagers. The teacher played baseball with them during noon and recesses; he was an old hand with children.

He drove with horse and buggy some fifteen miles to the school; passing our home he picked up my brother and me. On the way to school we tried to teach each other to count. The teacher could never pronounce "seven" in Swedish; that takes an extra trick of the tongue. We "picked-up" English fairly fast. I progressed quite well and was soon alone in the second grade. While sitting on the teacher's lap I read while he watched a group of teenagers do arithmetic problems on the blackboard. When I came to an unfamiliar word I stopped and he would look down and pronounce it for me. It didn't take me long to learn to skip the unfamiliar and continue. The teacher chewed large hunks of tobacco, so he had the coal hod handy for spitting.

The next year, in September 1909, school was held for an eight-month term in a newly built schoolhouse. We had a lady teacher who knew how to get things done. The enrollment increased, more teenagers. The teacher decided I could do fourth grade work. I also had the only classmate I can remember. He dropped out in the spring and never returned.

By the time I was in seventh grade I had taken and passed all state exams for seventh and eighth grade except one. My teacher then was a recent high school graduate. I decided to review all subjects and write the exams again in December. Evidently she thought that wouldn't keep me busy so she offered to teach me high school Ancient History, which I lapped up.

Then, she advised my parents that I should go to high school. She told them I could stay with her mother, a widow living only one block from the high school in Bismarck. I started the second semester. My teacher explained to the high

continued on next page

12

week trial it was demonstrated that prosecution witnesses bore private grudges against Wishek, and the charges were finally dropped. In Cass County a local rural school board was criticized for failing to buy an American flag. Angered by the fuss that developed over the matter, school board president Henry Von Bank told the teacher that he would as soon see a pair of trousers flying over the school as the flag of the United States. Von Bank's inappropriate remark led to his conviction under the Espionage and Sedition acts, although the judge in the case directed a not guilty verdict.[43]

The extent to which the war affected the rural schools is difficult to gauge, but the war undoubtedly put pressure on the immigrant families to learn English and demonstrate their loyalty to America. It was during this period that Mathilda Staael Smith's parents abandoned their native Danish and began speaking English in their home.[44] In some areas church services began being held in English. Immigrant families across the state bought Liberty Bonds, which the rural schools promoted.

During World War II the schools were once again called upon to assist the national effort by promoting bond sales and conservation practices. After the Pearl Harbor attack the schools assisted in registering young men under the Selective Service Act. Inculcating the principles of democracy and impressing loyalty to the nation and its constitution became salient features of a rural school education.[45]

The teacher and the school were not welcomed enthusiastically in every community. Some immigrants retained strong cultural identities with the old country and viewed Americanization as corruption of traditional values. The Germans from Russia tended to resist Americanization and placed less emphasis upon education than any other major nationality. Their experiences in Russia, where the government had reneged on promises made to them when they began migrating from Germany to the Black Sea area in the mid-eighteenth century, made them suspicious of government and somewhat clannish. They were loyal to their community and family, thrifty, hard working, almost fiercely materialistic in their desire to make a success of their new life on the northern plains. Attending school was not considered as important as working at home or on the farm.

There were numerous Germans from Russia who did value education and supported the schools, but the school terms in their communities were the shortest, absent rates the highest, and teachers frequently the least trained and poorest paid. As late as 1938 a teacher in rural Grant County entered a school where none of the German-Russian children knew English, nor even the order of letters in the alphabet. By the end of the year she had succeeded in awakening their interest in learning, but their native tongue remained in use outside of school.[46]

school superintendent that she had taught me ancient history and asked if I could earn one-half credit by taking and passing the semester exam. The superintendent agreed. Then she went to a local pastor who was starting a class in Bible history for high school credit that I was able to join. The course consisted of one intensive lesson a week. I finished my first semester with three full credits, so I appreciate that gem of a teacher.

Louise Jevne, teaching in a German-Russian community in Mercer County in 1937, received letters from parents requesting that their children learn English. She had older pupils translate the first reader, word by word, and drill it into beginners. The first eighth grade graduation in the school's history was celebrated during her tenure at that rural school. She and other teachers believe that the women wanted their children to be educated; the men wanted them home to work.[47]

County school superintendents often decried the immigrant's lack of attention to education. In McIntosh and Morton counties, both heavily German-Russian, county school superintendents complained that nearly all the rural school district officers were foreigners who could not keep school records and seemed to have little interest in learning to do so. Several county superintendents lamented the immigrants' reluctance to send their children to school and suggested that the state provide for stricter enforcement of the truancy law.[48]

The school bell above and the flag below are illustrations from the catalog of one of the most popular suppliers to schools large and small, Colburn's School Supply Company of Grand Forks. In 1914-15, the bells ranged from $7.00 for one 20 inches in diameter to $27.85 for a 520 lb. 30-inch big one; flags could be purchased for from $1.50 for one 3x5 feet to $6.80 for the largest, 8x15 feet. The bell was shipped directly from the factory; postage for the flags was 6 cents.

The compulsory attendance law was commonly flouted because there was no state official to enforce it. Parents who wished their children to avoid the school's influence or to remain home to work could falsify the child's age (only those age eight through fourteen had to attend) or simply not send the child to school. They were seldom reprimanded because only a school official, who was likely to be a neighboring farmer, would report truancy. Neil C. Macdonald, state superintendent of schools in 1910, attempted to persuade officials to enforce the law. He was a strong advocate of education and struggled sincerely to upgrade rural schools and to improve the attendance. Regarding nonattendance of farm boys, he wrote in his 1910 report:

> Back of this sordid business is contempt for law and back of this is the lust for money — is the belief in the ignoble sentiment, that money makes the man. And so we have many thousand farms with broad and well-tilled fields as the price of many thousand boys with narrow and ill-trained minds.[49]

There was some successful enforcement of the truancy law. Morton County Superintendent W. F. Lorin reported that when the Germans in the county were informed of the compulsory attendance law, they conscientiously sent their children to school "out of respect for law and experience with strict laws in their mother country."[50]

In some districts hostility to the school made it nearly impossible to find a boarding place for the teacher. Belle Berg was taken to the home of a Norwegian Lutheran pastor who had agreed to board the

A Country School Student and Teacher Remembers — Emma J. Cole

As a product of the prairies of Barnes County, North Dakota I have some "first-hand" knowledge of the early rural school. I was five in 1897 when I entered the first grade in District No. 80, an ungraded system, where we were taught to spell and write "c-a-t" the first day.

During the eight years I was there, I learned there were five races of mankind, that there are over two hundred bones in a human body, how to diagram a complex sentence, who was President and Vice-president during the Spanish American War, how to draw a good map of the United States, as well as a cross-section of the eye, tooth, ear, and heart, how stocks and bonds were figured, and how to write, spell, and do arithmetic problems.

Spelling-bees and "ciphering down" were favorite pastimes, not only at school but also in the community. There were "lyceums" for adults where debates were held, for fun. Two topics I recall were: "Resolved: that a clean, cross woman is more desirable than a good-natured dirty woman," and "Resolved: that a lantern on a dark, rainy night is of more value than an umbrella." Families attended these get-togethers, held mostly in winter so the bob-sled ride was part of the fun.

With but one year of advanced teacher training at the Normal School in Valley City in 1911, I was happy to get a contract to teach in a rural school belonging to the Hope Special School District, about seven miles from my home in Hope, North Dakota. Board and room was secured at a farm home half a mile from school, at three dollars a week of five days. My father paid cash, $785, for his first car, a 1911 Ford, so he could bring my sister and me home for weekends. She was teaching a few miles from Hope.

In our area, I feel that the country school system did its duty well and amply prepared children for high school. The Hope superintendent was amazed that those entering from rural areas were so well prepared for higher learning. I believe this to be quite characteristic of our prairie days. It seems as if the country school of early times did all that could have been expected or hoped for.

✍✍

teacher near a rural Mountrail County school. When the pastor discovered that she did not speak Norwegian, he ordered her to leave immediately. Kidder County Superintendent Orra Hurd reported in 1910 that it was very difficult to obtain teachers for eight schools in German-Russian districts because boarding places could not be found. Permits had to be issued to untrained local people in order to supply the schools with a teacher. Similar situations were common in other counties.[51]

Maude Youngs Carlson, who taught a number of different nationalities in different schools over the years, observed that it took several years in this country before the newcomers recognized the importance of learning the English language and American culture. For the first few years the immigrants believed it was acceptable if their children learned English, but they believed learning the native tongue was more important. Time, she believes, led to a realization that the mother country was a memory that could not be recreated in North Dakota. The children who had little or no recollection of their parents' native land learned the English language and acquired more of the trappings of American life as they grew older. Many of them became ashamed of their parent's brogue and tired of hearing stories of the old country. The rural school had set them on a course that made them American in speech and outlook; only their nationality remained Old World.

✍✍

The rural school set immigrant children on a course that made them American in speech and outlook; only their nationality remained Old World.

Endnotes

1. Elwyn B. Robinson, *History of North Dakota* (Lincoln: University of Nebraska Press, 1966), p. 146.

2. *Ibid.*, pp. 282-83.

3. Omon B. Herigstad, "The First Norwegian Settlement in Griggs County," *North Dakota Historical Society Collections* (1906), p. 138.

4. Marie Mynster Feidler, ed., *In Retrospect, Teaching in North Dakota: Recollections of Retired Teachers* (Grand Forks: Retired Teachers Association, 1976), pp. 176-77.

5. *Renville County History*, Renville County Old Settler's Association, 1976, pp. 306-07.

6. Thorstina Walters, *Modern Sagas: The Story of Icelanders in North America* (Fargo: North Dakota Institute for Regional Studies, 1953), p. 135.

7. Laura Bassett and Alice Smith, *Helpful Hints for the Rural Teacher* (Valley City: Bassett and Smith, 1924), p. 60.

8. North Dakota, *Biennial Report of the Superintendent of Public Instruction*, 1896, p. 265.

9. Walters, p. 105.

10. *Ibid.*, p. 103.

11. Letter from Mrs. Frank Hitz, New Rockford, North Dakota, February 18, 1981.

12. Feidler, p. 145. *Biennial Report*, 1898, p. 259.

13. Letter from Vera McCombs Fairbrother, Towner, North Dakota, February 22, 1981.

14. Letter from Lillian Church, Leeds, North Dakota, March 5, 1981.

15. Letter from Bruce Ormiston, Bowbells, North Dakota, February 22, 1981.

16. Feidler, pp. 179-80.

17. Letter from Clara Jacobs, Stanley, North Dakota, February 22, 1981.

18. Letter from Mrs. Frank Hitz, New Rockford, North Dakota, February 18, 1981.

19. Letter from Bertha Essler, Kenmare, North Dakota, February 25, 1981.

20. Letter from Dolores Bertsch Pfeifer, Harvey, North Dakota, February 25,1981.

21. Interview with Ida Romsos, Crosby, North Dakota, January 19, 1981.

22. Interview with Alida Siverson, Williston, North Dakota, January 14, 1981.

23. Interview with Julia Rindel, Crosby, North Dakota, January 19, 1981.

24. Letter from Mary Barr Wilson, Dunseith, North Dakota, February 15, 1981.

25. Interview with Maude Youngs Carlson, Minot, North Dakota, November 18,1980.

A Country School Student and Teacher Remembers — Irene L. Dawson

Beginning in 1911, I attended a rural school in North Dakota for eight years. Lenora Township School No. 1 in Griggs County was located one and one-half miles east of my farm home. I remember the county superintendent visiting our school one time. Bertha's family had moved. Lily and I were in the seventh grade. In the beginning of the school year, our teacher asked us to copy a lengthy outline pertaining to the new subject called hygiene, formerly physiology. We copied diligently as she wrote on the blackboard. It was a long outline and we were busy most of the day. After finishing we put our copybooks in our desks and never looked at them. No study was required nor were we ever tested.

One sunny day in spring some bright-eyed pupil looked out the window and saw County Superintendent K. tie his saddle horse to a telephone pole. Teacher was informed, and she told Lily and me to study our hygiene outlines. Mr. K. came in, and walked about the room asking questions of pupils. He picked up my outline and asked Teacher if we had used it in our year's study. Teacher nodded in the affirmative, she may have been too frightened to think straight. "In that event," said Mr. K. "I will give these girls a passing grade and it will not be necessary for them to take state board examinations." Soon in the mail came printed slips of paper for Lily and me stating that we had passed hygiene. Who were we to question the powers above us? Is it any wonder that Mr. K. is the only county superintendent I remember from my grade school days?

I graduated from Aneta High School in 1923. During my senior year, along with many girls in my class, I took the teacher training course that was available. I chose teaching in Hettinger County because there were no vacancies in my home area. Experienced, older teachers were hired for local schools. Salaries were greater in the west, ninety-five dollars per month was more money than I'd ever seen at one time. Then, too, "Distance lends enchantment."

I remember vividly my first day of teaching. What a shock! I walked to school, carrying a lunch pail for the first time in my life, also a bottle of water. I found a small building, with two windows on each side, double desks, a pot bellied stove, a blackboard and a teacher's desk and chair. There were no books of any kind, no dictionary, no maps, no clock, no shades nor

continued on next page

window curtains, and not even a splinter of wood if needed on a chilly morning. Fortunately I had a watch. Someone had washed windows and cleaned the floor.

Five clean bright pupils came carrying the tattered books that their older sisters and brothers had used. Parents furnished books for their children. The school district furnished chalk. I taught those five for about six weeks. After corn was picked and outdoor fall work was completed their brothers and sisters came. Sixteen pupils in the small room, such well-behaved kids, eager to learn.

We sang songs I'd written on the blackboard from memory and I read to them. I played outdoors with them. I wrote to the school board and asked for geography and history texts that were supplied. Parents provided new books for the little children. I didn't dare ask for a lot. I bought crayons and drawing paper. Several first graders spoke little English and I knew no German. With the help of pictures cut from magazines and the assistance of older pupils I got through to them. They were so eager to learn. I wished I'd had more experience. There were no Christmas nor Last Day programs. No parent or school board member visited school. The last day of school all pupils kissed me good-bye, even the big boys.

Sanitation was an unknown word for many country schools. There were outdoor privies. No water was available except what pupils carried from home. In one school after Young Citizens League was organized, one family who drove to school with a team would bring a cream can of water. The last hour on Fridays the girls and I would clean the room, dust everything, scrub the floor, etc. The boys picked up the debris in the yard and scrubbed the toilet seat and floor of their privy with a broom. The girls took care of the same chore in theirs. How those kids flew around. Even the little ones took pride in doing a good job.

I think the country school, with a caring, well-trained teacher, provided the "beginning" of a good education.

26. Interview with Bernard Solberg, Minot, North Dakota, December 3, 1980.
27. Interview with Olivene Koppang, Williston, North Dakota, January 19, 1981. Interview with Gladys and Delrey Webster, Killdeer, North Dakota, January 15, 1981.
28. Interview with Winifred Erdman, Minot, North Dakota, November 19, 1981.
29. Walters, p. 105.
30. Feidler, p. 129.
31. *Ibid.*, p. 130.
32. *Ibid.*, p. 175.
33. Letter from Phyllis Campbell, Dunseith, North Dakota, February 15, 1981.
34. Interview with Oscar Oium, Towner, North Dakota, January 6, 1981.
35. Letter from Mrs. Frank Hitz, New Rockford, North Dakota, February 18, 1981.
36. Interview with Gladys and Delrey Webster, Killdeer, North Dakota, January 16, 1981.
37. *Biennial Report*, 1896, p. 16.
38. *Ibid.*
39. *Biennial Report*, 1892, p. 592.
40. *Ibid.*, 1892, p. 12; 1896, p. 144; 1900, p. 65.
41. Feidler, p. 206.
42. Letter from Mrs. Frank Hitz , New Rockford, North Dakota, February 18, 1981.
43. Robinson, pp. 366-67; Feidler, p. 175.
44. Feidler, p. 179.
45. Frank W. Cyr, ed., *Rural Schools and the War* (Washington, D.C.: National Education Association, 1944), p. 1.
46. Feidler, p. 180.
47. Interview with Louise Jevne, Lansford, North Dakota, November 20, 1980. Interview with Gladys and Delrey Webster, Killdeer, North Dakota, January 15, 1981.
48. *Biennial Report*, 1896, pp. 248, 265, 273; 1898, p. 239.
49. Neil C. Macdonald, *Rural School Progress* (Bismarck: Department of Public Instruction, 1910), p. 20.
50. *Biennial Report*, 1910, p. 204.
51. *Ibid.*, p. 198.

I think the country school, with a caring, well-trained teacher, provided the "beginning" of a good education.

Lenora Schools — The Records

North Dakota Country School Legacy Documents

THE *GRIGGS COUNTY HISTORY* published in 1976 describes the schools of Lenora Township as follows:

There were four schools in Lenora Township. The oldest school, No. 1, [was] built in 1883. The first location was on SE¼ of Section 7. At that time it was Tande School in Greenwood Township. From this location it was moved to NW¼ of Section 15. The patrons of this school wanted it moved again and since permission was denied, decided to move it anyway, one night, using Iver Udgaard's mules, to a site on Section 17, near Simonson Farm. A number of years later it was moved to SE¼ of Section 4. When closed it was sold and moved away.

Lenora School No. 3 *(from the Griggs County History, 1976)*

School No. 2 was located on SW¼ of Section 26. Known at that time as Torfin School in Pleasant Township, [it was served] by Andrew Torfin as the first clerk. J.H. was one teacher in 1884 and O.H. Olson in 1885. This school was sold and dismantled.

School No. 3 is located on SE¼ of Section 11 [and is] known as the Huso School. It is still used as a Township Hall for voting and other doings. J.H. Thomas and F.A. Markwood were teachers in 1885. O.P. Strand was issued $150.00 for building this school in July 1885.

Pladson School No. 4 was located on NW¼ of Section 29. This school was also sold when closed and moved away. In 1914 Martha Hansen was the teacher, and G.W. Simpson, clerk of the school board.

Teachers in those early days taught a 3-month period and school was held in the spring, part of the summer, and fall. [The] teacher's salary [was] $30 to $35 and $40 [per month] for the upper grades.

1885 school board officers were T.A. Huso, Martin Johnson, Andrew Torfin and A.V. Johnson.

A teacher's duties comprised not only of teaching but all-around janitor [work] as well. Coaxing those old wood and coal stoves to start mornings was quite a chore, many times smoking everyone out. The teacher walked to school then as well as the pupils, some several miles, teaching all grades 1 to 8 with up to 30 students at times. [There were] the programs by the pupils — the every-so-prominent basket socials to make some money — examination and graduation time. There is always some nostalgia in memories of the one-room country school.

✍✍

The document below along with the Teacher's Final Report on the six students and the Daily Program and Classification were submitted to Griggs County Superintendent of Schools M.L. Johnson in May by teacher Edith I. Smith. Eighteen of the thirty-six books reported to be in the school library were purchased in 1919 for a total of $11.29, as indicated in the invoice from Northern School Supply of Fargo reproduced on the following page.

(SHSND
Griggs County (ND), Lenora School District Records, RS40171,
"Teacher Contracts" files, Box 3,
"Teacher Reports" files, Boxes 2,3,
"School Textbook" files, Box 4)

SUMMARY OF ENROLLMENT AND ATTENDANCE

a. Enrollment: Boys 4 Girls 2 Total 6
City boys....... City girls....... Total......
Farm boys 4 Farm girls 2 Total 6
(1) No. pupils enrolled in first 8 grades 6
(2) No. pupils enrolled in high school (above eighth grade) - - - - ......
City boys....... City girls....... Total......
Farm boys...... Farm girls...... Total......
(3) No. pupils completing 8th grade - 1
City boys....... City girls....... Total......
Farm boys 1 Farm girls...... Total 1
(4) No. pupils completing high school (12th grade) - - - - - -
City boys...... City girls...... Total......
Farm boys...... Farm girls...... Total......
b. No. days school was taught (All days for which pay will be received) - - 160
c. Aggregate days of teaching - - - 760
d. Aggregate attendance - - - - - 759
e. *Aggregate absence - - - - - 0
f. **Aggregate non-membership - - - 2.01
g. Average daily attendance (d ÷ b) - 4.7+
h. Per cent of attendance d ÷ (d+e) - 100%
Verification: See that d plus e plus f equals c. Also that a times b equals c.

1. No. visits of county superintendent - One
2. No. visits of deputy superintendent - 0
3. No. visits of school officers - - - - One
4. No. other visits - - - - - - - 34

1. No. books in library (not including text books) - - - - - - - - - 36
2. No. books per pupil in library - - - 5
3. No. books purchased this year - - - 15
4. No. loaned this year - - - - - - 0

No. months school was taught, including all legal holidays and other days for which pay will be received - - - - - - 8
Salary of teacher per month - - - - 90
Grades taught - - - - - - - - - 3-6-8
No. Classes taught per day - - - - 18

Is there a U. S. flag in your school? - - Yes
Do you use it as required by law? - - Yes

* "Absence" means illegal non-attendance.
** "Non-membership" means legal non-attendance.

TEACHER'S REPORT

School No. I of Lenora School District No. 14
County of Griggs, State of North Dakota

County Superintendent of Schools:
I hereby submit my report for the term beginning September 19, 192 1, and ending May 26, 1922
Edith I. Smith Teacher May 26,
Dated at Aneta, No. Dak. 1922

Report received May 29 1922
Duplicate sent to clerk May 29 1922
M L Johnson Co. Supt.

GENERAL STATEMENT

A. Teacher's Training and Experience
1. No. years completed above 8th grade 4
Graduate 4 year high school Yes
Where Aneta When 1921
Graduate Normal School......
Where...... When......
Graduate college or university......
Where...... When......
2. No. years experience ......
Country...... City......
3. Are you a member of the State Educational Association? ......
4. Are you a member of the N. E. A.?......
B. School Property
Repairs and supplies needed: ......

C. Community Center Activities
Have you in your school district:
(a) A Farmers' Club? no
(b) A Parent-Teacher Organization? no
(c) A Boys' and Girls' Club? no
2. How many school entertainments (not held in school hours)? three
D. Health Conservation
Have you in your school:
(a) Hot noon lunch? no
(b) Medical inspection by nurse? Yes
By doctor? no
(c) No. individuals inspected? 4
(d) No. individuals having defects? 4
(e) No. individuals having defects remedied? 3
(f) How many times was your school-room floor scrubbed this term? 4
E. Is your school standardized for aid? no

F-24　　◆ BISMARCK TRIBUNE, STATE PRINTERS

TEACHER'S FINAL REPORT

No.	Names of pupils admitted during the term, surnames first, in order in which they appear in teacher's register	DATE OF BIRTH			Boy	Girl	City pupil*	Farm pupil*	Grade in course in which pupil is working	Grade completed	Days present	Days non-membership	Days absent	Total days taught	FINAL STANDING IN SUBJECTS									
		Year	Month	Day											Reading	Writing	Spelling	Numbers or arithmetic	Language or Grammar	Geography	History	Physiology	Civics	Nature study
1	Carlson Anna	1911	5	30		X		X	2	3	147	13	0	160	7	9	9	9	9					
2	Carlson John	1908	12	21	X			X	6	6	144	16	0	160	80	88	88	81	83	88	85	89		
3	Simonson Myrtle	1909	12	18		X		X	6	6	151½	8½	0	160	92	95	98	93	95	94	95	95		
4	Simonson Victor	1911	9	29	X			X	6	6	155	4½	0	160	94	93	98	91	95	94	95	94		
5	Strom Gunnar	1908	12	3	X			X	6	6	133	27	0	160	91	93	91	90	92	92	91	92		
6	Enney Kermit	1909	3	24	X			X	8		28	132	0	160										

Daily Program and Classification

9:00	15	All	Opening Exercise	6
9:15	15	8	Arithmetic	6
9:30	30	6	Arithmetic	2-3-4-5
10:00	10	3	Arithmetic	1
10:10	20	6	Physiology	2-3-4-5
10:30	15	all	Recess	1-2-3-4-5-6
10:45	15	8	History	6
11:00	15	6	Geography	2-3-4-5
11:15	10	3	Reading	
11:25	20	6	History	1-2-3-4-5
11:45	15	all	Nature Study	1-2-3-4-5-6
12:00	60	all	Noon	1-2-3-4-5-6
1:00	10	All	Opening Exercise	
1:10	10	8	Agriculture	6
1:20	20	6	Grammar	2-3-4-5
1:40	10	3	Language	1
1:50	25	6	Reading	2-3-4-5
2:15	10	3	Reading	1
2:25	15	all	Recess	1-2-3-4-5
2:40	15	6	Spelling	2-3-4-5
2:55	5	3	Spelling	
3:10	30	all	Writing and Drawing	1-2-3-4-5-6
3:40	20	all	Study Period	
4:00			Dismissal	

		DEBIT	
1	Little Men	1	15
1	Little Women	1	15
1	Legends of the Red Children		30
1	Ailsa Paige		60
1	Inside the Cup		60
1	Riders of the Purple Sage		60
1	Cabin in the Clearing		50
1	Hans Brinker		50
1	Along the Mohawk Trail		55
1	Two Little Knights of Kentucky		50
1	New Chronicles of Rebecca		60
1	Call of the Wild		60
1	In The Camp of Cornwallis		60
1	Grimm's Fairy Tales		50
1	Don, the Runaway Dog		50
1	Ambulance No. 10		60
1	Famous Stories Every Child Should Know		60
1	Legends Every Child Should Know		80
		11	05
	Postage & Ins.		24
		11	29

The document on the right lists the "official" textbooks selected by a group at a Teacher's Institute in Griggs County. The schedule above submitted by Edith Smith along with the Report on the preceding page is much easier than most, for as the *Teacher's Final Report* at the top indicates, she had but three of the eight grades and a single student in the third and eighth — the rest of the students were in the sixth grade. The report in 1922 included a distinction between "non-membership" and "absent" — obviously indicating that all students not there were legally absent. Teacher Smith reports an active entertainment schedule: three were held during the year. She reported the obligatory U.S. flag was used as required by law. She also reported that none of the books in the thirty-six-book library were checked out, but they may have been read in class.

Teachers, Salaries, Terms and Number of Pupils
in Pleasant School District No. 14 and Lenora School District No. 14
in Griggs County, 1884-1909

Year	School District & School No.	Teacher	Salary Per Month	Term and Starting Date	Number of Pupils by Gender
1884	Pleasant No. 2	J. H. Thomas	40.00	2 mo. Sept. 1	
1885	Pleasant No. 1	O. H. Olson	40.00	40 days Oct. 5	
1886	Pleasant No. 1	J. H. Thomas	35.00	39 days Nov. 1	
1887	Pleasant No. 2	Laura Amlie	35.00	2 mo. May 2	9B 6G
1887	Pleasant No. 2	John M. Cochrane	35.00	38 days Oct. 31	
1888	Pleasant No. 2	J. H. Thomas	35.00	2 mo. Nov. 4	
1889	Pleasant No. 2	J. H. Thomas	35.00	2 mo. May 6	11B 10G
1889	Pleasant No. 2	J. H. Thomas	35.00	2 mo. Feb. 5	10B 8G
1890	Pleasant No. 3	Nellie Simpson	35.00	2 mo. Sept. 22	9B 6G
1892	Pleasant No. 3	Laura Amlie	35.00	4 mo. Apr. 18	
1893	Pleasant No. 2	Nellie Simpson	40.00	3 mo. Oct. 2	
1894	Pleasant No. 1	Samuel J. Andahl	40.00	3 mo. Apr. 3	
1895	Pleasant No. 1	M. H. Hagen	35.00	3 mo. Sept. 25	
1896	Pleasant No. 2	Hilda Lynner	35.00	3 mo. Apr. 13	
1896	Pleasant No. 2	Hilda Lynner	35.00	4 mo. Sept. 1	
1897	Pleasant No. 1	Henry Mickels	35.00	3 mo. Aug. 14	10B 12G
1898	Pleasant No. 2	George W. Weldon	37.50	3 mo. Apr. 4	
1898	Pleasant No. 2	Syver Simonson	32.50	2 1/2 mo. Oct. 18	
1899	Pleasant No. 2	Andrew Sansbum	37.50	3 mo. Apr. 17	
1899	Pleasant No. 2	Myrna Moffatt	37.50	3 mo. Sept. 18	
1900	Pleasant No. 2	Bertha Sonju	37.50	3 mo. Mar. 18	
1900	Pleasant No. 2	Myrna Moffatt	37.50	3 mo. Oct. 15	
1901	Pleasant No. 2	J. H. Corcoran	37.50	2 1/2 mo. Oct. 28	
1902	Pleasant No. 2	H. A. Farr	37.50	3 mo. Apr. 7	11B 2G
1903	Pleasant No. 2	Bertha Sonju	40.00	6 mo. Jan. 9	12B 5G
1904	Pleasant No. 2	Harvey Bradley	37.50	3 mo. Jan 11	
1904	Pleasant No. 2	Harvey Bradley	37.50	3 mo. Apr. 19	8B 6G
1905	Lenora No. 3	Letitia Winger	45.00	6 mo. Jan. 16	7B 5G
1905	Lenora No. 3	Charles L. Smith	45.00	3 mo. Nov. 7	7B 4G
1906	Lenora No. 1	Ada Linendoll	40.00	6 mo. Nov. 13	4B 6G
1907	Lenora No. 1	Annie Hanson	45.00	4 mo. Mar. 18	3B 7G
1908	Lenora No. 1	Lily Johnson	45.00	6 mo. Oct. 5	3B 4G
1909	Lenora No. 2	Kaia Torgerson	45.00	3 mo. Sept. 28	11B 7G

The table above and on the facing page lists the available information about the teachers, their salaries, the term and number of pupils for one school. The data supports conclusions made by several observers in this publication. First, there is evidence that teachers did not stay in one school very long — in this example, only one served three years consecutively and but a few two. Second, the chart reveals that students actually went to school for a very short time until 1920. Third, with the exception of a few years in the early 1920s, salaries were very low in terms of purchasing power.

Notice that salaries declined dramatically in the 1930s and that they did not really go up until after 1942. The numbers and names also raise interesting questions for the student of local history: why, for example, did Myrna Moffatt and Bertha Sonju teach every other year between 1899 and 1901 (Bertha Sonju also came back in 1903)? Why were there half-terms in 1914 and 1917-18? Why was the school term shortened to but three and one-quarter months in 1936? What brought about the doubling of the monthly salary between 1942 and 1943?

Teachers, Salaries, Terms and Number of Pupils
in Pleasant School District No. 14 and Lenora School District No. 14
in Griggs County, 1911-1950

Year	School District & School No.	Teacher	Salary Per Month	Term and Starting Date	Number of Pupils by Gender
1911	Lenora No. 2	Clarice Hanson	50.00	7 mo. Sept. 5	8B 9G
1912	Lenora No. 2	Bertha Klubber	50.00	3 mo. Mar. 26	5B 9G
1912	Lenora No. 2	Hilda Halvorson	45.00	7 mo. Sept. 3	8B 9G
1913	Lenora No. 1	Maggie Robertson	50.00	7 mo. Sept. 3	9B 8G
1914	Lenora No. 4	Martha Hansen	50.00	3 3/4 mo. Feb. 16	4B 6G
1915	Lenora No. 2	Maggie Robertson	50.00	8 mo. Sept. 6	14B 16G
1916	Lenora No. 4	Geraldine McClanathan	50.00	7 mo. Sept. 4	5B 3G
1917	Lenora No. 2	Mary Evans	60.00	3 3/4 mo. Nov. 21	10B 10G
1918	Lenora No. 4	Agnes O. Haugen	50.00	4 mo. Mar. 18	3B 3G
1918	Lenora No. 4	Alice M. Brandvold	75.00	7 mo. Dec. 2	
1919	Lenora No. 3	Eleanor Strand	75.00	5 mo. Feb. 17	9B 5G
1920	Lenora No. 2	Florence Otte	100.00	8 mo. Sept. 13	8B 12G
1921	Lenora No. 1	Edith I. Smith	90.00	8 mo. Sept. 19	4B 2G
1922	Lenora No. 3	Olga Johnson	75.00	8 mo. Sept. 25	5B 8G
1923	Lenora No. 3	Bertha M. Tollefson	75.00	8 mo. Sept. 4	5B 8G
1924	Lenora No. 3	Bertha M. Tollefson	75.00	8 mo. Sept. 8	6B 5G
1926	Lenora No. 3	Gerhard Ovrebo	80.00	8 mo. Sept. 20	
1929	Lenora No. 3	Ellen Jensen	70.00	8 mo. Sept. 8	
1930	Lenora No. 3	Elllen Jensen	75.00	8 mo. Sept. 15	
1931	Lenora No. 3	Elaine Greenland	70.00	8 mo. Sept. 14	10B 10G
1932	Lenora No. 3	Elaine Greenland	64.35	8 1/2 mo. Sept. 19	11B 11G
1933	Lenora No. 3	Vivian M. Hamre	50.00	Sept. 11	
1934	Lenora No. 1	C. A. Erlandson	50.00	8 mo. Oct. 1	6B 9G
1935	Lenora No. 3	Charlotte Houghton	65.00	8 mo. Sept. 16	6B 13G
1936	Lenora No. 3	Beatrice Starr	65.00	3 1/4 mo. Sept. 21	
1937	Lenora No. 3	Beatrice Starr	65.00	8 mo. Sept. 20	
1938	Lenora No. 3.	Mrs. P. A. Egge	65.00	8 mo. Sept. 14	
1940	Lenora No. 3	Phyllis Anderson	65.00	8 mo. Sept.	
1941	Lenora No. 4	Phyllis Anderson	65.00	8 mo. Sept. 8	
1942	Lenora No. 3	Phyllis Anderson	65.00	8 mo. Sept. 8	5B 8G
1943	Lenora No. 3	Edna Almaas	120.00	8 mo. Sept. 20	
1944	Lenora No. 2	Mary Jane Zimprich	125.00	9 mo. Sept. 4	
1945	Lenora No. 2	Mary Jane Zimprich	130.00	9 mo. Sept. 10	
1949	Lenora No. 2	Myrtle Pederson	180.00	9 mo. Sept. 12	5B 2G
1950	Lenora No. 2	Mrs. J. B. Forberg	180.00	9 mo. Sept. 11	

A Country School Teacher Remembers — Sylvia Syvertson Fogderud

My decision to become a teacher was made when I was in the first grade. I loved school and hated to miss a day. In those days we had no television or radio and no car, so much time was spent at home. One of our favorite pastimes was playing school and I liked being the teacher. I taught sixteen years in country schools; fourteen in town schools.

I began my college days in 1929 at Valley City State College. A course I took there which was es-

pecially helpful to me in teaching was one in rural methods. We traveled by car to a rural school north of Valley City for one month; half of the time we observed and taught some classes in the morning, the other half in the afternoon. At the end of nine months I received a second grade elementary certificate that could be converted into a first grade elementary certificate after teaching

continued on next page

Pupil's Final Examinations for March 1910

The Eighth-Grade Statewide Examination

from *The Westland Educator*: Volume 10, No. 1 (May 1910), pp. 23-25.

PHYSIOLOGY

(Answer any five questions)

The exam which all students from country schools took were delivered by the County Superintendent and supervised by the teacher.

The first striking aspect of the exam is that it was all in essay or oral form in the early years — no multiple choice or true/false.

1. Describe the heart as to location, size, shape and structure.
2. Analyze the blood and tell one function of each part.
3. *(a)* Describe five parts of the eye; (b) Discuss the care and protection of the eye.
4. *(a)* Tell the effect of alcohol upon the nerves, the stomach and the heart. (b) What is a narcotic?
5. *(a)* How should a school room be ventilated? *(b)* Name three cautions to be observed in breathing.
6. *(a)* Locate the lungs; give their size and functions. *(b)* How may tuberculosis be prevented?
7. *(a)* Of what use is athletics? *(b)* How is a drowning person resuscitated? *(c)* Why are mosquitoes a menace?

continued on next three pages

eight months and reaching the age of twenty. In July 1972 after taking evening classes and attending several summer school sessions, I reached my goal; I received a bachelor of science degree from Valley City State College.

Some of my most vivid memories include the following: In the Dirty Thirties the dust storms got so bad that the schoolroom was dark as night. We had no lights, so all work ceased.

I dreaded morning for fear of finding some drunks warming up in my schoolhouse. The door to one of my schools was always padlocked, but one night the padlock was broken. My portable phonograph that I had purchased for teaching music and some other personal items were gone. The school board put on several more padlocks and each time they were broken, so they decided to leave it unlocked. It was believed that people passing by used the schoolhouse for shelter. It was a very cold winter and travel was with horse and bobsleds only. What a relief to get there and find the building empty! Many mornings I found refuse from unwanted visitors.

A sixth grade boy standing with his back to the stove and his clothes started to smoke. Someone told him he was on fire. His classmate, a girl, said, "Oh! He is too green to burn."

Discovering that your students have started a fire on the dirt floor in the barn on a cold winter day so they could warm up!

When I started teaching getting a job seemed to me more important than the salary. During my early teaching years, 1930-1939, I began with a seventy-dollar-a-month contract and dropped to rock bottom in my fifth year. That year, 1934-1935, I taught Plainview School No. 98 in Barnes County for forty-five dollars a month. In 1938-

1939 I was teaching Greenfield School No. 1 in Griggs County; I earned sixty-five dollars a month for an eight-month term. The Plainview contract stated that I would teach from one to nine months, depending on funds. I taught the whole term, but received no salary for the last five months until the following fall when I finally was paid, but I received no interest. The school closed for a few years.

My income during those years explains why I had to find work during the summers I didn't go to school. I spent two of those summers working as a hired hand on farms. I say "hired hand" because I had to do both chores and housework. I started the day by milking the cows, separating the milk, and feeding the calves; then I returned to the house for duties there. The day ended as it had begun. Other summers I worked for shorter periods. My wages were five dollars a week, for a seven-day week.

Being a rural school teacher was very rewarding. Teacher and students became very close to each other, almost like a little family. The situation of a mixed age group was good. Children learned to mingle with others both older and younger. The younger ones learned so much by listening to the older ones. I liked teaching a mixed group because it kept me more alert. Had I been forced to teach in town schools all the time I would have quit long before I did. I could never have taken thirty years of that stress and strain. I was very sorry to see rural schools disappear and worked against it until the end.

≈✍

CIVICS

(Answer any five questions)

1. Explain the terms: *civil township, veto, subpoena, consul, naturalization.*

2. How are vacancies in the following offices filled: U.S. senator, governor, speaker of the House, school director, president?

3. Give the names of the men who fill the offices of governor of North Dakota, judge of your district, director of your school, senators from your state.

4. Explain how a bill becomes a law.

5. Name five county offices and five state offices, stating one duty of each.

6. Describe two measures before the present congress.

7. Name the state institutions and tell how they are governed and maintained.

Students were expected to know both the political process and the current political issues. In 1910, there was no possibility that a woman would be elected to any of the offices listed in "Civics, 3."

WRITING

(Answer the first and any other four)

1. Quote eight lines of a memory gem.

2. Explain muscular movement, full arm movement and finger movement.

3. Make out a cash account having three items on each side.

4. Write a letter of acceptance to a formal invitation.

5. Write an order for a bill of goods, and address the envelope.

6. Make out a draft on a St. Paul bank in favor of yourself.

7. Write the first ten small letters of the alphabet showing proper proportions, and describe how the first three should be made.

Every student memorized poetry and literature in every grade.

ARITHMETIC

(Answer any five)

1. Define power, root, rectangle, cube, cylinder.

2. Give a method of finding: *(a)* Area of a triangle. *(b)* Area of a circle. *(c)* Solid contents of a cylinder. *(d)* Hypotenuse of a right-angled triangle having the base and altitude given.

3. *(a)* Name and define two terms used in percentage. *(b)* Give method of solution of two classes of problems in percentage.

4. A commission merchant sells 800 barrels of flour, at $6.43 3/4 a barrel, and remits the net proceeds, $5021.25; what is the rate of commission?

5. A school building is insured for 5/8 of its value; the premium at 1 1/2% is $125.25. What is the value of the school building?

6. A note for $800.00 at 6% was given Aug. 1, 1907. On this note the following payments were made: $200.00, Feb. 16, 1908; $25.00, Dec. 28, 1908; $50.00, March 6, 1909. What was due June 30, 1909?

7. *(a)* How many gallons of water will a cistern hold which is 7 feet long, 6 feet wide, and 11 feet deep? *(b)* How many bushels of wheat will a bin contain which is 8 feet square, and 8 feet deep?

8. The real estate taxes of a certain farmer in this state amount to $84.89, where the rate of taxation for the year is 39.8 mills. What is the assessed valuation of his real estate?

The school prepared students for the practical world. There were no calculators.

GEOGRAPHY

(Answer the first and any other four questions)

1. Draw an outline map of North Dakota and locate the three principal railroads, four important rivers and all cities containing state institutions.

2. *(a)* What causes the change of seasons? *(b)* Discuss winds as to causes, kind, use.

3. Write a letter to a friend describing in detail an imaginary journey from your home to New York City, and then to Liverpool by steamer and from there a tour thru the British Isles. Speak of the climate, products, industries, people, cities, and scenery of the British Isles.

4. Why are so many people from our state going to Canada? Where is Canada? Compare the eastern and western parts of Canada as to surface, climate, and occupations.

5. What and where are the following: (1) Hawaii, (2) Pike's Peak, (3) Nile, (4) Chicago, (5) Alps, (6) Japan, (7) New Zealand, (8) Vesuvius, (9) Amazon, (10) Berlin?

6. Draw an outline map of the United States, locating the principal wheat, lumber, mineral, and cotton regions, the four rivers you consider the most important, the ten most important commercial cities and the two chief river systems.

7. Describe briefly the chief characteristics of the people of the following countries: Holland, China, Switzerland, Egypt, and Italy.

Question 3 presumes extensive study of other cultures and geographical areas and the ability to write in the style popular in newspaper features of the time which did exactly what the question asks of the student.

ORTHOGRAPHY

(Answer the first and any other four. Fifty-two credits will be given the first and twelve for each of the other four.)

Little has changed in teaching the complicated spelling of the English language in the last one hundred years — students memorized the words.

1. Spell list of words.

2. Write the following in sentences: *except, accept; receipt, recipe; there, their; ever, every; bear, bare; does, dose.*

3. Mark diacritically the accented vowel in twelve of the words in question one.

4. Write the plurals of the following words: *cactus, mother-in-law, company, turkey, piano, negro, radius, sheep, beef, woman, roof, chief.*

5. Analyze the following words and give root, suffix, and meaning of each: *circumflex, phonograph, transport.*

6. Write *(a)* synonyms of: *branch, bear, clad, calm, damage, brave; (b)* homonyms of: *fair, flew, miner, need, so, hair.*

7. Give and define twelve common roots and prefixes.

LIST OF WORDS

plateau	homestead	comet	indictment	agriculture
coulee	invitation	superior	studious	insurgents
hemorrhage	preparation	mortgage	assessor	
corpuscles	prairie	constitution	continent	
relinquishment	avoirdupois	revision	physiology	
materials	nationality	controversy	familiar	

HISTORY

(Answer any five of the seven questions)

The history part of the exam asks for much more than names and dates. Interestingly, only one of the seven questions focuses on "Great Men of the Past."

1. Write an account of the life and public work of Washington, Franklin, or Thomas Jefferson.

2. Write a sentence about each of the following named colonies telling when it was founded, nationality of the settlers, and any other important information about them: Massachusetts, Virginia, New York, Maryland, New Jersey, Georgia.

3. Indicate three important results of the French and Indian War. Indicate three important things gained by the adoption of the Constitution.

4. What was the "War of 1812" about? What was the "Era of Good Feeling"? What is meant by "Nullification"? What is meant by "Secession"?

5. Give the principle provisions of any two of the following: Compromise of 1850, Fifteenth Amendment, Wilmot Proviso. What is the "Spoils System"?

6. Explain any five of the following expressions: protective tariff, tariff for revenue, advalorem duties, strikes, boycott, "free silver, 16 to 1," financial panic, Monroe Doctrine.

7. Name the last five presidents in order (5), with dates of their respective administrations (5) and two events of each administration (10).

READING

(Answer the first question and any other four. Forty credits will be given the first and fifteen credits for each of the other four.)

"Thanatopsis" by William Cullen Bryant (1794-1878) continued to be memorized by eighth graders in North Dakota in country schools through the 1950s.

"To him, who, in the love of Nature, holds
Communion with her visible forms, she speaks
 A various language; for his gayer hours
She has a voice of gladness, and a smile
And eloquence of beauty, and she glides
Into his darker musings, with a mild
And healing sympathy, that steals away
Their sharpness, ere he is aware.

"So live that when thy summons comes to join
The innumerable caravan that moves
To that mysterious realm, where each shall take
His chamber in the silent halls of death,
Thou go not like the quarry slave at night,
Scourged to his dungeon, but, sustained and soothed
By an unfaltering trust, approach thy grave,
Like one who wraps the drapery of his couch
About him, and lies down to pleasant dreams."

1. Read orally the above selection (at the bottom of the previous page).

2. Explain "holds communion," "summons," "innumerable caravan," "silent halls." What is the antecedent of "she" in the second line?

3. Name five selections suitable for study in the seventh and eighth grades.

4. Write a list of five good books and give the author of each.

5. Write at least twelve lines of some selection you have learned and give the author of same.

6. Give lists of papers and magazines which you read regularly.

7. Write at least twelve lines on the event of greatest importance to you which has occurred during the last three months.

GRAMMAR

(Answer five out of seven)

1. "As they descended, Rip every now and then heard long rolling peals like distant thunder, that seemed to come from a deep ravine between lofty rocks, toward which their rugged path conducted." Pick out the different clauses or prepositions in this sentence, tell what kind each is, and what it depends on. What kind of a sentence is it?

2. Write a sentence containing a clause used adverbially. Write a sentence containing a prepositional phrase used to modify an object of a verb. Write a sentence containing two subordinate conjunctions. Write a sentence containing an adjective clause which does not contain a relative pronoun.

3. Write the following paragraphs with full punctuation, margins, etc.: mother I put all the nuts back every one he cried now the squirrels wont be hungry will they my dear little boy I am so glad said mrs howe that was so thoughtful.

4. Write the third person singular and the first person plural forms of the verb "sing" for all tenses of the indicative mood. (12) Give the principal parts of *beat, bite, cling, ring, hang* (to execute), *draw, lay, wear.* (8)

5. Write the following sentences filling each blank with the correct word:
   (Have or has) everyone found (his or their) book?
   Each pupil must obey (their, his or her) teacher.
   (Who or whom) were they? (Who or whom) did you see?
   (Who or whom) did you say wrote the letter?
   Probably I (will or shall) go to the party.
   We (will or shall) go in spite of you.

6. Parse the italicized words in the following sentence: The Roman people considered the Gauls *very* dangerous *enemies* and always *kept* money in the treasury *to use* in fighting *them.*

7. Give a definition of each of the parts of speech and use an illustration of each in a sentence.

Perhaps less than 1 percent of students attending elementary schools in the last decade of the twentieth century would even know what the word "parse" means, but there has been many revivals of teaching prescriptive grammar in the last one hundred years. The distinction between will and shall has all but disappeared in all but the most rigorously formal of English writing and speaking.

Students at the Gallatin School, Griggs County, in 1904 pose with their teacher beneath a sign which says "Work and Win." The teacher, H.A. Bemis (male teachers were almost always referred to with the initials of their first and second names rather than by given names), appears to be the type who would have his students well-prepared for the state examinations.

(Myrtle Porterville Collection NDIRS, NDSU)

Chapter 2

Rural Schools as Community Centers in North Dakota

Mary C. and Robert L. Carlson

THE RURAL SCHOOL IN NORTH DAKOTA served as a community center from its very inception. The school was, in fact, the product of community effort because people met to decide where to locate it, how to build it, and to select a board of local citizens to manage it.

In early North Dakota communities were small geographically. Because transportation was limited to horses or undependable automobiles, small communities of only a few miles in radius developed to serve the local residents' needs. A small town provided the relatively simple material requirements for the immediate rural area.

Local churches reflected the religious denominations of area settlers, and a nearby rural school educated the children.

To most settlers in rural North Dakota the community was, as far as they were concerned, the universe. Community life was relatively simple, but its cultural importance was enormous. The community originally supplied education that was later transferred to schools. Children received vocational training from parents; communities provided recreation in the form of local baseball teams or in the games and activities that accompanied picnics and other gatherings. The home and church were responsible for character education. Everyone knew everyone else; there was no history of the community except as it was being made. Within the confines of these small communities the school pursued the task assigned to it — to make children literate.

The school's primary responsibility was education, but its convenient location made it a natural gathering place for community functions. Because community life was vital to the individuals who comprised it, the school's role as a community center rivaled its pedagogic value.

Progressive educator John Dewey placed great emphasis upon getting the school to become a social center for the community. His ideas meshed with the personal experience that led Laura Bassett and Alice Smith to urge rural teachers to get the school tied to the community. "Participation on the part of the community in your school," they wrote in their fine little volume, *Helpful Hints For The Rural Teacher*, "is most desirable. It is the keystone of success." They included an entire chapter of advice for the rural school hostess in which they suggested that the new teacher encourage the formation of a community club and offer the school as a meeting place. "But let the school part be subordinate," they warned. "If you are wise, while you may still be the directing power in this new movement, you will not appear to be such, but will tactfully let the community feel its ability and responsibility in the matter."[1]

Doings in a North Dakota School Enterprise District, Mountrail County

Margaret E. Sheeley, Teacher

from *The Westland Educator*, 16:1 (May 1914), pages 31-32.

School opened here last September in a bare shack with an attendance of two.

First, the board were induced to purchase a set of about twenty tools. We used them in practical manual training, such as putting the school building in repair, putting in ventilators in our storm windows, making window boards, thus installing a home ventilating system, making a closet for individual drinking cups, a cover for the water pail, last but not least, a good book case.

Our attendance was never over seven, but we were always busy. Also rope was secured and the boys were taught the different splices and knots, and how to make rope halters, later on the farmers were shown how at our club meetings. The girls had plain sewing with raffia work for the little tots. Agriculture, drawing, business arithmetic, and writing, besides the common branches, were taught.

In November a free "Farmers' Library" was secured from Bismarck, 620 pamphlets from Washington, some year books, pamphlets from the N.D.A.C. [North Dakota Agricultural College, which became North Dakota State University] and plenty of good farm papers, the teacher subscribing for four and saving them all. Then came a steady diet of Farmers' Clubs for a week or two, the pupils prepared a short program and the people were invited to hear it.

After the program the teacher addressed the farmers on the value and benefit of a co-operative farmers' organization. We organized the Farmers' Industrial Club with fifteen charter members. We held meetings in the school house every other Friday evening this winter. Our club has been gaining in membership and confidence all winter, until now we have about thirty members and are doing good work. They have decided to plant Northwestern Dent Corn, are purchasing a Babcock milk tester, starting a milk ring. They have exchanged, sold and bought grain, hay, and seeds. They also are purchasing a pure-bred stallion, and have other business in view.

We have also decided either to consolidate or at least to build a decent school building for next year.

The school served as a community center in two respects: it offered school programs, and it provided a meeting place for gatherings not related to the school. Community activities at the school benefited local educational efforts by helping to engender popular support for education and to create an awareness of the school's needs. In return the school served as a social center and offered entertainment.

Christmas party
(Carrie Busby Collection, NDIRS)

Many schools offered a variety of entertaining programs, none more popular than the Christmas program. The festive highlight of the year in many localities, the Christmas program drew everyone. Parents beamed as their children performed and other local residents witnessed what was in most schools a mainly secular program of plays, songs, poems, and the inevitable arrival of Santa at the conclusion of the affair. The spirit of the season, perhaps, brought community camaraderie to its zenith at the Christmas program. Even bitter December weather did not deter the audience from attending. At Oscar Oium's 1914 Christmas program, every person in the community crowded into the school to view the students' efforts despite the forty-degree-below temperature. Occasionally blizzards on the evening of the program forced everyone to stay at the school overnight. At one school where this occurred, the program was performed a second time. Children wrapped coats about themselves and went to sleep on the floor; adults conversed or played cards the night through and returned home the next day.[2]

The community expected an elaborate Christmas program, and the teacher usually saw that they got one. Preparation for the annual event began as early as October in some schools, though that was unusually early. In most schools, however, practice of Christmas songs would begin immediately after Thanksgiving and rehearsals of plays, poems, and other recitations would gradually take up more time until regular instruction actually stopped altogether for the last few days before the program. Every child had some part in addition to group singing. Mothers helped if extra recitation was needed at home. By the time the long-awaited program arrived, even the youngest and shiest children could give a glib rendition of their assigned lines. No effort was spared to make the program a success. As one former student recalls:

> The Christmas program was probably the biggest event of the year. Everyone practiced for weeks to get the little skits, monologues, poems, and songs memorized. Program practice meant getting away from the hum-drum of regular lessons so it was a great treat. The school house was decorated with red and green streamers and hand-colored pictures with a Christmas theme.

> The stage had to be made and seating arranged. Each mother would furnish one or two white sheets for stage curtains and these were also dividers to make a dressing room on each side. At the program I'm sure the mothers had to check to see who had the whitest sheets. Usually they were finger-marked before the program started and eyes peeked from between them during the program. Planks were laid across the seats to make room for the parents, grandparents, and neighbors. Everyone in the community went to the Christmas program.

> The schoolhouse looked simply dazzling in the light of the gas lanterns. The tree was decorated with paper chains, popcorn, and tinsel and it had a star on the top. Sometimes the teacher would donate some colored glass balls. Little snap candle holders held the tiny candles upright on the

tree to complete the decoration. These candles were seldom lit because of the fire hazard, but they were pretty anyway, and the pine smell filled the room.

After we had all spoken our "pieces" and sang our songs, someone passed out the packages under the tree. Sometimes a wrinkled, sagging Santa did the honors and all the little children would scream and cry. We drew names to see who would buy each one a gift. The cost was usually under 50 cents. We always looked forward to the teacher's gift for us. There were sacks of nuts and candy for all the children and an apple for each grown-up. Then we had a sack lunch which the mothers prepared. The grown-ups had coffee out of the tin cups that were really hot to touch. The big boys always blew up their sacks and popped them in some girl's ear after they had eaten their lunch.

Then the curtains were taken down and the desks were pushed back and everybody sang and played the games like "Farmer in the Dell" and "Skip to My Lou." Little tots would go to sleep and Mama would make a bed for them on top of a bunch of coats on a desk top. This kept on until everyone was hoarse from singing and very tired. We'd all bundle up and go home where I'd dream the whole evening over again in my sleep.[3]

The Christmas program was a universal favorite in rural schools, but it was only one of several programs for the public. Local customs, ethnic backgrounds, and a particular teacher's fondness for a holiday or season gave individual schools some unique programs. At one Wells County school, for example, a child was selected to take charge of an Easter program to which only mothers were invited.[4] Pleasant Valley School in Bottineau County had a traditional Fall program and basket social after harvest was completed.[5]

At the Carkuff School in Mountrail County the Young Citizen's League presented two programs each year: one for the parents and another elaborate program with skits, recitations, readings and special music for the public. This was a popular program throughout the 1930s.[6]

The Missouri Ridge School near Williston held spelldowns and competition in solving arithmetic problems for the public. These events were sometimes accompanied with box or pie socials. Spelldowns were so popular in Nelson County in

A Country School Student and Teacher Remembers — Verna E. Holden Silha

I was six years old in the fall of 1923 when I started rural school, Holden No. 2 in Adams County. Water was always a problem. We carried what we needed in half-gallon tin syrup pails or went without. I envied the family of three who carried a gallon of water and still had drinks on a warm afternoon. I don't remember any washing facilities when I went to school. Later, when I taught rural school we made arrangements to haul it and put it into a heavy five-gallon crock with a spigot. That left us a little for the "wash-dish" where we all washed in the same water and wiped on towels we hung on nails. I changed this. I heated water on top the stove and we used two "wash-dishes," one for the boys and one for the girls.

During the winter months, most of us were often frightened by the monster, our jacketed heating stove. This unpredictable creature could "blow its top" sending smoke up to the ceiling and the kids to the far corner of the room. Usually it would settle down after one sneeze, but sometimes it didn't. Teacher had to know how to build and tend a coal fire. The materials, coal, kindling, and kerosene, were stored in an adjoining coal shed. One needed to know how to carry out the ashes, dump the wastebasket into the firebox, top that with kindling, and start it with some kerosene and matches. If you were lucky and had school board members and patrons who were kind-hearted your wood was furnished chopped. Bigger boys, too, were always helpful with these chores, but they did not assume the responsibility, that belonged to the teacher. Before I left rural school teaching, we had a propane heater and electric lights!

The high points of every school year were our programs and socials. I recall the bitter, sweet apprehension about who would buy my pie or basket at a social. And I remember singing *Jolly Old St. Nicholas* all by myself in the first grade. In my teaching years, the Christmas program was our favorite. How we would plan and decorate and work! Right after Thanksgiving we started practicing, after the last recess every day. We utilized every bit of talent we could muster and some we didn't have. Memorization of parts was imperative and it was a sorely chagrined youngster who forgot his part. Costuming added much to the fun, and best of all, the stage made of planks with sheet curtains stretched in front. Board members tended to this shortly before the great night. On that same

continued on next page

day these men would meet at one of the homes and fill the little, brown candy sacks with peanuts, a few mixed nuts, at least one Brazil nut, Christmas candy, peanut brittle, and one big old-fashioned chocolate drop. These sacks, and a box of apples, were passed around after the program, first to all youngsters and mothers of babies, and if there were enough, to the visiting teenagers who secretly hoped they wouldn't be missed. We always played to a full house! Not till many years later did I fully realize what a wealth of training and experience these youngsters were acquiring with their public performances. To live through the wonderful excitement of "opening night" and know the thrill of reaching a common goal by means of a combined and total effort was an enriching experience.

When I decided to go into teaching there were, for practical reasons, only three career choices for farm girls, nursing, secretarial work, and teaching. My sisters were teachers so there I drifted, too. All but one of my thirteen years teaching rural school were spent in Grainbelt Township in Bowman County. Our father faithfully "hauled" us three girls to our various schools and took us around to make personal applications. I found the president of my first school board stacking hay and offered to go up on the stack to get his signature on a contract. This appealed to him and I had my first job. With him on the stack was his son who later became my husband! My first salary was fifty dollars a month, fifteen for room and board left thirty-five — that made me feel rich.

It was not uncommon to teach one's own children which I did for most of their elementary grades. But it was unusual to take an infant along to school. My son "attended" when he was a little over one year old, along with diaper bags, bottles, etc. He was in his play pen corner for three school terms. Primary students enjoyed playing with him, and he was a very good, quiet baby. By the time he approached three he was beginning to decorate his corner walls with crayon markings.

≈≥ ≤≤

1896 that County Superintendent C. A. Hall, noting that the competition was "conducted with all the old time vigor of the eastern New England School," began attending the events to learn what parents and other community people thought of the educational system.[7]

Other schools staged programs that became popular and customary in various areas. Halloween, Valentine's Day, Memorial Day, Mother's Day, Arbor Day, Parents Day, and Washington's birthday were all celebrated in different schools with varying degrees of enthusiasm.

At Enid Bern's school in Hettinger County, May Fetes — an unusual program in rural North Dakota — were held with considerable pageantry. The event was performed in the traditional manner with a Queen leading a costumed procession of medieval court jesters, page boys, Queen's attendants, and ladies in waiting. A play such as Robin Hood and His Merry Men, and songs were performed on an outdoor stage. The Queen of May was crowned followed by the Maypole dance and recessional.[8]

School picnics were a feature of the last day of school in many rural communities. Pot luck dinners provided by neighborhood women, sack races, horse shoes, and games of all sorts celebrated the return of warm weather and, for children, the end of the school term.

Basket socials were a favorite form of social entertainment and fund raising in rural communities. Often held in conjunction with some school programs, these raised funds for the school or for needy neighbors in economic distress. At these gatherings a box or basket containing food for two people was prepared by each woman of the community. The men would bid for the privilege of consuming the contents of the basket in the company of the preparer, a woman whose identity was, theoretically at least, unknown. In practice most married men were able to discern the container prepared by their wives and, out of a sense of decorum, would bid a sufficient amount to purchase that basket.

The popularity of this event, however, lay in the potential for economic exploitation of the romantic suitor or husband. Humor abounded when it became apparent that a young man was apparently prepared to spend a considerable sum to earn the right to share lunch with the preparer of a basket whom the residents of a small community could easily deduce belonged to his wife or girlfriend. Other men would take the risk of bidding against the amorous man, gambling that they could drive his bid higher. The eligible young school teacher's basket often secured the highest bid.

As a social activity, the basket socials throw rural community life into relief better than many other functions. They were entertaining, and therefore popular, only because the community was so small and its inhabitants so well known to each other that the basket's anonymity was merely a fiction. The entertainment of the game lay not so much in eating lunch with a mystery partner as it did in detecting which husband was jealous enough to let another man force up his bid. In these respects the basket socials not only served to raise money for some community use, they also furnished information for gossip. Basket socials were most popular in newly settled areas where age differences were not great and where men outnumbered women.

In addition to school functions that attracted the community members, the country school served as a meeting place for a variety of gatherings that were unrelated to the school. Community clubs met at the school in localities that were enterprising enough to form an association. At the Brooklyn Consolidated School near Wheelock a community club met one Friday of each month for a social evening. The business meeting always preceded an entertaining program followed by a pot luck dinner. Parents usually provided the program in the form of a debate, skit or play. Everyone in the community came to the meetings, which were the social highlight of the month. There were always some members who could furnish music with violin, accordion or piano to entertain or to accompany group singing.[9]

The community clubs in rural schools resembled the parent teacher organizations that operated in town schools. Surviving records of the Twin Butte Community Club in Williams County offer a detailed look at the functions and activities of the rural community clubs and their relationship to the school. Membership in the club was open to those age fourteen and older for twenty-five cents annually. Membership entitled one to participate in the business meetings and hold office and practically mandated service on one of many committees that kept the club going financially and designed the program for each meeting. Programs were elaborate and imaginative involving a mixture of adult participation and entertainment by school children. A typical program included community singing, two or three readings — generally humorous or inspirational pieces—accordion and violin solos, and an address by a member who had news of community interest to impart.[10]

The Brooklyn School in Williams County was new in 1913. At the left are the school buses, which were placed on sleigh runners in the winter. Some even carried a small stove. *(SHSND)*

Debates were very popular and were held frequently. Topics debated include: "Resolved: that the Farm Woman Works Harder and has less Recreation than the Farm Man" (resolved in the affirmative by a panel of three judges), or "Resolved: that the Soldier Serves His Country More than a Farmer" (decided in the negative). The debate topics generally revolved around social questions of local interest and avoided weighty political or philosophical matters.

The club sponsored a local baseball team that played against other area teams at picnics and on summer holidays. Picnics were always accompanied by a wide range of organized outdoor activities, including horseshoes, croquet, and relays and sprints in boys, girls, men and women categories.

During the 1930s the club became very active despite the depression and the minuscule treasury. In December 1936, the balance in the treasury fell to $4.03, and it was decided to perform a play to raise money by selling tickets. In February 1937, the four-act play *Let Toby Do It*, featuring a piano solo between each act, was performed before eighty people in the Twin Butte School. The price of each ticket is not mentioned, but total ticket receipts for the play were $7.50. By the early 1940s the club had returned to relative prosperity, enabling the group to pay $4.54 to tune the school piano.

The records demonstrate that the Twin Butte club's welfare was closely tied to the school. As in most rural areas, the school was more than a convenient meeting place. It was a source of entertainment and focus of community social life.

Many rural school teachers recall that the exertions of the dance left them drowsy at school the next day to the delight of older pupils who understood and were quick to exploit the teacher's handicap.

Dances were a favorite form of community entertainment frequently held at the school. Desks were stacked by the wall and the school organ or piano, sometimes supplemented by a local violin or accordion player, was used for music. The school usually provided room for no more than two square dance sets, but that was generally sufficient for the size of the crowd. If the crowd was young, dances often continued until the early morning hours following a midnight lunch. Many rural school teachers recall that the exertions of the dance left them drowsy at school the next day to the delight of older pupils who understood and were quick to exploit the teacher's handicap.[11]

Political parties and farm organizations also met at the country school. These meetings, unlike the social gatherings, appealed to a certain group and rarely attracted the entire community.

The Nonpartisan League, a progressive farm oriented political movement that flourished from 1916 to 1922, occasionally used the country schools to hold organizing meetings. A movement that excited strong opinions, pro and con, the League and its opponents waged a bitter battle that divided some communities into cliques. That

Election Day at Beaver Creek Precinct, McIntosh County, November, 1940 *(SHSND)*

division naturally extended into the school itself where children of parents who favored one faction warred with those who favored another. On election day the school was usually the polling place, where political debates were eventually settled.[12]

Farmers Union local organizations often held their regular monthly meetings in the school. Although the farm organization was committed to specific goals and farm policies, their meetings included a program and a social evening resembling those of the community clubs. People attended the meetings who were not particularly involved in the farm organization's activities.[13]

Religious services were common in the schools in the early years before various denominations had constructed their own church. Weddings and baptisms were conducted in some early schools. The larger denominations such as the Roman Catholic and Lutheran were generally quick to construct a church in their community, but the smaller groups, Baptists, Congregational and others used the school until they could accrue sufficient funds to construct their own building. Evangelists also occasionally used the school building or grounds for revival meetings.[14]

A wide variety of other non-social meetings were also held at the country school. The Wheat Growers Association, cooperative organization meetings, Homemakers lessons, County Agent demonstrations or any meeting of community interest that required a meeting place was likely to be held at the school.

The country school was such a successful community center because it was the only place that was open to everyone. All members of the community, regardless of their religious or political affiliation, met on the school's neutral ground. In the process they established a community identity. A number of developments — easier transportation, the decline in rural population, the pressure to consolidate schools — eliminated nearly all the country schools by the 1960s. But the sense of community in many of those old rural school districts remains a living legacy of the North Dakota country schools.

✍

The country school was such a successful community center because it was the only place that was open to everyone.

A Country School Teacher Remembers — Elsie Bergman

When I was in the second grade, I decided I wanted to be a teacher. The idea remained with me while I was in the grades and high school. My first year of teaching was in the fall following high school graduation. I did attend college the next summer. My college education was attending summer sessions except for the winter of 1931 when I attended the fall semester at Minot, North Dakota.

My first two years of teaching were at Albert School No. 3 in Benson County; it has been torn down. Then, I taught at Albert School No. 1 for six years. This was my home school where I had received my grade school education. This schoolhouse was sold to Arland Paulsen. They use it as part of their home. The following three years I taught in Eldon School No. 3. That schoolhouse was joined to another schoolhouse in the district making it the township hall. Seven years of teaching was spent at Oberon. For six years I taught grades three and four and one year I taught grades one, two, and three. In 1943 I began teaching at a consolidated school at Isabel and taught there for nineteen years. We had two grade rooms and two years of high school. I taught the four upper grades and exchanged subjects with the high school principal. He taught my history and citizenship classes while I taught his English classes. But their high school closed and the pupils attended Maddock or Esmond high schools. My last two years of teaching were at Harlow where I taught grades five through eight. The following year I was offered the Oberon School, but because of my husband's poor health I remained at home. Thirty-nine years was a long time, but I enjoyed teaching.

Salaries were sixty to seventy dollars a month those first years, and there were eight-month terms. We didn't strike for higher wages, but each year the salary was increased a few dollars for which we were thankful. Living expenses were not so high as they are now. If I got a dress for ten dollars, I thought I was well dressed.

I can recall my first day of teaching. I was nineteen years old, and a couple of my pupils were four or five years younger, and about as tall as I. But they were all friendly and caused no trouble. I had fourteen pupils at the beginning of the term, but two more came later during the year. This was in Albert School No. 3. In Albert School No. 1, I had thirty-two pupils and all eight grades. Class periods were from ten to fifteen minutes in length. I do think the pupils did

continued on next page

Mary C. and Robert L. Carlson

Endnotes

1. Laura Bassett and Alice Smith, *Helpful Hints for the Rural Teacher* (Valley City, North Dakota: Bassett and Smith, 1924), p. 59.

2. Letter from Nancy Heinzer, Bismarck, North Dakota, January 30, 1981. Letter from Florence Newsom, Hurdsfield, North Dakota, November 11, 1980. Interview with Oscar Oium, Towner, North Dakota, January 6, 1981.

3. Copy of a letter written by Mrs. Jalmer Fagerland, Wildrose, North Dakota.

4. Letter from Florence Newsom, Hurdsfield, North Dakota, November 11, 1980.

5. Letter from Roy Olson, Willow City, North Dakota, February 25, 1981.

6. Letter from Hazel Satterwaite Evans, New Town, North Dakota, February 21, 1981.

7. Letter from Lawrence Poe, Williston, North Dakota, February 15, 1981. North Dakota, *Biennial Report of the Superintendent of Public Instruction*, 1986, p. 269.

8. Marie Mynster Feidler, ed., *In Retrospect: Recollections of Retired Teachers* (Grand Forks, North Dakota: North Dakota Retired Teachers Association, 1976), p. 152.

9. Interview with Alida Siverson, Williston, North Dakota, January 14, 1981.

10. *Twin Butte Community Club Record Book*, 1923-1944. Private Collection.

11. Interviews with Anne Lassey, Williston, North Dakota, January 14, 1981, and Alida Siverson, Williston, North Dakota, January 14, 1981.

12. Letter from Roy Olson, Willow City, North Dakota, February, 1981.

13. Interview with Dennis Stromme, Zahl, North Dakota, January 15, 1981. Letter from Cynthia Haberstroh, Lisbon, North Dakota, January 22, 1981.

14. Interview with Louise Jevne, Lansford, North Dakota, November 20, 1980. Interview with Dennis Stromme, Zahl, North Dakota, January 15, 1981.

learn by listening to the other classes. I seldom assigned homework, but I did expect them to do some homework if they were not capable of doing all of their assignments at school.

The school boards were always willing to supply necessary textbooks and supplies to carry on the classes. I do not think I dared spend too much for supplies because evenings and weekends kept me busy making seat work and pictures for the lower grades.

Each year I had a program and basket social to raise money for library books and playground equipment. Christmas programs were given each year for the parents and in the spring a Mother's Day program usually about the last day of school. Novelties were made by the pupils to present to their parents.

The rural schools were heated by a jacketed Waterbury stove. The room was quite comfortable except on windy or very cold days. Then the pupils were moved nearer the stove because the floor was often cold. The janitor work was taken care of by the teacher. Youngsters would beg to dust erasers while the teacher swept and dusted the room. Coal and wood were carried in buckets.

Sometimes the older boys offered to carry coal. Scrubbing the floor was done by the wives of the school board members or some other woman in the community.

I usually had a room with a family living close to the school that I often shared with a daughter of the family. I paid fourteen or fifteen dollars a month for board and room. I always lived with nice families that treated me very well.

I didn't think country school teaching was a lonely life, as I taught following high school graduation and we could not attend too many activities during high school. It was expected that a teacher should not "go out" very often during school nights. Weekends I spent with my folks; the schools I taught in were near my home. I stayed with my parents when I taught in Albert School No. 1. When I taught in Eldon School the people of the community put on a Farmers' Union play each winter. I participated in three of those three-act plays. That meant play practice once or twice a week and often on Sunday afternoons. It

continued on next page

was fun; we presented the plays in several nearby small towns.

One year I had two children that had recently arrived from Norway and they could not speak our language. But I was able to speak and understand Norwegian so we got along fine. Their mother told me that she wished she had time to attend school, but it was surprising how those children taught her to speak our language. The children learned very quickly and refused to speak the Norwegian tongue because they wanted their mother to be able to speak to others. Their father was able to communicate in our language. They were a nice friendly family.

In the Eldon School I set aside one hour each Friday for religious lessons. We called it our "Sunday School Class" because we used Sunday School material. There were no problems because all the students were Lutherans and so was I. But the second year that I taught at Eldon a Catholic family moved in so we discontinued our "Sunday School." I imagine that teaching a class like that would not be allowed today.

I organized a Young Citizens League. Pupils served as officers and meetings that included a program planned by a program committee were held twice a month. The organization taught them rules for conducting a business meeting and gave them responsibility. They enjoyed it.

We seldom had very much playground equipment the first years I taught, but we would bring balls and bats from home and have a good baseball game. We played games like Tag, Pom Pom Pull Away, Annie Over, Here I Come, Where From, and many others. In the winter time we often went to a small pond and skated during the noon hour or we would play fox and geese, make snowmen, or have a snowball fight.

Unless the weather was cold and stormy most of the pupils and I would walk to and from school. So, we did not need physical education classes; we got our exercise. There were no cars for us "to jump into and go."

Country school teaching never became monotonous because you were always busy and someone would always make a laughable remark. I often wished I had kept a notebook of some of the remarks made by some of the pupils, especially those in the lower grades. One day when a little girl came to school she was so surprised to see me using the dictionary. She remarked, "I thought you knew the meaning of all those words." I informed her that I had to study also and that I had a lot to learn yet.

One time a first grader propped his hand like a gun and went "bang" at a monkey he had made and put on the bulletin board. The other youngsters looked at me and I think I gave them surprise because I just laughed. They all joined in. This happened one of my first days of teaching and came so unexpectedly. Soon we were all back to our books working again. I always thought a good laugh would do us all some good.

Many changes have taken place in the schools since 1923. We did not have electricity at that time. Textbooks have improved in many ways and also teaching methods. Now, most schools serve a hot meal at noon. I recall when the teacher and pupils prepared a hot dish that consisted mostly of surplus commodities. We received rice, macaroni, canned meat, butter, and cheese. We had a kerosene stove and a double boiler in which to prepare dishes. I usually had an arithmetic class just before dinner; the pupils were sent to the blackboard, but every few minutes I would step back and stir the dinner to make sure it would not scorch.

I enjoyed teaching and attending a country school even if I had to shovel coal into a bucket and carry it to a jacketed stove. After four o'clock there were always floors to sweep and desks to dust. It did mean a lot of work being a teacher and custodian and often walking to school if weather permitted; but I hate to see these country schoolhouses demolished.

I'll always remember those friendly students. Enrollments were small so the pupils were more friendly because they all played together from the first grade to the eighth grade.

Teaching in country school left me with many good memories and friends.

In the Eldon School I set aside one hour each Friday for religious lessons. We called it our "Sunday School Class" because we used Sunday School material. There were no problems because all the students were Lutherans and so was I. But the second year that I taught at Eldon a Catholic family moved in so we discontinued our "Sunday School." I imagine that teaching a class like that would not be allowed today.

Chapter 3

Report on North Dakota Schools in 1911-1912 *

Neil C. Macdonald, State Inspector
of Rural and Graded Schools

THERE WERE IN ALL 156 SCHOOLS INSPECTED of which nineteen were consolidated, thirty-eight were graded, and ninety-nine were rural schools. In addition, twenty-three schools were visited during the year which were not recommended for inspection. These schools were on the line of travel and while the team was resting or the machine cooling, a short visit was paid to the schools. The attention of the pupils and the teachers therein was called to the provisions and benefits of the state rural aid law. I have been informed that some of these schools have since qualified for the state aid and will apply for classification. Of the schools inspected only six had met all the requirements when visited, one graded and five rural, four of which would classify as a second class rural and one as a first class rural. It is true that many had almost met the requirements, yet several were far from doing so. This certainly shows that the rural school is in urgent need of great and rapid improvement. There were schools recommended for inspection in three other counties but owing to the shortness of time and the scarcity of money these have not been inspected by me. The superintendents in the remaining counties did not notify me that they had any school ready for inspection which would be taken to mean that they had none. It is true that the superintendents have found it a very difficult matter to get accurate data regarding the schools that are ready for classification and so there are some counties that reported schools for inspection after I had been in those counties and in other cases I was called to inspect schools that were far from being ready for classification. Someone had evidently misinformed the county superintendents. The majority of my visits were very short as it was necessary to save time and money. Some counties that were on the line of travel or that could be more easily entered from another quarter were visited more than once. In visiting schools in several counties I passed through others where no schools were offered for inspection, and when possible consulted with the county superintendent regarding these matters. In all I traveled over 15,000 miles by rail and over 3,000 miles by horse and automobile livery.

A Country School Teacher Remembers — C. Ross Bloomquist

The Birtsell Number 3 schoolhouse in Foster County was old even when I started in the first grade in the Spring of 1914.

The schoolhouse yard of somewhat more than an acre was virgin prairie not absolutely level since the northeast corner next to the quarter line collected water after a heavy rain or during the spring thaws. During vacation time many species of prairie flowers managed to grow and bloom in spite of the childrens' efforts to wear out the grasses and plants during playtime. Among the flowers blooming in the summer there were two types of legumes or vetches with pale purple blossoms and bean-like pods which I never encountered elsewhere. We called them "buffalo beans."

Besides the schoolhouse there were three other structures on the school grounds. The ramshackle barn near the south boundary had in years past stabled the horses of children who rode or drove to school....In the distant past it had been painted red but most of the color had long since weathered away....We played in the barn occasionally on rainy days but its main use was as a place to hide behind during recess and noon time hide-and-go-seek games. The two outhouses, boys' and girls', were situated along the west boundary of the school yard. The girls' was directly west of the schoolhouse and the boys' about 30 feet further south. The rear of the two little houses also served as hiding places during games.

The schoolhouse itself was a simple frame structure about 20 by 30 feet with a single gable roof with a belfry at the east end. The windowless entry facing east also had a smaller gabled roof. The exterior had been painted white with

continued on next page

*From the publication by the North Dakota Department of Public Instruction, *First and Second Annual Reports of the State Inspector of Consolidated, Graded and Country Schools, 1913*, pp. 9-28. Neil C. Macdonald, Inspector. Part of the introductory statement and the section on "Regulations" of the *Report* was deleted and information in tables has been rearranged and placed along with text.

Neil C. Macdonald was born on Manitoulin Island, Ontario, Canada, March 17, 1876. He attended school in Langdon, and at age sixteen took the county superintendent's teacher's examination and received a state teaching certificate. He taught rural schools in Cavalier County for several years, became a student at the new Mayville Normal School, and received his first-grade teaching certificate in May 1896. He graduated from the University of North Dakota, attended graduate school at the University of Chicago, and after earning a solid reputation as a teacher and school superintendent he joined the Department of Public Instruction in 1911 as its rural and graded-school inspector. Intensely interested in improving rural schools he fought for "A Square Deal for the Country Boy" and promoted standardization and consolidation. Endorsed by the Nonpartisan League he was elected Superintendent of Public Instruction in 1916, but was defeated in an acrimonious campaign two years later. *[1915 Photograph, Special Collections, University of North Dakota]*

red trim around the windows, eaves and corners. It was never repainted during my days there. Both the north and south side had two windows placed symmetrically, the east wall had two flanking the entry. The west wall was blank except for the brick chimney protruding from the west gable.

The entry, windowless, except for the transom above the door, had hooks and nails to hang coats and caps. The lunch pails were set on the floor before the cold of winter set in. A small bench held a water pail with a dipper and the wash basin we all used. There was a hole in the ceiling through which there should have been the rope attached to the bell. The rope had long since worn out and was never replaced.

In spite of the windows on three sides of the interior, the schoolroom was dark and uninviting when school was not in session. The wood walls and ceiling painted a bluish gray were sometimes cleaned but never repainted during my years in attendance. No permanent pictures relieved the monotony of the dull walls. The floor was dark and splintery. A six inch high platform projected about five feet from the west wall. It stuck out a little farther in the center to give just enough space for the teacher's desk and the wastepaper basket.

A huge shiny black circular coal stove occupied a considerable portion of the north wall. I have never seen another quite like it. Basically it was a large pot-bellied stove enclosed in a sheet casing about five feet in diameter and the same height. The cast iron doors of the fire box and ash pit were flush with the case. Sharp, serrated or crown-like points decorated the upper edge of the case. Around the bottom at floor level vents which could be opened or closed by slides controlled the flow of heat around the fire box so that the room was heated by convection as well as radiation. The casing itself was a protection for the chlordane; it never became too hot to touch. No child was ever burned by coming into contact with the stove. Within the casing the dome over the fire box had a flat top. In winter when the stove was in use water in a pan or pot set on it would come to boil in a few minutes. The hot lunches were prepared there.

The pipe from the stove to the chimney came out only a few inches from the north wall. Protective metal plates shielded the pipe from the wall and ceiling. In a year the paint on the shields would become blistered by the hot gases radiating from the stovepipe. The shields failed to protect the walls one night in 1929, the walls caught fire and the building burned.

continued on next page

Attendance. In the schools inspected there were enrolled in the consolidated schools 1,668 pupils of which 784 were boys and 884 were girls. This made an average school enrollment of eighty-seven. In the graded schools there were enrolled 3,006 pupils of which 1,415 were boys and 1,591 were girls. This made an average of seventy-nine pupils per school. In the rural schools there were enrolled 1,931 pupils of which 857 were boys and 1,074 were girls. This made an average of twenty per school. The per cent of boys enrolled in the consolidated school was 47, and the actual per cent of attendance for all was 75. For graded schools these items were 47 and 76; and for rural schools these items were 44 and 64. It will be noticed in the rural schools that the enrollment of the boys is much smaller than that of the girls; though if the enrollment were taken in the winter months the number of boys would probably equal that of the girls. But the number enrolled in the upper grades would on an age basis average about two grades below that of the girls. The reason for this difference in enrollments is due to the fact that the majority of these schools were inspected during the time when there was work for the boys to do on the farm; and so these boys were kept out.

Country Boys. For sometime I have been impressed with the fact that the average attendance of country boys in the upper grades of the country schools is much smaller than that of the girls, while the attendance of the girls ought to be larger than it is. On two different occasions I invested time and money to look the matter up, but not until I took up the work of inspection did I realize that the difference was so great; did I realize that the country boy was deprived in such large numbers of his inalienable right to boyhood hours of play and years of study, during the period in his young life when it counts most for him. No one can object to a boy's doing light manual labor, provided he is not kept out of school to do so; but objections must be made when he is kept out of school to do labor of any kind. Youth is the time for play and study. It is the time when the boy should have an opportunity to complete the eighth grade. This course should be completed, if it is to count for the most, before his fifteenth year. This is the time when the mind should be stored with good ideas and high ideals concerning life and its responsibilities. Youth is the time for the boys to prepare themselves to enter largely and successfully into the discharge of their American citizenship.

In the ninety-nine rural schools inspected there were 389 available country boys between the ages of eight and fifteen inclusive who were non-members at the time of inspection or at sometime prior to it during the school year. Of the 264 non-attending boys in the graded and consolidated schools all but four were country boys. Up to the time of inspection the average non-attendance (non-membership) was forty-six days. This non-attendance was inexcusable and therefore was in violation of the law. The non-attendance of the country girls in the rural schools was too large, but that of the country boys was ten times as large. Of the 155 registers examined, the records showed that during a part of the fall months there were enrolled in the upper grades (fifth to eighth), 625 country girls and only 63 country boys. This means when compared to the number of girls on the roll that some 600 boys were not in school that ought to have been in school, and on a pro rata basis throughout the state, it means that over 18,000 were out of school. It means that with bodies of growing boys, tender of muscle and soft of bone, they were working on the farms assisting in securing the money to maintain the schools which they could not attend. Of ninety registers examined during the winter and spring months, the record showed that 357 country boys ranging in age from eleven to fifteen inclusive were kept out of school during the fall months on an average of 8 weeks each. This is a serious condition of affairs and one that is so common and of so long standing that many good people have come to look upon it as the usual and proper thing. There were a few schools of course, that showed conditions quite opposite to these. They were efficient in one essential respect at least. The low per cent of attendance of the country schools and country town school is due in a very large part to the non-attendance of the country boy.

This poor attendance of the country boy is shown in another way when we consider the small number completing the eighth grade. In the ninety-nine rural schools inspected only sixteen boys and thirty-eight girls had completed the eighth grade during the preceding year. This does not indicate that the country boy is stupid or is lacking in ambition and brain power, but that he has been kept

The stovepipe angled across the room to the chimney in the center of the west wall. The base of the chimney was supported on a wood platform about six feet above the floor. A cupboard under the platform was used to store spare text books. Slate blackboards on either side of the cupboard occupied the rest of the west wall. Several composition boards were attached to the other walls.

The teacher's desk on the platform was placed so that she faced the children sitting at their desks. The desk had a shallow center drawer where she kept her records. Chalk and supplies for handiwork and her personal belongings filled the side drawers. A row of text books held in place by bookends were lined up on the side of the desk toward the children. Six kindergarten-size chairs stood in a row on the platform to the right of the teacher's desk. The children sat in these chairs when they were reciting.

The pupil's desks of the combination type were new the fall before I started school. They were bright and shiny with a heavy durable coat of varnish which resisted the children's efforts to mar them. The backs and seats were light colored wood, the cast iron metal frames were black. The desk tops were reddish brown with a groove for holding pencils and never used ink well. Below the sloping tops each desk had a level shelf large enough to hold a half dozen text books, a few pencils, tablets of writing paper, crayons, and a paint box. Most of the desks had a hinged seat in front so that they could be arranged in files from front to back. There were in all about 25 desks of graduated sizes to fit all from the tiny first graders to the near adult eighth grade pupils. The arrangement of the desks depended on the teacher's wishes. Usually they were screwed to the floor in 3 or 4 files with the seated children facing the blackboards on the west wall. One teacher liked the desks of similar sizes paired to allow for wider aisles.

Compared to the classrooms of modern schools Birtsell No. 3 was a rather dreary place when school was not in session. The teachers did all they could to liven the atmosphere. They made curtains to cover the bottom third of the lower sashes on the windows. Colorful pictures drawn or traced by the primary children were tacked along the walls and black boards. On sunny days the light pouring in the east and south windows made splashes of glaring illumination of the floor and desks. The light reflecting from the shiny desk tops made bright spots here and there on the walls and ceilings and sometimes in the eyes of the children. On cloudy days the light coming in from three sides made dark

continued on next page

and light areas haphazardly across the room changing as the day progressed. In midwinter the sun was near setting by the time school closed for the day and the room was becoming immersed in shadow.

≈ ✍

out of school during a portion of the fall and spring months and so his sister and city cousin leave him far behind. Disgusted, and discouraged, he drops out when the compulsory law cannot reach him and often when he cannot do the sixth grade work. This small number completing the eighth grade shows a per cent somewhat above the average, but as a matter of fact the enrollment of these schools would indicate that at least 200 boys and 190 girls should have completed the course. These schools being above the average in this and in other lines, the results in other schools in these lines must be worse. On a pro rata basis, these figures would mean that some ten thousand boys that should have completed the eighth grade that year in the state failed to do so. I may add that available statistics analyzed and other data collected, all amply confirm these deductions.

During a portion of the fall and spring months many country boys are out upon the plows and upon the grain-tanks — boys kept out of school in order to get money to

Three friends: Loam Twp. School, Cavalier County, Blanche Welsh Shortridge, Teacher, 1922 *(NDIRS)*

assist in supporting the school of which they were deprived. They are kept out to plow the fields while they are unable to determine the area thereof, to haul grain to town while they cannot determine the value of the same. It is not fair and it is not just to the boy for a great state to permit such a wrong to be done to its future citizens. The boy is educated for and by the state, so if necessary the state should protect him in the days of his helplessness. This means in particular a better enforcement of the compulsory attendance law and soon a better law and, in general, the arousing of public sentiment in favor of a better deal for the country boy. In a few short years the government of this great state will pass into his keeping and if he has not acquired those powers of body and mind that come from years of study and hours of play, that control cannot have passed into the best of hands.

Then, too, the country boys must in a few short years make the largest contribution to support a family, church, school and state; while he of all children has received the least training, though he furnishes the largest per cent of school children of any age group. It is claimed that we are a wealthy state and if this be true it should not be necessary to draft the boys to add to that wealth. There are few cases where poverty forces the boys out of school. On the other hand there are many farmer-parents over this state who sacrifice a great deal that their boys and girls may complete the eighth grade and sometimes the high school and college; and they are the patriots in the best sense of that term. But there are others who are careless, or indifferent about this matter. Generally they plead scarcity of labor which means that labor is high priced. This can be answered simply by the statement that the money paid for tobacco in this state by farmers would more than pay the wages of hired men to take the place of boys who are kept out of school. Back of this sordid business is contempt for law and back of this is the lust for money — is the belief in the ignoble sentiment, "that money makes the man." The boys are developing the material resources of the state, that some may boast of ill-gotten gains, that some may accumulate wealth for its sake alone, while boys 14 and over do not know the multiplication table, and do not know whether Madison's administration is part of history or arithmetic, and do not know whether a Hambletonian is a flower or a horse, do not know whether loam is a chicken or a kind of soil, whether Whittier is the name of an Indian Chief or a great poet. These are some things I found out in the past year. And so we have many thousand farms with broad and well-tilled fields as the price of many thousand boys with narrow and ill-trained minds. There are a few of these boys, who, in spite of the great handicap, forge to the front, but the great majority never even make a start. Then there are a few score of boys who have splendid opportunities, whose farmer-parents sacrifice much; and those boys are the ones that we see and hear so much about while we never see the several thousand each year who fail to complete the eighth grade. These become the submerged nine-tenths. The problem of the country boys is in many ways the biggest problem connected with the rural school.

Many pages could be written upon this subject but suffice it to say that if the operation of this Rural Aid Law will save a hundred boys to the end that they may complete the eighth grade each year, it will have returned many fold to the state that provided these funds.

Teachers. In a majority of schools that I visited I did not find what I would call good teaching; and I did find evidence in a majority of a lack of scholarship including leadership. The rural school teacher is hard worked and under paid. She lacks scholarship and therefore leadership; she lacks professional knowledge and therefore professional zeal and interest. And yet for the money paid she is as good or better than the people are entitled to. She

Williams County Teachers, 1904 *(SHSND)*

ought to be paid more than she is now paid even with her present training. However, she ought to have more academic and professional training and, therefore, possess more largely the element of leadership and therefore be paid at least two hundred dollars more per year than she is now paid. Her lack of scholarship including leadership is shown largely in her failure to aid the superintendent in securing the classification of her school, in her failure to secure and hold the interest of pupils and patrons in the school, in her ignorance of the financial and scholastic resources of her school district and the means to utilize such, in her failure to have a normal percentage of her pupils of both sexes complete each grade each year with good passing grades, and in her inability to inspire her pupils with a high regard for knowledge and lofty ideals of conduct.

Salaries. The average monthly salary of the principals in the consolidated schools is $90.53, and of the assistants $60.37; and of the principals in the graded schools it is $84.16, and of the assistants $57.45. The average monthly salary of the teacher in the rural schools is $54.63. It ranges from $45.00 to $80.00 per month. The average salaries are too low even where the teachers comply with only the minimum requirements as to qualifications; and are much too low in the rural schools. Until the rural school patron makes up his mind to pay a higher salary, he must be content with a teacher inferior to the city school teacher.

Records. In visiting schools, I have found that the records in some cases are incomplete in several essential respects. This has been principally along the line of failure to keep a list of the kind of books, an up-to-date list of pupils enrolled in the several grades, a financial statement including the assessed valuation, the tax rate, and the value of the school property. These defects are very noticeable in the record keeping of the village or town principal. The great majority do not know anything about these items and they do not even know the qualifications of their teachers. I have been compelled to use from 30 minutes to one hour in getting data that had the records been complete could have been obtained in 10 minutes. I cannot see how any teacher can hope to be an efficient teacher in any community whether she be a rural school teacher or the village principal, who knows nothing about the material equipment or financial resources of her district, and who knows nothing about the grading and classification of the pupils or the qualifications of the teachers. You will notice that I have added this as one of the regulations in the list submitted. I found only two principals, one of which was a woman, and only one rural school teacher who had records that were approximately complete.

Library. I found many schools, both rural and graded, poorly equipped with general and reference books. Many of these were worn-out or out-of-date. In the graded schools there were, not including readers and other text-books, 5,731 books or an average of 150 books per school; and in the consolidated schools there were 2,734 books or 144 per school. In the rural schools there were 5,662 books or 57 books per school. A good library, however, presupposes and requires pupils that have been taught to read and that have been taught what to read. This cannot

"Organ and Pupils" *(Porterville Collection, NDIRS)*

be taught to boys or girls either who go to school only 4 or 5 months in the school year. It requires regular attendance and good teaching. It seems that the books in the libraries are not generally read, that is, those on hand, could be more generally read. I am unable to place the blame unless it is poor teaching in the subject of reading which may be brought into existence by non-attendance of pupils or lack of sufficient preparation on the part of the teacher.

Equipment. It is very evident that the rural and graded schools are not equipped as they ought to be, for I found less than a score that had met the requirements in the matter of equipment. In many schools I found that dictionaries were worn out or a cheap unreliable edition. This was also true of maps. I found a few schools that had drinking fountains installed, but the majority had the common drinking cups in use.

Course of Study. The requirements in domestic science, manual training and agriculture appear to be quite difficult for the small graded school to meet. And yet many schools provide equipment in self-instructing courses in order that classes might be organized in these courses. The subject of agriculture was taught in the majority of the schools that I visited and in a practical way. This is one subject that next to literature and reading it seems to me has a high, practical and cultural value. It seems too bad that boys and girls raised in the country with the great book of nature spread out before them should find themselves unable to read a word therein. I found many boys who could not tell me whether Scotch Fife was a weed, or a kind of wheat, who could not tell whether Duroc Jersey was a hog or a cow, who could not tell whether a Wyandotte was an Indian or a chicken, who could not give one good reason why they plowed or harrowed the ground; and yet they bore the marks — hollow chests, and stooped shoulders, of too much familiarity with heavy manual labor upon the farms. Some of these boys seemed to resent the introduction of a course in agriculture feeling that they knew all about it; and they do know too much about the manual side, but very little about the mental side. It did not take many questions to show them that they were ignorant of the rudiments of nature study or elementary agriculture. I found the teachers of this course unfamiliar with the subject in some of its aspects and in doubt as to how the classes should be organized. These, objections, however, will be overcome when the purpose of teaching this subject is understood.

School Grounds. In a great majority of cases the grounds do not present an orderly and attractive appearance. They are small, unfenced, and without trees. In many cases there is no sufficient room for boys and girls to play unless they go into a public highway or into plowed fields. In the open country the grounds should be at least two acres in extent and in town at least a block.

School House, Stanton, North Dakota, August 26, 1904 *(NDIRS)*

School Buildings. The majority of the rural school buildings that I saw and inspected were of the chalk box type with double cross lighting, unpainted, and set out upon the wind swept prairies, on a small plot of ground that was unfenced and without trees. The great majority of graded and consolidated school buildings, however, were commodious and were well kept. The little progress of the rural school during the last 25 years is shown strikingly in the failure to build proper buildings and to place them upon suitable school grounds. It is a very common sight to find a farmer's barn better suited to serve its purpose than you will find the country school house to serve its purpose. I did, however, find six rural school buildings in six different counties that were built along modern lines. They were a credit to the county in which they were erected and were worthy monuments to the good judgment of the men and women who paid for their erection.

Heating and Ventilation. With three or four exceptions, all the schools that were recommended for inspection had some one of the modern systems of heating and ventilating in operation. I found one home-made system that was not properly constructed and therefore, was of little use. The majority of rural schools used a "jacketed stove" while a few used the basement furnace. I did not find a patented system of heating that was not working in an excellent manner. I found several basement furnaces of the hot-air type that provided for the death circle system of ventilation. This matter of heating and ventilating is one that probably has more to do with successful school work than any other single piece of apparatus or equipment that can be found in the school.

Outhouses * — Laura J. Eisenhuth, State Superintendent of Public Instruction

I would here urgently call the teacher's attention to a growing evil that is abroad in all the land,—the filthy and vile condition of the school outhouses. I know of and have made complaint of school houses in this state where the outhouses were snowed full in winter, and too vile to enter in summer, leaving the pupils without the proper means to obey the calls of nature the whole day. No wonder that their brains are inactive, their digestion impaired and their circulation sluggish. And not only are they pest houses where disease is germinated, but they are immoral influences that burn and blacken the pure young souls of innocent children, and perpetuate and strengthen the evil in evil. This is no place for false modesty to prevent action. The law provides for these buildings, and it is your duty as teachers to see that the school where *you* teach has comfortable and convenient buildings, and *then are kept clean and free from all kinds of drawings and writings.* All over the land is going up a cry against these moral and physical abominations. Let North Dakota lead the van in purging and purifying them, and through them the health and morals of our children. This is a call to duty. I request county superintendents in visiting schools in their counties to make inspection, not only of the outhouses, but of the school walls, and make note of their condition to use in granting certificates where the fault is the teacher's, or reporting to the school boards for improvement.

✍✍

*Source: North Dakota, Department of Public Instruction, *Manual Of The Elementary Course Of Study For The Common District Schools Of North Dakota*, 1894, p. 99.

"Modern" outhouses built during the 1930s. *(NDIRS)*

Outhouses or Closets. I have found several outhouses that were not properly built and were not properly kept. I found also during the winter months several that were **filthy** and **obscene** in the extreme. There were seven schools including one rural in District N. 6 Cass County, that had the outhouses built on as a part of the school building. I made special inquiry into the matter of health and morals in connection with the use of these buildings and in each case found evidence to show that the health and morals of the pupils had been more largely safeguarded than where the other style was in use. Some schools are using the inside system of closets, but the majority still use the old fashioned two upright rectangular buildings built some distance apart and away from the school. At best they are far below the poorest inside closet. It is nearly impossible to keep them clean or free from obscene words and pictures. Then, too, young boys and girls will not use them when they should and especially is this so during severe weather. This means ill health and later on a body of low working power. The inside closet or outhouses built in as a part of the building where they can be under the care and control of the teacher and where the pupils are not exposed to inclement weather, are the proper solution to this problem.

✍✍

Table I
Percent of pupils completing the eighth grade during school year 1911-1912, per 100 enrolled in first grade eight years previous, in North Dakota

City Girls	80
City Boys	50
Country Girls	11
Country Boys	6

Source: North Dakota, Department of Public Instruction, First and Second Annual Reports of the State Inspector of Consolidated, Graded and Country Schools, 1913, p. 15.

Table II
Average length of term in days, and average number of days attended by each pupil enrolled, during school year 1910-1911

For rural schools in Province of Manitoba (1911)	200
For city schools in North Dakota	180
For rural schools in North Dakota	138
Days attended by each pupil enrolled in city schools in North Dakota	142

Source: North Dakota, Department of Public Instruction, First and Second Annual Reports of the State Inspector of Consolidated, Graded and Country Schools, 1913, p. 15.

Table III
Average salary per year of teachers during school year, 1910-1911

For rural teachers in Manitoba (1911)	$586.52
For city school teachers in North Dakota	$562.50
For rural school teachers in North Dakota	$340.00

Source: North Dakota, Department of Public Instruction, First and Second Annual Reports of the State Inspector of Consolidated, Graded and Country Schools, 1913, p. 22.

Table IV
Qualifications of teachers during school year, 1910-1911

For rural teachers in Manitoba (1911)	Second class professional—about 12 years of training
For city school teachers in North Dakota	Second class professional—about 12 years of training
For rural school teachers in North Dakota	Second class elementary—about 8 years of training

Source: North Dakota, Department of Public Instruction, First and Second Annual Reports of the State Inspector of Consolidated, Graded and Country Schools, 1913, p. 22.

Table V
Average tax rates during school year 1910-1911, in North Dakota

For city residents	21.3 mills
For rural residents	6.9 mills

Source: North Dakota, Department of Public Instruction, First and Second Annual Reports of the State Inspector of Consolidated, Graded and Country Schools, 1913, p. 22.

Table VI
Average monthly salary paid teachers, on a 12-month basis, during school year, 1910-1911, in North Dakota

Paid city school teachers	$46.88
Paid rural school teachers	$28.41

Source: North Dakota, Department of Public Instruction, First and Second Annual Reports of the State Inspector of Consolidated, Graded and Country Schools, 1913, p. 22.

Neil C. Macdonald, State Inspector

left, Buses at early consolidated school in Williams Co. @1903-1913

right, Brooklyn Consolidated School *(SHSND)*

The Benefits Of The Consolidated School

The benefits of the Consolidated School far outweigh any disadvantages that may be involved in the system.

The Six Major Benefits of this school when compared with the One-Room Rural School are as follows:

(1) *Better Attendance*—A 9-month term with 90 per cent attendance instead of 7.5 months term with 65 per cent attendance as in the average rural school.

(2) *Better Teachers*—Well trained teachers teaching a good school in place of a poorly trained teacher keeping a poor rural school.

(3) *Better School Work in the Grades*—Three times the number completing the eighth grade and doing work of twice the quality when compared with rural school results.

(4) *Better High School Privileges*—Ten times the number of country pupils completing the high school and at one-fifteenth the cost to the individual patron when compared with the old rural school system.

(5) *Better Organization*—A teacher with three grades and 15 classes daily instead of six grades and 30 classes and 15 visits per year of a supervisor instead of two, as in the rural school.

(6) *Better Civic-Social Opportunities*—A good place for various Clubs, Literary Societies, Social Events, Athletic Contests, Lectures and Art Exhibits, which the rural school has not.

The Twenty-five Benefits of the Consolidated School when Compared with the One-Room Rural School are the following:

(1) Increases the attendance.

(2) Makes the attendance more regular.

(3) Increases the enrollment.

(4) Keeps the older pupils in the school longer, giving a form of the continuation school.

(5) Provides high school privileges at one-third the cost to the community and one-fifteenth the cost to the individual patron.

(6) Makes possible the securing of better trained teachers.

(7) Improves industrial conditions in the country, including improved roads and farms.

(8) Results in higher salaries for better trained teachers.

(9) Makes possible more and better grade school work.

(10) Enriches the civic-social life activities.

(11) Conserves more largely the health and morals of the children.

(12) Increases the number of eighth grade completions.

(13) Provides adequate supervision.

(14) Reduces truancy and tardiness.

(15) Develops better school spirit.

(16) Gives more time for recitation.

(17) Increases the value of real estate.

(18) Produces greater pride and interest in country life.

(19) Prevents the drift to the larger towns and cities.

(20) Brings more and better equipped buildings.

(21) Eliminates the small weak school.

(22) Creates a school of greater worth, dignity and usefulness.

(23) Makes possible a more economical school.

(24) Provides equal educational opportunities.

(25) Gives much greater and better results in every way.

Source: North Dakota, Department of Public Instruction, *The Problem of Rural School Betterment,* Neil C. Macdonald, May, 1917, pp. 17-18.

left, Atkinson School Dist., Marion Twp., Griffin, ND

right, Eden Valley Consolidated School, No. 1, Renville Co.

Chapter 4

Education and Ethnicity: A Study of German-Russians and Norwegians in N.D.

Playford V. Thorson and William C. Sherman

UNTIL RECENTLY THERE HAS BEEN A POPULAR NOTION that there was — perhaps still is — a decided difference in matters of education between North Dakotans of Norwegian background and those who trace their roots to a German-Russian heritage. Elwyn B. Robinson's *History of North Dakota* quotes a German-Russian educator, Joseph Voeller, who wrote in 1940: "To this day the shortest terms, the poorest schools, the lowest teacher's salaries, the most inadequate equipment, and the most irregular attendance, are found in German-Russian communities."[1]

In contrast, Leona N. Bergmann in her *Americans from Norway* says in 1950: "No state university in the country has so many students of Norwegian stock as the University of Minnesota, which, like-wise, has many department heads and deans of Norwegian descent."[2] Neither Voeller or Bergmann seem to substantiate their claims with definite data. Still the assumption persists; the Norwegians supported education much more than did the German-Russians. What proof exists?[3]

Official reports rarely, if ever, mention national origins in educational matters, at least in a comparative sense. However, it may be possible to study the influence of ethnic heritage on attitudes toward education by examining closely a number of select counties which are made up predominantly of the particular ethnic groups. Four North Dakota counties have the highest proportion of citizens of German-Russian heritage

North Dakota County map showing counties of Norwegian (shaded) and German-Russian dominance (black)

— Logan, McIntosh, Mercer and Sheridan. Four others have the greatest percentage of those of Norwegian background — Divide, Nelson, Steele, and Traill.[4] (See *Appendix, Table I*, page 104.)

We examined educational data for the years 1910-1912, 1922-1923, and 1930 for the following reasons:

(1) homesteading was, by and large, completed by these dates,

(2) county lines involved had achieved their permanent form,

(3) the United States census and Superintendent of Schools documents were published at these approximate dates.

From a socio-economic point of view, all eight counties were still highly rural in nature at the time the data was collected. The basic type of agriculture, both grain and livestock, was similar. None had large towns of any size or institutions of higher learning which might affect attitudes towards education. Recognizing that the eastern Norwegian counties were settled somewhat earlier than the more centrally located German-Russian counties, we decided to balance this factor with Norwegian Divide County, one of the last North Dakota counties to be settled. Finally, we recognize that there were certain disparities in population and economic conditions between the German and Norwegian counties but we are satisfied that, for the purpose of this study, the differences are minor, not significant enough to invalidate the results of the investigation.[5]

We examined the United States Bureau of Census figures for the years 1910, 1920, and 1930. We also analyzed the reports of the North Dakota State Superintendent of Schools. In addition, we studied such other documents as college graduation lists and reports of selected public schools. Finally, we looked at historical literature.

In general, we have studied the two groups by comparing known aspects of the educational system which might be indicative of the differing national attitudes, aspirations, and achievements: the variance in physical plants, teacher and school personnel, school classifications, outside observer assessments, parental support, and student performance. We offer an analysis of a small school composed of both Germans and Norwegians in detail. We have also included several small reports of more recent educational records in an effort to assess contemporary trends. Convinced that the major contributive cause of observed variance is to be found in the groups' prior experience, we offer an historical survey of the background in Russia and Norway prior to emigration.

During the first quarter of our century schools were highly decentralized, procedures were varied, and many county educational programs were in their infancy. Considerable homesteading continued in Divide, Mercer, and Sheridan counties until 1910. As a result, school reports were often fragmentary. Yet some public documents are available. The first to be analyzed are those which deal with the physical plant: the facilities, buildings, rooms, and conveniences. As will be seen, the German-Russian counties compare unfavorably to the Norwegian.

One index of the acceptance of education in general and of a local educational institution in particular is the type and quality of school which a community builds and supports. An analysis of school reports in 1911 shows that only one "log and sod" school remained in the four Norwegian counties. At the same time, the reporting German counties, Mercer and McIntosh, had five and seven respectively, a total of twelve.[6]

Another indicator of community support is the number of schools which are erected with such niceties as a gymnasium. In 1923, the four German-Russian counties reported a total of eight

The Tramp Teacher

H. A. Tewell, Cando, N. D.

from *The Westland Educator*:
Volume 10: Number 10 (April 1909), pp. 12-14.

That sounds strange, indeed. But there is a great concourse of teachers who teach school on the "installment plan." They are on the tramp, tramp, tramp, north, south, east, west — anywhere from whose solitude the school bell, breaking the stillness, sounds better than the one she is used to. But that "somewhere" seldom, if ever, measures up to what you have heard, or your imaginary concept of such a place.

Certainly, I believe in one's bettering one's self, in whatever pursuit of life, when such time, place, and surroundings are opportune. Among other influences, one's conscience should be heard here, and then one's best judgment rendered accordingly.

Sometimes a teacher desires a wider range for her activities within the province of the school, and hence seeks such conditions.

Some prefer the town or the city school to that of the rural community.

Some desire a more congenial climate and environment.

Still others "love" to make an "annual move, or perchance it may be a semiannual one just because it is too 'utterly tame' where I am, and 'gee' I must change."

And yet there are others who, regardless of the wider range of vision and usefulness, the town or city schools, the more congenial climate and surroundings, the "love" of moving about — I say there are others who are "scenting" the "snaps" and seeking the "larger pay."

Any one of these may be honest in itself. All may be expedient and perhaps legitimate, but the reflex action, the certain influence on the performer might be unwholesome and have a tendency to lessen, in the teacher's mind and practice, the real object for which the school exists. And then, there is a world of on-lookers and sight-seekers outside our immediate sphere. Think, how about them and their criticism? Should we regard not only ourselves, but them also, and that with a true politician's shrewdness? Am I my brother's keeper is yet a terrible interrogative "about face" to the teacher, either excusing or accusing. One's motive should put at ease the inquirer or the doer. But how is one to divine the motive? Simply by taking careful note of how others have acted under similar circumstances and testing the fruitage of such actions.

Let me illustrate: One desired larger responsibilities — the opportunity came shortly from an unexpected quarter. After due consideration, from different points of view, she accepted the new and larger field, and in so doing cast honor upon it, proved herself a noble fellow-worker, and reflected credit upon her alma mater.

We knew a teacher who succeeded nobly in the rural schools, but failed ignobly in the town school — this could be multiplied by one hundred.

We had a high school teacher who sought the Pacific Slope. School opened on the first of September, and had been running three weeks, and on the Friday after-

continued on next page

noon of the third week this lady entered the office and in the one breath informed us that she had been elected to a position in the West and desired an immediate release from the written contract she had of her own volition placed her signature to — and made preparations to make her departure. She went — we did the best we could. She soon wanted testimonials from *us*, favorable to her of course, going to make another shift in about six months. Yes, yes, on the tramp, tramp, tramp.

I knew a place where the lady teachers desired very much to go — well-to-do bachelors were numbered by the score — but not so numerous now as they once were. Few teachers who began their labors here returned to tell the story — if they had a *chance* to remain to help make a home there. (I do not blame them for this always, but here, we tried to get one of these ladies to defer the culmination of her matrimonial quest till the close of the term. but, no, no. She married — and we did the best we could for the remainder of the term.)

We had as a grade teacher, a lady, who had been elected at a certain salary as teacher in a town — she accepted it. Shortly she was notified of her election at another town where she had failed to withdraw her application. She accepted this position also, and at the same time broke her contract at the first place. In a few days here came a notice of her election in our town school at an increase in salary over the second offer which was an advance above the first. She signed a contract with the board here where she had failed again to withdraw her application on securing the second position and broke her second contract. We were looked upon as perverters of the truth, thieves, robbers, and as violators of all professional ethics that ever existed —but we were innocent of the underhandedness of the entire scheme till too late — so we did the best we could under the conditions. Could you do more? There is such a thing as an honest tramp and an honest "tramp" teacher — but please deliver me from the dishonest teacher whether a "tramp" or otherwise.

However many objects one may have in store for present and future use, and however much they may be emphasized and utilized, these two should not be forgotten: First, as a teacher with a mission to perform and a specific work to *complete*, I must build for myself the *best record*, have the *best practice*; Second, I must as a loyal, devoted teacher and conscientious unit of *society* contribute all I am and have not only to the progress but to the *stability* of the teachers' possibilities and work.

Teachers, these cannot be realized by joining ourselves and influence to the Coxey-ite ranks with their whims, idols, and miserable failures.

We must be not tramps but "stayers" as long as it is expedient, help complete some part at least of the great superstructure we delight in denominating — Education — become a part of the struggles, the joys, the groans, the shouts of victory of a community!

If it is a sacrifice of salary and immediate advancement? Yes, often. It may be best if it is a sacrifice (apparent) of everything except principle and health. One should stay in his place until his work may be called the finished product. It is not only your duty to stay but your business to so have hold of matters and so manipulate them that you may be *sure* as to the time to quit it.

continued on next page

gymnasiums while the four Norwegian counties reported thirty-two. Divide, the late settlement county, had seven, while McIntosh, settled twenty years earlier, had two. (See *Table II*, Appendix, page 105.)

The German-Russian counties were often cited for deficiencies in the condition of the buildings and the various furnishings. A 1922 report includes descriptions of "bad or no curtains," "poor toilet facilities," "no wash basins or paper towels," and "lack of ventilation systems," in the German-Russian counties. In the same year, reports from the eight counties make it very clear that school districts in the predominantly Norwegian areas, "scrub their schools" significantly more than those in the German-Russian counties. (See *Table II*, Appendix, page 105.)

Among the best guides to both the level of support and the quality of education in a county is the number of school libraries and the quantity of books in the libraries. In 1912 the Norwegian counties had a total of 169 school libraries, while in the same year the German-Russian counties reported only fifteen. Even more indicative was the number of books in those same school libraries in that year. The Norwegian counties reported 18,547 books, while the four German-Russian counties listed a total of 1,138. Divide County, the late settlement area, reported 782 books in their twenty libraries, more than any single German-Russian county total.[7]

Eleven years later, 1923, the three German counties which reported, McIntosh, Mercer, and Sheridan, listed a total of 12,154 books, while Divide County alone had 11,082. The three Norwegian counties reporting in that year had a total of slightly more than 44,000 books in their various libraries.[8]

There is, however, evidence in the superintendent of schools' reports that the German-Russian county school authorities were concerned about their educational deficiencies. In the 1923 category of "sets of encyclopedias in schools," the Norwegian counties listed 339 and the German-Russian 208. But Logan County had more encyclopedias than any Norwegian county except Nelson, and the Traill County total, seventy-one, was below the Sheridan County total, eighty-one. On the other hand, the number of schools "not furnishing supplementary readers for the first six grades" show a serious discrepancy between the two groups: 156 schools in the German-Russian counties lacked such readers but only five in the Norwegian counties were deficient in this regard.[9]

It also seems clear that school consolidation of some type or another proceeded at a faster rate in Norwegian school areas. Whether such concentration of facilities enhances quality is a matter of discussion even in the present day, but for whatever it may mean, the reports say the following: 240 "one-room" schools existed in the Norwegian counties in 1923, while 364 such schools were reported in the German counties of that year.[10]

No master workman, having a contract to complete a certain task, deserts it till the last nail is driven and the last stroke is the finishing one, if he values his reputation, character and purse. Can we afford to do less? Will we do less?

The stability of the teacher's work, and its standing among the people who are taxed to support it, depend largely upon those who by years of ardent toil in one city, one school, one rural community, give definite form and direction to that school which must influence that people, which must inspire confidence in its constituency, in its real mission and its proper place among the world-wide civilizing agencies.

An Anglo-American school superintendent in German-Russian Logan County, Eva B. Farell, had observed earlier, "It is with much difficulty that the foreign population is convinced of the great necessity of good school houses and good schools, hence building is slow."[11]

A few years earlier, in 1896, a Napoleon School Board official wrote in a Logan County newspaper:

> Let us take a glance at our schoolhouses, or more appropriately, school caves. The greater number are being taught in Russian homes. These houses are what eastern people call caves or outdoor cellars; being built of sod and covered with clay. They are heated with Russian ovens and have no ventilation except the door. I know of a room of this kind in which there is one bed, a lounge, and a table; the family meal is spread three times a day on this table in the school room. No desks, blackboards or maps. True, we have a few good school houses, the best at Napoleon. Outside of Napoleon, we had but three months of school, the teacher receiving not more than thirty-five dollars per month.[12]

There well may be additional factors which affected the quality of the physical plants in the German-Russian communities: bad roads, varying economic situations, political intrigue, inept public officials, and discrepancies in tax structures. However, there remains considerable historical evidence that the plants were inferior to those in Norwegian counties.

A second general index of educational commitment are the qualifications of teachers hired and the salaries paid them by the two groups. People who seriously believe in education will try to find good teachers and pay them well. Contemporary documents indicate that school authorities were interested in quality education as is evidenced by the 1923 report of a County Superintendent of Schools: "Many of these (teachers from eastern states) are a disappointment. In one district last year we had persuaded the board to pay $55.00 and $60.00, thinking that thereby we could get better teachers, and there were four failures out of six. They had come to have a good time rather than attend to school work."[13]

The Norwegian communities paid their teachers at a higher level than did the German-Russian. In 1910-1911, the Norwegian counties which reported — Divide, Nelson, Traill — paid an average monthly salary of $72.60. This compares to $43.70 in the one German-Russian county reporting — Logan. The women in the three Norwegian counties received $54.80 and the German county paid its women teachers correspondingly $41.19.[14]

Table 1
1923 Teacher Salaries in Norwegian Counties

County	Divide	Nelson	Steele	Traill	Average
Men	131.87	156.07	157.01	163.56	151.00
Women	110.02	104.40	108.80	113.13	108.00

Table 2
1923 Teacher Salaries in German-Russian Counties

County	Logan	McIntosh	Mercer	Sheridan	Average
Men	96.10	89.21	107.12	81.10	93.00
Women	99.42	101.66	106.52	105.98	103.00

Teacher Salaries for 1923 are outlined in *Table 1* and *Table 2.*

Quite clearly, the Norwegian counties paid higher salaries to their teachers in 1923, an average of $151.00 for men teachers in the Norwegian counties and $93.00 in the German-Russian. The differences are substantial. Surprisingly, the women teachers in German-Russian counties fared comparatively better than their counterparts in the Norwegian counties. In fact, the women teachers in the German counties received almost the same average salary as the women teachers in the Norwegian schools. Moreover, the women teachers in the German-Russian counties received higher salaries than the men in the same school system: $103.00 for women and $93.00 for men.

What were the reasons for this variance? Were women teachers considered more effective in German-Russian areas? Were they more qualified and thus merited higher salary? Did German-Russian parents perceive school teaching as being a female occupation and frown upon male participation through a disadvantageous salary scale? A superintendent from Logan County gives us some insight into this. After complaining about the low salary increments, he says:

> This is an inconsistency familiar to all who have made a study of the remuneration of the common school teacher, yet on the whole the schools of Logan County are forging ahead and what is most needed is something to awaken the average school official to the fact that he is trying to employ people of education and natural pedagogic ability and in some instances with special training for the profession of teaching for less money than he pays a man to drive his team and to attend to his stock.[15]

In other words, farm labor was preferred to teaching; it paid more.

In terms of county superintendent salaries in 1911, the four Norwegian counties generally paid more than the German-Russian counties with one interesting exception, Divide County. The three German-Russian counties which reported paid more than twice the salary received by the superintendent in the Norwegian Divide County.[16]

If the payment of teachers is, as suggested in the various comparisons above, an indication of the degree of local support, the German-Russians viewed education in a less favorable light than the Norwegian citizens.

North Dakota teacher qualifications have varied through the years according to the mandates of the State Department of Public Instruction. We can say, however, that the teacher professional requirements were applied in each decade with an even hand throughout the state. It is, therefore, possible to compare the various counties as they procured the services of teachers with different qualifications. Here again, the German counties appear to be second best. Thus, reports show that in 1923 the Norwegian counties in graded rural schools and in the town schools were clearly attracting more college and normal school college graduates than their German-Russian counterparts. (See *Table III*, Appendix, page 105.) The reports further show that while in the one-room schools of villages and the open countryside, virtually no college graduates were teaching in that year in any of the Norwegian or German counties, with the exception of Mercer; nevertheless, far more normal school graduates were employed in this type of school in the Norwegian counties, nineteen, as compared to German-Russian counties, three. Of particular note, also, are the number of teachers in the reports who taught in one-room schoolhouses the entire term with either a permit or no certificate at all. In the four German-Russian counties, there were 128 such teachers. In the Norwegian counties there were only three. (See *Table IV*, Appendix, page 105.)

School records, unfortunately, rarely indicate anything of the ethnic background of teachers or officials in administrative rank, but such information would be of value. The question of unconscious bias, the projection of role models for students, and ultimately the encouragement of an upward mobility in the various groups could be ascertained with such information. While the subject is a complicated one, we have begun the exploration of the matter by making an ethnic name analysis of all the county superintendents of schools in the years 1923 to 1925.[17] We found that one-fourth of the county superintendents, including the State Superintendent of Public Instruction, were of Norwegian background; half of the superintendents were of Yankee or Anglo-American background; and the remaining tended to be primarily German. No one name was clearly German-Russian in background. For the eight counties of particular concern to this study, we can say conclusively that the superintendents in the German-Russian counties were not of that ethnic origin, while all the Norwegian counties had superintendents of Norwegian background. Indeed, a number of German-Russian counties had superintendents of Norwegian derivation. It is interesting to speculate on how the fact that the control of educational affairs by "outsiders" either at a state level or locally on the school boards, influenced German attitudes toward public schooling. We treat the question briefly in the Silva portion of this essay.

Another measure of school quality and ultimately of educational support is the variance in the classifications of the different schools as reported in the documents of the county superintendents of schools.

First, we looked at existence of graded schools. This more specialized institution was, in the past, considered better than an ungraded school. In contrast to the one-room school, they were required by law to meet higher standards in various categories: libraries, subject matter, departments, administrative offices.

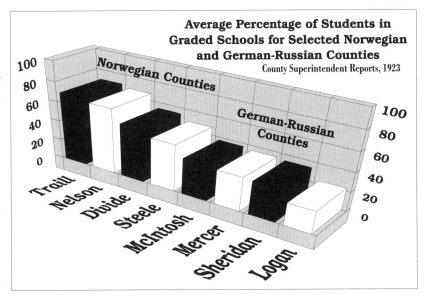

Average Percentage of Students in Graded Schools for Selected Norwegian and German-Russian Counties
County Superintendent Reports, 1923

In 1923 the graded schools were all in towns. In that year Norwegian counties had significantly more pupils in graded schools than the German-Russian counties. In

A Country School Teacher Remembers — Lillian Dinwoodie

My sixteen years of rural school teaching were confined to four schools: Hubbell School No. 3 and Hubbell School No. 1 in McHenry County; Bronston School in Riverview School District and Reservation School in Hawkeye School District in McKenzie County. I taught eight years in each county.

The salary for my first year of teaching Hubbell School No. 3 was seventy-five dollars per month; I paid twenty-four dollars for room and board. For my first year of teaching in McKenzie County, in 1930, I was paid ninety-four dollars per month; I paid twenty-four dollars for board and room. For five years during the Great Depression I taught Hubbell School No. 3 and received forty-five dollars per month; I paid ten dollars for room and board.

Shortly after Christmas during my first year of teaching, one of my students, Kenneth looked out of the window one morning and exclaimed, "Harold's coming!" I looked and there came Harold down the road carrying his lunch bucket. Harold, in his twenties, was a nephew of one of the neighbors. He had come from Norway to help his uncle farm. He was now coming to school to learn to read and speak English. I helped him with his reading. Often, Kenneth, a beginner, would sit on his lap and they would talk Norwegian. Harold attended school until it was time to get busy with spring work. Shortly before the end of the year there was a knock at the door one afternoon. I opened it and there stood Harold with a gift. He said it was for the help I had given him. It was a piece of Community Plate silverware. I still have it.

In the winter of 1935-1936 when the thermometer at Parshall, North Dakota recorded 60 degrees below zero I was boarding about two miles from my school. The man had an enclosed school bus that even contained a little stove. He had been a rural bus driver before he rented the farm. He or the hired man would take the little

continued on next page

the Norwegian counties there were 5,635 pupils in graded schools while in the German-Russian counties there were only 3,580. (The 1920 United States Census shows 39,670 total residents in the Norwegian counties and 32,882 in the German-Russian.) Divide County, the late settlement Norwegian county, had 1,131 pupils in town graded schools. This was greater than any one of the German-Russian counties. (McIntosh the highest, had 1,059.)[18]

A further index of community commitment to quality schools is revealed in a similar set of statistics found in a graph published by the State Superintendent of Public Instruction in 1926. The proportion of students in graded schools for Norwegian and German-Russian communities, including classified high schools are indicated in the chart at the left in these percentages: Traill — 70; Nelson — 67; Divide — 54; Steele — 48; McIntosh — 37; Mercer — 35; Sheridan — 34; and Logan — 23. In brief, the lowest Norwegian county had 48 percent and the highest German-Russian county had 37 percent of their students in graded schools. Again, it might be noted that Divide County, the latest county to be settled, was far above the earlier settled German-Russian counties. If the "grading" of schools has anything to do with determining the "quality" of schools, the Norwegian community schools were better.

The average length of terms as to numbers of days in graded schools, in towns, for 1923, differed little. Norwegian county schools averaged 180 days per year, German-Russian counties reported almost the same with 175 days.[20] The situation was quite different earlier, however, as seen in the *School Superintendent's Report* of 1911. The number of schools which taught "seven months or more" was far greater for the Norwegian counties — 264 Norwegian and 63 German-Russian. Comparison of the two sets of reports indicates that the German-Russian area schools in the twelve intervening years made great efforts to catch up in the length of term category, and they were quite successful in their endeavors.[21]

One basic and indisputable indicator of community support for education is whether young people are sent to school at all, and whether they persist in school once they started.

Table 3 (from the *1910 United States Census*) clearly shows that German-Russian parents did not send their children to school to the same degree as Norwegian parents. In every county, the German percentage of the total of students enrolled is less than the Norwegian.

Table 3
**Number and Percentage of Children in North Dakota Ages 6 to 14
Who Attended School in 1910 (U.S. Census)**

COUNTY	Divide	Nelson	Steele	Traill	Logan	McIntosh	Mercer	Sheridan
Total Children	891	2035	1516	2545	1448	1861	1064	1962
In School	667	1700	1250	2263	997	1021	643	1441
Percent	93.5	83.5	82.5	88.9	68.9	54.9	60.4	73.4

Table 4
**Percent of Children in North Dakota Ages 7 to 13
Who Attended School in 1920 (U.S. Census)**

COUNTY	Divide	Nelson	Steele	Traill	Logan	McIntosh	Mercer	Sheridan
Percent	93.5	95.2	91.0	94.8	88.0	94.0	94.5	96.1

A decade later, as seen in *Table 4*, the United States Census indicated that the discrepancy between the German-Russians and Norwegian counties had virtually disappeared. We may therefore conclude that, in so far as the "three R's" in grade school are concerned, by 1920 the German-Russian parents were as insistent as were the Norwegian parents that their children receive basic education.

The Norwegians attitude, however, differed from the German-Russian in the matter of schooling beyond the basics. It was a question of how much education was deemed necessary. In 1920 the total population of the Norwegian counties was 39,670 persons and the German-Russian counties numbered 32,882. The Norwegian population totaled about sixteen percent more than the German. *Table 5* indicates the number of students finishing eighth grade, the total in high school, and those completing high school. The large difference in numbers indicates a much higher percentage of students from Norwegian counties completing the eighth grade and going on to high school than can be accounted for by their slightly higher total population.

Table 5 (next page) reveals that, as they advance in years, the German-Russian students increasingly leave the educational system. For every ten Norwegian county children who finished the eighth grade, less than five did so in the

boy and me to school in this bus and would build a fire in the little stove. It was real cozy. In early February the man decided the snow was too deep for the horses so he quit taking us to school. He kept his boy home and I walked the rest of the winter.

When I taught in McHenry County most of my pupils were children of German-Russians. They were good students but were at a disadvantage their first years because their parents did not speak English to them at home. Recently I renewed my friendship with one of those former students. She tried to explain to me how the children all felt back in those days. It was less than ten years since World War I had ended. She said they were ashamed and humiliated to be called pro-German, they were ashamed of the language, and above all, they were ashamed of their German accent. They vowed to become proficient in the English language and rid themselves of it. They succeeded.

Only once did I have a beginner who would not speak to me in class. The two girls had much fun learning the new vocabulary in sentences on the board, playing games with the word cards, beginning to read in the pre-primers, and writing. Noel appeared to think that it was all foolishness. After a month, when he finally decided to talk, he knew it all. He had fun sitting there absorbing it all like a sponge.

🖎🖎

German-Russian areas. Likewise, for every ten Norwegian students in high school, approximately three German-Russian students were in the same level of school. Finally, for every ten Norwegian county students who finished high school, less than three did so in the German-Russian schools.

Table 5
Number of Students Finishing Eighth Grade, the Number in High School and the Number Finishing High School in 1923(Superintendent Reports)

COUNTY	Divide	Nelson	Steele	Traill	Total of N Counties	Logan	McIntosh	Mercer	Sheridan	Total of G-R Counties
Finish 8th Grade	154	151	186	220	711	57	49	65	110	281
In High School	267	498	245	586	1536	121	108	134	149	512
Finish High School	25	90	45	125	285	18	13	19	17	67

Table 6
Percentage of Norwegian and German-Russian Youth Aged 15-17 in School in 1910 (U.S. Census)

COUNTY	Divide	Nelson	Steele	Traill	Logan	McIntosh	Mercer	Sheridan
PERCENT	57	62	72	65	42	21	42	63

Table 7
Percentage of Norwegian and German-Russian Youth Aged 15-17 in School in 1920 (U.S. Census)

COUNTY	Divide	Nelson	Steele	Traill	Logan	McIntosh	Mercer	Sheridan
PERCENT	59.1	57.1	52.3	60.1	42.9	34.1	39.2	59.1

The information from the United States Census reports in *Table 6* and *Table 7* leads one to the same conclusion. A surprisingly small proportion of young people in 1910 aged fifteen, sixteen and seventeen were in school: 64 percent of the Norwegians, 42 percent of the Germans. A decade later, the percent of sixteen and seventeen year-olds were Norwegian, 57 percent; and Germans, 44 percent. Again, the German counties were decidedly less inclined to send their young people to school in the middle teenage years. One must remember in this context, that some teenage students, especially those who were born in foreign countries, were in the lower grades learning American basic language, history, and civics. Some may have had a good background in the elementary schools of Europe and were doing remedial work in the American schools of their newly acquired homeland.

The inadequacy of early schools distressed some German-Russians. One Mercer County gentleman, who came to the area after spending his youth in a South Dakota German area, wrote:

> The public school I had in South Dakota was worth less than nothing. My teacher did not know at the time a word of English and he did not know the ABC's. He was about a sixth grade scholar in the German Language. My father had a fairly good education in German, so he taught us children in German. It was not mine or my parents fault that I did not then learn English but after I found it was up to me to learn English myself and this I have done the best I could as you can see I am writing this myself and in my own hand.[22]

Another measure of educational commitment, as revealed in the county superintendent of schools' reports, is the number of parent organizations supporting the schools in the various counties. Such information is available for the years 1922-1923. The reports indicate that there were twenty-two parent organizations in the four Norwegian counties, while the German-Russian counties had nine.

Keeping in mind that the German counties had some sixteen percent fewer people, the number of reported parental visits to Norwegian county schools in 1922-1923 is still proportionately higher than the visits of parents to German-Russian county schools in the same year. In the Norwegian areas, 4,189 visits took place, while in the German-Russian counties 2,531 visits occurred. If parental visits reflect support for the student or the school, the Norwegian parents were clearly more supportive.

Some indication of the differing school performance of males and females within the national groups can be seen in several United States Census publications and also in an official North Dakota Education report. The *Twelfth Biennial Report of the North Dakota Superintendent of Public Instruction, 1910-1911*, indicates that in that school year, Norwegian girls seemed to be in schools in greater number than Norwegian boys. In the German-Russian counties, the opposite appears to be true.

Table 8
Number of Boys and Girls Enrolled in School in Selected Norwegian and German-Russian Counties in 1910-1911

COUNTY	Divide	Nelson	Steele	Traill	Total of N Counties	Logan	McIntosh	Mercer	Sheridan	Total of G-R Counties
Boys	664	1276	711	1528	4179	804	944	702	1296	3746
Girls	652	1233	885	1601	4371	749	819	514	1206	3283

We can only guess why the Norwegians were more inclined to send their daughters to school while the German-Russians seemed more ready to send the boys to school. Did the Norwegians feel that women should be more equipped to deal with the more "refined" aspects of life and that men needed agricultural skills which school could not give? The opposite problem comes up in analyzing the German-Russian statistics. Why school for the boys and not so much for the girls?

The *United States Census Report of 1910* in *Table 9* shows the illiteracy rate among foreign-born residents aged ten or above to be higher than the local native-born population. This is to be expected. Arrival in America was a recent thing; in fact, immigrants were still coming. Only World War I stopped immigration to North Dakota. The Norwegian counties, nevertheless, had less illiteracy than the German — 4.25 percent to 9.15 percent.

Table 9
Percent of Persons Age Ten and Over Who Were Illiterate in 1910 in Selected Norwegian and German-Russian Counties (U.S. Census, 1910)

COUNTY	Divide	Nelson	Steele	Traill	Average	Logan	McIntosh	Mercer	Sheridan	Average
Native White	1.40	0.01	0.03	0.20	0.36	2.10	6.60	0.06	0.09	2.55
Foreign-Born White	3.00	3.10	6.20	4.70	4.25	8.50	16.80	2.70	8.60	9.15

Table 10
Percent of Persons Age Ten and Over Who Were Illiterate in 1920 in Selected Norwegian and German-Russian Counties (U.S. Census, 1920)

COUNTY	Divide	Nelson	Steele	Traill	Average	Logan	McIntosh	Mercer	Sheridan	Average
Native White	00.1	0.30	0.20	0.30	0.23	1.00	0.60	0.60	0.60	0.70
Foreign-Born White	4.90	1.60	2.40	1.40	2.58	10.40	5.70	10.20	21.50	11.95

The census report of ten years later, in 1920, however, is very interesting. As can be seen, the Norwegian counties reduced the difference between native- and foreign-born, with the exception of the late homestead county, Divide. However, in the German-Russian counties, the gap widened, with the exception of McIntosh County.

Table 11
Percent of Males of Voting Age Who Were Illiterate in 1910
in Selected Norwegian and German-Russian Counties (U.S. Census, 1910)

COUNTY	Divide	Nelson	Steele	Traill	Average	Logan	McIntosh	Mercer	Sheridan	Average
Males	2.0	1.8	2.9	1.7	2.1	5.3	11.5	2.3	4.5	5.9
Female Literacy not Recorded in the 1910 Census										

Table 12
Percent of Males of Voting Age Who Were Illiterate in 1920
in Selected Norwegian and German-Russian Counties (U.S. Census, 1920)

COUNTY	Divide	Nelson	Steele	Traill	Average	Logan	McIntosh	Mercer	Sheridan	Average
Females	2.5	1.1	1.0	0.8	1.35	9.6	5.5	9.1	19.8	11.0
Males	2.9	0.7	1.0	0.7	1.33	5.5	2.8	5.4	12.3	5.5

A Country School Teacher Remembers —

Gladys Kieffer Hedlund

My mother decided that all three of us girls were to be teachers. She considered office jobs to be less honorable. I was only sixteen when I received my three-year normal diploma from Ellendale. It was considered equivalent to a high school diploma. Blanche Stevens, the county superintendent of schools of Dickey County, needed teachers to go to a German-Russian settlement at Fredonia. She sent me there to teach the children English and told me to concentrate on the Three R's. I had boys seventeen years old who couldn't read; they came only three months in the winter during the seven-month term. In spring all the children were put to work picking rocks out of the fields. Later, I attended Valley City Normal and Moorhead State Teachers College in Minnesota.

One year I shared a room, but not a bed, with an old grandmother who didn't speak English. She was in bed when I retired and arose after I did so I had little privacy. At another place I stayed with an older woman who was crippled. I brought in her coal and wood, washed the dishes, and helped with the dinner.

The country school system lacked money for books and materials. Some teachers spent half their small salaries on supplies from Northern School Supply in Fargo.

One can only conclude that the Germans were in no great rush to acquire fluency in the English language, at least for those who were over ten years of age.

The United States Census of 1910 and 1920 show the varying rates of illiteracy for adult residents of voting age (*Table 11 and Table 12*). The 1910 illiteracy of such males (females were not recorded) in the German counties is higher than that of the Norwegian counties — 2.1 percent Norwegian compared to 5.9 percent German. One must remember that settlement was not complete in these years and the figures include the native born population. *Table 12* (1920 census), taken after immigration had slowed almost to a halt, show illiteracy in the German counties — 11 percent — decidedly higher than the Norwegian — 6.5 percent.

Of special interest in *Table 12* is the difference between the illiteracy rates of males and females. In the 1920 census the degree of illiteracy in the Norwegian counties, whether male or female, is almost the same; in the German counties, the illiteracy rate among females of voting age or older is astonishingly higher than that of the males, almost twice as high. This is in accord with *Table 8* which shows that German-Russian counties had more boys in school than girls. The question of why literacy and classroom education should be valued more in the life of the German male than the female still remains. Perhaps the woman in the solidly German communities was not required by circumstances to learn the American ways; each little ethnic enclave was a community unto itself. The male, to the contrary, was forced to trade with "outsiders," could be drafted into the army, and necessarily had to keep abreast with American political and economic affairs.

The extent to which a national group enters the ranks of professional educators may be an indicator of the level of acceptance of schools and formal education. Young people tend to become whatever is honored in the home. What is discouraged they avoid. An analysis of the fifty-three names in the Directory of County School Superintendents for the years 1923 to 1925 shows that at least twenty-five percent of the officials had Scandinavian surnames, most of which were clearly of Norwegian origin. In contrast, only four superintendents had German names and these were most likely of non-Russian background. One-half of the fifty-three superintendents were of old American Yankee origins.[23]

Likewise, out of fifty-four students who received teacher certificates from the University of North Dakota in 1920, twenty-one had Scandinavian names. Since the vast majority of Scandinavians in North Dakota are of Norwegian origin, we must conclude that a good-sized number of the graduating students were Norwegian. German names on the list were few, and none were of German-Russian background.

An examination of the roster of graduates of two state institutions of higher learning in selected years gives further insight into the educational values of the two groups in question. We selected commencement lists for the University of North Dakota at Grand Forks in 1910, 1920, and 1930. We also looked at lists of graduates at Dickinson State Normal School (now Dickinson State University), which opened its doors in 1918; we examined names from the 1920, 1925, and 1930 graduation lists. A careful name analysis, using ethnic recognition tools and local compilations of family histories, made it possible to determine with a degree of accuracy the national origins of the various students. The results were sometimes surprising.

The survey of the University of North Dakota graduates in 1910 reveals that, out of 114 graduates, one-third had Scandinavian names, al-

A Country School Teacher Remembers — Loretta M. Stern

How did I get my first teaching job? Depression stalked the land in 1931. Teachers were plentiful and jobs were scarce. Two weeks before school was to begin (after doing a lot of praying) I got a contract to teach an eight-month school for $55 per month in a one-room school in Conklin Township, near Woodworth. To get this position, my father and I walked across a field where the president of the school board was plowing. I was wearing my best clothes. I applied for the job and got it! The school was in a German settlement where the people spoke German most of the time except at school. I stayed there two years to get a good recommendation and then left.

My first day of teaching was an anxious one. Even though I had had six weeks of practice teaching in a rural school near Valley City I had never lived on a farm. The school needed repairs, had old blackboards, out-dated textbooks, and no teacher's copies of anything. The desks were the type made for two upper-grade pupils and there were smaller ones for the lower grades. On the wall was a picture of George Washington and an old copy of the Ten Commandments and the Pledge of Allegiance to the flag; a flag was nailed to the wall. My first year I had sixteen students in all eight grades. My eighth grade boy was bigger and older than I. I didn't dare let him know I was a little afraid of him at first, but he turned out to be all right.

I had always lived in town and by the end of the first week of teaching I was so homesick I decided to hitchhike the twenty-two miles to Carrington, my home town. To make matters worse, it had rained the night before. I wore a bright red jacket and on my way to the highway I had to pass a herd of cattle that were grazing in the pasture. I kept looking straight ahead and walking as fast as I could. I even went out of my way to avoid them, but then I saw a car coming. I ran fast so I wouldn't miss it before it turned, thinking I might get a ride into town. The road was muddy and mud kept clinging to my saddle oxfords. Now and then I would stop and clean them. I fell and ruined a new pair of stockings. The car did stop, however, and I was given a ride into Carrington. I learned that the driver also was a beginning teacher. I had him drop me off at the Penny Store where I bought some new stockings and put them on before going home.

I boarded with a German family. The teacher's room was special, and I appreciated having it

continued on next page

alone. I had a kerosene lamp, but no indoor bathroom facilities. The two things I missed the most, having grown up in town, were electricity and running water. Having to live on a farm almost discouraged me from continuing teaching, but I did like school, so I kept at it in spite of the inconveniences. I knew how to ice skate and I had a warm ice skating outfit that I brought from home. On Saturdays I would go skating by myself on a frozen pond or slough. Sometimes there would be card parties on Friday nights. I learned how to play whist and enjoyed the progressive whist parties. Some homes had Friday night parties at which "parlor games" were played. Other farm homes cleaned out a room (moved furniture) so they could dance, usually to an accordion or fiddle. Floors were made slippery by sprinkling corn meal around. It was all new to me and I enjoyed it. There seemed to be plenty to do after one got acquainted and joined in. After a party a big lunch would be served, but electricity and running water were lacking.

The people where I boarded for $18 a month continually spoke German, unless they talked to me, and then it was in broken English. They would speak so loudly you would think they were mad at each other or talking about you. I was the only Catholic among the German Lutherans and Seventh-day Adventists which didn't help matters any. By spring, however, I could understand enough German to get the gist of their conversation and had learned enough words to converse a little.

At first country school teaching seemed a lonely life to me. I stuck with it because I liked to teach school. A farm was a quiet, independent, healthful place to live. One advantage in attending a country school was that the student could listen to all the other grades and learn by listening. "Listening is the beginning of learning!" Another advantage was that a single grade student could work at his own speed and level, and many times advance sooner than if he were in a larger group.

most all Norwegian in background. No German-Russian names were found. The totals and those that follow reflect all the degree programs at the University, whether in engineering, business, education, liberal arts, science, or graduate level. The proportions remained the same for the class of 1920. Fifty-two of the 156 graduates were of Scandinavian background, again predominantly Norwegian. No German-Russian names were present. In a third University of North Dakota group, the 315 graduates of 1930, we found a total of eighty-four Scandinavian names, mostly Norwegian — this represents 27 percent of the class. At the same time, only one definite and one possible German-Russian student was on the roster.

The absence of German-Russian graduates is especially remarkable because, during the years in question, at least 15 percent of North Dakota's population was of that nationality group.

Dickinson State Normal School was close to large concentrations of German-Russians. The school, smaller and more informal in style, should, thereby, have attracted a good sized number of German students. Certainly the Dickinson enrollment proportions should be greater than the more distant Grand Forks University of North Dakota. The graduate lists were of particular interest because the majority of its students, at least in the early decades, were destined for employment at various levels in the teaching profession. Hence, an analysis provides an additional measure of attitudes toward education within the two ethnic communities.

In 1920, twenty students graduated from the Dickinson school. Of that number, none were of German-Russian origins and six, or 30 percent, were of Scandinavian, for the most part Norwegian, in background.

Five years later, in 1925, of 106 graduates, 25 percent had Scandinavian names while no more than eight, or 7 percent, were of German-Russian origin. Finally, in 1930, of the 130 graduates, twenty-one (16 percent), were Scandinavian and only three were of definite and five of possible German-Russian ancestry. The German-Russian percentage, therefore, did not exceed 6 percent.

Norwegians in those earlier decades were a minority group in the southwestern portion of the state. Some were found at Taylor and northward to Dunn Center and a large number were present north of the Little Yellowstone River in the Alexander-Arnegard-Keene region. Others were found in Slope and Adams counties.

But in the aggregate, they numbered probably less than one-fourth of the German-Russian population totals.

The proportions of college graduates gives, without question, some indication of the varying attitudes toward education in the two groups. Virtually no German-Russians graduated from the University of North Dakota during the years in question. In the same school, a surprisingly large percentage of Norwegians, at least 30 percent, completed their course of study. Thirty percent is a good approximation of the proportion of Norwegians in the entire state population. Such a degree of participation in higher education by members of a relatively new "immigrant" group is quite unique. It is doubtful whether any other sizable North Dakota ethnic community can match that record.

The graduation record indicates that the Germans from Russia were reluctant to attend school beyond the level of necessary basic skills. Even when offered the opportunity close to home in Dickinson, they were, at least in the early decades of the century, hesitant to take advantage of a college education.

The observations made above are substantiated by a study of German-Russians done (by co-author William Sherman) in 1965.

> In 1921, the University of North Dakota had one student of German-Russian ancestry among the 1,215 in attendance. Voeller found only two at that University among the 1,828 who attended in 1940. (404 of Norwegian background, 424 from the British Isles and Ireland.) These figures are amazing when one realizes that there were, without a doubt, from fifty to a hundred thousand German-Russians in the state in these years. Times have changed, however, for this author, in a hasty check of the *University of North Dakota, Student Directory* for Fall 1964, found over fifty students of this ancestry among the Catholics enrolled. No doubt the total of German-Russian students is several times this figure.[24]

Dayton School, 1890, three miles south of Tolna on Sheyenne River in Nelson County *(SHSND)*

Endnotes

1. Elwyn B. Robinson, *History of North Dakota* (Lincoln: University of Nebraska Press, 1966), p. 267.

2. Leona N. Bergmann, *Americans From Norway* (New York: J. P. Lippincott Co., 1950), p. 97.

3. The question of ethnicity and its relation to education has seldom been studied, at least in Great Plains states. No serious investigation of the comparative performance of any North Dakota groups has been made. Certainly no investigation of the behavior of North Dakota's two leading groups, Norwegians and German-Russians, has ever been undertaken. Some few paragraphs and occasional references, have been published concerning individual groups, but no real analysis or explanation of alleged differences has been made. As will be seen in this study, Height and Giesinger make brief mention of education in the Russian homeland. Aberle is defensive, George Rath makes only a scattered reference to schools, Adolf Schock is sympathetic and Voeller is highly critical of German popular support for education in North Dakota. On the Norwegian side, Nora Fladeboe Mohlberg's works underline the high priority which Norwegian families placed on education, as does Aagot Raaen's memoir, *Grass of the Earth*. Duane Lindberg's research attests to the concern North Dakota's Norwegians had for both public and private education.

4. The choice of these counties is based on United States Census reports for foreign born and mixed parentage in 1910, 1920, and 1930. A more recent unpublished study of rural and small town ethnic totals by William Sherman was also used. (See Table I in the Appendix.)

5. The population differences are not of great consequence; in 1920 the four Norwegian counties had an average population of 9,902, the German-Russian counties averaged 8,649. The economic differences may, at times, affect the variance as far as school facilities and salaries are concerned. (See Table I in the Appendix.) The date of settlement and the vagaries of weather certainly influenced the economic worth of the farm families. Nevertheless, it seems that the German-Russian counties had less total farm property value than the eastern Norwegian counties. For this reason, the authors will continually refer to the Norwegian Divide County whose agricultural worth was comparable to the German-Russians. It must also be remembered that the state of North Dakota, from even the earliest period, was making some grants to rural and graded elementary schools in every county, and that high schools, in particular, were receiving aid.

6. North Dakota, Department of Public Instruction, *Twelfth Biennial Report of the Superintendent of Public Instruction to the Governor of North Dakota* for the two years ending June 12, 1912, E. J. Taylor, superintendent, p. 91. Cited hereafter: *Superintendent Report*, 1912.

7. *Ibid.*, pp. 124-25.

8. *Superintendent Report*, 1922-23, pp. 190-91.

9. *Ibid.*, p. 190.

10. *Ibid.*, p. 184.

11. *Superintendent Report*, 1898, p. 246.

12. *Diamond Jubilee Book*, Napoleon, North Dakota, 1959, p. 11.

13. *Superintendent Report*, 1912, pp. 183-84.

14. *Ibid.*, p. 105.

15. *Ibid.*, p. 179.

16. *Ibid.*, pp. 164-65.

17. *Superintendent Report*, 1926, pp. 10-11.

18. *Ibid.*, 1923, pp. 186-87.

19. *Ibid.*, 1926, Exhibit D.

20. *Ibid.*, 1923, pp. 186-87.

21. *Ibid.*, 1912, pp. 100-01.

22. August Isaak, "Personal Story," Unpublished, *Mercer County Old Settlers History*, Beulah, North Dakota, 1926.

23. *Superintendent Report*, 1926. pp. 10-11.

24. William Sherman, "Assimilation in a North Dakota German-Russian Community," (unpublished M.A. thesis, University of North Dakota, 1965), pp. 78-79. The 1921 figure is from John M. Gillette, "Economic and Social background of the University of North Dakota," *The Quarterly Journal of the University of North Dakota*, XII, No. 1, p. 41. The 1940 figure is from Joseph B. Voeller, "The Origins of the German-Russian People and Their Role in North Dakota," (unpublished M.S. thesis, University of North Dakota, 1940), p. 76.

Case Study: Silva, North Dakota *

Playford V. Thorson and William C. Sherman

SCHOOL DISTRICTS MADE UP OF EQUAL proportions of students from Norwegian and German-Russian backgrounds are rare in North Dakota. The ethnic concentrations seldom are adjacent to each other; however, one particular district has been studied with a degree of care. And the conclusions drawn can be applied to some of the previously discussed issues.

Almost the entire life history of the Silva grade and high school is available through public records. Some 2,053 students, the pupil-year count, included 1,070 of Norwegian background and 983 of German-Russian ancestry.

The grade and high school began with the combining of several country schools in 1913. Though the school continued until the 1950s, the data used in this study deals with the years until 1940. Since settlement in the area took place in the 1890s, the time period represents second and even third generation activities. The Silva village tended to be predominantly Norwegian, perhaps 85 percent; however, the surrounding country areas embraced both Norwegian and German-Russian farm families. The school opened with eighteen students in grade school. In 1924, the high school had an all time high enrollment of thirty. The twelve grades averaged about ninety students through the ensuing years, with a record enrollment of one hundred four students.

*Portions of the study were presented by Walden Duchscher in an unpublished paper at the Conference on the History of the Red River Valley and Northern Plains, April 28, 1972, Fargo, North Dakota. That report is on file at the State Historical Society, Bismarck and at North Dakota State University and the University of North Dakota libraries.

Playford V. Thorson and William C. Sherman

Table 13
Enrollment and Absentee Records of the Silva Grade School, 1915-1941

SELECT YEARS	NORWEGIAN STUDENTS					GERMAN-RUSSIAN STUDENTS				
	Male	Female	Total	Percent Absent	Average Days Absent	Male	Female	Total	Percent Absent	Average Days Absent
1915-16	08	09	17	6.5	11.6	03	01	04	13.3	21.3
1920-21	21	22	43	4.1	07.4	26	21	47	07.1	12.8
1925-26	13	19	32	1.2	02.1	20	16	36	10.7	19.2
1930-31	18	19	37	1.3	02.3	15	18	33	08.5	15.3
1935-36	20	18	38	1.0	01.8	22	25	47	04.4	08.0
1940-41	15	14	29	5.9	10.7	22	25	47	07.7	13.9
TOTAL ALL YEARS 1913-1941										
	421	413	834	4.2	07.4	415	433	858	07.3	13.0

Table 14
Enrollment and Absentee Records of the Silva High School, 1920-1941

YEAR	NORWEGIAN STUDENTS					GERMAN-RUSSIAN STUDENTS				
	Male	Female	Total	Percent Absent	Average Days Absent	Male	Female	Total	Percent Absent	Average Days Absent
1920-21	06	06	12	4.3	07.8	01	01	02	02.2	04.0
1925-26	06	09	15	4.2	07.6	00	02	02	01.4	02.5
1930-31	05	07	12	2.9	05.2	03	05	08	05.7	10.3
1935-36	04	07	11	2.3	04.1	04	03	07	04.7	08.3
1940-41	11	06	17	6.2	11.1	07	04	11	06.9	12.5
TOTAL	32	35	67	4.0	07.1	15	15	30	4.2	7.5

Enrollment and absentee records of the Silva grade school for five-year intervals are presented in the following table.

As can be seen, the enrollment of both German and Norwegian pupils in 1920-1921 and the ensuing years was about equal. German-Russian girls tended to be present in slightly greater numbers than boys. The opposite is true among Norwegians. The differences are probably too slight to be significant. Absenteeism, however, is quite clearly more prevalent among the Germans. German students were absent 7.3 percent of the time and Norwegian children missed school only 4.2 percent of the time.

The Silva High School date presented in *Table 14* shows a different picture; hardly any German-Russian students were present until 1930, and even after that they were only a little more than half the numbers of the Norwegians. The male and female totals for both groups were much the same and the absentee percentages showed little difference. The study does seem to show that, when the German-Russian boys or girls went to high school, they were just as conscientious about attendance as were the Norwegians.

These figures are consistent with the earlier findings of the study when Superintendent of Public Instruction documents and census reports were analyzed. Germans went to high school in fewer numbers than Norwegians.

The Duchscher-Sherman study of the Silva School discovered some very decisive differences. During the years from 1920-1922 to 1939-1940 a surprisingly low proportion of the German-Russian males, 39.6 percent, who entered the first grade actually finished the eighth grade. The female German-Russian figure is about the same as the Norwegian (See *Table 15*, facing page). The remarkable percentage of male German-Russian boys leaving school is contrary to the state-wide data which showed German males stayed in school longer than females.

Clearly, more Norwegian young people continued on into high school than Germans. If German boys, a small minority, finished grade school, they were more inclined to go to high school than were the German girls. For the girls, completing grade school was a definite goal, 85.4 percent made it; but after the goal was achieved, only 56.1 percent went on.

The Silva study provides a unique opportunity for some analysis of the comparative performance of the two groups as they confront the various subject matter disciplines. The record of every student in every year was determined and the respective grades were assessed (*Table 16*).

As can be seen, the German-Russians scored almost the same as the Norwegians. With the lesser emphasis placed on education in the German-Russian home observed earlier in the study, one might expect the German average scores to be much lower than indicated. It shows that these children were, practically speaking, comparable to their Norwegian peers. The high school scores, too, are remarkably similar (*Table 17*).

The scores in English and reading are of particular interest, for Duchscher-Sherman say that the great majority, if not all, of the German students spoke German in their homes and began to seriously use English only on arrival in the first grade. In spite of this, the English scores in grade school were 83 (German) versus 85 (Norwegian) and 83 and 87, respectively, in reading. In high school the English scores are even more remarkable, for German students' average scores came to 88 and Norwegians received an average score of 89. This indicates that initial difficulties in the transition period from the German language home to the English grade school must not have been serious or long-lasting.

The above data is the first definite measure we have been able to obtain in regard to actual classroom performance. For the most part, the Germans did almost as well as their Norwegian counterparts. In ability, diligence and performance they seem much the same.

A reoccurring question is whether the national background of school personnel affected students' performance. Norwegians and others were often in the educational establishment; German-Russians were not. Silva was no exception.

From 1913, with the consolidation of the township school board, until 1940, a total of twenty-six different citizens were elected to serve

Table 15
Percentage by Gender of Students at Silva Who Finished Eighth Grade and Entered High School After Finishing Eighth Grade

	NORWEGIAN STUDENTS			GERMAN-RUSSIAN STUDENTS		
	Male	Female	Average Total	Male	Female	Average Total
Entered First Grade and Finished Eighth Grade	80.9	86.7	84.0	39.6	85.4	63.0
Entered Silva High School After Finishing Eighth Grade	88.0	78.0	83.0	68.4	56.1	62.0

Table 16
Average Grade School Scores in Selected Subjects for School Years 1917-18 to 1940-41 at Silva

	Reading	Writing	Math	English	Average Grade
German-Russian	83	85	81	83	83
Norwegian	87	86	85	85	86

Table 17
Average High School Scores in Selected Subjects for School Years 1922-23 to 1934-35 at Silva

	English	Math	History	Average Grade
German-Russian	88	83	88	86
Norwegian	89	89	89	89

A Country School Teacher Remembers — Mabel Wenstrom

I graduated from Rugby High School in 1921. My parents had no intentions of sending me to college. They told me when I learned the value of a dollar they would help me financially if I wished to continue my education. The best way to learn would be to take a job, make some money and save it.

In June Louis Larson, president of the school board in Hendrickson District, five miles west of Rugby and near the village of Turnbridge, came to our home and asked me to teach one of the rural schools in that district. I had taken one semester of psychology, one of pedagogy, and practice-taught a spelling class in the fourth grade for about four weeks during my senior year. So I was qualified.

In the decade following World War I there was a great shortage of teachers. However, when Mr. Larson found out I was only seventeen years old he hesitated. But my school record was good, so he secured a teacher's permit from the State Department of Public Instruction, good for four and one-half months until I was eighteen, and I was on my way. My salary was to be ninety dollars per month.

continued on next page

Summer flew swiftly and the first Monday morning in September found me at the desk of my little rural school. One of my patrons had told me that Charles Vaughn, fifteen, was undecided as to whether he should enroll in school or try to date the teacher. His parents and the state school attendance law evidently helped him with his decision. He showed up bright and early that first Monday morning — the tallest of the lot and singularly good looking.

As the children began coming in the front door carrying their dinner pails, they stopped and stared at the new teacher. Finally they were all there — twenty-three of them, and for the first time since I had taken the job I was really scared. I smiled and said, "Good morning." They smiled too, and we seemed to be friends.

The first day went very badly. I managed to get in all eight reading classes, eight arithmetic classes, and my language or English classes, but four o'clock came before I had taught any geography or history to say nothing of hygiene or physiology, as it was called.

I cried myself to sleep that night, softly, so my landlady would not hear me, and hoped my eyes would not be red in the morning.

The second day was hardly any better, and that evening after school I caught a ride home to Rugby. At the supper table I informed my parents that I had quit and I wasn't going back. Complete silence, I thought I had won, but at 6:00 a.m. my father called me, and after breakfast took me back out to the school in our Model A Ford. He also sent the county superintendent of schools to see me.

Gentle Sara Guss was a lifesaver. She made out a program for me to follow and taught me how to combine classes and alternate subjects. She advised me to give a little extra time to my seventh and eighth graders, as they were required to pass state-given examinations in May.

As the days went by I became very fond of my little charges, especially the primary pupils. My one little first grade boy could speak no English, only German. That was no problem, since I too was of German descent, and if he said *crut* instead of toad when he was reading aloud, I knew that he knew. He was a very intelligent child and before long he was ahead of his classmates.

I did not realize how lucky I was. I did decide if I ever saved enough money to go to Teachers College, I would specialize in primary grades.

Frank Hornstein, who lived on the farm just across the road from the school, built the fire in the school room heating stove for five dollars per month.

on the school board, for a total of 108 member-years on the board. Of the twenty-six board members, twenty-five were Norwegian and one was a German-Russian who served for only one-member year. Norwegian board members served for 107 member-years; moreover during the twenty-seven-year period, eleven men served as board president; all were Norwegian.

German-Russians did slightly better in terms of the position of principal. Of fifteen who served in that capacity, three or 20 percent were German-Russian, eight or 53.3 percent were Norwegians, and four or 26.7 percent of other nationalities.

Few German-Russian teachers were employed in the Silva school system. Of fifty-four teachers employed during the twenty-seven-year period only five or 9.3 percent were of that nationality, thirty-three or 61.1 percent were Norwegian, and sixteen or 29.6 percent were of other nationalities.

Bus drivers for the system submitted closed bids for their jobs and could submit only one bid for the route in his area. Low bidders for each route, of course, received the job. Interestingly enough drivers came from both groups. Of thirty-four bus drivers sixteen or 47.1 percent were German-Russian, eighteen or 52.9 percent were Norwegians. The closed bid system was also used in hiring school janitors. In this instance German-Russians were completely unsuccessful. During the entire period only six janitors were employed; all were Norwegian.

Why, if the school's student population was relatively equal, was almost the sole membership of the school board Norwegian? Why were the teachers preponderantly Norwegian, and why were all the janitors Norwegian? Why were the bus drivers almost 50 percent German-Russian? Certainly, a part of the answer has to do with the peculiarities of local politics. One does get the distinct impression that the German-Russians didn't want to get involved in school questions. The considerable number of grade school students of German background argues to the presence of a sizable German population. It would seem that they could have insisted on a greater share of responsible elected positions if they had wished.

continued on next page

A more fundamental question arises: did the high percentage of Norwegian teachers have any effect on the slightly lower scores of the German-Russian students? The answer would seem to be no. The teachers did not favor either ethnic group. Upon study of numerous individual cases, Duchscher, a native of Silva, says the range of a German students' grades was consistently the same from year to year or class to class no matter what the nationality of the teacher might have been. If in a given year, a student fell far below his average score, the entire class was also below their prior average. Rather than a question of ethnicity, we probably see here the differences in the scoring system of individual teachers.

Differences between the two groups were most obvious in the "political" aspect of school life. Silva school board members were, with one exception, entirely Norwegian. All the janitors were Norwegian, so also were most of the teachers and the majority of the principals. It seems that Norwegian citizens looked at the school with great concern and, in a way, saw it as their own special preserve. The German-Russians, on the other hand, proved to be often uninterested in school management affairs.

Records clearly indicate that only a small proportion, slightly over one-third, of the German-Russian males finished Silva Grade School during the years under study. The German-Russian females survival rate was twice that number. In contrast, the great majority of Norwegian males and females completed grade school.

Surprisingly, if the German-Russian male finished grade school, chances were very good, over 80 percent, that he would at least enter high school. Only half of the German-Russian females entered high school. Lists of those who actually *graduated* from high school were unfortunately not available.

Attendance records and achievements in various classes show that the German-Russians did not do quite as well as their Norwegian counterparts; average absences were higher and marks were lower in every category. But the differences were not great. Contrary to the generalizations some North Dakota writers have made, the differences in Silva between the performances of the Germans who did go to grade and high school and

My first payday was a red-letter day. My friend Tillie Tofsrud and I went to Devils Lake on the train to go shopping. We both bought lovely black velvet dresses. Mine cost thirty-eight dollars, and hers cost even more. By the time I paid for board and room, I did not have much money left. It was quite evident that I had not learned the value of a dollar quite yet. Maybe my parents thought I was a slow learner.

I spent most of my weekends at home. If I could get to Turnbridge by 5:00 or 5:30 p.m. on Fridays I could catch a ride to Rugby with Mr. Tweet who operated a general store there and lived in Rugby. One Friday in January when there was too much snow to drive cars on side roads, I caught a ride to Turnbridge with a patron in a bobsled, drawn by two horses. They somehow became frightened and ran away full speed across the fields. I climbed out the back end, landed in soft snow, jumped up and ran to Turnbridge as fast as I could go so as not to miss my ride with Mr. Tweet.

My father often brought me back out on Sundays but in the spring when the roads were blocked or very muddy, I came from Rugby to Turnbridge on the train. One of the farm boys in the neighborhood was usually willing to meet the train and bring me to my boarding place. After an especially rainy week Lawrence Bell met me at the depot with his horse and buggy. He liked to tease me, sometimes unmercifully, and this Sunday when I thought I had had it, I became very angry at him, and asked him to stop the horse so I could get out and walk home. He calmly drove off the road into the middle of a huge mud puddle or slough as it was called, stopped the horse and said, "O. K. You may get out and walk home."

After we sat there for what seemed like hours, I suddenly saw the humor in the situation, and we both began to laugh. Inside of myself I reflected on what a wit he really was, not only this time, but other times as well.

The end of May came, my seventh and eighth graders, being diligent workers, as well as intelligent, passed their state exams — 65 percent was the passing grade. The school board elected to rehire me for the next school year.

The second year was much easier and by spring I had saved three hundred dollars.

The fall of 1923 found me enrolled at Valley City Teachers College. In March my parents loaned me $150 to complete the school year. My primary special was a dream come true.

I also attended a rural school in Pierce County. I believe I received a good education. Through the years I have felt that the rural

continued on next page

their Norwegian fellow pupils was only a matter of several percentage points. Considering the almost exclusively German-speaking home life and the low priority given institutionalized education in the German-Russian family the performance of the two student groups were remarkably similar.

❧ ❧

Silva Consolidated School @ 1917 after eaves, throughs and downspouts installed *(Edith C. Lysne, Rugby, ND)*

school students held their own when they entered town and city schools. In the rural school I attended, I was the only German child while all the others were Norwegian. During World War I they really persecuted me. They wouldn't play with me and they talked Norwegian all the time. I would cry. I told my dad. He went to town and bought me a fifty-dollar Liberty Bond and told me when they ignored me I should ask them if *they* had a fifty-dollar Liberty Bond. No one had. So that really helped. For the most part my rural school days were happy days. And oh, how we cried when our parents moved to town when I was in seventh grade.

❧ ❧

I believe I received a good education. Through the years I have felt that the rural school students held their own when they entered town and city schools.

Chapter 5

Two Months in "Little Russia"

Jessamine S. Slaughter

AKEM IS THE NAME OF A RUSSIAN SETTLEMENT in Southeastern Emmons County, North Dakota. The name is not, as might be supposed, of foreign origin, but was invented by a patriotic Dakotan, taking the first syllables of the Dakota, and Emmons, thus naming it after the State and the county.

It was my lot to spend two months in this unique settlement as a teacher; and, although the recollections are not unpleasant and the experience is valuable, yet the memory of it is as if I had been exiled for two months from my native land. A letter from the school superintendent of Emmons County offering me the school, gave me no hint as to the character of settlement or the terrible isolation to which the teacher must necessarily be subjected. So I departed from my Bismarck home in good spirits, little dreaming what was in store for me.

A journey by stage-coach landed me at Emmonsburg, a little postoffice and stage station on Beaver Creek, fifty miles south of Bismarck and thirty miles west of my destination. The postmaster is an intelligent Frenchman, married to an Indian wife. They had a comfortable home and he and his family made my stay there very pleasant. His daughters had been educated at a convent and were really accomplished girls. As the weekly stage which conveyed the mail to Dakem had left, Mr. Archambault took me there by private conveyance.

Along the river and the shores of Beaver Creek there was scarcely a hint of snow; but as we journeyed eastward the evidences of a recent heavy snowfall became apparent, and rendered traveling difficult. When we reached Winchester we exchanged our buggy for a sleigh, or "jumper," as it is called in the parlance of the country. The postoffice here is kept by three maiden sisters from New England, who successfully conduct a store, a farm and a ranch. It is said they do all their own farm work and "break in" and tame their own horses, and all their surroundings bare evidence of Yankee thrift.

From there we proceeded to the postoffice of Omio where we had dinner. The postoffice is in a tiny sod shack in a most desolate spot, on the bank of Horse Head Creek. The country around here is very rough, and rugged buttes of fantastic shape shut in the prairie landscape. The postoffice was kept by a lady whose face bore evidence of great sorrow. Her experiences at this place had indeed been very sorrowful. Her husband had deserted her, and the previous summer her little crippled son had died, her daughter had been drowned in the creek that flowed past the door, and her daughter's husband had committed suicide near this spot. Her remaining son, a youth of seventeen, was serving a term in the Bismarck penitentiary for murder, he having killed a Russian who had taken his pony away. Her loneliness and sorrow excited our warmest sympathy.

Resuming our journey, we pressed eastward through the drifts, which now became higher and more formidable, requiring strenuous efforts of the horses to break through them. As we neared our destination we met Mr. Braddock, the postmaster at Dakem, and his family, accompanied by a young Russo-German and his sister, enroute to a housewarming and dance given by an American. As Mr. Braddock was the school clerk and stated that the school board were to meet at his house next day to sign the contract with me, and there being no place else to stop at, we were perforce obliged to turn back and accompany them.

All the settlers for miles around were there; even the melancholy postmistress of Omio was present and joined in the festivities. A family of Bohemians were there, coming a distance of ten miles. The music was furnished by two members of the family of the host, who played violins, and the dancing was of a spirited character. A hot supper was served about midnight, after which vocal music was well rendered by the daughters of the family. I was so weary I fell asleep in the midst of it, and when I awoke at daybreak the party was still dancing merrily as though fatigue were unknown to them.

In the morning I started for Dakem with the Braddock party. The vehicle we rode in was an open box-sled, made comfortable by straw mattresses spread on the bottom. Mr. Braddock's house is a large two-story white one and it was a surprise to

Linda
Slaughter
(SHSND)

"Two
Months in
'Little
Russia'" was
published in
*The
Northwest
Magazine*,
January,
1893,
pp. 3-6.

Linda
Slaughter
came to
Dakota
Territory with
her military-
physician
husband in
1871. Writer,
first
postmaster,
homesteader
and teacher,
she stayed to
live, make
and write
North Dakota
history.

see such a well built structure in such a lonely situation. He and his family, I learned, were the only English-speaking people in the settlement.

In the afternoon, the school board of Dakem arrived, and with all due solemnity the contract which bound me to teach the district school for two months was signed and sealed. The president of the school board was a benevolent and kindly appearing old man clad in typical Russian costume. He wore a coat of sheepskin made in the "old country" and worn with the tanned side out; the maker of the garment doubtless assuming that he knew more about the proper arrangement of such covering than the sheep that had originally worn it. He wore a pointed fur cap and heavy home-made shoes of cow-hide. The other members were similarly dressed. Our business being concluded, they led me to the sled, or "schliddy," as I now must call it. The schliddy, a square, low affair filled with straw, had no seat; so I stepped in and they motioned me to sit down on the bottom; then they piled straw around me and placed a sheepskin robe over my lap. Two of them seated themselves a little in front on either side of me on the edges of the robe. The third one stood up in front and started the oxen forward on a trot of which I did not suppose such usually slow-going animals were capable. In this way we journeyed the five miles intervening between us and our destination, my future boarding place. As we launched out on the white billows of the prairie I glanced back, and saw Mr. Braddock's house rapidly disappearing in the distance. My feelings at that moment were probably akin to those of a ship-wrecked sailor who sees a friendly sail vanishing in the distance.

None of my companions spoke English, but they kept up a rattling conversation among themselves, every now and then giving me a friendly nod as if to assure me everything was all right. Presently we espied the house, which looked like a black spot among the miles and miles of snowy prairie. On arriving there, my limbs were so benumbed from cold and the cramped position in which I had ridden that I could scarcely stand. I felt as if I were in a foreign land, and as I realized that this lonely spot was to be my home for two months, a feeling of homesickness almost overcame me. But an old woman came out, greeted me in a motherly fashion and led me by the hand into

A Country School Teacher Remembers — Laroy Bobzien

There were a number of incentives that led me to the field of education. Both of my parents were fortunate to have received eight full terms of rural school training and insisted that much of our daily living activity be scholarly and somewhat academically oriented. Early on we were provided with good books, daily newspapers, and monthly magazines to read. My mother spent many winter evenings teaching us songs, poems, and recitation for special occasions. There were also frequent family discussions of radio news and entertaining programs.

A second important incentive was generated by a number of dedicated and talented teachers through grade and high school. Having an outstanding first and second grade teacher, she taught both grades in the one-room school, was largely an exciting experience right from day one. Over the many years I spent in all phases of public school education it always seemed to me that my first grade teacher, Myrtle Weber Cartis, ranked number one. Our school superintendent my senior year was Gottlieb Phlugrath. He had considerable expertise in the classroom and high motivational qualities. With his help I became instilled with a desire to become trained as a teacher; especially in view of the fact that a teacher's training institution was close to home.

Limited opportunity and harsh economics also played a part in my decision to try teaching. It required only three quarters of training at a state teacher's college, and the Ellendale facility was located only seventeen miles from my home. Then too, my mother had two sisters living in Ellendale; they opened their homes to me and provided food and shelter that could be repaid at some future date if I was fortunate enough to get a contract to teach a rural school.

I began my teacher training at the Ellendale State Normal and Industrial College in early September 1932. During the three quarters of training I took methods courses in various subjects and was introduced to student teaching. During the last quarter of training critic teachers allowed students to handle actual classroom teaching for three weeks.

I was fortunate enough to get a contract to teach a rural school in the Coteau Hills eight miles west and a mile north of Forbes, North Dakota. The wages were $45 per month and for only a seven month term. Those were bare minimums allowed by law in North Dakota in the early 1930s. I taught two terms in that school district and finished both terms in March so I

continued on next page

could attend the spring quarters and the summer sessions of 1934 and 1935, thereby completing my requirements for the state two-year Standard Normal teaching certificate.

The old school I taught my first two years was only 20 by 24 feet with a small entry for storing clothes and lunch buckets. A large coal burning stove with a warming jacket around it took up about 10 percent of the floor space. There were sixteen students enrolled in all eight grades. There were four of the old fashioned, but sturdy, double-desks that accommodated two students per desk and ten single seated desks.

Absenteeism was somewhat high during the three cold months. There were first and/or second graders in three families that lived several miles from the school and if the weather was bad or threatening, or if one of the youngsters was ill the parents hesitated to send them. There were also two fifteen year-old boys in grade eight who seldom came to school. They would be sixteen before the school term ended and could quit at that age. Not much attention was paid to truancy or absenteeism in many of the schools at that time, although as country teachers we faithfully reported it to the county superintendent of schools and to the clerk or director of the school we taught. My recollection is about an average attendance of 12 or 13 of the 16 enrolled. Winter weather is generally more severe in the hills than in the flat country and 80 percent attendance was regarded as acceptable.

My boarding place was 1 3/4 miles east of the school I taught, but there was no direct road to the school. I simply cut across country, up and down hills, preferring that route to following a road that was roughly twice as far. Walking west on cold and blustery mornings was often an endurance test of physical strength, but it did help keep one in shape.

Another aid to keeping physically strong was a well-balanced diet of good home grown and home prepared foods. Then too, there would be some occasions for extra walking and jogging. The eight miles distance from my boarding place into Forbes, where my parents lived, was largely down hill the first four miles; I often made that trip on foot when the weather was reasonably nice on Friday. In those days I carried a dollar Pocket Ben watch. On a quiet day I could make that trek in an hour and twenty minutes.

The school's physical inventory was meager that first term. Twenty feet of slate blackboard across the north end of the room, a half dozen erasers, a box of chalk, and a very limited number of very old and tattered text books made up the teaching aids inventory. There was a small budget of $5 a month provided to purchase additional materials. On weekends I would contact the county superintendent of schools and my old high school superintendent, enlisting their help in getting any additional materials they could find for me.

Fortunately, they were very helpful and I managed to conduct from twenty-five to thirty individual class sessions per day, for the eight grades. This required some grouping of the upper grade classes. For example, grades seven and eight would have geography and history in one class and mathematics in another, or grades three and four might have grammar, spelling, and penmanship in one group. Grouping and alternating these combinations depended upon student's abilities and individual progress. The only place I felt that one needed to adhere to a constant well-planned program of instruction was in the first two grades.

continued on next page

the house. The house, buried to the eaves in the snow, was a long, low structure built of sod and plastered on the outside with a mortar made of cow-dung and pebbles. Paths dug through the immense drifts led to two doors, in one of which a cow stood, gravely surveying the landscape. Through the other door we entered the living rooms of the family.

The outer room was a little shed, piled to the ceiling with straw and stacks of dried cow-dung, which they used for fuel. The next room was a small, dark kitchen with one tiny window. In it were a bunk-bed, table, crockery, stools and a small iron stove. A little boy sat on the earth floor beside a small, square opening in the sandstone partition industriously thrusting straw into this opening from the stack by his side. This was the door of the Russian stove. As we entered the next room—the "best room"—I saw the stove itself. It was built of sandstone, plastered over with ashes and sand and painted a dark red. It was about six feet in height and two feet in breadth and width. The rest of the family, which consisted of the old lady's husband, two grown sons, a married daughter and her two little children, sat on low stools, with their

The first year I taught I had three first graders who understood and spoke only a few words of English and the second year there were two more, so it seemed imperative to me that one must put the major emphasis in that lower grade level.

During my fifth year of teaching, 1937-1938, I taught a nine-month term for $50 per month in Elm Township, Dickey County. While my salary hadn't grown appreciably I did receive an important fringe benefit, free family living quarters in the basement of a new type country school. The school was larger, roomier, had inside chemical toilets, was heated by a furnace, had facilities for washing, and perhaps most important of all there were new textbooks, encyclopedias, and dictionaries. There were ten students and six grades. Everything was better in every way that year, but I decided to try teaching in a small town school in South Dakota the following year because I was a married man with an infant daughter and the $80 per month wages looked immensely better than the job I had.

I had secured that position through an agency, but unfortunately it had not advised me completely about the school district's financial situation. Within a week I was advised by the school board president that the district had no money and that all teachers would be paid by warrant. A little investigation revealed that those of us in need of immediate cash for living expenses would be unable to get more than 50 percent of the value of the warrant and that the problem would probably continue throughout much of the school term. Although the teaching assignment and conditions were quite acceptable, economic necessity brought us back to our living quarters in Forbes, North Dakota, after less than two weeks teaching in that small town in South Dakota. For the balance of September and for most of October I worked on a Works Progress Administration (WPA) project until I was hired to complete the school term by a rural school just four miles from Forbes.

The next fall I returned to Elm School No. 2 that I had previously taught in 1937-1938. Although there was no increase in wages the move resulted in several economic advantages. We moved on to a rent-free farmstead, with a small set of buildings, 1 1/4 miles from school. Although we had to look after the upkeep of the house and the outbuildings we also had free use of about ten acres of fenced pasture land. We managed to get two milk cows and a hundred chickens and they provided a small supplement to my teaching income.

One family with three students moved away just prior to school opening, so I started the school term the first week in September 1939 with only three students, all boys. It was indeed a pleasant

continued on next page

backs against the stove. They arose and greeted me as cordially as the grandmother had done. The women were heavy-built and broad shouldered, with dark hair. They were dressed in typical Russian costume, short full skirt, loose blouse, heavy shoes and red handkerchiefs over their heads. The men were tall and dressed in sheepskin garments similar to those described before. The children, a boy and a girl, were dressed like their elders.

Toll, Emmons County School, 1903 *SHSND*

This room had a board floor; the walls were whitewashed and adorned with colored pictures of saints and Madonnas, which with a crucifix and rosaries, indicated their religion. Several large willow baskets of home manufacture swung by hooks from the ceiling and contained the extra clothing of the family. Two large bedsteads, piled high with feather-beds, stood in the room. Light was admitted through two small windows set deep in the sod wall. The windows were double, hermetically sealed, admitting no air. The women left the room and busied themselves in preparing their evening meal. Presently one of them opened the door into this room, ejaculating "Alla," which I afterward found was equivalent to "come in." The men at once repaired to corners of the room, crossed themselves, muttering prayers. The women and the children did the same. This I found was their invariable custom, both before and after meals. Then we sat down to supper, which consisted of boiled potatoes, boiled pork and boiled sauerkraut, served in earthen crocks. They all expressed the greatest surprise at my refusal to take coffee, and when the grandfather cut off a large quantity of the fat pork and placed it on my plate, my inability to eat it gave them all the greatest concern; but when I explained that I wanted a little of the "roth," or red portion of the meat, their cheerfulness was restored. Then I had a cup of milk, and with some excellent bread and sauerkraut I contrived to make a square meal.

After supper I began to feel very sleepy; so, summoning up my knowledge of German, I managed to made the old lady understand that I wished to retire. She nodded her head but went on with the basket making. Soon I repeated my request and she arose and went into the next room, whence the sounds of hammering and sawing had issued for some time; following her, I found that my bed was in process of manufacture. The men were building it out of lumber. Soon it was completed and brought into the next room and placed against the wall. Two fat feather-beds were placed on it, one

year, being able to give so much individual attention to each student in uncrowded and ideal teaching conditions in one of the new, well-equipped rural schools.

The next year I began the school term with six students, all boys. Again it was a pleasant, highly satisfying experience in an ideal rural school setting for the first six months of the term. Then, two families moved from the area and for nearly three months I had only two young brothers in school. It was an uninspiring experience and the three of us were somewhat relieved when the term ended and the school was declared closed until such time as at least six students returned to the area and the school could be reopened.

This marked the end of my rural school teaching. I was married and had one daughter when World War II broke. I had taught as little more than eight terms of rural school and decided to leave the teaching field until the war was over and some family stability could be reestablished.

I felt fortunate to have small numbers of students in all but three of my eight years teaching rural school. I began nearly every school day, for the five terms I taught in older school buildings, building a fire with a small stock of kindling and a dash of kerosene to which small pieces of coal were added as the kindling grew hotter. As the building was warming I began doing the cleaning chores, sweeping the uncovered floors, doing some dusting, and wiping down the blackboards. The students took turns in the late afternoon cleaning erasers, preparing some small sticks of kindling, and bringing in a scuttle of coal. I usually had another twenty to thirty minutes to make some class preparations for that day for the upper grades. Much of the class preparation for the lower grades was done in the evening at the place I was staying. I cut a lot of catalogs, magazines, and funny papers those first two terms in an attempt to devise teaching aids that appealed to the younger students.

From 9:00 a.m. until 10:30 a.m. we ran through a series of classes no more than 8 to 12 minutes in length. Even though I had dutifully posted a formal daily program of every class and activity it was seldom that we could adhere to it because giving every student in each class an opportunity to read and receive teacher help that an individual student might need would vary with the material and the number of students present that day. Usually grades three, four, and five had a busy work exercise in penmanship or writing practices.

Recess at 10:30 a.m. was a welcome break for student and teacher alike. The 15-minute break tended to be more like 20 minutes by the time all were back at their desks. The focus, then, was generally on mathematics, with a large part of the work being done at the blackboard. Crowded conditions and limited materials during my first two terms meant that students received little attention some days. However, a buddy system was worked out occasionally that was quite helpful. Fourth and fifth graders helped second and third graders, seventh graders helped first graders, and eighth graders helped sixth graders.

I well remember the confusion and circus-like atmosphere that first noon hour when I announced: "You may all get your lunch buckets." Chaos resulted when about 14 students dived into the small 8 by 8 foot entry looking for buckets and suitcases of food. I soon learned the necessity of letting three or four students at a time, beginning with grades one and two, march in almost military fashion to the entry-storage area to get their lunch bucket and take a quick hand-wash, which was optional. Sometimes a family with several students brought lunch for the entire family in one small suitcase, others brought separate gallon-pails or a lunch bucket.

One family with five students brought lunch in a small suitcase. A typical lunch consisted of half the suitcase filled with large slices of homemade

continued on next page

bread and a few homemade cookies, a jar of home-made pickles and the other half filled with large pieces of smoked and precooked, country-style sausage. To this day my appetite can be sharpened by just thinking of the pleasing odor that emanated from that case of food when the oldest girl, Clara, began that noon-meal ritual by serving Emma, the youngest; next, the twins Herbert and Arthur; then George and finally herself. It marked the beginning of my rural school "happy hour."

Enrollment ranged from 5 to 8 students, in no more than four grades, during five terms that I taught. That permitted me to carry out a well-planned program including some organized physical education, art, and music programs. I was particularly proud one school term when I had 5 students and they all played in the harmonica band. For 50 cents apiece, every student bought a standard notes Hoehner mouth organ and I arranged the note music for harmonica from a small book of music I purchased. Their favorite song was *Oh Susanna*.

Equipment and supplies in three of the five schools I taught were literally non-existent. Although my own resources were too meager to allow me to buy needed materials I managed to get a modest supply, off and on throughout the school term, with a bit of help from Dickey County Superintendents of Schools Faith Stevens and her sister Blanche, from some friends and relatives, and from older, teacher friends who were more than willing to be helpful.

Discipline was a problem in two of the five schools I taught. Before signing a contract the first year I had a short interview with Jake, the director of the school. My training and general qualifications were quite acceptable, but he had one concern. He asked me if I felt up to whipping the two biggest eighth grade boys at the same time. To him it was an important question and he needed to judge my confidence when I answered. He knew I was only 18 years and 6 months old, was between 5 feet 8 and 9 inches tall and

weighed no more than 175 pounds. He also knew that the two large boys were 15 years and 6 months old, with one of them being almost my size and the other one perhaps a little larger. The boys had established a reputation as "bullies" the previous term. They were two to three years behind the grade level ages found in many of the country schools; however, that was not unusual in country schools in the "hills" where seven-month terms were common and absenteeism for older boys was also common. Jake was aware that many teachers had trouble maintaining discipline. Because resignations in the middle of the school year were common and because there were nearly two applicants for every school during the thirties he preferred one that he might judge as being the most successful in completing a full and productive school term.

I don't know if my "yes" radiated confidence or whether what I said was more satisfactory than those to whom he may have posed the same question. Whatever the reason he was satisfied and the contract was issued.

As it turned out the discipline problems were few and then only in the first several weeks when a few test cases arose. For me it was reassuring to know that I could expect full support from the school board and parents. The first episode occurred at an outdoor, afternoon, recess activity about the second week of school. One little boy in grade four advised me that the two boys planned setting me up during a Pom Pom Pull Away game. I decided I would be prepared to do what was necessary to prevent any humiliation in the presence of the rest of the students and asked him to post himself in a position to give me a signal as to which one I could expect first. When the signal came I was ready for him and had a firm grasp on the collar of his coat when the second boy came rushing in. Swinging the first boy around to meet the headlong rush of the second unsuspecting

continued on next page

for me to sleep on, the other for covering. In this downy bed I slept soundly until awakened in the morning by the old lady trying to arouse her two sons, who slept in the next room, by shouts of "Alla oof, Nicolouse! Alla oof, Yohannes! Alla! Alla!"

After the family had gone through their usual prayers, we sat down to a breakfast of fried sauerkraut, fried pork and fried potatoes. After breakfast we started for the schoolhouse, two miles distant. The "schliddy" we rode in was a primitive affair. It was made by nailing short boards over two small logs which were placed parallel to each other. Across the center was placed a gunny sack, stuffed with hay for the horse's dinner. This sack was my seat; the driver sat down in front of me and the two little children behind me. The sensation of being dragged along so close to the ground at such a rapid rate was very unpleasant. The sled had no protection at the sides, so I was in constant danger of falling off. The others seemed to have no trouble in preserving their boy was enough to create a jolting and somewhat stunning collision. In a matter of seconds the rest of the students arrived on the scene to find two boys somewhat dazed and held in firm grasp.

It was a perfect time for me to practice some elementary psychology I had learned in Professor Phlugrath's and Professor Fuller's classes. I explained very briefly to my captive audience that the two big boys had been good sports, but had a little more growing up to do before they engaged in rough games older people played. In due time they would be able to do very well in those sports.

There were only a few disciplinary problems after that, and then not serious in nature. They usually arose on the schoolground, out of earshot, and were somewhat ethnic in nature, occurring when I was not present giving supervision. One of the four German-Russian families and one family of Finnish descent had learned to speak first in their native tongue and had learned English after they began attending public school. Sometimes it was difficult to explain that not understanding a language someone is using does not necessarily mean they are speaking to you in a derogatory or demeaning manner. Of course, they were perceptive enough to know that the older brothers and sisters and sometimes the parents were intolerant of people who used a different tongue. The result would be a verbal skirmish at times and even angry physical confrontation.

Some of the younger students delighted in reporting certain differences that needed resolution. At times a fair and just hearing was diminished sharply by the handicap of working in three different languages. Within a few months I had learned enough profane and offensive words in Finnish and German-Russian to handle rural school jurisprudence with some acceptable degree of fairness that enabled me to maintain discipline conducive to a pretty good learning atmosphere. Even-handed discipline was something I had experienced in my family when I was growing up.

During my eight years of rural school teaching I did not consciously stress American values—equality, helpfulness, kindliness, freedom, efficiency, practicality, patriotism, democracy, individualism—primarily because it was a heavy imposition on one's time. The time-ghost hung heavily over a teacher's shoulder almost the entire seven hours you had students in your charge each day. What I did and what I suspect most rural teachers did was to set good examples and thus, unconsciously or subconsciously, give favorable exposure and explanation to the common values that were responsible for making America great. I believe the results were somewhat ineffective at the time, but when I compared them to results achieved from a well-planned and conscious stressing of a number of the above mentioned values during the last five or six years I spent in the classrooms in city school system, there was no question in my mind but that we made greater contributions as teachers in rural schools in the 1930s than we did in larger school systems from 1963 to 1973.

Sanitation facilities and the availability of water were always problems. At one facility we had no well. We had no water other than drinking water carried from home and a gallon or two of extra water students brought for emergency purposes.

One unhappy incident tells it all. A little first grade girl and other students in her family arrived a bit late one morning. The youngest had suffered an upset stomach the night before, but insisted she felt good enough to attend school. Just before the afternoon recess she took quite ill and her sister very quickly ushered her to our only outdoor sanitation facility. They did not make it in time. After the afternoon recess I asked the older brother to get the team ready and the five of them left for home. The little one was feeling somewhat better but had to ride home nearly three miles in some very dirty and uncomfortable clothing. It would have been so helpful had we had plenty of warm water and a private place for her to be cleaned up. After that I took it upon myself to keep a bag of clean cloth handy and a pail of water warming on the big stove, just for such emergencies. I also got some extra water storage.

Since there was only one outdoor toilet to accommodate us all some ground rules were necessary. Because our little moon-in-the-door outhouse was in poor shape, the door and the hinges were "kaput," and because it accommodated only two people, the following rules for its use applied:

continued on next page

equilibrium, but every time the sled made a lurch, with the irresistible impulse of self preservation, I made frantic clutches at the broad shoulders of the driver in front. This made the children titter and was very embarrassing to us both. But presently he moved the long, red worsted scarf that encircled his waist so that the loops in which it was tied came directly in the back, and signed to me that I could cling to that. With this scarf as a life preserver I managed to maintain my position on the hay sack till we reached the schoolhouse.

From various directions across the prairie similar sleds were seen approaching, bringing in the children of the settlement. These little sleds, like our own, were of the most primitive description. Most of them were drawn by a single ox, while one which held a tiny boy and girl was drawn by a gaunt looking cow which contributed her milk at the noon hour for the children's luncheon.

The school was kept in a farm house, a low sod building almost buried out of sight among the immense drifts. I was met at the door by a friendly woman dressed in

only the girls used it, no less than two and no more than three girls were to use it at the same time, two girls could utilize the services and one girl held the door in place and kept it shut.

The facility the boys and I used was a small three- to four-stall barn. The dozen boys felt comfortable with it because that was what they used at home most of the time. There was a fair amount of graffiti carved on the inside walls of the barn, much of it by students from former years. It was often the secret desire of the boys in their last year to add something to the collection and I had a couple of boys who had a strong desire to contribute. It required some of my time, but with a little volunteer help from a couple of lower grade boys we managed to keep the problem to a minimum, thereby frustrating the boys who felt they had been deprived of a right to add their names to the list of those who had been involved previously in such forbidden activities.

They were not be to denied, however, other attention-getting pranks they thought entertaining and harmless. The most exciting from the older students' point of view was the "fountain trick." The barn sat roughly 50 feet to the east of the school and as we looked out the two east windows we could see a knothole in the siding, about two feet up from the bottom barn sill. One afternoon recess a number of boys had gone to the barn to relieve themselves before returning to the classroom. One of the younger boys came rushing into the school and shouted: "Look at the barn and see the fountain." He had aptly described what was taking place. Quite a strong fountain-like flow was coming from the knot hole. As I look back on the handling of that particular "no-no" I think how resolving an incident of that nature, as large as it seemed to loom at that time, was a "cream- puff" compared to those things laid on guidance counselors and other school personnel in the late sixties and seventies.

The first two years of teaching I stayed at a boarding place; one year my wife and I stayed with a farm couple who rented a bedroom to us and included three meals a day with them and their infant child. The elderly farm couple, Frank and Mrs. B., I stayed with my first year out were the finest of the old breed of pioneer farm family and had a home with 600 to 700 square feet of floor

space. They had boarded "the teacher" for at least twelve years and always provided the best they had. There was no running water, no indoor sanitary facilities, no electricity, no daily newspaper or magazines, and mail service only three times per week. The house was immaculately clean all the time. My bedroom and bedding were always clean and comfortably warm when I went to bed. The sanitary facilities were the old-fashioned crock chamber potty in each bedroom. Frank referred to them as "hoogle boogles." Mrs. B. kept them fresh and clean at all times.

There were two small bedrooms about 9 by 10 feet on the west side of the house. Mrs. B. used the north one and I used the south one. There was a very small living room with an old-fashioned hard coal heater and also a small kitchen-dining room area with a large old-fashioned range stove used for cooking, baking, and heating. Off to the northeast corner of the kitchen was another very small bedroom, perhaps no larger than seven by nine feet, containing a single bed used by Frank.

All of us slept on feather-tick mattresses and covered up with feather-tick mattresses through the months of cold weather. The reason for such warm bedding soon became obvious. The couple, in their early sixties, burned nothing but wood and used it with discretion.

Mrs. B. was up at six o'clock every morning to start fires in both stoves. She was definitely the ramrod of the outfit and would allow neither her husband nor me to help in any way around the house. She had her daily routine well laid out and had assigned a number of outdoor tasks for her husband to carry out every day. His first duty was to take two buckets down to the spring, some 40 yards away, and bring up about 6 gallons of spring water so she could start breakfast and make a gallon of fresh spring-water coffee.

The water in the large tea kettle on the big stove had become warm enough by 6:45 a.m. so that I could begin washing and shaving and preparing for my walk to school after a hearty breakfast. While I was eating a typical meal of sausage, eggs, oatmeal, and homemade bread, Mrs. B., as her husband addressed her, was making my noon lunch that consisted typically of two large sand-

continued on next page

77

Russian costume who conducted me into a small, dark room—dark, because the snow outside reached above the window. In this room was a small cooking stove surrounded by stacks of fuel. Several large bins of wheat and flaxseed occupied one end of the room. A calf was tied in the other. The school room, which was also the living room of the family, adjoined this. This room was plastered over with ashes and sand, and the floor was of earth. A long board table stood on one side of the room, with a long bench on each side of it. On the other side of the room were two featherbeds, on one of

wiches, cold beef or cold pork roast, generously layered between slices of homemade bread. There was also a large piece of pie or cake, and piece of fresh fruit. In the thermos was fresh milk. Oftentimes it was cold enough by the time I reached school to contain a lot of frozen crystals. I seldom had to concern myself about not having cold milk to drink at noon lunch.

During the long winter evenings there was little to do after the evening meal. Frank and I would sometimes read for a half hour and then I might correct papers or make lesson plans for another half hour.

By 8:00 p.m., however, we were ready for the card game. Their favorite game was three-handed pitch, sometimes called euchre or high, low, jack and the game. Their version of the game became very exciting within minutes after the first bid. Both were daring bidders and were highly skilled players. They were cut-throat competitors determined to give no quarter; they brought the action to fever pitch before the 10:00 p.m. closing deadline.

It was our evening recreation Monday through Thursday and once every five or six weeks they would invite enough neighbors to have a party of three tables, with four at each table playing pitch. Partners were rotated, individual scores were kept, and prizes were awarded. It was a delightful and different kind of experience, encompassing pleasant fellowship, fine food, and comedy.

When Frank played cards with anyone but his wife he became excited and almost hyper with enthusiasm. His demeanor would alternate from daring, to raucous, to cunning, to humming, to table rapping, to mirthful and joyful laughter, and then back to a rhythmic rapping of knuckles on the table to emphasize the triumph of having made his bid.

I sometimes thought that country school teaching was a lonely life my first two years because of a degree of isolation much higher than I was accustomed to. It never gave me the feeling of loneliness, however, that so many of my teacher friends experienced, especially those who taught farther back in the hills during severe winters.

Almost every weekend I was able to be with my parents in town, where there were a number of recreational activities available. They operated a

recreation hall and had shown silent movies every Saturday night for many years, but by 1930 they were discontinued; talking pictures had arrived in the towns near us. They did continue to hold public roller skating on either Friday or Saturday night and they also held public dances every two or three weeks. So I would have my date lined up on most weekends to go dancing or skating. With teaching wages as poor as they were I consider myself lucky indeed to enjoy recreation for little or no cost on many of the weekends.

Getting paid during my first two years of teaching was somewhat of a problem until I rose to the occasion. Our system of payment, every fourth Friday, was to go to each of the three board members who signed the checks, a trip of about ten miles. Since the school district treasurer was a Seventh-day Adventist and would not sign my paycheck after sundown and because we didn't observe day-light savings time in those days I devised a payday schedule that enabled me to meet the treasurer's terms. I received permission from my director to shorten the noon hour and had my father or some member of the family waiting to pick me up at 3:30 p.m. After failing once to make it in time I never missed again.

It was my good fortune never to have been subjected to unreasonable or unwarranted rules by local school boards. I was never visited by any member of the state department of education; school board members visited me on only two occasions, asking about services I might need; parents seldom visited, other than for special programs. The no more than half-dozen parent visitations in eight terms were short, friendly, and social in nature, with one exception. One concerned father came to inquire about a behavior and discipline problem he believed his daughter was having. After a discussion he was satisfied that it wasn't of the serious nature his daughter had led him to believe. He came to the afternoon Christmas program about a month later and enjoyed himself immensely, along with other parents. I usually had at least one and sometimes two county superintendent visitations during five of the eight years of teaching rural schools.

continued on next page

which was a baby girl whose dress was a miniature copy of her mother's, even to the handkerchief around her head. Some of the scholars sat on the benches, others stood with their backs against the whitewashed stove, their ages ranging from five to twenty. A few of them had some knowledge of the English *First Reader*, but the majority did not know their alphabet. In arithmetic, however, they were all fairly well advanced. Presently the head of the family and one of the school board came in and sat down on the low stools with their backs against the stove, and smoked cigarettes and listened to the recitations with rapt attention.

Our family had friends and relatives who taught rural school during the 1920s. I recall one instance in the later 1920s when the Ku Klux Klan burned a cross on the south edge of Forbes, the town where I grew up. My parents remarked about the shame of having something like that happen in our community. I was too young to get the full impact of that incident, but I do recall some concerns that were voiced by three female, rural school teachers in that area. The young ladies, who were at our home visiting my mother's younger brother and sister echoed my parent's views. They voiced concern about the KKK attempts to exert pressure on all our schools to adopt programs they regarded favorable to KKK teachings.

Sifting through material I recorded and saved from my teaching days I get the feeling that an honest and viable "value system" regarding public school education has eluded us. I recall an outstanding educator, Dr. Larry Hagen, telling us in the summer of 1965 that progress was indeed slow and that as long as the classroom teacher continued to be relegated to a minor role in our society nothing much by way of improvement could be expected, the best of teacher training programs notwithstanding. Another outstanding educator, Dr. Louis Wagner told a group of graduates the next summer that until those best qualified—those well-trained teachers on the firing line day in and day out—could be allowed their proper role in decision making with both dignity and assurance of job security, the public school systems would remain for the most part poorly conducted and lack progressive viability. My personal feeling would be that both gentlemen were correct in their assessment of future public education problems.

During four of the seven years I taught rural school in Dickey County, we maintained an active Young Citizens League (YCL) program, largely through the County Superintendent of Schools' office. Monthly communications from the office informed us of upcoming activities. Dues were modest and small fund-raising activities were held to help defray expenses. Our local unit elected officers and we managed to maintain a fair

amount of interest each year in the organization. It served very well as a teaching aid in promoting social involvement and self-worth—both essential items in the teaching of our youth. It was especially helpful in the rural school of the "Thirties" when children of poor families experienced very little social contact outside the home.

In four of the five different rural schools in which I taught no prayer exercise took place. No one asked for it but the Ten Commandments did hang in the school room. In one rural school in which I taught the Ten Commandments were not displayed. The five families served by that school never asked that they be placed in the room or that prayer be used in any of our daily exercises. This was true even though four of the five families attended church regularly. During those eight years of teaching rural school in the thirties I had the feeling that my students and patron families were almost instinctively aware of the need for separation of church and state. Needless to say, it was comforting and pleasing to me as a teacher. I was busy enough devoting all the time I could muster to aiding those with learning difficulties let alone sorting out literal interpretations of our national constitution. The subject of prayer or religion never came up except in an occasional social science or natural science class discussion and then never in rancor but in the spirit of pursuing natural curiosity. I firmly believe constitutional guarantees under our form of government will always be closely examined and forced into controversy in our public schools but I can state in all candor that I had not a whit of it to contend with in eight terms of rural school teaching.

In many instances in my eight years of rural school teaching experience nothing was wrong with the country school—in light of the many failings public school education in our towns and cities exhibit today. Did the country school provide a "good education"? On a scale of one to ten, the country schools of the 1930s in this area, would rate an eight. On a scale of one to ten the Class B schools in this area from 1953 to 1973 would rate no more than six to seven.

Glanavon
School (1897-
1898),
Glanavon
Twp.,
Emmons
County
*History of
Emmons
County*, p. 48
(SHSND)

At noon-time the books were laid aside and a dinner of boiled sauerkraut, boiled potatoes and boiled pork were served on the school table for the family and myself. After which the woman went to clean out the stable part of the house. Her husband meanwhile shoveled the snow off the roof and cut paths through the snow to the straw-stacks. I thought her the more expeditious worker of the two. In the afternoon another "schliddy" arrived, bringing four small boys and their father. This man could speak a little English, and when I asked him the names of his children he drew himself up proudly and answered, tapping each little black head in succession, "Yackob, eleven; Koll, ten; Gottleib, nine; Augoost, eight."

"A nice family," I remarked.

"O, got plenty more at home smaller as these," was his reply.

"Are you Russian?" I asked.

At this he made a great show of indignation and answered, "No indeed! He was not a Russian; he was a German. If I had ever seen a Russian I would quickly see the difference; the Russians were savage people—wild, like Indians."

He said further that his people lived in Odessa, Russia, their ancestors immigrating there from Germany a hundred years before. They had preserved their nationality and their German customs intact. They were obliged under the Russian laws to send their children to Russian schools and to speak the Russian language and to conform to the national customs of the country. But their children were always taught at home to read and speak German and to love the Fatherland.

When the school dismissed our sled was brought around to the door. The horse having eaten all the hay, there was only the empty sack for a seat; and, although this was not so comfortable, I found it attended with less peril of diving overboard.

In this way, for two months I journeyed to and from school; but in a very little time I had learned to preserve my equilibrium as well as the others, and also my equanimity when the "schliddy" upset, as it did almost every day. During these two months of February and March there were many storms and occasional blizzards which made the trip a hazardous one. Rough as this daily journey was, I believe it to have been the means of preserving my health; for if I had been confined to the close air of my boarding place or schoolhouse it must have proved injurious. I always got home with a keen appetite for the sauerkraut, pork and potatoes which formed the unvarying bill of fare for the whole term, and which at first had seemed so coarse and unpalatable.

With my life among the people I soon became quite content. My work in the school room soon became interesting, as the children were docile and eager to learn and the parents greatly interested in having them learn American ways. I soon learned that underneath their rough exterior they had kind hearts and were all animated by a sincere desire to make my stay among them happy and comfortable to the extent of their resources. Being intimately associated with their home and family life I became familiar with their habits and customs and learned to respect the homely sincerity of their religious and national customs. They are religious at all times, but 'tis on their national fast that the deep religious tendencies are most strongly marked. This fast, called "Bpost," begins seven weeks before Easter and is ushered in by a three days' carnival, or "farewell to flesh." These three days are celebrated by dancing and feasting. Great preparations are made; the best clothes are put in order and the shoes carefully blacked.

Their manner of polishing shoes deserves special mention: The brush is dipped in sweetened cold coffee; the iron dinner pot is inverted and the brush rubbed on the soot that adheres to the bottom of it. The brush is then rubbed vigorously on the shoes and the result is a polish resembling the sides of a brand new stove.

The neighbors assembled in the evening at my boarding place, which was the best in the settlement. They danced on the earth floor in the kitchen, to the music of a mouth organ. The round dances are the favorite, danced to a very quick time. The dancing was remarkably graceful, considering their heavy shoes, the earth floor, and the limited space. All danced, from the grandfather to the tiny child. Two little boys then danced a "soldier's dance." The men, instead of walking up and asking the women to dance simply beckoned across the room to the partners they wished, who quickly joined them. One dance, called "Boobna," was most laughable. A tall young fellow stood in the center of the room with an inverted broom in his hand. The company joined hands and formed a ring around him. He gave each one a word to call out, such as "Grites," "Schier," "Ixta," etc. A little boy then played on the mouth organ and was accompanied by a man who kept time pounding furiously on the table with his bare fists. The dance began by the leader shouting "Boobna, Boobna, Boobna," pounding on the floor with the broomstick; while the company danced around him, shouting the words that had been given them. The sound of the different words," Schier, Schier, Schier," "Grites, Grites, Grites," "Ix, Ix, Ix," and other queer words shouted in different tones with the unceasing bass tone of "Boobna, Boobna, Boobna," from the leader, together with the ridiculous postures of the dancers, made it the most comical scene I ever saw in my life. This boisterous dance continued until the dust rose in clouds from the earth floor and the dancers were too much convulsed with laughter to proceed. After the

A Country School Teacher Remembers — Earl H. Kruschwitz

As a high school graduate in June 1929, faced with a situation of no money, no job, nor anything to look forward to, my thoughts turned to further education, which I thought might hold out as a possible direction to go.

There were four members of our family in the graduating class. I might add that instead of four sets of announcements and four high school annuals, there was to be one of each to share. We were able to get separate pictures, which cost $6 a set. Lest I forget, there were no class rings either.

When a classmate asked me if I had purchased my graduation suit, I said, "I can't afford one, and my folks don't have that kind of money." Next time we came to orchestra practice, my classmate said to me, "I talked to my dad, and he said that you should come down to his store and pick out one." (That clothier was none other than Herman Stern of Straus Clothing Company in Valley City.)

I bought a suit with no money down and only the promise to pay, as I could, any amount I could, until paid for. I got a job teaching that fall and paid the account in four months.

Our dad "scraped" up enough money to pay our registration ($12 a quarter) fees at STC, and we all four attended summer school, earning Second Grade Elementary Certificates.

Then September came—the two sisters and the brother got rural schools, and I didn't! Finally on the last day of September, I received a telephone call from Hettinger County Superintendent Martha Bratcher. She stated that they needed someone to teach in Steiner School District, who could cope with a tough bunch of students. These students had been too much for the two teachers the previous year, and the school term was cut short.

Her question was "Do you think you can accept the challenge?" My answer was, "I weigh 190 pounds and I'm built of steel! I believe I can." I was authorized to use any type of punishment necessary short of "killing" them. She would not approve of that.

On October 2, 1929 I began the 7-month term at $95 a month, which was a $15 premium. I borrowed $15 from M. S. Ward to buy gas to make the approximately 300 miles from Valley City to Burt, North Dakota.

continued on next page

I didn't kill anyone, and I stayed the full time. I did "floor" one student and again later, I trounced him but good! For that I had five boys (17-20 years) threaten me, by placing a note in my mail box, telling me that they would "visit" me, and I accepted the challenge. They did not come. I had a sharp hatchet and a coal pick-ax handle, and I would use either or both, if necessary.

I had a very good year and successful, too. I had 37 students in all eight grades. My four beginners could not speak English—just German-Russian. With pictures we learned each other's language.

It would be an incomplete story if I omitted the following account. My landlady and her husband took me to Burt, just east of Mott, one Friday night. I took the train to Valley City via Mandan. All was well. I returned by train again to Burt in a blizzard. Since the storm was raging, I had to stay in Burt until Monday morning. The snow had ceased to fall, but a 15-25 mile per hour wind from the northwest and plenty of snow to blow around made driving impossible. I caught a ride with the mail carrier, but he found it impossible to continue and about 1/2 mile out of Burt, he turned back. I got out of his car and walked. I walked north 8 miles, facing the storm! It was 30 degrees below zero. It had taken me from 9:00 a.m. to 6:00 p.m. to walk those 8 miles. I still had 4 more miles to go. A telephone call informed my people of my whereabouts, and they came with team and bobsled to get me. We got "home" about 9:00 p.m. and had school the next day. I had to make up that Monday loss the end of April. No days off, and no sick leave. That was an extremely valuable experience, however, I wouldn't want to repeat it.

Some time later we attended a county teachers' meeting. The county superintendent had visited my school. It was a requirement at that time. At this meeting, County Superintendent Bratcher had me stand. She then said, "You should visit Mr. Kruschwitz's school! He has the neatest school I have ever visited!"

So you see rural schools can be a challenge.

dancing was over they all sang, and sang well, too. Many of them had sweet voices and the natural gift of song. After they had sung the Russian hymns, soldiers' songs and German ballads, they urged me to sing. I complied by singing *Die Wacht am Rhein,* which pleased them greatly.

After the three days of "Bpost" were over began the seven weeks of fast. For seven weeks they were not allowed to eat meat. In this country they are permitted to eat it three times a week, but very few avail themselves of the privilege. Considering the intense cold, the hard work performed by these people and their limited food resources, the abstaining from meat is proof of their sincerity, as it involves a sacrifice that no one unfamiliar with their daily life can appreciate. The nearest church is at Eureka, too far distant for them to attend in winter, so religious services are held at their homes until they shall be able to build a church in their own settlement.

Every evening, during the fast, the family at my boarding place knelt down and the grandfather read prayers while the rest made the responses. The prayers are short and it is a matter of pride with them to repeat a large number. On one occasion as I knelt—as I always did at the family devotions—the exercises were unusually tedious, so I fell asleep and was mildly reproved therefor' by the good old grandmother, who informed me that they had read and responded to 237 prayers and that I had slept through most of them.

The mode of courtship and marriage among these people is wholly different from our American customs. There is no "falling in love," or courting, or other nonsense. The whole affair is managed by the friends of the parties concerned. When a young Russo-German sees a girl whom he wishes to marry he makes no advances toward forming her acquaintance, but sends a friend, who presents his case to the girl and her family. The friend discourses of his good looks, his worldly prospects and the amount of his possessions. If the girl and her family are willing they in turn inform him of the amount of her dowry, which is usually a cow and articles of household use. These preliminaries being arranged the couple are married, at once, and frequently without having exchanged more than a word with each other.

One incident that came under my own observation while at Dakem was that of a young girl who had been in service at Bismarck and who came down on a visit to her parents. A young man in the settlement heard of her arrival, and, although he had never seen her, at once sent a friend to propose marriage. The offer of the young man proved satisfactory, but the family demurred because, having lost their crop of flax the previous fall, they were unable to give their daughter a cow, to which all brides are entitled. The young man came himself next day to say he would marry her anyway and wait a year for the cow. The day after this, they went to Eureka and were married at the church. It is seldom that the business-like overtures of marriage are rejected by the girl or her family. But when this does occasionally happen, strange to say, the would-be bridegroom feels no ill-will toward the girl, but all his dissatisfaction is directed toward the friend who managed his side of the affair, as he believes that had his own merit and the advantages of the union been fairly represented to the girl the result would have been different.

Barefoot children in a Country School, from the Porterville Collection *(NDIRS)*

Interested in my school work, the two months soon sped away. The closing day of school was observed by pleasing exercises by the children and their parents also took part in it. I parted with the children with regret, for they had become greatly attached to me.

Nothing was now left for me to do but to draw my salary and pay my board bill. No contract had been made as to the amount I should pay for my board. I supposed it would be the usual monthly charge of $10 which teachers in country districts expect to pay. But I was greatly surprised to find they had kept an itemized account of expenses; and had counted every potato I had eaten and every cup of milk I had drank. My board bill, in the preparation of which all the family had assisted, was a document so unique that I have preserved it. Here it is, translated:

School Teacher's Board Bill, Two Months.

Sleeping in bed two months	$3.00
Riding to school behind horse two months . . .	3.00
Eating 57 potatoes at 1 cent each	.57
10 quarts of sauerkraut at 10 cents	1.00
17 pounds pork at 12 ½ cents.	2.12
4 loaves of bread at 25 cents	1.00
Drinking 108 cups of milk at 1 cent a cup . . .	1.08
All	$11.76

I was greatly dismayed by this formidable list of eatables that I had consumed, and was in no-wise comforted by my conscientious landlady's assurance that she had not charged for the full amount, because what was left on my plate was always given to the pigs and chickens and was a clear gain to themselves. But I paid this bill cheerfully, bade my kind entertainers adieu and embarked in an ox-team for the stage station and soon reached my Bismarck home, none the worse for two months' isolation in "Little Russia."

Jessamine S. Slaughter

Recess

above left, Children around a Maypole *(Busby Collection, NDIRS)*

above, Rural School near Milton, *(Hulstrand, NDIRS)*

Snow picture above, Noon Horseplay at Nuen's School, 1920, Billings Co., 19 miles north of Medora, Ada Rue, Teacher *(SHSND)*

Left, Williams Co., Gamache School, 1907, J.W. Dwyer, Teacher *(SHSND)*

Chapter 6

Education in the Norwegian and German-Russian Homelands

Playford V. Thorson and William C. Sherman

The Norwegians

THE QUESTION POSED BY THE EVIDENCE given above invites an explanation. Why did the Germans from Russia lag behind the Norwegians in their educational endeavors in North Dakota? We are convinced that the answer lies in the conditions that existed in their homelands on the eve of their departure and the atti-

Playford V. Thorson and William C. Sherman

A North Dakota Country School Student Remembers — Ruth Marie Holden DeSart

I started attending country school, Holden No. 2, in January 1918. In my community schools usually took the name of the township; Holden Township in Adams County was named after my father at the time it was organized. Many townships, including Holden, had three or four schools. I turned six in December of the previous year. We spoke Norwegian at home, but I had the advantage of knowing English when I started. I picked it up from my sister who was two and one-half years older than I. I went through the first and second grades in that half year; I was ready for the third grade in the fall of 1918. I graduated from the eighth grade in May 1924. Hannah Olson was my favorite teacher, doubtlessly because I knew her the best. She was very fair in her treatment of pupils, I think this was the quality I appreciated most.

From the first through the eighth grade I studied reading, spelling, arithmetic, language (English), history, geography, penmanship, agriculture, and physiology. Classes were short, only a few minutes in length. I did not have any "worst subjects." Not one of my teachers could play the old parlor organ in our school, although some of them did try to sing. We had very little instruction in art.

Often I was the only one in my class. For a while in seventh grade I was in a reading class with a boy four years older than I. Having no brothers, and in those days often little contact with neighbors, I got the impression that boys were incredibly stupid, because this classmate could barely read. However, my father was one of those lifelong, avid readers, self-educated. He had a good-sized library in our home, from which neighbors borrowed books. My mother had been a teacher.

I don't remember school being especially "exciting," except when we gave a Christmas program. It was certainly not "boring." It was all we kids had, our window on the world, limited as it was. Our teachers did not assign homework. At least I never had any. When I came to school a few minutes early, I helped the teacher with little chores around the schoolroom — we considered this a privilege. We had no radio until we were grown up, no television, no young people's organizations of any kind.

It's hard to say if going to country school made any difference in my upbringing, since I had

tudes they brought with them to North Dakota. What remains then is first to describe briefly the education and milieu in Norway and among the Germans in Russia; second, to try to discern the differences; and finally, to determine *how* these differences affected their attitudes and achievements in education in North Dakota.

These two groups come from cultures which had *some* things in common. Both were overwhelmingly rural in character, what the anthropologist might call "folk societies," as distinct from "modern secular" cultures. They both adhered, by and large, to old-world confessional churches, particularly Lutheran or Roman Catholic. Loyalty tended to be to the family, the church, and to a place instead of a nation. While these similarities are not unimportant, the *differences* between Norway and South Russia during the late nineteenth century far outweigh the similarities.

While the Norwegians achieved independence from Denmark in 1814, they were forced to accept a dynastic union with Sweden the following year. They did, however, govern themselves internally with a fairly democratic constitution for the time; and, as the century wore on they, together with other Europeans, became increasingly nationalistic: they took pride in being Norwegian. Even if poor, they were free. Indeed, the Norwegian farmer had never been a serf, as had most peasants on the continent, and during the nineteenth century this *tradition* of freedom made them welcome settlers in the new American Republic. They came from Norway, land of the heroic Vikings. Now, of course, the great age of the Vikings had passed into oblivion nine hundred years before, but the romantic movement in literature and history revived it. From the mid-1800s, in Scandinavia, England, Germany, and the United States, scholars and laymen alike were extolling the virtues of the Vikings who were characterized as rugged, daring, hard-working, and reliable. So when Norwegians came to North Dakota, this was, at least in part, some of the baggage they brought with them. One need only peruse the national origins quota as set forth by the immigration law of 1924: Norwegians were welcome; eastern and southern Europeans, not to mention Orientals, much less so.

continued on next page

From the standpoint of education, a happy by-product of this Viking mania was the fact that a good deal of the ancient literature dealt with Norway; sagas, epic poems, and pagan myths were all popular fare by the latter half of the nineteenth century in Norway. We should not, of course, imagine that every Norwegian immigrant to North Dakota was steeped in the literature; still, most were aware of the heroic past. Another spur to literacy, and ultimately some education beyond the "three R's," was Bible reading. While the Norwegian priesthood saw it as their mission to interpret God's word, the layman was expected to read the Bible and Luther's catechism.

Education in Norway, as elsewhere, had always been a church affair; however, beginning in the 1700s the concept of a state or secular system was at least advanced. In 1739 the state attempted to establish elementary schools throughout Norway, supported by a general tax. In theory, schools were to be set up in every parish. Because of the extreme poverty of rural Norway, however, this did not become an accomplished fact until well over a century later; but, a start had been made, espe-

nothing with which to compare it. It used to be said that the valedictorians in the town high schools came from country schools. Whether this was, or one of those defensive myths, I do not know. We did know our teachers personally, usually calling them by their first names.

Nostalgia is tricky. One tends to remember the good, and forget the bad things. I think it safe to say we had neither the temptations nor the special advantages of a city school.

I remember one incident that could have been tragic. When I was in the fifth grade my sister was in charge of heating a pail of cocoa, sitting on a sort of shelf on top of the stove. She was trying to pry up the lid on the pail when it came off suddenly, and the contents flew up in her face. My Dad had seen to it that there was a telephone at school as soon as there were telephones in the neighborhood. We called home, and he took her to the doctor as fast as he could. The doctor was familiar with a new method tried in World War I. He applied some sort of wax to her face and left it on until the skin healed. When they removed the wax, her face had only one tiny scar.

cially in the towns. Although there was a tradition of a free peasantry from Viking times in Norway, only 3 percent of the land was arable, so most farmers were forced into fishing and timber cutting to survive. The population explosion of the 1700s and 1800s meant even less land for more people. There was, in fact, a large class of landless farmers who were cotters. So, while there were schools in the towns, there were few in the overcrowded and hard-pressed rural areas. The rugged nature of the terrain and the isolation of many farmsteads made it twice as difficult to establish schools. One solution to this was the "ambulatory school," teachers traveling from one isolated farm to another. A beneficial side effect of the system was that parents, grandparents, and other relatives learned something as well.

The single most important development in promoting a free and compulsory educational system was the advent of the constitution of 1814. If the general adult population was to be, in the last analysis, the ultimate authority, then their education became an inescapable obligation. The real foundation for a widespread school system in the rural areas was the law of 1860 requiring elected officials to establish seven-year elementary schools in each parish and to offer more than the "three R's" and religion; some history, geography, and general science were to be offered as well.[1]

Moreover, a very large number of the early Norwegian settlers in the state had spent sometime in the United States before arriving in North Dakota. While the language of the home and church was still Norwegian, they had acquired some knowledge of the English language and of American institutions in Minnesota, Iowa, Illinois, Wisconsin, or South Dakota first.

The illiteracy rate among the immigrants was extremely low. It is clear that when large numbers of Norwegians left their homeland in the years from 1870 to the First World War, the state system of education was well established. Norwegians were

A Country School Teacher Remembers — Clara Haakenstad

My first day of teaching was a day I shall never forget as long as I live. I had graduated from a four-year high school that spring and attended a term of summer school at Minot, but was unable to get all the courses required for a certificate. The county superintendent suggested I take the teacher's exams, which I did and passed.

The school was a one room with a small shed for wood and coal. All had been painted and cleaned with freshly starched curtains on the windows. It looked very attractive. I was nervous and excited and felt like the greenhorn that I was and became even more so when the twenty-three youngsters came with their lunch pails, tablets, and pencils. I did know two of the families but the rest were strangers.

I rang my little hand bell at 9:00 a.m. and asked them to find their desks until I could check on the size. I introduced myself, then got their names, ages, and grade.

Next we had opening exercises consisting of singing some of the songs that they were familiar with. I found there were many good voices and they seemed to enjoy singing for which I was thankful. Then we found the books we needed; I had them read to find out what they were capable of. The little first graders were taken care of first, then later as I worked with the others I let them draw and color pictures. We also did some work in numbers and arithmetic.

At noon we ate our cold lunches, then we went out to play. There was no playground equipment available so we played softball, Prisoner's Base, Last Couple Out, Nispstick or Farmer in the Dell, always a favorite of the little tikes, and many other games. We took turns choosing games; it worked out very well. After the first days of playing softball I was so stiff I could scarcely get out of bed in the mornings, but after a while I limbered up and could really enjoy their games.

Dismissal came early the first day so I could make up a program to follow and make plans for the rest of the week. With so many pupils, and having to teach all grades the time fixed for each class period was short. I later combined grades, especially in language and health.

It was late when I got home the first day and I was worn out physically, morally and spiritually. I told my mom if I ever lived through that

continued on next page

moving from "folk" society to a modern one, and the schools were important in this transition.

There were forces additional to the existence of state schools at work in Norway which did much to encourage a positive commitment to education. Historians of Scandinavian societies during the past century have accorded a high place to what they call the democratic "folk movements," or a type of popular volunteer association. They had a direct influence on the educational values of the rank and file. These movements, each encompassing large numbers of people, and often overlapping in their membership, experienced their greatest popularity during the same years that saw the largest influx of Scandinavians to the new world. The movements, all with local and nationwide organizations, included the temperance-prohibition movement, trade unions, political parties, cooperatives, women's suffrage, and the adult education and folk high school movements. Because they were all reformist in character, an important part of their work was to form study groups and schools with the purpose of persuading their opponents and the uncommitted. No less in Norway than in Denmark and Sweden, all of these movements had their night classes, short courses, itinerant lecturers and publications. So, for the large number of Norwegians who could not attend the state schools beyond the required seven years, there were many other opportunities for post-elementary school learning. Ingrid Semmingson had this to say about these organizations in Norway:

> The popular movements and voluntary organizations were forged by the middle class, and later by the working class. These were an expression of and conversely, effectively furthered the urge of, the social groups for self-assertion. . . . Religious movements were the first popular movement in the country districts. In political life organizations appear for the first time at the Parliamentary elections of 1851. . . . These various clubs or organizations were to form a school of citizenship. This provided an experience of democracy and taught the responsibilities of citizenship.[2]

Of particular importance for the rural districts of Norway according to Semmingson were the "folk high schools."[3] These were very informal schools for farm youths in their late teens or early twenties: no exams, no admission requirements, just a boarding school to discuss current issues with a teacher during winter months on an informal basis.

In all of these movements young Norwegians of fairly low social and economic origins learned how to debate issues and, ultimately, how to persuade others as to the virtue of their cause. There can be no doubt that many Norwegians who came to North Dakota were at least aware of these many societies, if not actual members. Attitudes in America toward education, and one might suggest, toward political involvement, were affected by these popular movements.

In conclusion then, it is clear that the educational milieu in Norway during the period of emigration to North Dakota was a lively one for the lower classes. What remains then is to make a connection between that milieu and the North Dakota experience of the Norwegian immigrant.

Charles Anderson, a scholar who treats immigration history to the United States in general and the assimilation process in particular, singled out the Norwegians for their ability to adapt to the American mainstream:

> As steadfast Protestants, reliable Republicans (except for a brief episode with the Populists), vociferous opponents of slavery, zealous Prohibitionists . . . , and persons steeped in agrarian virtues, Norwegian Americans have never threatened the ideology of Anglo-Saxon America. On the contrary, Norwegians have been among its utmost strident advocates.[4]

Anderson points out that "They experienced no great difficulty in acquiring the educational and vocational skills required to compete successfully in American Society, and once they possessed these prerequisites, they were allowed to use them, to the fullest." An important part of our thesis in this essay is that the Norwegians who came to North Dakota brought with them the "prerequisites."

Of course, the school experience of the Norwegians in North Dakota was not entirely positive. There were Norwegians who put very little into their schools, or at least the very minimum. In the central part of the state at the turn of the century, we read of one Norwegian-dominated school

year I'd never teach again, but she encouraged me by saying it would get better and it did.

It wasn't very pleasant to go to the toilet as it consisted of two outhouses. In the winter the banks of snow would get plenty high around them. We had a basin, cold water, soap, and paper towels for washing our hands. Water was carried in from the homes.

Since my first school was in my home district and close to my home, I decided to stay at home. I purchased a new Model T Ford. That was both fun and exciting, but later in the fall when the rains came my fun came to an end. Because the roads lacked gravel at that time I'd be stuck in the mud at times. Sometimes help would arrive and other times I'd have to walk home to get aid from my brothers.

The county superintendent would come regularly and sometimes the little ones were afraid of him or her; they'd end up with a "crying spell" until they realized that they wouldn't be hurt. School board members would come to visit but not very often. They were never critical but tried to be helpful which I appreciated.

In the schools I taught in we had the Ten Commandments posted in the room and I would refer to them from time to time. I often times read a passage from the Bible and had a little prayer for opening exercises and at noon I'd read good books from our library. I noticed that children coming from Christian homes were easier to discipline. Most of my country pupils were Lutherans so I had no problems with religion.

I had language troubles sometimes because many times the first graders did not know English. They spoke mostly Norwegian or Swedish. I understood both so I could explain things in their native tongue. I do remember an interesting incident related to the language problem. A little first grade girl came from a home where her parents spoke Norwegian only. One day in health class we talked about good food and I said "carrots" were good for us. She went home and told her mom that teacher had said to eat "rats." The next time I visited with her mom she told me she was puzzled about what we discussed in class. I explained to her and we had a good laugh.

At one of my schools one of my fifth grade girls could always fake answers to questions, especially in history. The following was her reply to my question, "Why did Christopher Columbus set sail in 1492?"

"Columbus was so old he couldn't work anymore so they put him in a boat and let him sail."

I did teach a six-month term during the Depression in the Badlands, Marquris No. 30 in

continued on next page

McKenzie County, where I lived in the school-house and boarded with a widow on a ranch. She had two boys and together with a neighbor boy the experience was more like teaching private school. My salary was twenty dollars a month, but I had free board and room with a bonus at Christmas. I enjoyed my teaching there; the people were so nice and friendly.

I didn't get paid until the night before I left. I wrote my folks one time earlier and told them I was "flat broke" and they were not to look for any more letters. My next letter from my dad contained a sheet of stamps.

What I dreaded most about teaching country school was starting the fire in the stove in the early morning in order to get the room comfortable. I didn't like any of the janitor work and detested the monthly scrubbing of the floors that had to be done without compensation. Emptying chemical toilets was always a detestable chore. Things got better with the coming of electricity, furnaces, good drinking fountains, and indoor water toilet systems.

≈≤

where the author never saw a parent visit the school, where parents were reluctant to buy textbooks, and where there were neither pictures on the walls nor curtains on the windows. She continues that there was never any playground equipment; the building was primitive and poorly maintained, and the nearest well for water was a half-mile away. Finally, she reports that in her years at the school there were never any library or reference books, only a dictionary on a stand.[5] This, however, was a description of a fledgling school in a pioneer setting. For the Norwegians as for everyone else, the home, crops and livestock came first. Nevertheless, the evidence given earlier in this essay suggests that, once the hardest years were behind them, the Norwegians did show a penchant for education.

In this regard, a Lutheran scholar of English-speaking background is quoted by E. Clifford Nelson in his study of the Norwegian Lutheran Church. The theologian, an observer of early twentieth century Great Plains Norwegians, said:

> And how they love education. How they will plan and how ready they are to sacrifice and to suffer that their children may have an education. I actually saw large families living in sod shacks on the open prairie sending a boy or a girl to Concordia College (Moorhead, Minnesota). Am sorry to say that I have not seen anything like this among the Germans.[6]

When asked what one quality isolated the Norwegian immigrants in North Dakota from other European immigrants, Nora Fladeboe Mohberg, chronicler of Norwegian pioneers in the state, wrote that she held to her

> . . . original ideas that their love of reading is the key to their viewpoints on a number of subjects. . . . Thus I have arrived at the conclusion that Norwegians go into politics because they feel that something should be done — so they go ahead and try to do it. The people I have known best are not social climbers, but are more likely reformers from the pulpit, the press, or public office.[7]

It is, of course, true that Norwegians have dominated state elective offices out of all proportion to their numbers in North Dakota. The lowest percentage is for the office of governor; 30 percent have been Norwegian. This requires an explanation. In describing the early years of the Sons of Norway Lodge, in Fairdale, Rosanna Gutterud Johnsrud, a poet, writes:

> . . . it was a most happy and enthusiastic lodge and we young ones quickly caught the magic of its Norse spirit. Special inspirational speakers awakened our awareness of the cultural values of our heritage. The best in music and song was shared — and all in the Norwegian language. A fine library was established in the lodge — it was there I first read Ibsen in Norwegian. The lodge early began presenting plays.[8]

It is not entirely insignificant that Ibsen is best known for his social dramas. There were Sons of Norway lodges throughout the state.

The church was the primary organization for the immigrant, and its role as an agent for educating the transplanted Norwegians can scarcely be over-estimated. In

1883 the Bang Lutheran Church in Steele County founded the Bang Reading Society. According to its constitution it was "organized for the purpose of purchasing good books and establishing a library and promoting the reading of same." Later a Young People's Literary Society was organized at Bang Church to engage in debates, music and readings.[9] Altogether some twelve Norwegian Lutheran schools for higher learning were founded in North Dakota. By 1922 only two were still in operation.[10] A few of the better known were Grand Forks College, Oakgrove Academy in Fargo, and Bruflat Academy at Portland.

Social gathering of Norwegian-Americans in Finley about 1910 (SHSND)

The foregoing illustrates one thing. There is some basis for the image which North Dakota's Norwegians have of themselves, that they have a commitment to education beyond the basics. There is a certain substance behind the image. The best known memoir to come out of the Norwegian community in North Dakota is Aagot Raaen's *Grass of the Earth: Immigrant Life in the Dakota Country*, published in 1950. If there is one theme in her story, it is surely the drive to become an educated person. While her story is by no means typical, it does serve to personify an aspiration for education which was deep in the hearts of many North Dakota Norwegians.

The evidence discussed above, while important, would be incomplete without mention of a final, and vital, factor in this study. A significant number of Norwegian pioneers to the state were either born in America or had spent some years in other states before arriving in North Dakota. In a more comprehensive account of Norwegians in the state this is referred to as "delay time." Well before statehood in 1889, and certainly after, there were attorneys, physicians, business men and educators, both men and women, who had acquired their professional training in other states before arriving here. Beyond this, some of the children of the earliest settlers went off to other states to pursue professional studies, and some returned. These professional and business Norwegians were "role models" for their fellow countrymen and women in the state. Germans from Russia in the state did not have this advantage. They were exclusively "off-the-boat" immigrants, while many of the Norwegian pioneers had a substantial "American" experience before arriving, hence the importance of "delay time" as a factor promoting education.

Yet another aspect of this prior American experience was the presence of journalists and novelists. Over the years there were some fifty-five Norwegian language newspapers in North Dakota. Most were short-lived, but *Normanden*, in Grand Forks, and later Fargo, lasted from 1887 to 1954. Many in the state subscribed to *Decorah Posten* or to Minneapolis and Chicago Norwegian-language newspapers. While these papers promoted interest in "Norwgianee," they also encouraged the immigrant to adapt to American ways — including education. Beyond the journalists as role models, there were novelists writing in Norwegian, such as Simon Johnon, H.A. Foss and Jon Norstog. All of the above suggest the ability of the Norwegian in the state to achieve a rapid acculturation in the host society which, of course, included as much education as possible.

Endnotes

1. George M. Wiley, *The Organization and Administration of the Educational System of Norway* (Oslo: 1955), p. 25.

2. Ingrid Semmingson, "The Dissolution of Estate Society in Norway," *Scandinavian Economic History Review* No. 2, 1954, pp. 199-200.

3. *Ibid.*, pp. 199-200.

4. Charles H. Anderson, *White Protestant Americans From National Origins to Religious Group* (Englewood Cliffs, New Jersey: 1970), p. 69.

5. Barbara Levorson, *The Quiet Conquest, A History of the Lives and Times of the First Settlers of Central North Dakota* (Hawley, Minnesota: 1974), pp. 114-118.

6. E. Clifford Nelson, *The Lutheran Church Among Norwegian Americans* (Minneapolis: Augsburg Publishing House: 1960), Vol. II, P. 113.

7. Letter To Playford V. Thorson, March 27, 1977.

8. Letter to Playford V. Thorson, October 10, 1978.

9. Duane R. Lindberg, *Men of the Cloth and the Social Cultural Fabric of the Norwegian Ethnic Community in North Dakota* (University of Minnesota: 1975), p. 102.

10. *Ibid.*, p. 98.

11. Playford V. Thorson, "Norwegians," in *Plains Folk: North Dakota's Ethnic History* (Fargo: Institute for Regional Studies, 1986), pp. 203-204.

The Germans from Russia

ANY DISCUSSION OF THE LEVEL AND CONDITION of educational enterprises in the German villages of Russia treads on sensitive ground. The three generations who lived in Russia, from about 1800 to 1900, necessarily form a background for the tender matter of German-Russian performance in the United States. Echoes of prejudicial remarks and biased comments rebound throughout the question. George P. Aberle reacts sharply to American criticism. He says, "By the time the schools opened in Russian villages, the colonists had some of the finest elementary schools in the country . . . high schools, gymnasiums, and several colleges."[1] Other students of the subject are not so sure, at least in terms of the first half century of colonization. (We speak here of the Black Sea Villages, for they are the forebears of our North Dakota Germans.) Joseph S. Height, and several other authors, refer to the first five decades, until at least 1860, as the "dark years," and he calls it a time of "frustration and stagnation . . . of decadence and regression."[2] Many of the first adult Dakota settlers left Russia in the 1870s and 1880s, so we must conclude that their formative years were during this dark period. This fact alone may have some bearing on their subsequent attitude toward the American educational system.

But let us take a closer look at the first Russian decades. When the German settlers arrived in the Black Sea areas, they were faced with enormous physical and cultural difficulties. The erection of a school system was a small part of a total adjustment problem. The mere question of physical survival was of immediate importance. They entered, with little support, a primitive land, far away from their original homeland; an unfamiliar environment with inadequate roads, meager housing, and a difficult agricultural situation. The death rate in the first years was appalling. Schools, at least quality schools, were a luxury which the first generation could not afford. The question of survival overrode all other considerations. The land, the work, the building of home and village, these were the pressing problems. As Frederick Jackson Turner would say in a later context, the frontier bred practicality; the niceties of culture were secondary.

In the first years of settlement, illiteracy, at least in many villages, was the rule and not the exception. Johannes Brendel, writing of the Catholic Kutschurgan colonies, lists the ratio in 1812. Elsass Village had 89 percent illiteracy; Mannheim, 79 percent; Kandel and Selz, 72 percent; and Strassburg, 64 percent.[3] Other villages must have reflected something of the same.

When German colonists went to Russia, they made a decisive break with Germany. They all but severed the taproot to the parent culture. Mail and other forms of communication were rare. German educated professionals were absent from the migration. The Germans found themselves in relatively isolated villages, far from the artistic and scholarly centers of the homeland. Likewise, the villagers, jealous of their traditions, had little contact with Russian institutes of higher learning. The literacy and scientific advances which thrilled the population of Germany as the century proceeded were unknown to much of the *Volksdeutsche* of Russia. Few if any figures of intellectual stature captured the imagination of the survival-minded villagers.

Students and teachers from a German-Russian Mennonite school near Munich in North Dakota pose in their classroom about 1912. The German-Russian Mennonites were the first of the *Volkdeutsche* to come to Dakota. They first arrived in 1872-73. (Cavalier County Historical Society)

When they arrived there were no public schools. Height says, "Throughout the one hundred year history of the colonies, the government never contributed a ruble of tax money to the building or operation of the village schools."[4] The first educational establishments were primitive and were usually under the aegis of the clergy. Often the Church sexton was the schoolmaster. The Roman Catholic villages had an additional disadvantage in that the clergy for the first two generations tended to be Polish in background. Adam Giesinger says that Polish priests "left the schools in the hands of colonist schoolmasters who were often ignorant and incompetent."[5]

Protestant villages also had difficulties. Even in the rather late year of 1859, a survey of Grossliebental district schools, seven Evangelical and four Roman Catholic, showed an average of two blackboards, one abacus, a dozen ABC primers and one hundred sixty tablets per school. This meant one textbook and one slate for every four children.[6] Nevertheless, the Protestant schools fared better than the Roman Catholic. Neglect of education by disdainful Polish clergy was not a burden in the Protestant villages. Many authors observe that, though educational conditions were still primitive, Protestant areas made some small advances while the Roman Catholic colonies lagged behind in the earliest decades.

Governmental, clerical and environmental forces may have hindered the growth of schools in the villages, but the blame must also be put on the attitude of the

A Country School Teacher Remembers — Esther Busch Bernard

My mother and father came to North Dakota and built a house on the prairie in 1905. Both had lived in Wisconsin and Mother had finished the eighth grade, but my dad had to help with farm work and finished the fifth grade. Both had learned to read and write and did a lot more reading than most and we subscribed to a number of magazines when I was growing up. My mother was especially anxious that all of their children have at least a high school education. She used to say we could always wash dishes and scrub floors for a living, but if we had an education we would have a greater choice.

My dad was a member of our rural school board as long as I can remember. When they got single seats in the classroom he brought home some of the double seats and we set up a school situation in the barn loft. We spent many playtime hours brushing off the cobwebs and playing school with the discarded seats and also the old textbooks and bits of chalk that came from the schoolhouse. I remember we even had a piece of broken slate blackboard in our play school. My mother thought it would be wonderful if we would all be teachers. There was no high school in our area at the time, but the Sisters of Saint Joseph would come around in the late summer to recruit students for their boarding school in Jamestown, North Dakota. They told our parents we could earn part of our board and room by helping with dishes and scrubbing floors, so both my older sister and I got a very thorough high school education at the academy in Jamestown.

I was sixteen when I finished high school, so I went to the Valley City State Teacher's College during the winter quarter in 1927. I was granted a Second Grade Elementary Certificate that was valid for two years. A friend helped me get a contract in her home district when I was eighteen years of age. At that time I weighed under a hundred pounds.

That first year of teaching was a disaster. I had thirty pupils and at least five of the boys were fifteen years of age and repeaters. That meant they hadn't passed the state examinations that were required at that time. I looked like one of the students and had problems getting the children to come in off the playground when I rang the school bell after recess. When they did get into the building there was bedlam and by Christmas time the board members

continued on next page

villagers themselves. Apparently, they saw little value in formal education. Geisinger says, "By default, and through the power of the purse, control lay in the hands of the colonists themselves . . . the conservative peasant mentality, suspicious of all innovation, saw no need for educational frills."[7] Brendel concurs when he says, "The colonists . . . , being materialists . . . , didn't get excited about their schools. Also they were stingy with their money." They preferred leaving their sons and daughters possessions, particularly land, rather than education.[8]

A serious and continuing difficulty was the fundamental lack of teacher training. Ultimately, the villagers wanted German teachers in their classrooms and lecture halls. But the institutions of higher education were either far away in Germany or were Russian schools which meant, in either case, a young man or woman was forced to leave their family or people and spend long periods of time in alien circumstances. This fact, coupled with the low salary and prestige allotted to school employees, continued the lack of adequate teacher training. Eventually, about mid-century, at the insistence of some leaders, particularly some clergy, and the Russian government, several teacher colleges were established. No popular reform or rank and file betterment movement swept the German areas at the time. There was nothing like the Norwegian "folk movement" experience. On the contrary, it seems that the pressure to change came from outsiders, even from the Russian civil officials. Conrad Keller, in assessing the educational problems of the villages almost one hundred years after settlement, said in 1904, "Another consideration that also speaks unfavorably for striving for education of the colonists is that almost always the initiative for founding a school comes not from themselves but from other persons."[9] A Protestant school was founded in Bessarabia in 1844, and this institution began to provide teachers.[10] The establishment of a seminary in 1857 at Saratov helped with the education problems of the Roman Catholic clergy. By the 1870s teachers' colleges, some under both Protestant and Roman Catholic auspices, were producing a steady flow of graduates and much was being done to alleviate the situation. Brendel says, "In the beginning of the 1880's the education system experienced a renewal, and there developed more interest than prevailed before."[11] The political scene was deteriorating; Russian culture was being imposed, and a series of *Landamtschulen* and other such institutions developed to supplement the village schools. Increasingly, the Czar's government insisted on higher standards, much with an eye to enforcing the Russian language and culture. For many Germans the school became an instrument of an alien way of life. A rebirth was taking place, but by this time the Germans were leaving for America.

Arrival in America meant conditions both the same, yet different. Again, a primitive prairie; again, the struggle to survive with its corresponding emphasis on work, the land, the family, and the *dorf* (village). Again, the Germans found themselves in an alien world, thousands of miles from Russia and completely out of touch with modern Germany. It was almost a repeat of the scene which their ancestors faced in previous generations. Schools were primitive and other matters took first place. Nina Farley Wishek remembers her early country school in McIntosh County, "It was the usual tan-grey sod building with only one room in which to live, eat, sleep and have school."[12] For the early Germans in south central North Dakota, long hours of work, harsh winters, and muddy springs took their toll in educational matters. Wishek says, "In the early days, the schools were short terms, usually two months, never more than three."[13] Frequently, incompetent individuals were the only ones to accept teaching jobs. Adolph Shock quotes a teacher in the German school whose official report went as follows: "My ame (sic) has been this winter to learn my students all of the English I posebel (sic) could."[14] In 1906, Jessie Tanner says, "Some of the German-Russians do not send their children to school, complaining that teachers fail to understand them and neglect them."[15]

Again there was the fear that the public school, the bearer of English language and Anglo-Saxon traditions, would lessen the contact with family and people, those ever-necessary supports which alone had brought them through the harsh years of Russia. Schock says,

> This American system caused some apprehension among the communities, fearing that the German language would ultimately be entirely replaced by the English language, so that

asked me to resign so they could hire a man to handle the big fellows. I was a bit chagrined, but glad to be relieved of that job. I went back home to lick my wounds and wait for a better break.

The first day of my third year of teaching a brown-eyed nine-year-old boy came to the door of the school to take a look at the teacher. He ran out onto the playground and I heard him telling the other children, "She licks!" That incident made discipline much easier during that term. He had evidently heard about me from the neighboring school where I had just finished my second term.

The second year of my teaching career saw the beginning of the Depression and jobs were hard to find. I finally got a job in a German-Russian district near Wishek, North Dakota. This was another large school, about thirty pupils, but I was determined not to let this bunch get the upper hand, so things went a little smoother. It was a seven-month school and I think my salary was forty-five dollars per month.

One stormy evening a high-pressure salesman came to the schoolhouse after school and in order to get rid of him I signed a paper to get a ninety-dollar set of *Classroom Teacher.* I thought I would be able to break the contract, but found that was impossible, so I had to pay for the set. I did use them a little, but ninety dollars was a high price to pay.

The following year I went to a neighboring school with a seven-month term and earned forty-five dollars per month. I had twenty-four pupils and a pleasant boarding place with an English-speaking family. In both schools most of the beginners spoke only German, and it took at least two years before they really got anything out of the English. Since that time radio and TV have helped a lot with the language problems, but this was 1930 when there was little radio and no TV in rural areas.

The first year in the area I stayed with a German-Russian family. They had a new house, but it had very poor heating facilities and we spent most of our waking hours in the kitchen where the range was used to bake bread and heat the house. I remember waking up to the smell of burning cow manure as the children were sent out to gather buckets of cow chips on the hot summer days and these were used for fuel during the winter months. The food was wholesome; most of the time for breakfast we ate oatmeal with hot milk, homemade bread, and some kind of dried prunes or raisins. I took my noon lunches to school in a gallon syrup bucket and if we weren't careful to air out the bucket it didn't smell right.

continued on next page

I taught in several different schools over a period of about eight years; I finally got a job in a small town school. That was the year I got married and the contract I taught under stipulated that if I got married I would be out of a job. I finished the term and got married during the summer. My salary during those years ranged from forty-five dollars per month for a seven-month term to fifty-five dollars per month for a nine-month term, in my first town school. Board and room ranged from twelve to fifteen dollars per month, and if the family I stayed with was of another religion they usually saw to it that I got to my church on Sunday.

Supplies were meager, especially in western North Dakota, and many times students had to share books and materials. Getting pencils and papers together was difficult as money was in short supply in the school and at home. We used both sides of a sheet of paper and did a lot of blackboard work. We had to be careful of the chalk supply and were lucky if we got hard chalk instead of the soft, dusty kind.

Most of the schools I taught in had a jacketed stove and a supply of coal. We were lucky if there was kindling and paper to get the fire going. We tried keeping fire overnight during the week and sometimes banked it with ashes to keep the coal from burning up overnight. We burned mostly lignite coal and that took a lot of coaxing and meant a lot of ashes to haul. Some contracts directed us to carry the ashes a certain distance from the school and that was a sensible suggestion because one school I recall had a huge ash pile right by the schoolhouse door. The hot ashes could have set the building on fire if weather conditions were right. We had to watch for grass fires in the fall, too.

I recall standing too close to one jacketed stove. I burned the back of a wool skirt and had to be careful to keep it from falling apart before I got home that night. It was so cold in the building I didn't realize it was that hot behind me. Many mornings it would be below zero in the building, especially on Monday.

Copies of the Ten Commandments were present in some of the classrooms. Many times they were hung so high nobody could begin to read them, so I often hung them at a lower level. We sang patriotic songs for opening exercises and had programs of such holidays as Lincoln's and Washington's birthday, Easter, and Christmas. Many of the songs and poems stressed values and the book of poems published by the state department of education contained many choice verses, many of which were memorized.

continued on next page

in time the German heritage would not only be lost but children would become estranged to their parents.[16]

As seen in the U.S. Census and Superintendent of Public Instruction reports cited in Chapter 4, a distinction must be made between education which was a matter of vocational skills and those studies which are often called the "fine arts" or the "humanities." The life of a successful farmer or a village artisan involved a thorough knowledge of the trade and this necessarily meant the ability to read, write, and "figure." Parents in German-Russian counties accepted education to the fifth and sixth grades. All the census data indicates that by 1920 the proportions of students attending school from the ages of seven to thirteen, whether in German-Russian or Norwegian counties, ranged in the ninety percent categories. (See *Tables 3, 4.*) In matters of high school enrollment, however, the German-Russian students, at least until the 1930s, dropped well behind their Norwegian counterparts. College attendance for German students was almost unheard of in those same years. Education beyond the requirements of farm and craft type of skills was frowned upon. Only in one area was it accepted, the seminary and the convent and clergy-training schools. In both Roman Catholic and Protestant villages, such a possibility was highly regarded. But here, too, one gets the impression that these institutions may have been seen as a type of clerical trade school.

The failure of German-Russian families to encourage extensive formal education was not all a one-sided affair. The Germans, coming from the Ukraine, bore the stigma of the Russian peasant. Many Anglo-Americans of the time tended to look with some disfavor on the arrival of Eastern European immigrants. Certainly, they were not embraced with warmth and welcomed into the intimacy of full American life. The German-Russian had no Viking or romantic past, but rather bore the image of a dull, long suffering, primitive peasant worker. The school officials themselves did not always have the compassion of Nina Farley Wishek. Thus, the non-German superintendent of schools in German-Russian Stark County complains in 1906:

> Approximately 80 percent of the people of the rural districts were recent arrivals from foreign countries and were generally illiterate and clannish

and decidedly indifferent to the establishment and patronage of the public school.[17]

One wonders whether the doors of the state's high schools and colleges were opened as widely for the German young people as they were for Norwegians and other immigrants from more acceptable North European countries.

Yet even in the earliest decades there were those who saw a certain ability and eagerness in the German students. Nina Farley Wishek says, "I found the children alert and eager to learn."[18] University of North Dakota German Professor Bek says in 1915:

> It is interesting to observe the descendants of the Ruszlaender when they are given an opportunity for education in our schools. . . . They reveal an aptness and a zeal.[19]

A kind of watershed in educational aspirations seems to have come about during the years of World War II. A series of events happened that changed the perspective of both parents and children. It may have been in the 1930s with the disastrous dry years. Perhaps then German fathers, especially those with large families, began to doubt the wisdom of seeing the future exclusively in terms of farming and small town life. Thomas Cummings suggests a change was taking place in the late 1930s. After studying enrollments, library statistics, and the apportionment of funds he says,

> Inference from these figures should lead the analyzer to the conclusion that, education was valued by the German-Russians of McIntosh County and that if there was any opposition to education earlier in the century, it was overcome by the late 1930's.[20]

What Cummings may have detected could have been the first robin of that summer. The authors are convinced that by the 1950s a dramatic shift had taken place in the German-Russian perspective. Whether in response to the mid-thirties drought or the sudden increase in land values, the expanded horizons of World War II or the GI Bill, something had happened. German boys and girls began to finish high school in great numbers, and many went on to the state's colleges and technical institutes. In 1942, Adolph Schock, writing perhaps from personal experience, makes a comment that may be central to the question:

> Children were appraised in terms of their economic value. Not until the problem of giving each son a farm arose would parents turn their attention toward education and the advisability to having their son enter a profession.[21]

Most districts I taught in had water fountains in their schools; directions from the health department that were posted reminded everyone to wash their hands. The supply of paper towels was meager, but you did the best you could. In the rural school I attended we had outdoor toilets, but by the time I started teaching many schools had indoor chemical facilities that some school board member came to charge at regular intervals. I remember one fellow badly burned his hands from careless handling of the strong disinfectant that was used.

Almost every contract stipulated that the teacher was to do the janitor work and scrub the floor once each month or as needed. We had to sweep out every night and once in a while the district supplied sweeping compound to hold down the dust. I remember using chunks of wet paper and even snow to keep down the dust when sweeping compound was unavailable. Janitor supplies were meager and were expected to last the whole term.

For entertainment I usually attended programs at neighboring schools. One time I went to a house party and before the evening was over at least three inches of "Russian Peanut" husks [sunflower seeds] covered the dance floor. They were a staple in the area. Many families raised them in their gardens; they couldn't have bought that many. Once in a while the local church would sponsor a bazaar or card party and one community had a cake and coffee party one day of each month in the church basement. We were served luscious cakes and lots of them. Once in a while there was a basket social to make money. I remember how upset one fellow was when he got a pig's tail and nothing else in the basket he bought. It about ended the basket social season.

My dad was very nice about bringing me home to spend a weekend when the weather was good and my parents always came to bring me home for holidays.

✍✍

✍✍

Endnotes

1. George P. Aberle, *From the Steppes to the Prairies* (Dickinson, North Dakota: Privately Published, 1965), p. 47.

2. Joseph S. Height, *Paradise on the Steppe* (Bismarck: North Dakota Historical Society of Germans from Russia, 1972), p. 211.

3. Johannes Brendel, "The German Colonies in the Kutschurgan Region," *Heritage Review*, Vol. 10, No. 2 (April, 1980), p. 25.

4. Height, p. 211.

5. Adam Giesinger, *From Catherine to Khrushchev* (Battleford, Saskatchewan: Marian Press, 1974), p. 216.

6. Joseph S. Height, *Homesteaders on the Steppe* (Bismarck: North Dakota Historical Society of Germans from Russia, 1975), p. 255.

7. Giesinger, p. 177.

8. Brendel, p. 25.

9. Conrad Keller, *The German Colonies in South Russia, 1804 to 1904*, Vol. 1 (translated into English by A. Becker, Saskatoon, Saskatchewan, 1973), p. 82.

10. Giesinger, p. 177.

11. Brendel, p. 26.

12. Nina Farley Wishek, *Along the Trails of Yesterday* (Ashley, North Dakota: The *Ashley Tribune*, 1941), p. 180.

13. *Ibid.*, p. 182.

14. Adolph Schock, *In Quest of Free Land* (San Jose: San Jose State College, 1965), p. 154.

15. Jessie Tanner, "Foreign Immigration into North Dakota," *North Dakota Historical Society Collections* I (1906), p. 144.

16. Schock, p. 153.

17. North Dakota, Department of Public Instruction, Superintendent of Public Instruction, *Ninth Biennial Report*, June 1904-June 1906, p. 327.

18. Wishek, p. 181.

19. William Godfrey Bek, "Some Facts Concerning the Germans of North Dakota," *The Quarterly Journal of the University of North Dakota*, V No. 4 (July, 1915), p. 334.

20. Thomas J. Cummings, "An Examination of the Lubell Thesis: A Statistical and Historical Sketch of McIntosh County, North Dakota, 1936-1940" (unpublished M.A. thesis, University of North Dakota, 1972), p. 145.

21. Adolph Schock, "In Quest of Free Land," *Rural Sociology*, VII No. 4 (December, 1942), p. 441.

A Country School Teacher Remembers — Phyllis George

The incident I recall best occurred when I was staying in a neat German-Russian home. I had no means of communicating with the family except through the young son who was thirteen years old and spoke some English. I arose unusually early one morning. When I went to breakfast the lady of the house was cleaning her false teeth in the dipper that was used for drinking water. The rest of the year I learned to like coffee.

❧❧

Recent Developments

A SHIFT IN GERMAN-RUSSIAN ATTITUDES may, perhaps, have begun in the late 1930s. It certainly came about in the post-World War II years. The Cummings study of McIntosh county, reported above, detected something of a change and Sherman, previously cited, found it quite clearly at the University of North Dakota in 1965. Germans had, for whatever reasons, begun to attend college in sizable numbers.

To check the validity of these reports, the authors studied Northwood High School, located on the edge of Traill County, and Napoleon High School, located in German-Russian Logan County. The study covered the years 1957 to 1961. The graduating classes of those years were similar in their ethnic proportions; Northwood was slightly more than 80 percent Norwegian and Napoleon had the same ratio of German-Russians.

The Northwood school reports showed that 69 percent of the graduates in those years went on to "college or technical school."[1] The predominantly German-Russian school at Napoleon reported that 60 percent of the graduates "went on to a four year college."[2] In fact, some of the Napoleon graduates went to highly rated schools; two attended Harvard. The Northwood figure contains students who went to "technical schools;" the Napoleon total is for "four year college." One could probably say that the college bound proportions were much the same for the two schools. Perhaps, the Germans exceeded the Norwegians.

Napoleon was, and is, a farming town whose population numbered 1,078 in 1960. Northwood, in a little more affluent farming area, was a similar town with a total of 1,195 residents. In neither town did there seem to be institutions or unique activities which were capable of unduly influencing the educational aspirations of the young people.

What is abundantly evident is that the totals show an astonishing change in German-Russian attitudes. In 1940, the University of North Dakota was said to have had only two German-Russian students in the entire enrollment of 1,828 students.[3]

A Country School Teacher Remembers — Esther Aljets

Why did I become a teacher? From my first day in school, I wanted to be a teacher. My teacher was my idol. I also had two relatives who taught in rural schools. They lived in the schoolhouse so they came to our place often for weekends. They spent a great deal of time telling me stories and teaching me nursery rhymes which I loved to hear. I thought it would be nice to become a teacher and storyteller.

Because college training wasn't required to enter the teaching profession when I graduated from high school in 1924 I taught a year before I enrolled at Valley City State Teachers College. After that first year I continued to teach rural schools for ten years. Every summer I went back to school until I received my Standard Diploma; my mother would often tease me by telling me I taught nine months, went to school three months, and vacationed the rest of the time.

I taught in the Birtsell District in Foster County the first two years for eighty dollars per month. I stayed at home because the school was only three miles away. From 1926 to 1931 I taught in the Wyard District, also in Foster County. My sister taught in the same district so we drove from home during the fall and spring, but stayed in some nice homes during the winter months or when the weather was bad. One time, because the houses were small and the families were large, I shared a room with four girls in the family. My salary was ninety dollars a month plus another five dollars for doing janitorial work. Later, my salary was raised to a hundred dollars, very good for a rural school salary.

continued on next page

At the end of these five years, the depression was beginning and the board decided that they couldn't continue paying such a salary. I decided to look elsewhere and accepted a salary of eighty dollars a month and concluded that I was very lucky because many rural teachers were getting only sixty or sixty-five dollars a month. I had just received my first month's salary when the bank where the district kept its money closed; after that I did receive my eighty dollars per month but had to wait several days to get it.

The first school I taught in was made from an old house; the schoolroom was L-shaped and had windows on three sides. Although two stoves were used to keep the room warm it was still so cold that we kept our overshoes on all day during the cold weather. Later the building was sold to a farmer from southwest of Sykeston who used it as a residence.

Although I had lived on a farm I had never "hitched up" a horse. In fact, I worried more about "hitching up" the horse than I did about getting my first day of school off to a good start. I did get to school early in the morning, but many of the pupils were already there and so was the president of the school board. Twenty-six pupils in all grades except the eighth were there to greet me. An eighth grade student who was helping at home started school somewhat later. I combined classes as much as I could, but still had about thirty short classes every day. I never assigned homework; in this way the pupils were kept busy while I conducted other classes.

One family was responsible for hauling water to school; it was brought in a five or ten gallon cream can and kept in a water cooler. Toilets and the woodshed were separated from the schoolhouse; after a winter snowstorm the teacher had to do a lot of shoveling. I usually kept a pail of coal and some kindling wood inside so I could start a fire in the morning. Once or twice during the school year I would scrub the floor.

The schoolhouse was used for various programs, basket socials, and other school entertainment. We always had a Christmas program; this would bring out the entire community. The little schoolroom would be packed. Declamation contests were held once a year. The pupils in the district would meet at one school and compete for the county contest; mothers would come to these contests. Because one school was not equipped with modern lighting fixtures patrons brought gas lamps or lanterns when programs were held at night.

Since I lived on a farm I didn't have to adjust to rural life when I began teaching; I never found

continued on next page

100

Yet twenty years later, a German-Russian school is found sending 60 percent of its graduates to college. The change is dramatic. Furthermore, an informal check of teachers who taught in other German areas found that something of the same was happening elsewhere.

To verify the data, a survey of the Napoleon graduates of 1970 was made by studying the publication of that class as it gathered for its tenth anniversary reunion in 1980. Fifty-seven had graduated in 1970 and of that number, thirty-two or 56 percent had gone to either a four-year college or to a two year college or technical school.

The well known German-Russian pattern of determination, personal discipline and hard work which had previously been oriented toward life on the farm and in a small town, by the 1960s was also being directed toward college and professional level activities. The diverse paths of Norwegian and German-Russian aspirations seem to have merged in the present.

Summary

WHEN SEEN AS A WHOLE the German-Russians in the counties and schools studied above were decidedly less interested, less supportive, and less involved in the state's educational enterprises. Joseph Voeller's assessment, mentioned at the beginning of the essay, was substantially correct: "To this day (1940) the poorest schools, the lowest teacher's salaries, the most inadequate equipment, and the most irregular attendance are found in German-Russian communities."[4]

In terms of the school plant and its physical condition the German counties were slow in development and hesitant in support. During the early decades of settlement they were not generous in their teachers' salary scales, although women teachers fared better than men, they did not insist on teachers with the highest qualifications, and they were less concerned about developing such things as multi-graded, town type schools.

In the first one-third of this century, the German-Russian counties had twice the amount of adult illiteracy as the Norwegians. Less than half of the proportions of children finished grade school among the Germans as did so among the Norwegians. Perhaps only a third as many entered high school and less than that number actually graduated.

The negative contrast stops, however, in terms of attendance in the first years of grade school. By 1920, the German-Russian averages in the seven to thirteen school enrollment category equal the Norwegian. There are clear indications that the basic skills usually acquired in elementary school were considered just as important among Germans as among Norwegians.

In general, the German-Russians viewed education beyond the basic "three R's" as superfluous; high school, college, and in many families even the last several years of grade school, were of little value.

The absence of Germans in the ranks of school administrators or even on school boards is most evident. Perhaps the whole question of education was viewed as the province of "other people." The reverse side of the picture may also have been a coolness on the part of the educational establishment to encourage German-Russian participation.

A change, however, seemed to be taking place as the decades of North Dakota residence proceeded. Here and there, indications appeared in the basic reports, that education was seen of increasing importance. By 1960, as the Northwood-Napoleon school comparison shows, the Germans were abreast of the Norwegians in college attendance.

country school teaching a lonely life. I was invited to all the parties in the neighborhood and when the family I was staying with went to the theater or to town they invited me to go along. In fact, many times I'd rather stay at home. I kept busy taking correspondence courses, reading, and sewing.

My last three years teaching in a rural school was in the Cathay District in Wells County. This school was in a German-Russian settlement and to them school was just a place to go if they could think of nothing else to do. I would go and work until noon and if no one came I would go to my boarding place. In one year there were twenty such days.

Parents were always welcome to visit the school. In Wyard School District the school board visited the school once a year. The County Superintendent visited twice a year, once in the fall and again in the spring.

The children in a rural school had an advantage over the town school children. They often listened to other classes recite and so they got an education by doing so. Of course, the disadvantage was that most of the time there was only one pupil to the grade so they had no competition.

The rural teacher didn't have the discipline problems the town schoolteacher had. Rural children weren't exposed to the temptations that the town children were. Most farm children had chores to do and I think the 4H clubs gave them interests that kept them busy. They weren't always looking for something to do.

My mother who was born in Missouri had an eighth-grade education; my father who was born in Kansas didn't have a chance to get as much. But, both wanted their eight children to get a good education and made sacrifices to get them educated.

We found no evidence that the German-Russian young people were less capable of education than Norwegians. The Silva study informs this conclusion. On the contrary, it seems that the matter was basically a cultural thing; the German attitude toward education, from a pre-democratic life in an alien environment in Russia, was different than the Norwegian.

The Norwegian participation in North Dakota's educational life during the first few decades of the century is truly a remarkable thing. Given the fact that, in contrast to the German-Russians, many had the advantage of a few prior years of life in such states as Wisconsin and Minnesota, they seemed to have plunged into the American scene with amazing rapidity. If university enrollment and the occupancy of key positions in the educational and even political hierarchy is a measure, they exceeded other large ethnic groups by far. It must be remembered that other immigrant peoples, too, had lived for a short while in eastern states but were absent from the school leadership scene. The name analysis of school officials and college graduates showed Norwegians standing shoulder to shoulder with residents of early American and British Isles background. The literacy rate and the proportion of young people attending high school in the Norwegian counties compares favorably with and often exceeds that of counties with a high Anglo-American population. Apparently, many Norwegians agreed with the sentiments of Paul Hjelm Hansen, the Norwegian journalist whose praise of the Red River Valley brought many settlers to North Dakota. In 1869, Hansen said:

> I believe that it is the sacred duty of the emigrants who wish to make this country their future home . . . to become united and assimilated with the native population of the country, the Americans, to learn the English language and to familiarize themselves with and uphold the spirit and institutions of the Republic. The sooner this comes about, the better.[5]

We believe that the source of the difference in the two groups' attitudes toward education can be found in their prior experience both in Russian and in Norway. On the one hand, the Germans were an isolated and threatened group, little affected by the "modern" events of contemporary Germany or Russia. They were a rural-minded folk society trying to survive under difficult circumstances. Norway, however, was a whirl of movements: nationalism, pietism, secularism, and grass root romanticism was part of the scene. There was a thirst for learning, social advancement, and personal achievement which was unique. The Norwegian immigrants to America apparently saw the North Dakota school as among the best of ways to success.

Finally, by the 1960s, the achievements of the two groups begin to converge. When the possibility of life on the land became a less possible and less attractive option, the German-Russians began to see high school, college and technical school attendance as a necessary part of a successful life.

Endnotes

1. Letter, Superintendent Robert E. Sheppard to Playford V. Thorson, May 11, 1981.

2. Interview, Superintendent Gilbert Holle, May 1, 1981.

3. William C. Sherman, "Assimilation in a North Dakota German-Russian Community," (unpublished M.A. thesis, University of North Dakota, 1965), p. 79.

4. Joseph B. Voeller, "The Origins of the German-Russian People and Their Role in North Dakota" (unpublished M.S. thesis, University of North Dakota, 1940), p. 36.

5. Theodore C. Blegen, ed., *Land of Their Choice: The Immigrants Write Home* (Minneapolis: University of Minnesota Press, 1955), p. 446.

*B*ecause I had good citizenship training throughout my years in rural schools, high school, and college, I was determined to instill that in my rural pupils. I tried to teach them the importance of attaining good marks, to work for better things in the future, and to strive for suc-cess for themselves and others by obedience to laws, kindness to others, patriotism to our country, and becoming an individual to be ever admired in our society.

"And There's a Reason," proclaimed the headline for the cartoon on the front of *The North Dakota Farmer* magazine of October 15, 1917 (published in Lisbon, N.D.) — the man is MONEYBAGS, who says, "As far as I can see this rural school uplift is all bosh. What was good enough for me is good enough for the boys and girls nowadays." Comments the editor, "Strange how a little extra tax will distort vision."

When a push was on for consolidation in North Dakota in 1917, many rural schools were in a sorry state — in Norwegian areas as well as those predominantly German-Russian. Moreover, both groups were concerned with the economic future of their children and the usefulness of education to economic well-being.

Appendix — Table I

Table I U.S. Census 1910									
COUNTY	Divide	Nelson	Steele	Traill	COUNTY	Logan	McIntosh	Mercer	Sheridan
Total Foreign-Born	1843	2955	1985	3632	Total Foreign-Born	2364	2638	1735	3104
Total Foreign-Born Norwegian	1154	1886	1310	2854	Total Foreign-Born German-Russia	1811	2479	1404	2499
Percent of Foreign-Born Norwegian	63%	64%	66%	79%	Percent of Foreign-Born German-Russian	77%	94%	81%	81%

U.S. Census 1920									
COUNTY	Divide	Nelson	Steele	Traill	COUNTY	Logan	McIntosh	Mercer	Sheridan
Total Foreign-Born	2290	2230	1369	2649	Total Foreign-Born	2269	2337	2239	2284
Total Foreign-Born Norwegian	1318	1489	921	2077	Total Foreign-Born German-Russia	1772	2189	1794	1862
Percent of Foreign-Born Norwegian	58%	67%	67%	78%	Percent of Foreign-Born German-Russian	78%	93%	80%	82%

Rural Households in Selected Counties in 1965 by W.C. Sherman									
COUNTY	Divide	Nelson	Steele	Traill	COUNTY	Logan	McIntosh	Mercer	Sheridan
Total Households	619	843	701	1025	Total Households	696	678	565	690
Norwegian Households	449	550	518	715	German-Russian Households	616	655	456	556
Percent of Households Norwegian	73%	65%	74%	70%	Percent of Households German-Russian	88%	97%	71%	81%

U.S. Census					
	Value of All Farm Property in Dollars		County Population		
COUNTY	1910	1920	1910	1920	1930
Divide	5,647,007	25,117,517	6015	9637	9626
Nelson	21,841,555	37,223,242	10140	10362	10203
Steele	20,758,421	34,462,903	7616	7401	6972
Traill	28,886,708	46,457,967	12545	12210	12600
Logan	9,993,823	19,784,319	6168	7723	8089
McIntosh	11,775,792	22,470,283	7251	9010	9621
Mercer	7,398,696	18,090,166	4747	8224	9516
Sheridan	13,104,617	17,993,100	8103	7935	7373

Appendix — Tables II-IV

Table II
County Superintendent of Schools Report, 1922 — Physical Plant

Number of Schools in each county	Divide	Nelson	Steele	Traill	Logan	McIntosh	Mercer	Sheridan
With Gyms	7	4	10	11	1	2	1	4
Seats Wrong Size	5	0	11	6	25	0	3	0
Not Scrubbed Once a Month	—	0	25	15	91	103	73	77
No or Bad Curtains	6	0	9	3	9	0	23	0
With Inside Toilet	54	9	19	31	5	2	0	11
No Inside Toilet as Required by Law	0	0	2	0	0	0	0	0
No Wash Basins or Paper Towels	0	0	0	17	74	97	66	13
No Modern Ventilation System	17	13	7	14	84	89	67	67

Table III
County Superintendent of Schools Report, July 1922-July 1923
Teacher Qualifications in Graded Schools in Town

Number of Teachers in each county	Divide	Nelson	Steele	Traill	Logan	McIntosh	Mercer	Sheridan
High School Graduate Only	8	15	10	9	3	7	18	9
Normal School Graduate	20	35	16	36	15	21	7	14
Teacher College Graduate	6	27	15	25	5	7	5	5
Teacher Proficiency Certification	26	61	31	62	22	27	16	20

Table IV
County Superintendent of Schools Report, July 1922-July 1923
Teacher Qualifications in One-Room Schools in Town and Open Country

Number of Teachers in each county	Divide	Nelson	Steele	Traill	Logan	McIntosh	Mercer	Sheridan
Normal School Graduate	7	4	2	6	0	0	1	2
College Graduate	0	0	0	0	0	0	2	0
Teacher Proficiency Certification	2	4	2	6	0	0	2	0
Teaching Entire Term on Permit or Holding No Certificate	2	0	0	1	12	65	47	4

Chapter 7

Teachers: Their Roles, Rules, and Restrictions

Warren A. Henke

By December of a new term many school patrons in a community most likely had decided whether their school board had "picked a lemon" or a "live-wire" to teach their children. Similarly, teachers had probably decided whether they were in a livable, friendly, and supportive district or whether they were "hopelessly buried." Likely, the decisions were made before everyone became truly acquainted. Some no doubt speculated if the board, in vying with other boards, had indeed secured the best schoolmarm. Others in the community surely wondered how proud their children would be when they said, "Lookit OUR teacher!"

Understandably, Robin M. Williams, Jr., in his interpretation of American society, concluded that:

> . . . teachers are often held to special standards of conformity and propriety; for there has been a close historic association between school and church in this country; and the latent social functions of the school are, in fact, similar in several respects to those of religious organizations. Willy-nilly the educator deals with values; he has exceptional opportunity to examine the unexamined axioms of the culture and interpret its crucial but vulnerable symbols. Since society is so largely equivalent to consensus, those who deal with values and beliefs as part of their occupational role—ministers, judges, writers, some artists, social scientists, teachers—touch upon the sensitive fringes of social order. In part for this reason, persons who deal with the beliefs and values that the community feels basic to its existence are the object of special surveillance and concern.[1]

Since education was not specifically delegated to the federal government by the United States Constitution, it fell among the powers reserved to the states. North Dakota's first legislature formalized its constitutional requirements for education. Administered by the State Department of Public Instruction, county superintendents, local school boards, and individual teachers, this layered administration of education in North Dakota decided what rules the teacher would have to follow, what role teachers would play in a community, and what "special standards of conformity and propriety," if any, would be applied to them. Over time, North Dakota developed a fairly elaborate set of "Duties of Teachers" that not only mirrored certain aspects of the local culture but also reflected a wider national one.

The state took responsibility to determine what the teacher taught, what the student learned, and what content, intended and unintended was given to its young citizens. Through its adopted curriculum of orthography, reading, spelling, writing, arithmetic, language lessons, English grammar, geography, United States history, civil

A Country School Teacher Remembers — G. C. Leno

I was a teacher for 43 years and all of my teaching experience was in North Dakota schools. There is very little in elementary, secondary, or higher education in which I did not come in direct contact. In retrospect, my most memorable experience was the three years that I taught in a one-room country school. Perhaps most memorable because it was my first experience in teaching and also perhaps because all of my first eight grades of school were also in a one-room rural school setting.

The teaching certificate that I received after attending a state teachers college for one year stated that I was qualified to teach in a rural school. However, in my own mind, I was not completely convinced that this was true, had it not been for my own experience as a student in a country school I would have been very skeptical indeed. During my three years of rural teaching, I do not know from what reservoir of knowledge I drew most; that which I learned at college, or what I recalled from my own earlier experience.

My first application for a teaching position was in 1935 in the midst of the Great Depression. Several schools were in need of teachers, but only those which were located in the most remote areas of Kidder County, or so it seemed. I applied to several of the schools and was hired by the North Merkel School District for a salary of $45 a month, over a seven month period along with the stipulation that, "said teacher keep reasonable hours." I assumed that this was in reference to my personal life. The warning was somewhat ludicrous since there was no opportunity to spend a "wild night" out unless it were with the jack rabbits. The nearest town was 12 miles distant, and I did not own an automobile.

I discovered later that the district was extremely poor, most of the residents were on welfare of one kind or another, and taxes were left unpaid. There were several instances when I was issued a warrant, which could only be cashed at a discounted rate. Banks found this practice to be a lucrative source of income, collecting on the full amount of the warrant when it became negotiable, as well as the interest on the delayed payment. At the time, I was grasping for straws for a firmer grip on the future and sacrifices of one kind or another seemed to be in order including an income, no matter how small it was. Back in the depression years, no amount of money was "small." In spite of a limited sal-

continued on next page

ary, I always paid my bills and had enough money remaining at the end of the year to attend an eight-week summer session at a state teachers college. Fortunately, my rural living expenses were small. I paid nine dollars a month for board and room and had no automobile to maintain.

My father came periodically to the school on Friday afternoon to take me home for the weekend, but in general, I stayed in the community weeks at a time especially after the weather made travel difficult. On occasions, I would catch a ride to one of the neighboring towns on a weekend, but only stayed briefly. When roads became impassable, I would solicit the help of the mailman who was kind enough to make small purchases and deliveries for me. I recall the winter of 1936 being an exceptionally hard winter plagued with deep snow, extremely cold weather and subsequently little travel. Even the mail had difficulty getting through. Delivery was made with a mail sled, comfortably enclosed and pulled by two horses. Since the end of the route was some distance from its origin, the mailman had a fresh team waiting for him for the return trip.

Prior to the beginning of the school year, I had made arrangements for room and board at a farm home not far from the school. Before I arrived for my work in my first year, I was informed that there would be a slight delay before I could occupy my room, and that temporary arrangements had been made for me to live with a neighboring family. I arrived at this other place at the appointed time and moved my personal belongings into the room. The farm couple was very gracious and it was evident that considerable preparation had been made for my coming. Most noticeable, was a perceptive odor that I noticed when I first entered my room. Later on in the evening, I saw the relationship between the odor and some little guests that also occupied the room. I was made aware of their presence when I lit the kerosene lamp that was on my bedside table. I observed an irregular pattern of spots on the wall paper that I had not noticed in the day time. I also observed that the spots rearranged themselves and upon closer observation, surmised that they were bedbugs. Bedbugs were not uncommon in those days and so this did not come as a complete surprise. The strong medicinal odor that I perceived when I first entered the room came from a bedbug repellent that had been liberally sprinkled about the bed and bed frame. Apparently it worked because I was never bitten by the insects. It was none too soon, when I was informed that my permanent quarters were ready for occupancy.

continued on next page

government, physiology and hygiene, the teacher gave students a common set of ideas, beliefs, values, and skills.[2]

To make sure the state's educational mission was carried out in the best possible manner the Department of Public Instruction told teachers that "the people of the neighborhood will watch with interest the 'new teacher.'"[3] Making a good impression was possible if teachers heeded many of its suggestions. They were asked to consider their arrival time in the community before the beginning of the term. Should they arrive Friday afternoon, Saturday afternoon, Sunday afternoon or Monday morning? They were also reminded of the many things to do before school started on Monday morning: find a boarding place, unpack, know the name of the school clerk and the president of the board, and become acquainted with several families. Besides that, the schoolmarm or schoolmaster should visit the school house, study the previous year's register, become familiar with the pupils' names, arrange the teacher's desk, and have the room aired and dusted. Teachers were also asked to think about: "What place does 'opening of school' have in the life of a child?" A successful opening day also included having made a tentative program. When the opening day finally arrived the department suggested teachers "greet each child with a smile," know their names, and "know what to talk about when all are in their seats."[4]

To be able to do that, efficiently and well, one of the more important responsibilities of the teacher was becoming familiar with the state *Course of Study*. Developed by the State Department of Instruction, it was a fairly detailed outline of each subject studied, month by month, for grades one to eight. Included were suggestions for teachers, workable devices they could use in the classroom, and books they were urged to master. It also contained guides for nature study and physical education and selections for memorization. To many, it became the "Bible."

The state's curriculum reflected the national culture, but the inclusion of health studies mirrored local concerns about the use and abuse of alcohol, stimulants, and narcotics. Prohibition, a thorn in the side of the body politic for years, was approved by North Dakota voters in 1889 by a narrow margin—18,552 to 17,393. Shaky as the victory was prohibitionists made sure their kind of morality, teaching "scientific temperance," became part of the curriculum. As early as 1890 teachers were directed to give

> . . . special instruction concerning the nature of alcoholic drinks, stimulants, and narcotics and their effect upon the human system, physiology and hygiene. . . . their effect upon the human system shall be taught as thoroughly as any branch is taught, by the use of a textbook, to all pupils able to use a textbook. . . , orally to all other pupils. . . . , a sufficient time, not less than fifteen minutes shall be given to such oral instruction for at least four days in each school week.[5]

The lower three primary grades were also instructed orally in hygiene, at least three lessons per week for ten weeks in each school year.[6] Prudent teachers complied with the law. Those who disregarded it could lose their jobs; their teaching certificate could be revoked for failing to give this instruction.[7]

Some patrons and county superintendents were watchful. State Superintendent of Public Instruction Emma Bates noted in her biennial report that "there are some, but not many, exceptions to compliance with the provisions of this law in the letter. The spirit of the law is not always fulfilled as it might be."[8] She believed, however, that teachers did their best. Classroom instruction, she said, should aim at teaching students "to refrain from all injurious habits. Next, having the right desire he must have the properly disciplined will-power to execute his desires."[9] At least one teacher, Signe Hanson, took that sort of suggestion very seriously. Teaching in a one-room school in the Red River Valley she had all her students sign the pledge to never "smoke or drink," having organized it into a Temperance Union.[10]

Anti-liquor forces persuaded the 1917 legislature to designate a special day to promote their cause. On Temperance Day, the 3rd Friday in January of each year, teachers had to set aside at least one hour for instruction and "appropriate exercises" pertaining to the history and benefits of prohibition and the prohibition laws of North Dakota.[11] Although North Dakotans legalized the manufacture and sale of beer in 1933 and legalized the sale of liquor in 1936, the law establishing Temperance Day remained part of the code for many decades. It was repealed in 1993.[12]

Uppermost in my mind was the beginning of school and my need to make preparation for it. I went through the past year's enrollment in order to determine the number of children I could expect, the number that would be in the various grades, as well as the specific classes and grades for which I had to prepare. After making this determination, I sorted out the different textbooks that I would need for each of the grades. I soon discovered that textbooks, teaching supplies, and related teaching equipment was at bare minimum and the district had very little money to make new purchases. Library books for recreational reading were almost non-existent. I recalled my rural school experience and remembered that the teacher had periodically obtained books from the state librarian. I investigated the source and followed the same procedure. Children and adults made generous use of this new source of recreational reading.

The first day of school finally arrived! I awoke early that morning after having spent a restless night in anticipation of what was to come. I ate breakfast while my lunch bucket was being packed, and left for school. While I was walking, I thought of every possible bit of preparation that I may have overlooked. I had memorized

continued on next page

Sennev Nertrost Whipple, County Superintendent, Wells County, 1914-1920
(Martha P. Tatem Collection, SHSND)

the names of the children and tried to picture who they were and what they looked like. When I arrived at the school, I built a fire to take the chill off the classroom, put up the flag, and went over my day's routine. I would frequently gaze out of the window to see if anyone was coming, although it was much too early, then continued with my preparations. Finally, after what seemed to be a long time, I saw a group of youngsters walking towards the school. From their antics it did not appear that they were very much concerned about the start of school.

Much of my concern and worry on the first day of school was groundless. Following a period of getting acquainted, the boys and girls who were my students, also became my little friends. A trusting form of relationship developed, a bond of confidence that remained throughout the years that I was their teacher. I was now their TEACHER, and that is what they called me.

My classes were small but still needed my full attention. During scheduled periods throughout the day, I would call each class to the recitation bench located in front of the room and near the blackboard. The children brought their books, seatwork and related materials with them. I would provide supplementary materials such as maps, globe, use of the blackboard or whatever other materials would enhance the instruction. The blackboard was especially useful for spelling or arithmetic exercises because the teacher could detect learning difficulties that might exist among the students. (In contrast to today's classrooms, there was no electronic equipment available, not even a duplicating machine.)

On Friday afternoon, starting at 2 o'clock, the class routine was changed. Until dismissal time, this period was used by the children to engage in self-directed creative experiences. If a holiday was approaching, it was used to prepare a program for it. Other than that, the children could plan their own projects. These may have included water color painting, the use of construction paper for original designs, and several other projects of one kind or another. Several boys brought coping saws and apple box sides. The boards were used to cut out a variety of gifts and toys. Also high on the list was to make relief maps of continents using old newspapers soaked in water. After the maps dried, different colors were applied to denote the different elevations.

The school, by tradition, was expected to prepare a Christmas program. It centered around Biblical stories and the students portrayed the characters in the different events. The songs, in general, were also of a religious nature. At that

continued on next page

The uppermost layer of educational administration in North Dakota always promoted patriotism. In her biennial report to the governor Emma Bates declared that it was gratifying "to see the flag, loved at home and honored abroad, floating from the rural school house." She insisted that because of North Dakota's large proportion of foreign residents that it was "eminently proper to keep, as an object lesson, the emblem of our national honor, of our national sacrifices, of the blood and money spent for national preservation, before the eyes of the children and future citizens of our beloved commonwealth." She urged all teachers, if feasible, to celebrate Memorial Day each year with appropriate exercises.[13]

If one duty of the teacher was to promote "scientific temperance" in the local community, another was to teach and advocate patriotism. As Dan Rylance notes:

> All readers emphasized the positive features of American government and the individual contributions of American presidents. Special days were set aside to honor Washington and Lincoln. Teachers and students fondly remember these as important events in the yearly cycle of activities. Criticism of the role of government or negative personal aspects of American leaders were not part of the educational process. The American government and its leaders like the parents of the school children must always be treated with respect and trusted. Helen Barrett who taught in Stutsman County and served for many years as deputy county superintendent of schools recalled 'for the one room school, almost a page of ancient history, I have a warm feeling.' It was there that "patriotism and the golden rule were taught."[14]

Issuing a circular to all schools in 1906 the State Department of Public Instruction urged them to celebrate the bicentennial anniversary of Benjamin Franklin's birth. That day "should not pass" the circular declared, "without some recognition from the schools of this state, of the services rendered this nation at a time when it tried men's souls to be patriotic."[15] Some two decades later, in 1929, the legislature deemed it appropriate to begin teaching the United States Constitution in all public and private schools, beginning not later than the eighth grade.[16]

Country school teachers also found themselves preparing particular materials and programs for other special days which broke their daily routine: Parents Day, Good Citizenship Day, Lafayette Day (October 19, 1898), John Marshall Day (February 4, 1901), Illiteracy Day (November 20, 1924), Flag Day (June 14), Bird Day, Play Day, and Arbor Day.

Seeing a need to improve playground equipment for rural schools, Mary Beatrice Johnstone, who taught in a one-room country school as early as 1885 and became Grand Forks County superintendent of schools in 1913, developed the County Play Day Movement. Designed as community get-togethers held at the close of the school year they were organized on the principle that participants play *with* each other instead of *against* each other. The occasion was meant to promote widespread participation, not to determine interschool or individual championships where only the best competed. The Department of Public Instruction believed that "EVERY child in school should have an active part in the PLAY DAY PROGRAM." It thought Play Day should permit mass participation in: mimetic exercises and story plays, rhythmic exercises and singing games, competitive games, stunts and contests, posture parades in which all students participated, athletic games, and individual athletic events.[17]

Intended for the planting of trees to foster interest in the preservation of forests Arbor Day was first observed in Nebraska in 1872. First observed in Dakota Territory in 1884, North Dakota governors issued annually an Arbor Day Proclamation. Public schools organized special events. The suggested program for 1892 opened with selections about trees taken from the Scripture, followed by prayer and song. Declamations, remarks by visitors, and a short address were recommended and school children were asked to vote for a favorite flower. Activities on the school ground focused on tree planting. In 1891 Arbor

time no one thought that Christmas could be celebrated in any other way. Following the program, gifts were exchanged and everyone in attendance spent the evening in neighborly conversation over a cup of coffee and lunch provided by the families.

Needless to say, spring never came too soon. Balmy southern winds melted the snow, and roads became once again passable. Spirits among young and old rose and everyone was looking forward to the end of the school term. However, eighth graders had one more hurdle to complete before the school year ended for them. In those days, the state required that eighth graders must successfully complete state examinations in certain subject areas. The tests were prepared by the State Department of Education and administered by the local teacher. Most rural schools ended their school year several weeks before the scheduled examinations were to be given, therefore students had a waiting period during which time they could prepare for the finals. In addition to having his textbooks available for review, the teacher would also provide him with copies of previous tests on the same subjects. Although the exact subject matter was likely to be duplicated in the new tests, it did give the student a sense of performance that was helpful when he took the final tests. Students usually "made" it and all was well. In general the public concept was that children trained in rural school did as well, or better in high school, as their city counterparts.

In retrospect, my rural teaching was a character and professional building experience. It provided me with the opportunity to see myself as a teacher and as a person, working and living in close harmony with the community. Under no circumstances would the reality of this relationship have been as evident as in this little country school.

What happened to the one-room rural school is the same that happens to all man-made institutions. Once they have served their purpose, they gradually fade away. However, they remain as part of our great heritage!

✍✍

Day was observed by 274 schools. Pupils planted 1,703 trees and cast 2,478 votes for the Wild Prairie Rose as the state flower. Its nearest rival was the Lily with 487 votes. To many early educators Arbor Day meant more than just planting trees. They believed that: "Next to familiarity with great books, an acquaintance thus formed with nature will tend most to the development of a refined and noble character." During the early decades Arbor Day was one of the more significant, special days in the school year.[18]

A Country School Teacher Remembers — Grace Brittner

My teacher training began in the fall of 1932 at Dickinson Normal School. [Dickinson State University] It was a difficult time for farmers, and I could never have gone to school had it not been for the National Youth Administration, a federal government program that provided work for needy students. I was allowed 40 hours of work per month for which I received $10. I washed dishes in South Hall, morning and night, and on Saturdays I mopped and waxed what seemed like miles of halls, cleaned bathrooms, and cleaned the rooms of the housemother and the dean of women. We were allowed to go home one weekend a month if we had completed the allotted number of work hours. This was not always possible. Neither was it easy to find a ride. It was much too expensive for my folks to make the trip very often.

Life was difficult with money so very scarce. I lived at Stickney Hall, the light housekeeping dormitory. For food, I depended mostly on the supply I brought from home, potatoes, home-canned meat and vegetables, beans and bread. This was quite satisfactory if I could get home once a month to replenish my supply; however, I was so hungry for a wider variety, I hardly dared to go into a grocery store when my friends went shopping. I remember one time I weakened and bought a package of six cinnamon rolls that cost

continued on next page

Floyd Henderson, Teacher, Melby School, 6 miles SE of Dunn Center (*SHSND*)

While teaching, perhaps as many as forty-five classes per day or preparing for a special day, teachers were also obligated to master and keep the *Teacher's Register*, certainly one of the more burdensome tasks of country school teachers. Along with the *Course of Study*, it provided an almost minute by minute account of a school's daily plan, for what should happen and of what actually took place in that school on a given day. It contained the teacher's daily program, monthly review records, final examination records and student classification, a visitor's log, a record of visits by the county superintendent, and an extremely detailed account of student attendance and punctuality. The attention paid to the latter reflected a national pride, as expressed in Horatio Alger novels with their many references to the virtue of employees showing up every day on time.

To keep the *Register* satisfactorily, the teacher had to "master" the following set of instructions:

In marking attendance place month and day of month over appropriate columns. Opposite "a.m." and "p.m." record the attendance and tardiness of each half day respectively. Enter E in proper place to designate when pupil entered school and L to designate the time when pupil left school. If pupil is present at roll call, leave the space blank. If absent, draw a vertical slanting line (/). If pupil is tardy and enters after rollcall, draw a horizontal line across top of vertical or slanting line. T to represent tardy.

If a pupil is absent for five or more consecutive days, he should be marked L (left) on the day on which the absence began and E (Entered) on the day on which he returns. Draw a horizontal line (-) through all the spaces from the beginning of a term of school until a pupil enters school and from the time of leaving school until re-entering, or until the close of the term, as the case may be. These days so marked by a horizontal line are designated "days of non-membership." The days marked by the vertical lines are designated "days of absence," and the days left blank are designated "days present" or "days of attendance." All totals should be carried out in "Summary." The formula given at foot of Attendance page furnishes all information needed in making up "Summary." If a term should exceed four months, enter pupils' names on every other or on every third page.[19]

Puzzling out the directions and becoming adept at keeping the *Register* was a daily and necessary chore. It was the basis for an acceptable *Teacher's Final Report* that had to be submitted at the end of the term, under the threat of forfeiting their last month's wages if they failed to do so.[20]

Country school teachers were subject to many other rules and regulations. They had to give notice to the county superintendent of the time and place of the opening of school, had to hold a valid certificate or permit or forfeit wages, and had to display the flag on the school house in seasonable weather. Teachers were given the right, if notices were sent to parents or guardians and some member of the school board, to suspend pupils for as long as five days for insubordination, habitual disobedience, or disorderly conduct.[21] Revocation of their teaching certificate could result because of incompetence, immorality, intemperance, cruelty, crime, breach of contract, refusal to perform duties, or general neglect of the business of the school.[22]

Although most of the duties of country school teachers were explained by state law, their status and relationship to the larger community were affected by other factors. Teachers' salaries were never more than adequate in North Dakota; their wage and salary levels were always low compared to other professions. Teaching was ordinarily a female occupation in the state; in 1894 they constituted 66 percent of the work force; 84 percent in 1915; 78 percent in 1936; and 73 percent in 1952. Generally, women teachers received lower salaries than men. The extent of the difference was often determined by the attitude of the ethnic community in which teachers worked. Logan County, settled mainly by German-Russians, paid its male teachers an average of $36.58 per month in 1894; Grand Forks County, settled mainly by Norwegians, paid its male teachers an average of $45 per month. Female teachers received less; $32.98 per month in Logan County and $39.50 per month in Grand Forks County.

10 cents. I'm sure I enjoyed them although I felt very guilty about spending a dime for them.

I remember especially one time when I had not been home for over a month, and money was unusually short because I had been required to buy a book for a class. My food supply had dwindled to almost nothing, and my money was gone. After pondering my dilemma, and going rather hungry for a few days, I decided I'd have to tell my parents and see if they could help me, as there was always plenty of food at home.

They began planning when my letter arrived. All the money they could "scare up" to send was $2, and they knew that wouldn't go far in buying for the rest of the month. They decided it would be best to use the money for gas, and take food to me, so they all went to work. I'm sure Mother, at least, must have worked far into the night. At daylight the next morning, there were no lights on the car, Dad started out with the precious cargo. When the dormitory was unlocked, the housemother told me I had a caller. There was my dad, laden with boxes and wearing a big smile. The first box I opened contained food that was ready to eat, fresh bread, big molasses cookies, fried chicken, baked beans and squash. Never had food tasted so good! The other boxes contained foods to supply my locker, and the box in the cold storeroom.

I hope I thanked my dad properly, he had made a long cold 50 mile trip in an unheated car. I think perhaps my eagerness to get at the food eliminated much chance for conversation. Men were not allowed in the dormitory, except for the lounge, so he didn't even have a chance to see me unpack my boxes. However, I'm sure a letter of love and gratitude must have gone out in the next mail.

Salary inequalities because of location and gender continued over time. The farm depression of the 1920s was followed by the Great Depression of the 1930s, which was deep, devastating, and disheartening for thousands of North Dakotans. After the drought of 1934 New Deal programs continued to provide some kind of security to the one-third to one-half of the state's people who were on relief. School districts struggled to keep schools open; in 1934-1935 some 592 schools were unused. Practically all were one-room schools; most closed because of insufficient enrollment.[23] Average monthly salaries of teachers plummeted. A federal survey of nine counties revealed the following percentages of decrease: Sheridan, 47; Mountrail, 44; Slope, 42; Logan, 42; Mercer, 40; Sargent, 36; Grand Forks, 35; Griggs, 29; and Bottineau, 22.[24]

In 1936, Logan County paid male teachers an average of $64.12 per month and female teachers $49.09. Grand Forks County paid males $143.22 per month and females $91.92 per month. In 1952 Grand Forks County ranked second in average salary paid teachers and Logan County last. The statistics reflect accurately economic conditions: while both counties lowered salaries during the Great Depression, Logan County was much harder hit than Grand Forks County in the Red River Valley where some rains came.

Opperud School, Williams County, about 1903-1913 (*Martha P. Tatem Collection, SHSND*)

During the period teachers did their part to keep schools open. By accepting low salaries and warrants—promises by school boards to pay a stated amount when money became available — teachers indirectly subsidized education in North Dakota. In many cases, teachers were forced, in order to live, to sell their warrants for as little as ninety cents or less on the dollar. If one could "hold on," warrants were redeemed eventually for face value. Many, if not most of the school districts, issued warrants during those bleak and jobless days. However, one survey of rural education in North Dakota during the depression concluded that "while teachers' salaries and other expenses have been drastically reduced, there is no indication of board members foregoing their regular stipends."[25]

As early as 1921 one district in southwest North Dakota paid by warrant. Agreeing to "stand all discounts on warrants issued on this contract" Mrs. James Ruggles taught Heisler School in Alred School District No. 2 in McKenzie County in that year. Teaching School No. 3, Plainview School District No. 31, in Benson County in the northcentral region, Ruth Jacobson in 1933 agreed: "to hold some of her warrants for a reasonable time if lack of funds make it necessary to require it." In the southeast the financial situation was no better. Two years later Irene Anderson and the Kennison School District in LaMoure County signed a contract agreeing that "in case school funds are depleted she agrees to wait for salary to accept certificate of Indebtedness." Northcentral districts were also issuing warrants. The same year World War II broke out in Europe, Clara Haakenstad who was teaching in Eidsvold School District No. 7 in Bottineau County agreed "to accept registered warrants if the district is unable to provide the cash." Districts in the state's northwest corner were also suffering from lack of funds. Teaching School No. 13 in Lexington School District No.13, Divide County, in 1940 for $100 per month, J. H. Gohrick agreed that he would "take [his] own discount on warrant."[26] School boards in the southwest section used different ways to pay their teachers. Short of cash in 1940 the school board of Solon School District No. 8 in Hettinger County could pay Allyne Anderson only half her salary, $60 per month, in cash and the other half in registered warrants.[27] Sometimes districts had to combine resources to meet their payroll. Moline School District No. 27 in McKenzie County joined with Alred School District to pay Hazel Thompson Burns $45 per month for an eight-month term in 1934. The former paid $9, the latter $36.[28]

Teachers had little job security during the 1930s. Signing a contract for $45 for an eight-month term to teach School No. 3 in Clark School District No. 22 in Hettinger County in 1933, Amanda Schmidt agreed that the "School Board or Teacher may close school by giving a ten (10) day notice." Four years later she agreed to teach School No. 4 in E Six School District No. 10 in Slope County for a similar term for $60 per month. Her stay, however, was uncertain. The board had included the following provision in her contract: "School board can close or discontinue any school at will."[29] The Tepee Butte School District in Hettinger County hired Frank Schieber to teach School No. 1 for an eight-month term for $55 per month in the fall of 1933. He had to do the janitor work and agreed to the following contract language: "Contract to run one month at a time. If District runs out of funds, Board may close school at any time unless a satisfactory agreement can be made with the teacher to hold school warrants until uncollected taxes are paid."[30]

Teachers often had to wait for part of their salary even if money was available. Some boards were reluctant to pay the teacher the full monthly contracted salary until they were satisfied the teacher would "work out." Teaching School No. 3, Krossna School District No. 39 in Emmons County in 1932 for $65 per month, Julia Romany-shyn agreed to receive $55 the first two months, $65 the next three, and $75 the last two. Grace Sheppard instructed youngsters in McIntosh County in 1934 for $45 per month. Her contract "further provided" that "the clerk shall retain 10% of the salary until mutual termination or expiration of this contract." Bernice Whitney who taught for $55 per month in 1937 in Stutsman County accepted a similar provision in her contract: "10% of teachers wages will be retained to be paid when teacher has completed her term." Sometimes school boards insisted on an economic "hold" on instructors to assure their returning the next term. Teaching a nine-month term in Nelson School District in McLean County in 1920 for $125 per month Leonard Cox agreed: "Salary to

A Country School Teacher Remembers — Gertrude C. Berg

I chose teaching because I could attend school and work at the same time. I paid my own way. There was a great deal of playing school in our home. I finally realized that was how my mother learned English. A high school education qualified one to teach in the 1920s. One could get a Second Grade Elementary Certificate. The highest degree I was granted was a Bachelor of Arts; I had half my time in for a Masters in Library Science.

I was nineteen years old when I began teaching. I graduated from Litchville High School in May 1923 and that fall I began teaching my first school, Ransom County Bear Creek No. 4, which was in my family's home district. I boarded at home. My father was president of the schoolboard and he purchased anthracite coal for the school. This kept a fire overnight. I made a new fire on Monday mornings.

I walked two miles to and from school. In the winter I wore leggings that had been knitted by my mother. They came up to my hips. I wore my brother's sheepskin coat and mittens that were made from horse hide. Inside these I had home knitted mittens. I never felt better. The walking was good therapy. Our lunches that were packed in syrup or lard pails often froze, however, and we had to set them near the stove to thaw.

My first day of teaching was a very quiet one. It was more or less a tutoring affair. Only three girls came; they were sisters in grades one through three. Later four big boys entered and another boy who was too ill to attend very often also enrolled.

On sunny days, during the noon hour, the big boys would sit on the south side of the schoolhouse. That was the wall next to which stood the jacketed coal stove. There was a vent in the wall and I could always hear what the boys were saying. One day one boy said, "Let's have some fun harassing the teacher this afternoon." Another answered, "If you do I'm going to clean up on you."

One autumn day we went on a field trip along a creek near by. We left at noon after eating our lunches. When we returned, it was about 2:00 p.m., the county superintendent was there. He was rather disturbed because I was not "keeping school."

At the Wild Rose School in Burleigh County during the 1925 school term the schoolboard furnished canned goods for days when there were blizzards and we could open one can each

continued on next page

day for hot lunch. There was a kerosene stove and lamps at this school and we may have had one of the first hot lunch programs in the state. We brought our own lunches to go with the hot dish.

I didn't get to town during this eight-month school term. If I wanted to purchase anything, I'd send money with the mailman who would purchase what I needed.

The family I boarded with was nice to me. They subscribed to several magazines that I had the pleasure of reading. They had a stone house that was warm, but there was no indoor plumbing. I cut my own hair which was bobbed and straight.

There was one major social event in the community during this school term. A dance was held at a neighbor's farm, about five miles away. I rode to the dance with a peddler who had a wagon drawn by mules. I don't recall how I got back. I did stay overnight with the other teacher in the district.

I stayed in private homes while teaching rural schools. I received board, room, and laundry for a reasonable price. The food was plain, but tasty. There was home-made bread, but few vegetables and fruits. There was an apple, orange, or sauce in my lunch bucket besides sandwiches, cookies, or cake. I did not share my room except during my third year when the daughter came home weekends. I enjoyed her. I made my own bed and wiped dishes. This was not required.

When I taught the Kinservik School in LaMoure County I stayed with a poor family. The upstairs of their house was not heated; consequently, at school I would melt snow or save water that I had brought and after 4:00 p.m. I would lock the door, draw the shades, and take a bath whenever that was needed.

The main event at that school during the school year was a school program and a basket social. The money that was raised was spent for library books.

Country school teaching was not really a "lonely" life for me. It was my usual life. At the places I stayed at I became one of the family and we were happy. Dates were few. In my second year of teaching a daughter and two sons who worked at road construction stayed home during the winter. The four of us went to some dances.

Weather was not a special problem in my rural teaching. If there was a blizzard, we just stayed home. In my third year of teaching in western North Dakota I was told to stay in the schoolhouse during a blizzard or a prairie fire

continued on next page

be paid on 12-month basis. 10th and 11th month pay to be given with the ninth, reserving 12th until teacher returns in the fall."[31]

Attending a County Institute, usually for one week, was one of the contractual obligations of the country school teacher, and perhaps one of the more enjoyable. Schools closed and the board paid his or her regular wages; nonattendance, however, meant forfeiture of pay. Isolated for periods of time in the desolate bleakness of North Dakota's winters, possibly boarding at a place which furnished her with an unheated room, having few opportunities to confer easily with fellow teachers or seek advice from superiors, and sometimes not being able to converse with patrons, many teachers valued the Institute as an opportunity "to get out." It provided inspiration, an opportunity to socialize, and a chance to get practical, tangible helps, examples, and suggestions that could be brought back to their school. Institutes were important for other reasons. Communities holding one could both demonstrate their hospitality and benefit economically by providing room and board for the attendants; most county seats and other towns did not have sufficient hotel rooms to accommodate the teaching force of a county for a week. Furthermore, commercial clubs or businessmens' groups might impress the visitors of the community's generosity by organizing sightseeing trips to points of natural or historic interest, thereby strengthening the teachers' understanding of the state's geography.

Teachers' Institutes had their roots in territorial history. Recognizing a need to improve teachers' skills the Dakota Territory Board of Education spent $600 each year, in the several years before territorial division, employing persons of "learning, ability, skill and experience" to conduct them. The cost of two-week institutes was limited to $60; regular institutes were five-day affairs.[32]

Younger and less experienced teachers needed additional training in such subjects as reading, orthography, arithmetic, geography, and grammar. Professional educators thought the institute a necessity even where opportunities existed for training teachers in normal schools and colleges. What the County Institute did was to bring educators from those kinds of institutions, along with county superintendents, local school administrators, and personnel from the state department of education, together with classroom teachers, for comparing notes, exchanging views, and learning new methods.

Focusing on "Form Lessons And Geography, Number Lessons and Arithmetic, and Language Lessons and Reading," the 1892 institutes, for example, devoted about an hour each day to the subject matter under consideration. Time was also spent on opening exercises, subject matter drills, group singing, discussions by teachers, and lectures by the Conductor of the institute.[33] Conductors gave at least one evening lecture at each institute; county superintendents scheduled additional evening lectures if funds were available, allowing one evening of the week for a social gathering where teachers and townspeople mingled. State Lecturers, John H. Worst, who later became president of the Agricultural College (North Dakota State University) and Joseph M. Devine, who became state Commissioner of Immigration in 1923, addressed both teachers and citizens during institute week on the subject of patriotism and citizenship. Thirty-nine separate institutes were held that year, mostly in May and June. The state institute fund paid Conductors $5 per day; the county institute fund paid $25 for institute expenses.[34]

Louise and Mary Gutherie returning to Stady after attending Teacher's Institute in Williston, June 1910 (*Martha P. Tatem Collection, SHSND*)

During her two-year tenure, 1895-1896, State Superintendent of Public Instruction Emma F. Bates traveled by rail and stage 26,993 miles, visited 67 institutes held in 34 different counties, and gave from 1 to 6 lessons at each institute in an effort to improve the educational climate of North Dakota.[35] Asked to critique the 1895 institutes, teachers told Bates they valued them but wanted more specific work, in fewer subjects, at future sessions. In particular, they wanted to focus on English. In response, the state superintendent outlined the work for the 1896 institute, giving four periods of the six, in each day of institute, to work in English on John Greenleaf Whittier's *Snow Bound*. Teachers who attended that institute focused on reading, critical analysis, grammatical construction, and oral and written reproduction of the poem, section by section.[36]

Response to studying *Snow Bound* was mixed. At the institute held in Bismarck in April 1896, Conductor William Moore found that, because of previous training, some teachers "accomplished much" of what the state superintendent intended. Others, however, "on account of deficient

and to keep the children there. Language was not a problem for me. I could speak Norwegian and in my second year of teaching made use of the language.

I did janitor work at all the rural schools I taught in and it was also understood that if I married I would resign my position. No school board member ever visited my schools. The county superintendent visited once a year, but in my third year of teaching that person failed to do so. I left each school on my own; I think I was expected to ask to return if I so desired.

I don't think there was anything wrong with the country school system. It served the "times." It provided a "good" education for what was needed at the time. Students had to really study. Sixty-five percent was passing in state exams and I made it my task to encourage the students to want to pass those final exams. I was from a rural school and I held my own in high school and kept a good average. Although I worked for my board and room, I took part in more activities than most.

I'll always remember Johnny who didn't start school until late one September because there was plowing to do. My landlady told me that Johnny was a terror. Many teachers had left the

continued on next page

117

district because of Johnny. One morning I saw him coming over a hill. The sun shone on his red hair. When he came closer the freckles stood out loud and clear. Johnny saw a gopher and gave chase. It disappeared into a hole and Johnny was down on his knees hoping it would come up. There was a well under the schoolhouse and a pump in the entry. Fortunately, I had trapped gophers in my youth. I pumped a pail of water, ran out, and poured the water into the gopher hole. Up came the gopher and Johnny caught it in his hands. He looked up at me. I got a beautiful smile. We were friends all year.

educational qualifications, accomplished little." At the Cavalier County Institute at Langdon in June, Conductor W. E. Johnson discovered that teachers "showed a lack of study and reading in this line and an inability to appreciate such literature." Nevertheless, by the end of the institute they "were very much interested...and seemed to get a great deal of good out of its study." Johnson reported that the teachers attending the Ramsey County Institute were "very much interested," but he thought shorter selections would be better. After studying Whittier's poem at the Cando institute he concluded it "most practical because it directly affects the teacher herself, not merely her intellect, and we teach what we are, after all." Rolette County teachers, according to Conductor J. E. McCartney, were "very enthusiastic in this work." Many Conductors failed to report their institute's reaction to *Snow Bound* but commented on other aspects. Of the twenty-two teachers at the New Rockford institute, H. W. McArdle observed "a lack of thorough preparation on the part of a few," but "the interest, professional spirit, and enthusiasm," of the group "was good." Commenting on the virtues of the thirty-four teachers attending the institute at Cooperstown, he said, "So far as I could judge from observation and association, the moral influences of these teachers would be good, with the exception of one or two cigarette smokers." Local citizens, he said, did not attend the institute generally.[37]

Although the superintendent realized that not much academic advancement could be expected in five days she believed that the time spent in institute and the value received was commensurate with the expenditure made.[38]

The institute played a major role in the most effective campaign to improve rural schools to date. In 1917, Neil C. Macdonald, the leading crusader for school improvement and consolidation, organized "Better Rural School Rallies" in every county of the state. The mass meetings consisted of a week's institute for rural teachers, followed by a one-day exchange of views for school board members. Over 6,000 teachers and a like number of school board members attended the rallies; Governor Lynn J. Frazier, who had taught rural school, spoke at 22 of them.[39]

Attendance figures indicate the importance teachers attached to the County Institute and provide insight into the make-up of the teacher corps. Of the 8,057 teaching positions in North Dakota in 1920, 5,200 or 65 percent of the teachers who filled them attended institutes in 1920. Of the 5,200 enrolled, 92 percent were women, 8 percent were men. Of that number 3,643 or 70 percent were one-room rural school teachers; 9 percent completed the eighth grade; 58 percent completed high school; 17 percent were elementary normal school graduates; 9 percent were advanced normal school graduates; 2 percent were college graduates; 13 percent were teaching on permits only; and 2 percent had taught without certificates.[40]

Bertha R. Palmer, superintendent of public instruction from 1927 to 1932, brought the "round-up" type of institute—which required the presence of all teachers at the same course regardless of their previous training, experience, interests or needs—to an end. In the fall of 1927 she changed the program, completely reversing the procedure for Teachers' Institutes. Demonstration teachers were brought into a county for five days. The new program of demonstration-conferences was planned especially for teachers in the rural schools. By this time twelve weeks' attendance at normal school after graduation from high school was required for the lowest grade certificate. More than half of the teachers in the state worked in rural schools and only one of the five teacher training schools prepared teachers to understand and handle the conditions peculiar to the one-two-and three-teacher schools. Palmer thought the new system would fulfill the need for specific, practical, and concrete help with problems met with every day by "twelve week" teachers. Under the new program county superintendents arranged for a visiting or demonstration teacher to meet with small groups gathered in one-room schools. Morning classes were taught by the demonstrator, assisted by one or two local teachers, chosen by the county superintendent for their expertise. After the noon-day lunch students were dismissed and the morning classes were discussed and analyzed in terms of methods and procedures. Daily programs were examined, remedial measures were considered, and helpful books and materials were recommended during the afternoon conference.[41]

The program's first year was gratifying: eleven demonstration teachers visited 340 schools, held 188 conferences, and met with 4,639 teachers. Forty-six county superintendents responded favorably to the new program; three thought otherwise. Teachers, too, supported the new program. Of 614 teachers who responded to a call in 23 select counties to critique the new plan, 597 were favorable, 300 of whom declared they received more and better help than from any other sources of training previously experienced. Furthermore, Palmer calculated the cost and concluded that the new program was economically beneficial for all concerned. One-day teacher conferences rather than five-day institutes saved each community four school days per teacher, or about $92,780. Not attending a five-day institute saved teachers $69,585; they did not have to spend $15 for board and room. The county, too, was better off. In 1925 the average cost per county for an institute was $108.45; under the new plan the average per county was $63.81. Even the state department benefited. From 1922 to 1925 it spent each year $5,300 for institute Conductors, instructors, and for summer school lecturers. In 1927 it spent $4,464.82, including pay for all summer school lecturers.[42]

For many years the institute and the demonstration-conference were the most important and practical ways for teachers to up-grade their skills. Most teachers, eager to get advanced training, were unable to leave work to attend school during the time rural schools were in session. Many could and would, however, attend a short term of from four to six weeks in midsummer when the rural schools had a harvest vacation. Summer sessions were held at the University of North Dakota in the early 1890s. Eventually, all of the state's institutions of higher learning would offer summer courses; for the most part they replaced the Teachers' Institute and the demonstration-conference. Teachers attending those early summer sessions, "in unexpectedly large numbers," considered them "profitable and helpful."[43]

Going to Teacher's Institute in 1915-16 from Hague to Linton — Charlotte Borchert (middle), Nell Johnson (right), unidentified (left) *(NDIRS)*

A Country School Teacher Remembers — O. Emma Blumhagen

In the fall of 1923 I received a wire with this offer. There was a rural school in Mountrail County, North Dakota that needed a teacher. The position would pay $90 a month for a seven month term. I was to meet the county superintendent in the train depot in Minot. I was leery about going to Minot, yet I accepted the offer. I arrived at the Minot depot, but no one was there to meet me. The depot seemed very large and scary to me. I walked around the station and saw a small showcase with jewelry in it. What a temptation, I thought. However, I walked away from it and sat down on a bench where I could watch the door. It was in an area where I could see the showcase, too. Soon a young lady appeared on the scene near the showcase. Shortly thereafter I saw a man approach her and say to her, "I'll trouble you for the ring you took." I assumed he was a police officer or a detective. She said to him, "What ring?" He reached into her pocket and took out the ring. It also crossed my mind she may have been working there.

After a time I was met by County Superintendent Larson who came up to me and told me who she was. She took me with her to her home in Mountrail County. I met her folks and was cordially welcomed. The following day she took me to her Uncle Hans Larson's home that was very close. It was here I boarded and roomed for the school year. He was a member of the school board. My room was satisfactory; I had a kerosene lamp, a wash bowl, a pitcher, and other necessities.

I was somewhat afraid when it came to signing my contract because he tried to lower the wage. I told him the amount in the wire was $90 a month; I also showed my first grade elementary certificate from Valley City State College. I compromised and signed for $85 a month. Someone in the community suggested to me and the other teacher who taught in another school that we put our applications in for the consolidated school in the area. I didn't. I knew I did not wish to return another year; I wanted to go on to school.

The first thing I did was to go over to my school to get organized for the opening day. It was a beautiful autumn day and it was only a short walk. When I arrived at the schoolhouse I inspected the windows and decided how I was to ventilate the room and arrange it to take advantage of the lighting. After examining the jacketed stove I decided I was capable of operating it satisfactorily during the winter months. I also

continued on next page

Almost all the wisdom of the world is in books. Realizing that no one could ever read all the good books that had been written, Superintendent of Public Instruction William J. Clapp in October 1890 thought it timely to organize a State Teachers' Reading Circle. Several sections of the state had established county circles and others were demanding the formation of a state circle. He was willing to assume immediate responsibility for prescribing a plan of organization and a course of reading, but hoped that state educators would then sponsor it. In a meeting two months later, however, the State Teachers' Association passed a resolution authorizing and requesting the state superintendent of public instruction to assume the entire direction of reading circles. In doing so educators rejected an early opportunity to accept responsibility for their own professional development.

Making basic plans Clapp declared: "The object of the reading circle shall be the improvement of its members in literary, scientific and professional knowledge, and promotion of the habits of self-culture." He appointed county superintendents as county managers, chose the books for the course of study, laid out a four-year course, and promised to issue diplomas to those completing it. Any teacher could become a member, and fees from the state teachers' examination would be used in paying necessary expenses.[44]

The 1891 legislature codified the state superintendent's actions and directed county superintendents, under instructions from the state superintendent, to organize either county or district institutes or reading circles, held at least one Saturday each month. Teachers were obligated to attend "or forfeit one day's wages for each day's absence" unless excused.[45]

The first two books chosen for the four-year course were *Selections from Hawthorne and His Friends* and Page's *Theory and Practice of Teaching*. Clapp's successors chose the following to complete the four-year course: for 1892, Fiske's *Civil Government of the United States*, Ogden's *Elements of Ethical Science*, and *Evangeline*; for 1893, White's *Elements of Pedagogy*, and *Schoolmaster in Literature*, and for 1894, *Lights of Two Centuries* and Andrews' *Elementary Geology*. To qualify for a diploma teachers had to answer successfully a series of questions each year on the assigned texts and submit their certificates of completion to the state superintendent. For example, after reading *Elementary Geology* the examination required teachers to "give the theories of separate creations" and explain the "theory of evolution."[46]

Clearly, taking a reading course was not the highest priority for state teachers in 1890-1891. Only 481 of 1,982, or 24 percent, enrolled. Of that number, only 125, or 26 percent of the enrollees completed it and received a certificate, just 6 percent of the state's teaching work force. The numbers of persons completing the course of reading, listed by county name, were:

Cass	40	Nelson	6
Cavalier	20	Ramsey	6
Emmons	4	Sargent	6
Foster	3	Towner	6
Kidder	17	Traill	5
LaMoure	19	Wells	3
Logan	3		

The following term, 1891-1892, 758 teachers were reading the course, in 1892, 590. During the closing year of the four-year course, 1894, only 300 of 2,200 teachers, or 14 percent were reading it. State Superintendent of Public Instruction Emma Bates found it "lamentable, dear teachers, that in the face of the effort that was made in the beginning of this work in its organization and early development, in the face of law upon our statue books, that the matter at the close of the first four years' course should show such results."[47]

Because of the initial lack of enthusiasm, Bates planned to visit county superintendents, "to create anew an interest and enthusiasm in the work" and to urge them to begin the new course work "with higher ideal, more persevering spirit, more earnest purpose for self-culture." She believed the new texts, White's *School Management* and Gray's *How Plants Grow*, "sufficiently attractive to inspire" educators. White's text should "prove profitable and interesting"; Gray's, a "delightful little book," should help teachers and pupils "learn the beautiful truths concerning plant life." Prodding educators she told them that 2,000 teachers in Minnesota and 1,500 in South Dakota were members of reading circles. She was confident that "teachers of North Dakota are as progressive, as enthusiastic, [and] as desirous of acquiring greater intellectual activity . . . as are the teachers of any other state." They also possessed a higher professional spirit.[48]

Hoping to secure libraries for all schools and to create a desire on the part of the pupils to read books of "real merit," the state department encouraged county superintendents and teachers to establish and promote Pupils' Reading Councils. To get a Reading Circle Diploma in 1903-1904, Stutsman County pupils, for example, had to have completed the sixth-grade state course of study and in grades two through seven had to have read twelve books, six of which were required. Eighth graders could get the diploma by reading *Irving's Sketch Book* and five other books selected

surveyed the library and checked the class register; I had ten students in the first four grades. Then, I sat down to write my lesson plans. After I finished them I returned to Larson's place.

There, he told me how to start the fire in the school stove and how to bank it. He also told me to let it go out over the weekend, but reminded me that I had to go over late on Sunday afternoon to start it again. I was also informed that part of my job was to supervise the playground.

I loved my work and I loved all my pupils in my one room rural school house. My county superintendent told me that my discipline was very good and I tried my best to be a successful teacher. I was down on my knees every night, praying to God that I would not fail to teaching the pupils he had placed in my care.

A Country School Teacher Remembers — Ruth Dahlia Buchmiller

Anyone who has taught in or attended a North Dakota rural school must have a feeling of nostalgia as he passes one of the few remaining little rural schools on the North Dakota prairies. Fresh from high school in Kenmare, North Dakota in 1921, I signed my first contract to teach a school three miles east of my home in Norma, North Dakota. Faithful old Topsy pulled my little buggy to the one room schoolhouse. A barn, two outhouses and a small coal shed seemed very adequate. One thing impressed me. In the back of the register that I found in the big drawer in the teacher's desk was an exhortation to teach the children the dangers of smoking and drinking. A teacher who smoked or drank would not have to wait until the next year to get her walking papers. I received $90 a month the first year. In 1923 I intended to go to college but things didn't work out that way. I had waited too long to apply for schools so I had to take a rural school between Sykeston and Woodworth at $60 a month. The man where I boarded informed me that each fall the young men in the neighborhood came by and looked through the kitchen window. If they liked the looks of the new teacher they would knock at the door and say, "We were just going over to Kuskies to get a hair cut." Sure enough, here they came, in droves. Each time I had a hard time keeping a straight face. The one I married came from further away, closer to Sykeston. I think one of the drawbacks in having rural teachers with only a high school education was their lack of education in methods, especially first grade reading methods.

from the lists for the sixth, seventh, and eighth grades. To receive credit for any book pupils had to pass a "reasonable test" on the book's subject matter; for all students after the fourth grade the test was written. School boards had authority to appropriate annually between $10 and $25 for libraries in each school. Books for the 1903-1904 Course of Reading in Stutsman County numbered 29 and cost $14.53. The required book for the second grade entitled *Big People and Little People of Other Lands* cost 30 cents. Fourth graders were required to read *Stories of American Life and Adventure*, cost 50 cents; sixth graders, *Fifty Famous Stories Retold*, cost 35 cents. After tenuous starts both the State Teachers' Reading Circle and the Pupils' Reading Circle became successful programs promulgated by the State Department of Public Instruction.[49]

Professional educators realized the importance of both Teachers' Institutes and Reading Circles. Rural teachers were poorly trained. In the early decades of the state's history, each fall, half of them were beginners. Not many normal-school graduates wanted to teach country school. What little training most rural teachers received they acquired from attending institutes, enrolling in reading circles, or going to summer school, if they could afford it.

An early effort to improve teacher preparation occurred in 1905. That year the legislature established a minimum salary of $45 per month for teachers holding a Second Grade Certificate. Teachers holding lower grade certificates could not be paid a salary equal to or more than upper grade certificated teachers. School boards did not necessarily have to pay uniform salaries to teachers holding comparable certificates.[50]

In 1921 the state tried again to improve public school teacher preparation by tying qualifications to salary. Although the 1921 state legislature was split between the Nonpartisan League (NPL) and the Independent Voters Association (IVA) it passed such legislation. Applied to all teachers entering the profession in the public schools after August 31, 1923, the law demanded, as a minimum requirement, that teachers hold a diploma from an approved four-year high school course or its equivalent, and meet all certification requirements. The following minimum salaries for a minimum amount of training for a school year of nine months were established:

● the minimum wage for a teacher with less than four years of high school training and who taught in the state before August 31, 1922 was set at $720 ($80 per month),

- high school graduates were to receive not less than $810 ($90 per month),

- graduates of normal school courses of one year beyond the four-year high school were to receive not less than $1,000 ($111.11 per month),

- two-year normal school graduates or those who held a second grade professional certificate for life would receive $1,100 ($122.22 per month),

Morton County, Moltzen School Dist. Number 1, 14 miles NW of New Salem, Miss Ethel Chitty, Teacher, 1913 *(SHSND)*

- graduates of three-years of normal school or those holding a first grade professional certificate for life would be paid $1,200 ($133.33 per month),

- a graduate of a four-year program should receive at least $1,300 ($144.44 per month).

Salaries were also to be increased over these minimums at the rate of $50 per year for five years. Hiring teachers with less training or failing to comply with the act could result in school officers being fined $25 to $200 for each separate offense.[51]

The legislation, really an unfunded mandate (the state provided no additional funds to support it), was passed when North Dakotans were caught up in a period of educational change, political volatility, and economic uncertainty. The situation did not bode well for the law's future.

School districts participating in the consolidation movement were saddled with additional expenses. A dramatic increase in the amount expended to transport pupils to and from school had occurred, $560,000 was spent in 1919, $877,000 in 1920.[52] To complicate matters the Bank of North Dakota suffered a liquidity crisis during the winter of 1920-1921 and failed to release school funds it held. Furthermore, because citizens were slow in paying their taxes some districts found it necessary to issue warrants to pay teachers. An opinion issued by the attorney general's office, however, caused difficulties for those receiving them. No longer were teachers' salary warrants considered "preferred warrants." Under those circumstances it was feared that many teachers, unable to support themselves without pay, would be forced to quit, or choose to quit. During the crisis Bottineau citizens guaranteed payment of its teachers' salaries and in another community teachers were given free room and board by a hotel keeper. Although Superintendent of Public Instruction Minnie J. Nielson reported that no schools had closed and that she did not anticipate any would, she said there had been some "close calls."[53]

Moreover, the farm depression in North Dakota was not conducive to sustaining widespread support for the minimum training and salary law. Farmers had produced a paltry 61 million bushel wheat crop in 1919; and wheat prices dropped from $2.35 a bushel in that year to $1.01 in 1921. Farmers also owed a total of $286 million in farm mortgages in 1920; 25 percent of them were tenants. At the same time some farmers and ranchers began leaving counties north and west of the Missouri River.[54]

Warren A. Henke

A Country School Teacher Remembers — Agnes Hagen

In the fall of 1935 I started teaching at $45 a month, for an 8-month term, in the Bear Creek School in Northland Township. The school was located near Fort Ransom in Ransom County. There were 29 students enrolled in all eight grades. The first day of teaching was so scary. Twenty-nine faces looking at you, wondering what you would do. I sized up the group, those big eighth grade boys, would I be able to handle the group? One little first grade boy sat in his desk, clenching the side of his desk top, crying at the top of his voice. I tried to look calm, but I, too, wanted to cry. Pretty soon an older sister came over to comfort him. He told her he wanted to go home.

Some schools had telephones but the Sand Prairie School near Kathryn did not. When a blizzard struck around noon one day some parents came early to get their youngsters. At dismissal time one could not see very far. I knew the children, three boys from three families, who were still at school would be there all night. We all spent the night in the building. The boys bundled up in their coats and slept well. The wind howled and blew so hard the building shook. I kept wondering what I would do in case of fire. We were about a mile from any home. At the homes the parents of these boys didn't sleep. They had walked the floors. They had no idea whether we were out in the blizzard or safe in a building. The next week we had a telephone installed in the school building.

One of the favorite past times at noon hour was snaring and trapping gophers. After the well was dug students tried to drown them out. When one was seen racing toward a hole all nearby holes were plugged and water was poured into the open one. Eventually the gopher emerged and was captured. Maybe sometimes I was guilty of extending the noon hour so they could get their gopher. Here was cooperation, team work, and enthusiasm and the boys needed the few cents they got for each gopher tail. [Bounties were paid at that time to help eradicate the rodent.]

Pranks on the teacher were not uncommon. Can you imagine the frustration of coming to the school house the day after Halloween to find an entire row of desks, they were on wooden slats, strung up on the flag pole? The pranksters did remove the books and papers. The desks were well tied. I went inside and started my dusting when one of the parents brought his

continued on next page

124

Additionally, North Dakotans had just emerged from a vicious and divisive recall election. Politics and financial strain brought public expenditures under scrutiny. Shortly after he ousted NPL Governor Lynn J. Frazier in the hotly contested recall election in October 1921, IVA Governor Ragnvold A. Nestos inaugurated a statewide economy movement by telling a meeting of the state's county commissioners at Jamestown in January 1922 that the tax burdens of the people of North Dakota had to be reduced. He called on them to approve a program of economy and declared that "all political subdivisions, as well as the state itself, will have to bear its share of the burden." Although he advised the commissioners that "we cannot afford to slash and curtail the expenditures for education so as to injure this important cause" and noted that severe cutbacks in library expenditures would seriously impair its mission, he told the assembly that in the preceding five years, 1916-1920, the total general property taxes levied for township purposes had increased 56.25 percent and for school purposes 117.60 percent. The increase for schools was the highest for all subdivisions and also for the state.[55]

Throughout the state taxes and the minimum training and salary law caused considerable discussion and protest. In January 1922 at the Tri-State Grain Growers Convention in Fargo a large number of farmers caucused to discuss the tax situation. The group approved a resolution calling on all taxpayers in each precinct of the state to meet on February 2 to elect a delegate to confer with county commissioners to consider how to reduce next year's budget.[56] The Sargent County taxpayers' meeting held at the courthouse in Forman was "a grand success." A resolution opposing the teacher training and salary law was adopted unanimously. It declared that it "places such a burden on the local school districts that it is becoming impossible to obey the law and maintain our public schools and that said law does not tend to raise the efficiency of the schools and takes away from the local authorities any discretion." Another resolution called for its repeal and called upon local legislators to work actively to repeal it. Additional meetings were to be held later.[57]

Taxpayers in LaMoure County were also unhappy with the law. The *LaMoure County Chronicle* headlined: "COUNTY TAXPAYERS IN

MASS MEETING," "Teachers' Minimum Wage Law Unpopular." One taxpayer told his fellow citizens that government expense had increased so enormously that a point had been reached in North Dakota "where you can levy taxes, but you can't collect them." He disclosed that delinquent unsold taxes exceeded $150,000, that in normal times only $10,000 to $15,000 were carried over annually. In Ovid Township alone, he told the audience, the total tax burden had increased $8,747.46 from 1916 to 1921. School taxes had gone up $2,263.54.[58]

youngsters. He helped me get the desks inside. I believe some younger married men in the community had a hand in the trick.

One notable change that occurred during my teaching career was the coming of TV. Sometimes youngsters watched too much at home and would then fall asleep during class. Another change was the availability of commercial seat work and the many workbooks that were also available. Sometimes I think they were overused. Installation of modern heating systems, the standardization of school terms, redistricting, and the beginning closing of one room rural schools were also significant changes.

One school board was deeply concerned about the situation. The Hillsboro School Board urged all boards in Traill County to attend a meeting to "discuss means of adjusting teachers compensation and of lowering the cost of school maintenance." It concluded that teachers' salaries had reached such a high level that they placed an "an uncommon burden on the taxpayers." Besides, wage reduction was "widespread in all other professions and lines of work." The board resolved to petition the next legislature to lower the minimum teachers' wage and revise the schedule. The board acted only after considerable thought "and upon conviction that united action...will offer relief to the taxpayers and need work no injustice to members of the teaching profession." The board declared it did not want local teachers to feel it "under-estimated the value of their services to the school and the community." Rather, they were "well-pleased" with them and hoped sincerely they would return next term. However, because of "the heavy burden of taxation that is doubly hard to bear in these times of great financial stringency, we feel it our solemn duty to take steps to lower the cost of maintaining our school. We are not seeking to lower the compensation of teachers to an unfair level but we would like to have it follow the downward trend that is so noticeable in all other lines of work."[59] The *Hankinson News* was like-minded. It believed that the law should be modified and that a reasonable minimum salary should be retained but that salaries should reflect "existing conditions."[60]

Meeting in February 1922 Divide County tax payers voted unanimously to retain it. They were interested in how to attract better teachers, not how to reduce teachers' salaries. Recognizing that some reduction in school expenditures was necessary the gathering thought "the pruning process should not be applied to the root of the tree. Better cut off a few unnecessary branches."[61] Although at a meeting of township and school officers at Forman on March 9 no resolutions or definite plans of action were adopted to reduce taxes, the sense of the gathering seemed to be to "cut off" a branch, reduce school terms by a month. At least seven friends of education attending that meeting objected to that approach. They insisted that "to reduce taxes at the expense of the rising generation should not be thought of, because we feel that any normal parent with children growing up is more interested in their future welfare and success than in any other thing on earth." Their approach was to ask the county commissioners to reduce the current $30,000 bridge levy to $4,000, the previous level. They also suggested discharging the county agent and the club leader, but meeting their contracted salary obligations. They believed the county could make progress with fewer bridges, no county agent or club leader, "rather than lower the standards of our schools.[62]

Not everyone in the state agreed with those approaches. Two momentous meetings in Nelson County sealed the fate of the teachers' minimum training and salary law. Blaming the legislative committee of the North Dakota Teachers' Association for the passage of the law, a conference of school officers and other political subdivision officials at McVille decided to initiate a movement for repeal. Petitions were prepared and plans made for their circulation.[63] At a follow-up meeting at Lakota on March 7, 1922, called by the county commissioners, "taxing officers and other citizens of Nelson County" drafted a set of eleven resolutions. Two were crucial for the law's future. Resolution seven declared that the assembly approved of "the movement to repeal the teachers' minimum salary law, as it is wrong in principal and tends to destroy merit. That unless a material reduction in wages of teachers can be had, many of our school districts will be unable to provide schooling for their children, the wage scale being out of proportion to the ability of the taxpayers to pay. That we believe the teaching profession should do its share in the general re-adjustment of the times and as conditions become more normal and stablised (sic) work up on a system of merit." Resolution nine stated that "sentiment should be worked up for a State Taxpayers' Association believing that much good could be gained by an association of this kind. Excessive taxation has been the ruination of communities and the downfall of nations. The evil exists in our state and we should check it before it gets too large a root and gets beyond control."[64]

Stark County School, February 1942 *(NDINRS)*

Eventually the State Taxpayers' Association secured enough signatures on an initiated petition to put the issue to a vote of the people on June 28, 1922. Both opponents and proponents mounted intensive campaigns to influence the voters.

Some local communities thought they would have to increase taxes to comply with the law; others were determined to "keep control of the schools in the hands of the people." To them, the law took the right of bargaining out of the hands of the school boards. They ought to be free to negotiate salaries without legal restrictions. Also, the law was economically unsound because it was not based on the law of supply and demand. Because of necessity or the desire to teach in a certain locale, for whatever reason, qualified teachers would accept less than the legal minimum salary. Opponents also believed that the high cost of living was attributable primarily to public expenditures, that school taxes constituted the major share of their tax burden, that the major item in school budgets was salary, that teacher's paychecks were too high, and that the law was designed to bring about and maintain high salaries. In the interest of economy the law had to be repealed. Skeptics suggested that the law provided no real incentives for teachers to do their best work or to improve their scholarship. Most doubters, however, believed some kind of teacher training or qualification law was necessary and desirable.[65]

Mounting an intensive campaign to retain the law, educators and their friends insisted it was, above all, a minimum training law. It was designed not to protect teachers but to benefit the schools and safeguard the children of North Dakota, particularly those who were attending rural schools. They needed protection from the large number of unqualified rural teachers under 19 years of age. More experienced, efficient, and better trained teachers were needed, the only way to get them was to make it impossible for young girls without training to teach. The law would also tend to reduce teacher turn-over. A study in the fall of 1921 revealed "that the typical woman teaching academic subjects . . . had less than five years of experience and is teaching for the first year in her present position."[66]

A Country School Teacher Remembers — Martha J. Holler

Religion played an important part in the lives of the children. A teacher had to be on the "alert" if they were of different faiths. Sometimes the children would begin quarreling over whose religion was right. That had to be taken care of quickly to prevent fights. Prayers were offered before meals; each day the children took turns saying grace. The Catholics said it "their way" and the Protestants recited "their way." There was never any problem. It was my duty to see that there were no other representations on a particular wall except the Ten Commandments. That was done for emphasis.

Defenders of the law charged that equal educational opportunity was nonexistent in the state, rural school children were being discriminated against. During the campaign Attorney A. M. Kvello, president of Lisbon's city school board, cited a specific example of what he considered unequal educational opportunity in Ransom County. "I have in mind," he said, "two of our richest townships adjoining each other. One has four ancient, single room, poorly equipped, and poorly ventilated school houses; one of which is taught by an eighth grade graduate and housing thirty-six pupils. School terms have until this year been only seven months in each year, and now eight. The most influential citizen of that township is an open advocate of six months only, and all in the sweet name of saving a bit of tax money. And also of $65.00 a month teachers openly boasting of the fact that not one teacher in that district gets over $95.00 a month. Across the line is the finest equipped and most economically operated consolidated school in the county, with highly educated and trained teachers. And this discrepancy of opportunity is made possible by the heretofore granted privilege of each board largely setting its own standard of school efficiency."[67]

Teachers also argued that they did not need salary laws to protect them because they could quit teaching, go into other work, and be paid more, if they wanted to. A survey in Valley City showed that the business world was paying more than any teacher received for equal training and ability. Teachers discovered that beginning store clerks with no educational requirements and "mediocre ability" were paid $75 a month, or $900 a year. Hotel waitresses were being paid $85 per month, or $1,020 per year; and teachers with experience and two years of professional training were receiving less than stenographers who were being paid from $90 per month if employed in the court house or as much as $150 per month if working as an insurance clerk.[68]

Proponents also argued that adequate salary schedules were important. Good salaries would induce the country's best people to enter the educational profession permanently instead of following other pursuits, and schedules would make incomes definite and more stable. Besides, salaries should be high enough to enable teachers to spend summers in advanced study, without having "to borrow or 'ask Pa' for the funds for such a purpose."[69] Although conceding that their incomes had risen in the recent past educators claimed that because the cost of living had increased substan-

Rural school near Osnabrook *(Hulstrand Collection, NDIRS)*

tially since 1914 and the tendency toward inflation had been noticeable since 1918, few teachers, in reality, had had an increase since 1914.[70]

Another major argument used to persuade voters to retain the minimum training and salary law was that it would not reduce taxes in any appreciable amount. At a mass meeting of LaMoure County taxpayers who gathered in February 1922 to discuss ways to reduce public expenditures the law came under heavy fire. Responding to the criticism, County Superintendent of Schools Mabel Osborne challenged the opponents' arguments by noting that 154 of the 166 currently employed teachers in the county were being paid more than the law required.[71] Other proponents argued that over 80 percent of the teachers in the state were paid more than the law required and that salaries for the next school term would remain the same in over 90 percent of the towns. Proponents also suggested that lowering the total amount paid all teachers in the state by about $1 million would not affect the salary law in the state.[72]

Supporters of the law offered other reasons to retain it: it was not class legislation because other public employees' salaries were set by law; minimum salaries and schedules were not new, many states had adopted similar plans; most of the tax money spent on education remained in the local community; North Dakotans were spending more on luxuries than they were on education; and the argument that school boards should be free to set salaries without legal restrictions was not well founded because the state required districts to maintain schools, prescribed by law the length of the term, and determined the subjects that were taught.[73]

On July 28, 1922, voters decided the fate of the minimum training and salary law. Accepting the arguments of the opponents, they repealed it by a vote of 101,167 to 70,372, or 59 percent to 41 percent.[74] The law was in effect from July 1, 1921 to July 28, 1922, its merits were never tested. Its repeal was significant for several reasons: continued improvements in teacher preparation through legislation would be slow, almost glacial; a combined minimum preparation and salary law would never again be enacted by the state legislature; teachers continued to be their own chief negotiator; school boards were left to "dicker" with individual teachers, to offer the least they were willing to pay; and gender inequality insofar as salaries were concerned would continue.

Countless dedicated teachers including those in country schools, however, continued to pursue their education. For many the goal was attending normal school for two years or eventually getting a four-year degree. Many did just that.

Americans familiar with the importance and significance of the words *I Do* in marriage ceremonies and legal proceedings can appreciate the teachers' concern with the words *Provided, That* or *PROVIDED FURTHER* or *FURTHER PROVIDED* found in a Teacher's Contract. The first two combinations spelled out aspects of current school law. The latter combination held special significance, perhaps as important as the offered salary. It was followed by several blank lines in a contract and when filled in spelled out the many and varied demands made upon the individual. The board could insert any provision, not contrary to law, deemed advisable that would reflect the values, moral standards, and concerns, including economic, of the local community. Those provisions reflected the teacher's duties to the local society and in many cases determined her own lifestyle.

Aside from teaching the daily schedule, keeping the register, or preparing for a special day most teachers did their own janitor work. Probably the most detested duty was complying with the law covering the cleanliness of seats and walls in the outdoor toilet. The state department offered several suggestions to enable the teacher to adhere to it: keep the door closed; keep fasteners in good repair, especially during the winter to prevent the facility from filling with snow; sprinkle ashes in the vault to prevent an accumulation of flies; cut newspapers and old catalogs for toilet paper; and inspect the facility daily to prevent writing on the walls. The department concluded that "the conditions in the toilets are the key to the moral standards in the community. The best influence of the best teacher during the five hours each day may be entirely overcome by the conditions in the toilets."[75]

Although some teachers might hire some rugged country boys to build the fire during cold weather, minimum wages precluded most of them from doing it. Besides, some districts insisted that only the teacher be entrusted with that chore. It was almost a universal and understood rule that teachers serve as janitors. Ordinarily, they were not compensated for custodial duties.

Few school boards recognized in contract language the added chores that cold weather brought. At least one in Towner County did. Marie Wendt taught School No. 17 in Howell School District No. 17 for $100 per month in 1931. She agreed to do the janitor work "until cold weather sets in." Then the board "employed and retained until Apr. 1st or longer" a janitor "at the pleasure of the board; depending on the weather at that time." Recruited by Hawkeye School District No. 14 in Divide County in the northwest corner of the state, J. H. Gohrick, in 1937, taught a nine-month term for $80 per month and was willing to do "all janitor work without extra pay, floors to be scrubbed at least 4 times during the school term." Sometimes, however, custodial duties paid extra. Hired by the Freitag School District No. 65 in McLean County in 1915 Leonard B. Cox agreed to teach and serve as janitor for $60 per month. When he taught in the Regan School District in Burleigh County in

A Country School Teacher Remembers — Hazel Thompson Burns

While I was growing up I never thought of teaching school. I had always wanted to be a stenographer. When it came time to go to college, it was decided that I should go to Minot State Teachers College. My father's sister lived in Minot and I could stay with her. Of course, I thought the college would offer a secretarial course, but I was informed the first day that it taught *how* to teach secretarial courses and I was asked why I didn't take a one year rural teacher's course, teach a year, and then decide what to do. As a result I taught for twenty-seven years and missed only five days of teaching.

There were too many teachers at the time that I went to college in 1929-1930. I sent out many applications in the spring of 1930, but most schools were rehiring the same teachers. In October, a friend's father who happened to be on a school board called me and asked me if I'd teach their school, Pleasant View School in McKenzie County. He had fired the teacher. She had an eighth-grade education and had her pupils drawing and coloring most of the time. Another method that was apparently unsatisfactory was to teach one subject for an entire week and then teach another the next week.

I had five pupils at first, but two moved away. In the spring I told my landlady that she may as well send her four year old boy to school. He was the youngest and the six other children in the family were all girls. He was a precocious child and learned a lot. Whenever his Dad asked him what he had learned that day, he would say, "I've got it in my pocket." An elderly man by the name of "Lucky George" had taught him to smoke cigarettes and while standing on his head in a corner he could blow smoke rings. His Dad told him that he couldn't smoke while in school or his hair would turn green! I caught him just once with cigarette papers and a Bull Durham sack of tobacco in his shirt pocket.

Almost every country school had a pump organ. I had had only eight piano lessons and hadn't learned the bass clef so I played the treble clef with both hands and since few people in the community could play, they probably never knew the difference.

Sometimes a pupil stayed with me at the schoolhouse. That was very satisfactory as the schoolhouse was always warm when the children came in the morning. I could eat what I wanted, etc. I had no car so had to depend on

continued on next page

the neighbors or the mailman to bring me groceries. My little nine year old bed partner and I put rocks the size of your head on the heater each morning. Then when night came, we wrapped them in bath towels and put them under the covers at the foot of the bed. As a result, we had no cold feet.

I had never heard of hot lunches when I first started teaching, but every day, my landlady would send a quart of beans, peas, etc. We also brought scrubbed potatoes to school. At recess we put each potato in a baking powder can, shake down the stove ashes over the cans and at noon, we would have a tasty baked potato. Some years each family would take one day a week to serve and would bring a hot dish of some kind. I furnished for everybody one day also. Someone had to watch the food on the stove so that it didn't burn; usually an older girl would sit on a high stool with her book on her lap and watch the food. We received many things like flour, grapefruit, ham, dried eggs and other surplus commodities from the county hot lunch program during the Great Depression. Sometimes we received big crates of grapefruit that we could not begin to eat before they got too old so I'd divide up the surplus and sent them home with the pupils. At that time not too many country people had eaten grapefruit. One lady told me that she had tried fixing them many ways, all cooked and her family just would not eat them! One thing that we all refused to eat were the dried eggs. They just did not smell good.

1934 he was paid $70 per month plus "free house and fuel" and earned an additional $10 per month to do the "janitorial work." As the Great Depression deepened, Cox's salary dropped; in 1936 he signed a contract with the Estherville School District in the same county for $60 per month, but with no "free house and fuel," and no extra pay to be the janitor. By 1940 his salary was increasing; at his school in Oliver County (School No. 1 in Butte School District), he was earning $75 per month plus "free fuel and use of the teacherage" for serving as the janitor.[76]

Employed in 1921 by River View School District No. 4, McKenzie County, Mildred Lamphier was paid $100 per month and was "allowed four dollars per month for sweeping floors and building fires." In 1943 in a neighboring county, Dunn, Julia Hurinenko was instructing youngsters in School No. 2, Badland School District No. 14, for $115 per month. She agreed: to get "Fires started and school house warm by 8:45 A.M. Floors scrubbed once each month or $2.50 will be deducted. Toilets kept sanitary." Some miles to the east in McLean County the school board of Fort Berthold School District No. 86, in 1931, retained Hazel Houghtaling for an eight-month term at $65 per month; she agreed to scrub the schoolhouse floor three times during the term. She was paid $5 for each scrubbing.[77]

Teachers who remember their "janitorial work" delight in the description of Valborg Fisher who began her teaching career in a one-room school in Morton County in 1925. As she wrote *In Retrospect*:

"I Remember the Floors."

At that time I was expected to do all janitor work, so the floor stands out in my memory. It was a black splintered floor, full of slivers and dirty grease. I swept it with a straight broom. When it was scrubbed it absorbed all the water.

The next floor showed some improvement in that it was dark brown with fewer slivers. It had been oiled during the summer. I was still using a straight broom. Then the floor improved to a sliverless, light brown varnish. A sweeping compound could be used with a push broom, but oily spots would show if the compound wasn't removed quickly.

Later someone had the idea of painting this floor. That made for easier cleaning, but by spring it looked horrible because the paint had worn off in so many places. Tile on a cement foundation was really an improvement. Now the children could sit on the floor, and best of all, this floor came with a janitor. Small area rugs found their place in library corners, reading nooks and special places. These could be washed if necessary.

Today, we find school rooms with wall to wall carpeting. Huge vacuum cleaners do the work that I had to do under trying conditions after putting in a full day of teaching.

How can I forget the floor![78]

Teachers might also remember incidents similar to the one related by Harvey M. Sletten of Fort Ransom who remembers almost not being re-hired because, as the farmer with whom he boarded put it, "The board reckons as how yer a fair to middlin' teacher, but you've burned jest too derned much coal this winter."

Sletten reported "A tinge of bitterness creeping through shocked disbelief. My school stood on a hill—utterly naked and exposed to frigid winds."

The farmer admitted that "The younguns have all learned to read tolerably well, but you've burned jest to dern much coal this winter. That buildin' of your'n is as drafty as long-handled underwear with the trap door down. It always takes some more coal, but nothin' like you burned up."

But the farmer liked Harvey, so he did a little investigating in Paradise School District in Eddy County that spring of 1933. Both he and Harvey were happy when the farmer could come in one day and announce, "Well yer hired back! Seems as how the feller that hauled coal to yer school got a mite light fingered. Part of each load went into his own coal shed at home."[79]

Country school teachers will not forget the floor, the problems with the stove, or the restriction on their social life. Many teachers were the object of what Williams calls "special surveillance." Hilda Ellilngson remembers *In Retrospect*:

> When I became a teacher, it was an idealistic type of work. Teachers were respected; we commanded respect from the pupils as well as from people in the community. Certainly, what we did, with whom we associated, what we wore, what we said and how we taught were common topics of conversation, both constructive and destructive, in any community. At this time the success of a teacher was determined by how well she could heat the school room with the damp lignite coal afforded her; how many pupils passed the State Board Examinations and how well she disciplined. Her conduct in the community was another thing that was well weighed. No drinking, not smoking was the rule; and her associates were approved or disapproved. We were expected to join the Homemaker's Club, to attend the nearest church, even though it might not be of our own denomination, to sing in the

A Country School Teacher Remembers — Lillian A. Nelson Desmond

Nineteen twenty four, what a wonderful year! In June I graduated from a two-year course at Jamestown College with a special certificate to teach. I was ready to apply for a teaching position in a rural school, though I was not quite eighteen. By chance, I went to Eldridge to inquire about vacancies and found a school board meeting in progress in the office of a local elevator. I was told a new school was being started to accommodate four families who had had to transport their children five miles to the closest school. I was hired. Why? I think because my father was well known, having threshed in the area; maybe because the father of the president of the board had "courted" my mother when she arrived as a young lady from Iowa in 1883.

When I visited the "school" I found it to be a replica of the room in which the board was meeting when they hired me. It was the office of an old grain elevator, 10 by 14 feet; it had three ordinary windows, one in each of the south, east, and west walls. The west half of the room was taken up by four double desks. In the northeast corner was an old-fashioned teacher's desk. In front of it were two kindergarten desks and a zinc-jacketed hot air heater. The room had one door; when opened it barely missed the stove, but it surely was convenient when adding coal or wood to the fire! A small shed sheltered the door entrance, and also provided a shelf for the inevitable wash basin, water pail and tin cup, wood for kindling and a bucket of coal. There were two makeshift outdoor toilets and a three-sided stable to shelter riding ponies and a stack of wood. A bin of coal was found beside the schoolhouse door. The textbooks were surplus used ones from other schools. There were two wall maps, a hand bell, three erasers and half box of chalk. A blackboard covered the north wall. The building had no foundation. It had been moved out on the prairie and leveled with stones at the corners. It had no screens or storm windows, and it was not "banked up" until January. It was 30 degrees below zero for three weeks before Christmas, so the 10 students sat with coats and overshoes on, around a red hot stove, but they were still unable to keep warm. I frosted my heels in the schoolroom because there was no room for me around the stove.

The night before my first day of school was memorable because I was kept awake all night by bedbugs. I roomed and boarded at a farm

continued on next page

choir, teach Sunday School, coach or take part in home talent plays and be a participant in any other activity that might arise. No one thought of going home weekends, something we had learned from a college professor, who termed such teachers "suitcase teachers," and heaven forbid that we should be labeled such, for that was little short of a plague.[80]

Many school districts expected teachers to maintain high moral standards and be community role-models. Teaching in northcentral North Dakota Elsie Maurer's contract from Superior School District No. 19 in Eddy County in 1930 fixed her salary at $90 per month; however, there was "no dancing allowed in said school." Julia Ann Romanyshyn may have been the originator of America's current favorite hackneyed expression: "Thank God Its Friday." Spring Creek School District No. 18 in Billings County in southwestern North Dakota paid her only $65 per month for a seven-month term in 1931, while insisting that "the teacher will not stay out evenings from Sunday to Thursday inclusive." In 1935 in the southeastern section of the state, Irene Anderson who taught School No. 3 in Kennison School District, LaMoure County, for $60 per month not only had to "refrain from midweek dancing parties" but also had "to be at her residing place by 11 o'clock P.M." Southcentral school patrons also expected their teachers measure up to their expectations during the school week. Vera Daniels, who taught School No. 2 in Finn School District No. 11 in Logan County in 1937 for $50 per month agreed to "Stay away from dances parties etc during school days." Two years later restrictions in that county were relaxed slightly. Grace Sheppard who taught School No. 2 in Willowbank School District No. 2 was granted "one night out in the school week for social pleasures." Her salary was $60 per month. Some school patrons in northeastern North Dakota were also concerned about the public image of their teacher. Pembina School District No.1 hired Rita Mae Rene in 1938 to teach School No. 1 for a nine-month term for $70 per month. To earn her salary she had to agree "not to use tobacco, beer or intoxicants in public nor to frequent places where beer and intoxicants are sold nor to attend 'late' parties on evenings prior to school days."[81]

How did one school board protect the daily routine and the larder of a school patron willing to board and room the teacher? They resolved that worry by controlling both the teacher's eating and sleeping habits. For $95 a month Nora Connell consented in 1927 to teach School No. 1 in Belfield School District No. 10, Stark County, for an eight-month term. In addition to doing her own janitor work and firing up the heating plant by 8:30 a.m., she agreed that the board would withhold $5 per month, that amount to be paid when her final report was completed and accepted. And according to her contract she consented to retire "by 9:00 o'clock P.M. and be up at 6:00 A.M. [and she] Must only eat three meals a day." For whatever reason two districts in North Dakota did not want their teachers fixing lunch in the school. Just north of Stark County, while teaching an eight-month term in School No. 5, New Castle School District No. 33 in Dunn County, for $90 per month in 1928, Eleanora Rue promised that she "would not board in school building." The school board of Pherrin School District No. 30 in Williams County was willing to pay Lillian Togstad $90 a month for nine months to teach School No. 1 in 1930. She also guaranteed the board to serve as janitor for an extra $10 per month and assured them she would have the schoolhouse warm in time for school. Having settled on the major provisions of the con-

home 1 1/2 miles from school. I was given the hired girl's room because a new addition where my room was to be was incomplete. For six weeks after the bedbug night I slept with the farmer's wife until my room was ready. It had no heat and during the winter the walls became covered with a half inch of frost. The home was not modern.

tract the board also insisted that "your lunch must be carried to school."[82]

Clara Bakke may have been one of the most physically fit country school teachers in 1929. She taught School No. 1 in Maple River School District No. 114 in Cass County for $85 per month. She had to produce at least one program during the term and "play outdoors with pupils 25 minutes each day when weather permits." One school district was concerned about daylight saving time during World War II. Teaching in Herman School District No. 8 in Sargent County in 1942 for $85 per month Vera Fox taught "on new time till Nov. 1st, then old time until April 1st. Then new time remainder of term." In the 1960s some districts began to realize the importance of fringe benefits. In addition to her regular salary ($460.44 for 8 months, $460.48 for the balance of a 37-week contract) Hazel Moxley was paid a travel allowance of $180 by the New School District No. 8 in Williams County.[83]

In the 19th century in Kansas "one Kansas county announced that it would employ 100 women teachers who would pledge to remain unmarried for three years. Another countered with the offer that it would hire 100 women teachers who would pledge to marry within one year. The county that received the most response is unknown."[84] It is unknown if any North Dakota counties engaged in a similar contest. While recognizing that the schoolmarm was a civilizing force in the community some school districts in North Dakota prohibited teachers from marrying during their term of employment. In 1938, in Ramsey County, Lake School District No. 5 paid Cora Aasmunstad $65 per month for a nine-month teaching term. The board was willing to pay her $5 per month additional for janitorial services but was reluctant to see her marry. Her contract declared "that marriage violates this contract and the board reserves the right to discontinue this agreement." The board that managed School No. 4 in Lippert School District No. 54 in Stutsman County was more rigid. Bernice Whitney taught there in 1939 for $70 per month, but her contract declared that "if teacher marries during school year her contract becomes void." The board that hired Edna Edinger to teach in School No. 3 in Greatstone School District No. 52, McLean County, was like-minded, declaring "that this contract is void if said teacher

A Country School Teacher Remembers — Lillian Erickson

I graduated from Starkweather High School and later enrolled at Valley City State Teachers College where I earned a one-year teaching certificate in the spring of 1934. My first job offer was from the western part of the state at $45 a month. Then another offer came at $55. This made my father decide to send me back to school and there I attained my two-year Standard Certificate. I was in my glory.

I accepted my first job offer in Ramsey County, a rural school in Royal Township, close to my parental home. It was an exciting and I would say a successful year. Success to the extent of surviving four days in the schoolhouse during a severe snowstorm. The children were picked up early because of the storm. A load of coal was also to have arrived that day, but delivery was interrupted by the storm. I was left with four lumps of lignite and a woodpile out by the outhouse. My sister Evelyn was living with me then. We had a few necessary facilities in one end of the schoolroom. It grew so cold in the room that we decided to move to the furnace room, where we wrapped ourselves in quilts and sat and waited to be rescued. Our water ran out and food was low. Worse yet the coal was gone. We ripped a double blanket into strips to tie together to make a rope. We tied it to the doorknob and tied the other end around my waist. I did find the woodpile, but what a struggle to get some pieces back to the schoolhouse. The fourth morning broke with a heavy drifting and it was very cold. We decided to chop up a few desks for more fuel. No sooner had we emptied the desks when we heard a loud "whoa" and a voice saying, "Is there anyone in there?" We were rescued by close neighbors. As dirty and sooty as we were we quickly donned our coats, grabbed a few clothes, and were off to warmer quarters. The first thing we did was try to call our parents to let them know we were okay, but the telephone lines were down.

I look back with a warm and grateful heart to my 36 years of teaching. God was good to me to fill my life with beautiful people to work with. It was an honor to know parents entrusted their children to me. I feel warm toward my many school board members. It turned out that I applied for only two schools that I taught; the other schools were offered to me. That was half of my rewards, being asked to teach in their schools.

School District 11, Towner County — used as Bethel Township Hall for about ten years, sold for a home in the 1950s — school barn, outhouses *(NDIRS)*

marries during term." While most anti-marriage pro-visions are found in womens' contracts at least one man agreed to such a proviso. Arthur Grafsgaard as-sured the board of Bryan School Dis-trict No. 20 in Griggs County in 1940 that he would "not marry during [the] school year." They agreed to pay him $65 per month to teach the youngsters at the Iverson School.[85]

If these teacher rules and regulations seem unreasonable or extreme to the modern reader, the following gleaned from the files of the Barnes County archives might seem equally so to many, or perhaps sensible or silly, to some:

● "The Board requires that at least half of the week-ends must be spent in this town."

● "This contact not subject to cancellation."

● "Contract for an indefinite term but not to exceed 9 months."

● "He shall share a room at the teacherage with the other man teacher." (In female contract)

● "Contract to be renewed each month."

● "Teacher to open school with prayer and Bible reading each morning at least 10 minutes." "Personal social relations will not be tolerated between teacher and pupil.""The teacher is limited to playing of Inde-pendent basketball to one night each week during school term."

● "School Board will hire janitor for 3 months, but the janitor's salary ($5 per mo.) will be deducted from teacher's pay."

● "No partiality to be shown any of the children in any way at school."

● "Teacher will receive a bonus of $5.00 per month at end of term if she puts forth her best efforts and everything goes satisfactory at the school during the year." (Salary was $50 per month)[86]

A teacher's role in the community was not always confined to classroom du-ties. Irene L. Dawson graduated from Aneta High School in 1923, took a teaching training course offered to seniors, received a second grade elementary certificate, and began teaching. She taught a total of 10 1/2 years in Hettinger, Griggs, and Morton counties. At one of her boarding places the man of the house asked if she could drive horses. She replied: "I can if they are not wild." Satisfied that she could handle a team he asked her to help in transporting three wagon-loads of wheat to market, 14 miles distant. The son took the lead, followed by the teacher and the father, all had three-horse teams. The three waggoners had a lunch of bread, cheese, and bologna in the village store, no café was available. She remembers delighting in the all-day trip, enjoying the outdoors on a beautiful day. Lillian Erickson, a Starkweather High School graduate, taught for 36 years. She remembers having to act as baby-sitter. "Often a five year old was dropped off to spend a day in school while the parents made a trip to the county seat." Margaret Tangedahl who taught some 30 years in country schools, mostly in Mountrail County, decided to paint the walls and ceiling inside of one of her schools, "as it needed it badly. I'd paint in the evenings after I had my work done and at times painted some before the children came. I think I got $5 or $10 for this work. Those were hard times. I also had a telephone installed myself."[87] Floyd Fairweather, who lived near Souris, remembered that the local school board "thought nothing of dismissing school in the afternoon so the teacher could sing at funerals."[88]

Country school teachers were given much advice. Don't be a snob; don't go just to teach, but also to learn; don't pretend . . .

Country school teachers were given much advice. Don't be a snob; don't go just to teach, but also to learn; don't pretend, be yourself, because children are quick to recognize a fraud; make the community your community; and, by example, leave in that community lasting expressions of kindness, compassion, and open-mindedness. If Robin W. Williams, Jr. is right when he says that "persons who deal with the beliefs and values that the community feels basic to its existence are the

Concludes on page 137

A Country School Teacher Remembers — Mertis Searles Fritz

Everyone was beginning to feel the pinch during the Great Depression. The drought was showing its severe effects in western North Dakota where my parents were farmers and ranchers. As luck would have it, they had taken out an insurance policy for me when I was about 14 years old. It had a cash value of $95 in 1932. The policy was converted to cash. I took a light housekeeping job, scrimped "like heck," and made it through one year at Dickinson State Teachers College, earning a One Year Rural Certificate. The incentive to enter the field of education was economic, not from the standpoint of income, but because it was as much education as I could afford.

All my teaching, 11 years in rural schools, was done in Dunn County. My first job paid $50 a month for an 8-month term. I always stayed at home when I was teaching, the first few years at my parental home. I rode horse back to and from school, 4 miles each way, cross-country, on a trail most of which was unmarked. To keep from freezing in 30 to 40 degree below zero weather I wore men's felt shoes with heavy cloth overshoes, wool knee socks, two pairs of lined trousers, sweaters, a man's overcoat, heavy wool cap and scarves. My hands were the first to get cold so leather mittens, lined with wool knitted mittens, were a requirement. Even then, I would sometimes have to beat them on the pommel of the saddle to get the blood to circulate. The biggest problem with all this clothing was dressing and undressing. In no way would a female teacher be allowed to teach wearing trousers. So, I had to keep dress clothes at school and change when I got there. Then, in the evening, it was back into all those riding clothes. Another problem was getting on the horse with all that weight.

One school I taught was located in very rugged country directly west of the Killdeer Mountains in Dunn County. It was set back from the main road about 1 1/2 miles. The trail to the school wound down through deep ravines and up over the steepest of hills. One student lived with her father near the top of one of the mountains about 3 miles from school. She was about 8 years old. They would ski to the bottom of the mountain and then would walk and ski where possible the rest of the way to school. Her father would go home and then return to get her in the afternoon. She missed very few days of school.

After the third month of school the board notified me that they were out of money. School

continued on next page

would continue but they would pay me with registered warrants. I would send them to the State Capitol where they were converted to negotiable checks, but the amount was reduced by 10 percent. My $50 warrant was reduced to $45.

During my teaching career I had as few as 4 pupils and as many as 28. Grade levels ranged from first to eight. To be a good rural school teacher you had to be a good organizer, especially with eight grades. The first grade had to be taught separately, but other grades could be combined in several subjects. Children often helped one another, and I believe they learned much from observing other grades.

Supervision of teachers was certainly lacking. The county superintendent probably visited once or twice a year. School board members never visited. If you needed something you had to go looking for them. I wasn't aware of the state department [of education] in my earlier years. Parents did visit in some schools. Generally you were pretty much on your own. Rural schools could provide a good education, but it depended on the teacher and the desire of parents and board members to demand the best of the teacher. In some instances patrons and board members took no interest. The pupils suffered if the teacher wasn't dedicated to giving her best.

✍ ✍

Carrie Busby aiming a pistol from the school house *(Carrie Busby Collection, NDIRS)*

. . . be yourself, because children are quick to recognize a fraud; make the community your community; and, by example, leave in that community lasting expressions of kindness, compassion, and open-mindedness.

object of special surveillance and concern," country school teachers would have done well to adopt Marion White Currier's

COMMANDMENTS OF THE COUNTRY TEACHER

Thou shalt adopt this country school,
Here with nature, quiet and bleak;
Inside some gloom and musty books,
A spell of loneliness and mystique.

Thou shalt keep a tidy room
All janitorial duties to perform:
Sweep the floor, clean boards and dust,
Fire up and keep it comfortably warm.

Thou shalt devote and dedicate.
You're a teacher, a social symbol high.
Be satisfied with modest bed and board,
Though for salary, you almost cry.

Thou shalt instruct every single child
Some oral, some written and some outlined.
To read, to spell and do arithmetic;
Flash cards could almost do the trick.

Thou shalt discipline very wisely.
Promote and master basic skills.
Use ingenuity, with determination too,
For leadership with a satisfied will.

Thou shalt glide softly about the room.
Remember the contract and the code.
Every child should work and share,
Doing his portion of the load.

Thou shalt pray for heroic courage
To always abide by the Golden Rule;
The gratitude of work is salvation,
A tribute to the Country School,
That slowly passed away.[89]

What exactly was the country school teacher's place in American society? Perhaps, Maude Frazier, a teacher in Nevada, answered the question best. "Early in the 1900's, women teachers suffered most of the restrictions of nuns, with none of the advantages they enjoyed. . . . Nobody defined exactly what a teacher's place was, but everyone knew she should keep it."[90]

🖆✎

Endnotes

1. Robin M. Williams, Jr., *American Society*, 3rd. ed. *(New York: Alfred A. Knopf, 1970)*, *p. 328.*

2. North Dakota, *Laws of North Dakota*, 1890, c. 62, sec. 130.

3. North Dakota, Department of Public Instruction, *Rural School Management*, 1923, p. 14.

4. *Ibid.*, pp. 13-14.

5. *Laws of North* Dakota, 1890, c. 62, sec. 130.

6. *Laws of North Dakota*, 1911, c. 266, sec. 271.

7. North Dakota, *Compiled Laws of North Dakota*, 1913, sec. 1374-1375.

8. North Dakota, Superintendent of Public Instruction, *Fourth Biennial Report*, 1896, p. 17.

9. *Ibid.*, pp. 17-18.

10. University of North Dakota, Chester Fritz Library, Elwyn B. Robinson Department of Special Collections, Country School Legacy, Dan Rylance, "Reading, Writing, Arithmetic and Recitation: The Curriculum of the One Room Country School," p. 12.

11. *Laws of North Dakota*, 1917, c. 234.

12. *Laws of North Dakota*, 1993, c. 190, sec. 1.

13. *Fourth Biennial Report*, 1896, pp. 15-16.

14. Dan Rylance, pp. 11-12.

15. *Ibid*, p. 12.

16. *Laws of North Dakota*, 1929, c. 210.

17. Nellie R. Swanson and Eleanor C. Bryson, eds., *Pioneer Women Teachers of North Dakota* (Minot: *Ward County Independent*, 1965), p. 11. Johnstone was born in Glencoe, Minnesota on April 14, 1870. Her family moved to Grand Forks in April 1883. In May 1885 she began to teach a one-room village school, teaching for six summers while continuing high school and enrolling at the University. After graduating from the University with Phi Beta Kappa honors she became the principal at Buxton. After two years she served as principal at Thompson for one year, at Hillsboro for five, and at Grand Forks for thirteen. She was also instrumental in effecting legislation providing for school nurses. Department of Public Instruction, *Manual of Physical Education for the Elementary Schools of North Dakota*, 1931, p. 51.

18. North Dakota, Department of Public Instruction, *Arbor Day Pamphlets*, 1892, pp. 4,5,12,13; 1894, pp. 3-5. The Wild Prairie Rose became the official flower for North Dakota in 1907.

19. North Dakota, North Dakota Historical Society, Local Government Records, Burleigh County, Estherville School District, Box. 1/1.

20. Laws *of North Dakota*, 1890, c. 62, sec. 128.

21. *Ibid.*, sec. 132.

22. *Compiled Laws of North Dakota*, 1913, sec. 1374-1375.

23. United States, Federal Emergency Relief Administration for North Dakota, *Survey of Rural Education in North Dakota*, n.d. [1935?], p. 24.

24. *Ibid.*, p. 29.

25. Ibid., p. 33.

26. University of North Dakota, Chester Fritz Library, Elwyn B. Robinson Department of Special Collections, Country School Legacy, Contracts.

27. Local Government Records, Hettinger County, Superintendent of Schools, Teacher's Contracts, Box 10/12.

28. Country School Legacy, Contracts.

29. *Ibid.*

30. Hettinger County, Superintendent of Schools, Teacher Contracts, Box 10/12.

31. Country School Legacy, Contracts.

32. Dakota Territory, Board of Education, *Common Schools of Dakota*, District System, Compiled from the Various Enactments of the Legislative Assembly from 1877-1885, p. 57.

33. North Dakota, Department of Public Instruction, Circular No. 36., *Institute Manual and Notebook*, 1892, pp. 1-6.

34. *Ibid.*, Circular No. 37, 1892, pp. 1-4. The county institute fund originally consisted of all money received by the county superintendent from examination fees. In 1890 the state created the State Institute Fund by allocating $50 each year to each organized county in which there were ten or more resident teachers. By 1920 the appropriation was increased to $100 each year to each organized county.

35. *Fourth Biennial Report*, 1896, p. 10.

36. *Ibid.*, p. 13.

37. *Ibid.*, pp. 317-331.

38. *Ibid.*, p. 14.

39. Elywyn B. Robinson, *History of North Dakota* (Lincoln: University of Nebraska Press, 1966), p. 305.

40. *Bismarck Tribune*, February 5, 1921, p. 8.

41. North Dakota, Superintendent of Public Instruction, *Twentieth Biennial Report*, 1928, pp. 8-9.

42. *Ibid.*, pp. 24-29.

43. *Fourth Biennial Report*, 1896, p. 10.

44. North Dakota, Superintendent of Public Instruction, *Circular No. 7*, 1895, p. 61.

45. *Laws of North Dakota*, 1891, c. 56, sec. 7, 22.

46. North Dakota, Superintendent of Public Instruction,*Circular No. 2*, 1895, p. 30; *Circular No. 7*, 1895, pp. 63-64.

47. *Circular No. 7*, pp.63-65.

48. *Ibid.*, pp. 65-66.

49. North Dakota, Stutsman County, *Pupils Reading Circle Prospectus for 1903-1904*, pp. 2-7.

50. *Ibid.*, *Laws of North Dakota*, 1905, c. 100, sec. 695.

51. *Laws of North Dakota*, 1921, c. 112. The Nonpartisan League controlled the Senate, 25 to 24; the Independent Voters Association controlled the House, 59 to 54. The Senate vote on the bill was 45 to 3 in favor. The negative votes were cast by IVA members. In the House the vote was 57 to 42 in favor; of the 42 negative votes 31 were cast by IVA members. *Senate Journal,* 1921, p. 516; *House Journal*, 1921, p. 735. At a recall election on October 28, 1921, the first recall of state officials in the United States, IVA candidate Ragnvold A. Nestos defeated NPL Governor Lynn J. Frazier in a close election, 111,434 votes to 107,332.

52. *Bismarck Tribune*, January 22, 1921, p. 1.

53. Rozanne Enerson Junker, *The Bank of North Dakota* (Santa Barbara: Fithian Press, 1989), p. 84. *Bismarck Tribune*, January 19, 1921, p. 5; *Kenmare News*, March 17, 1921, p. 1; Robinson, p. 349.

54. Robinson, pp. 371-379.

55. *Bismarck Tribune*, January 19, 1922, pp. 1,7.

56. *Sargent County News*, January 26, 1922, p. 1.

57. *Ibid.*, February 9, 1922, p. 1. The taxpayers also recommended that new public works projects be suspended for two years or until conditions improved; that all political subdivisions and public officials cooperate to reduce public expenditures, that the county commissioners submit to a vote of the people continuance of the levy for agricultural extension work, the employment of the county agent and club leader, and that all county officials devote their time to the business of their offices.

58. *LaMoure County Chronicle*, February 9, 1922, p. 1.

59. *Hillsboro Banner*, February 24, 1922, p. 1.

60. *Ibid.*, March 24, 1922, p. 2.

61. *The Associated Teacher*, March, 1922, p. 15.

62. *Sargent County News*, March 30, 1922, p. 1.

63. *Hillsboro Banner*, March 3, 1922, p. 1.

64. *Lakota American*, March 23, 1922, p. 1. Other resolutions: (1) reduce taxes "to save the property owner from financial ruin"; (2) all taxing officials should "practice the utmost economy in making levies"; (3) commended the county commissioners for building federal, state, and county roads, especially the latter; (4) abolish the Motor Vehicle Department, return motor licensing functions to the Secretary of State's office; (5) amend the motor vehicle law, return vehicle license monies to the county to build and maintain roads; (6) repeal the legislature's authority to exempt any and all classes of personal property by amending the state's constitution; (8) abolish a class subsidy by repealing the tax exempt status of government, state, and municipal and other bonds, by amending the national constitution; (10) urged the next legislature to thoroughly survey all state institutions and commissions with an eye toward abolishing the unnecessary; (11) sent copies of the resolutions to daily and county newspapers in the state. The resolutions committee was composed of: J. G. Gunderson, N. O. Hougen, W. C. Hagler, J. J. Schindele, O. S. Hove. The State Taxpayer' Association was incorporated in December 1922. Its purpose: "To investigate questions of taxation imposed upon the taxpayers of the state, to secure and disseminate accurate information among the members and the public in general on that subject, with the view of causing a material reduction of the heavy tax burden now existing; to make recommendations relative thereto to the taxing officers in the state and other interested bodies and to aid in promoting and securing economy and efficiency in the administration of public affairs. To call public meetings, promote auxiliary organizations and to propose and cause to be initiated and adopted such Legislative enactments and constitutional amendments as it may deem necessary to attain its objects and purposes." Incorporators were: J. G. Gunderson, Aneta; E. J. Weiser, Fargo; W. C. McDowell, Marion; T. Welo, Velva; A. L. Martin, Sentinel Butte. North Dakota, Secretary of State, *Non-Profit Corporations*, Vol. 1, p. 399. In 1934 the North Dakota Taxpayers' Association was incorporated by John Conrad of Erie, Harrison Garnett of St. Thomas, and John Dawson of Mandan. *Ibid.*, Vol. 2, p. 563. In 1958 the North Dakota Taxpayer's League, Incorporated was founded by Keith V. Bacon, William M. Trepanier, and Fritz Nelson, all of Grand Forks. *Ibid.*, Volume 7, p. 118.

65. *The Associated Teacher*, June, 1922, pp. 7-8; May, 1922, p. 15; November, 1922, p. 23.

66. *Kenmare News*, June 8, 1922, pp. 1,8; *The Associated Teacher*, May, 1922, p. 7.

67. *The Associated Teacher*, April, 1922., pp. 10-11.

68. *Ibid.*, p. 24.

69. *Ibid.*, May, 1922, p. 7.

70. *Ibid.*, pp. 4-6. The National Education Association concluded that the cost of living increased 71 percent from December 1914 to December 1921. To match their buying power in 1914 teachers' salaries in 1921 should have averaged 171 percent of their 1914-1915 salary.

71. *Ibid.*, February, 1922, p. 26.

72. *Kenmare News*, June 8, 1922, p. 8.

73. *The Associated Teacher*, May, 1922, pp. 10, 12, 15; February, 1922, p. 13. State Superintendent of Public Instruction Minnie J. Nielson pointed out that for the year 1919-1920 most of the money spent for education was returned to the local community: 90 percent of the $6,238,154.79 spent for the salaries of 5,057 teachers; all monies spent for transporting pupils, $876,876.10; and the total amount spent for paying the salaries and expenses of 11,275 school officers, $220,583.16. In addition $5,992.81 was spent for evening schools and the $274,722.02 in interest paid on bonds went into the state apportionment fund. Nielson also noted that for the same period North Dakotans spent $29.74 per capita on luxuries and other nonessentials (theater tickets, candy, soft drinks, ice cream, perfume, cosmetics, automobiles) while spending only $19.72 per capita on education.

74. *Laws of North Dakota*, 1923, Initiated Measures, Repeal of Teachers Minimum Training and Salary Law, p. 548.

75. *Rural School Management*, 1923, p. 9.

76. Country School Legacy, Contracts.

77. *Ibid.*

78. Marie Mynster Feidler, ed., *In Retrospect* (North Dakota Retired Teachers Association, 1976), pp. 104-105.

79. *Ibid.*, pp. 112-114.

80. *Ibid.*, p. 138.

81. Country School Legacy, Contracts.

82. *Ibid.*

83. *Ibid.*

84. *The Great Plains Newsletter*, Vol. 4, No. 3, September 1982, p. 2.

85. Country School Legacy, Contracts.

86. *Ibid.*

87. *Ibid.*

88. North Dakota Historical Society, Timothy John Austin, "Reminiscences of Teachers and Students in The One-Room Rural Schools of North Dakota," Seminar Paper, Minot State College, April 1976, p. 7.

89. *In Retrospect.*, p. 98.

90. Andrew Gulliford, *Country School Legacy: Humanities On The Frontier* (Silt, Colorado: Country School Legacy, 1981), p. 22.

Sod School in Western Divide County, 1910 *(Hulstrand Collection, NDIRS)*

Chapter 8

Teacher Examinations

Superintendent of Public Instruction
State of North Dakota
W. L. Stockwell, Superintendent
Ninth Biennial Report, 1906

THE FOLLOWING PAGES include the rules governing examination of teachers and the examinations themselves used in North Dakota in 1905-1906. It was the responsibility of the county superintendents to administer the examinations, and as the document which follows indicates, the Department of Instruction was most concerned that there be no cheating: ". . . Our readers return papers to us which indicate too great a similarity, and we have frequently called the attention of the county superintendents to these matters. Certainly there is nothing that needs to be more thoroughly safeguarded than examinations of this character." The following pages duplicate the layout and design of the 1906 document. The *Report* of 1906 begins with a summary:

EXAMINATIONS OF CERTIFICATES

During the past biennial period examinations have been held under the provisions of section 740 (amended) and the result of these examinations is as follows:

First grades... 84

Second grades... 1,718

Third grades... 1,923

Failures... 3,466

Appended are two sets of county examination questions, and also a set of primary questions:

TEACHERS' EXAMINATION.

October 27,28, 1905.

RULES AND REGULATIONS.

School teachers who took teacher's exam in Dunn Center, Fall, 1914 *(SHSND)*

The department has made an endeavor to revise the rules and regulations governing the matter of teachers' examinations, and we have eliminated a number of same which have previously appeared.

However, we desire to impress upon all county superintendents the necessity of having these examinations conducted in such a way that there can be no possibility of any irregularities. Occasionally our readers return papers to us which indicate too great a similarity, and we have frequently called the attention of the county superintendents to these matters. Certainly there is nothing that needs to be more thoroughly safeguarded than examinations of this character. You will therefore use every measure in your judgment necessary to have all perfectly fair and honest.

Candidates and examiners should read carefully, and must comply strictly with the following:

Rule 1.—Questions are in sealed envelopes and must be first opened in the presence of the class after candidates are in their seats, and this paper has been read by each candidate.

Questions on one subject, only, will be handed candidates at a time, and until this subject is completed or time limit called.

A Country School Teacher Remembers — Eleanor Burdict

In 1924 a high school graduate could teach in a rural school without any further education. The training I had for my first year of teaching was so very inadequate. During my senior year in high school I took a methods course, forget the title, that stipulated that there were *two* methods of teaching beginning reading. One was the "word method" and the other the phonic. *That* was my training! I was hired to teach the "home" school and began teaching in September 1924. I was not 18 until in October, so my first month of teaching was with a permit. I did not know whether to feel sorrier for the children or their teacher. Ever summer, thereafter, until 1929, I attended Valley City State Teachers College. There, I took all the electives that I thought would help me with my teaching. During the winter term in 1929 I was granted six weeks leave of absence from my teaching job and again attended Valley City College. There, I did my practice teaching. In August 1929 I graduated from the two year course at the school, obtaining what was then called a Standard degree.

The school *Register* was a book that remained in the teacher's desk from year to year. It contained the previous teacher's daily schedule. A teacher could model hers after it, or make any changes she wished.

Schoolboard members were seldom visitors. I don't believe they were especially interested as long as there were no complaints from parents or teachers. Parents did come, rarely. Fathers were usually *too* busy and mothers often had no means of transportation.

If one found a child who was not working at the level he was expected to be, perhaps she or he would require extra help. It could cause much friction if a child were held back. I was always available for help before or after school. In fact, *sometimes* I would *insist* on it.

The first two years I taught I stayed at home. In Grant County I shared a room with two daughters, sleeping in a single bed. I did help with the household chores, not because I was expected to but as a change from the school room routine. When I had a room of my own I was expected to take care of it. At one place where there were many cows to milk I sometimes milked as many as six cows in the evenings. The lady of the house was always glad of a helping hand in the kitchen also.

During my first year of teaching I was visited by County Superintendent Minnie J. Nielson

continued on next page

Rule 2.—The program for this examination, which accompanies the questions, must be followed. The examiner will announce the time of beginning to write on each subject; also, the time of closing. Immediately upon announcing close of period the examiner shall collect all papers written on the one subject and seal same in an envelope, provided by the department of public instruction, arranged according to the number of applicants and properly labeled for identification, and place them in a secure place (so as to be able to certify "that no person saw or had an opportunity to see, handle or alter them after they were handed in by the applicants").

Rule 3.—The examiner will offer no explanation of any question or the meaning of the same.

Rule 4.—Each applicant must be supplied with paper and with pen and black ink. Papers must not be folded or rolled, and if an applicant writes on more than one sheet for a subject, his papers should not be pinned or fastened together in any way. Superintendents or examiners will kindly see that this rule is followed.

Rule 5.—The county superintendent will see that all papers written in the county are forwarded, prepaid by express or registered mail, plainly addressed to the Superintendent of Public Instruction, Bismarck, N. D., not later than the third day following the examination.

The standing in writing will be marked upon the general appearance of papers.

The following regulations in regard to acceptance of standings will be observed by the Department of Public Instruction:

First—No credit will be given unless the applicant has received normal standing since attaining the age of sixteen years.

Second—No standing from either of the normal schools or from the normal college of the university will be accepted, which was received more than two years prior to the date of the examination at which the same is presented, unless the applicant is a regular accredited student of one of the said institutions, under which condition the standing may be presented within three years of the time the same was received.

Third—No standings will be accepted for second or third grade certificates which are less than 80 per cent, and no standings will be accepted for first grade certificates which are less than 90 per cent.

CERTIFICATES SHALL BE OF THREE GRADES.

Third Grade—The third grade certificate is good for one year. A person will not be allowed to teach more than fifteen months on third grade certificates. The applicants must be eighteen years of age. To obtain a third grade certificate the applicant must average 75 per cent in reading, writing, orthography, language lessons and English grammar, geography, United States history, arithmetic, civil government, physiology and hygiene, and theory and practice, and must not fall below 65 per cent in any of them.

Second Grade—The applicant must be eighteen years of age. To obtain a second grade certificate must average 85 per cent, and must not fall below 70 per cent in any of the same branches.

who found fault with my seatwork method of teaching combinations to first graders. I let them use pegs to find the sums! The technique was later used in modern math. She also criticized my many pictures on the walls. She understood my motive though when I took one down and showed her they covered holes in the plaster. She played games with the children at noon. She was a grand lady!

First Grade—The applicant for a first grade certificate must be twenty years of age, and must have taught successfully twelve school months. To obtain a first grade certificate the applicant must average 90 per cent, and not fall below 75 per cent in above branches, and must average 75 per cent and not fall below 65 per cent in physical geography, natural philosophy, algebra, geometry and psychology.

Hereafter it will be impossible for any candidate for first grade certificate to complete the examination at one time. The number of applicants for first grade certificates is so small that it seems best to make the program conform more largely to the needs of the greater number, viz: those writing for second and third grade certificates. Candidates for first grade certificates will be able to write upon the subjects for a second grade at one examination and then complete the advanced subject necessary for a first grade certificate at the next examination. The fee once paid covers both examinations for first grade; there will be no additional fee.

Candidates who fail in any subjects at this examination or those who desire to raise their grades may write on the subjects in which they fail at the next examination. No additional fee will be charged for the second examination. If examinations are not satisfactorily completed upon two trials all standings will be canceled. In all cases the applicant's number at the previous examination should be submitted with his papers.

County superintendents in remitting fees for examination will forward the amount by draft, express or postoffice money order, which amount in every case must equal $1 for each applicant.

If you remit by personal check add to the sum a sufficient amount to cover exchange.

W. L. STOCKWELL,
Superintendent of Public Instruction.

The Cass County Teachers' Institute, 1894 *(Porterville Collection, NDIRS))*

PROGRAM FOR TEACHERS' EXAMINATION

October 27,28, 1905.

FRIDAY, A. M.

Reading Rules and Regulations...9 to 9:10

Preliminary..9:10 to 9:30

Second and Third Grade Subjects.		First Grade Subjects.
Arithmetic....................................9:30 to 11.........................Algebra
Civics...11 to 12........Physical Geography

P.M.

U. S. History.............................1:15 to 2:35.....................Geometry

Geography...................................2:35 to 44...... ....Psychology

SATURDAY, A. M.

Language and Grammar...9 to 10:15

Physiology and Hygiene..10:15 to 11:15

Reading...11:15 to 12:15

Orthography...12:15 to 1

(C. E. October 27, 1905.)

PRELIMINARY.

No credits assigned on this paper.

1. Have you read the rules governing this examination?
2. What is your age?
3. How many months of school have you taught, and where?
4. Are you a citizen of the United States? If not, have you resided in the United States during the last twelve months?
5. *(a)* Are you a graduate of a college or university? If so, of what institution? *(b)* Are you a graduate of a normal school? Of what school? *(c)* Are you a graduate of a high school? Of what school?
6. What was the grade of your last certificate and where held? How many times have you held the same grade certificate and where?
7. How many months, if any, have you taught in the state on third grade certificates?
8. What special training have you had for the work of teaching?
9. What teachers' association have you attended during the past year?
10. What books on teaching have you read?
11. Do you subscribe for and read regularly any educational journal? If so, what?
12. What does the law require with regard to teaching *(a)* hygiene and effects of stimulants and narcotics, *(b)* civil government, *(c)* physical culture?
13. Did you attend institute or training school last year? If not, why?

Pictures above are sections from photograph below of the Griggs & Steele County Picnic. *(Porterville Collection, NDIRS)*

14. Are you a member of the North Dakota Teachers' Reading Circle? If not, do you expect to join the reading circle? The department urges every teacher to become a member this year. Are you familiar with the course of study for common schools in this state?

Hand the county superintendent $2 with the preliminary paper. The statutes require every candidate to pay a fee of $2 for examination, whether successful or otherwise.

(C. E. October 27, 1905)

LIST OF WORDS TO BE SPELLED.

develop	phonics	embarrass
proceeding	initiative	judgment
sheriff	superstitious	kerosene
syllable	Panama	Bismarck
expense	alcohol	precedent
Manila	arrangement	deceive
separate	prairie	believe
munitions	apologize	Roosevelt
pedagogy		

(C. E. October 27, 1905.)

ORTHOGRAPHY.

1. Of what value is a knowledge of syllabication? How would you teach it?
2. *(a)* Use correctly in sentences each of the following words and give a hononym *[sic]* of each: aisle, clime, claws, draught. *(b)* Give a synonym of each of the following words: courage, high, wealthy. *(c)* Give an antonmy *[sic]* of love, success, fine.
3. Exemplify the use of three prefixes and explain their force or meaning.
4. Illustrate by words and indicate by diacritical marks: *(a)* four sounds of a; *(b)* two of g; *(c)* two of c; *(d)* two of e.
5. Spell list of words to be pronounced by examiner.

(C. E. October 27, 1905.)

Gusta Wermager, Teacher, Williams County, Dist. 69, School No. 3, @1903-1913 (Martha P. Tatem Collection, SHSND)

READING.

Note: Answer any five questions and only five; if more than five are answered credit will be given on the first five answered.

1. How may the reading lesson be utilized in teaching: *(a)* Patriotism; *(b)* kindness to animals; *(c)* courtesy?
2. In teaching reading what use may be made of: *(a)* fairy tales; *(b)* biography; *(c)* historical sketches? In which grades may they be used to advantage?

3. *(a)* If your pupils have access to a well selected library how may they be taught to use it profitably? (b) Mention some of the benefits of a free public library.
4. Define: *(a)* elementary sound; *(b)* phonic analysis; *(c)* supplementary reading; *(d)* word method; *(e)* emphasis.
5. *(a)* What preparation of a reading lesson should a fifth grade pupil make?
(b) How do you determine a perfect recitation?
6. Name the author of the following: Barefoot Boy, Snow Bound, The Scarlet Letter, Merchant of Venice, The Hoosier School Master.

Souvenir for 1900 school term of School District No. 15, Mabel Township, Griggs Co., Louise C. Kaas, Teacher (enlargement below) *(Porterville Collection, NDINRS)*

7. *(a)* Write four questions such as you would ask a class studying the poem from which the following selection is taken.

> The way was long, the wind was cold,
> The minstrel was infirm and old;
> His withered cheek and tresses gray
> Seemed to have known a better day;
> The harp, his sole remaining joy,
> Was carried by an orphan boy.
> The last of all the bards was he,
> Who sang for border chivalry;
> For, well-a-day! their date was fled,
> His tuneful brothers all were dead;
> And he neglected and oppressed,
> Wished to be with them and at rest.

(b) In which grade might the poem from which the above is taken be studied profitably? *(c)* Name the poem from which this selection is taken. Name the author.

(C. E. October 27, 1905.)

LANGUAGE AND GRAMMAR.

Note: Answer any five questions and only five; if more than five are answered credit will be given on the first five answered.

1. (a) What is meant by the antecedent of a pronoun? Illustrate, using more than one kind of pronoun. (b) Compare: noble, good, able, cleanly, bad.

2. Illustrate in sentences: (a) Noun clause; (b) adjective clause; (c) adverbial clause; rewrite the sentences, changing each clause into an equivalent phrase.

3. Give the principal parts of the following verbs: Bid, bite, drive, seek, fight, drink, cleave, slay, awake, mean.

4. Combine the following sentences into one and tell whether your sentence is simple, complex or compound: Washington crossed the Delaware. He crossed the river at night. The river was full of floating ice. The night was dark and cold. He surprised the enemy. He took many prisoners. He lost only two men.

5. (a) Illustrate in sentences two uses of the infinitive; (b) analyze your sentences.

6. What is the difference between the conjugation and the synopsis of a verb. Give a synopsis of the verb "have" in the first person plural, active voice, indicative mood.

7. (a) Define: Case, tense, comparison, declension, preposition, antecedent. (b) What is meant by a redundant verb? A defective verb.

(C. E. October 27, 1905.)

Teacher with students *(Porterville Collection, NDIRS)*

GEOGRAPHY.

Note: Answer any five questions and only five; if more than five are answered, credit will be given on the first five answered.

1. *(a)* What two river systems in North America are the most important commercially? *(b)* Name five cities on one of these rivers and state for what each is noted.

2. Define: *(a)* Latitude; *(b)* longitude; *(c)* give the approximate latitude of the east boundary and the longitude of the south boundary of North Dakota.

3. Give two reasons why the Panama canal will be of great benefit to the United States. Mention some of the principal difficulties to be overcome in the construction of that canal.

4. Compare New York and North Dakota as to population, aggregate wealth, commercial industries, manufacturing, education.

5. Draw an outline map of North Dakota and locate your county, its county seat, the state capital, the three largest cities. Estimate the value of this year's crop of grain of various kinds in North Dakota.

6. Name the leading products of Ohio, Georgia, California, Missouri, Maine. Name the capital of each.

7. Name and locate three large cities of Europe favorably situated for commerce; three large cities of the United States favorably situated for manufacturing. Of what educational value may a visit to Washington, D. C., become?

(C. E. October 27, 1905.)

Souvenir for 1897-1898 school term at Cooperstown, Griggs Co., H.A. Faar, Teacher (enlargement below) *(Porterville Collection, NDINRS)*

UNITED STATES HISTORY.

Note: Answer any five questions and only five; if more than five are answered, credit will be given on the first five answered.

1. Name three Europeans who made voyages to the New World before the year 1500 A. D., and mention discoveries made by each.

2. Name two Englishmen who made unsuccessful attempts to found a colony in America. (a) Name two Englishmen who made successful attempts to found colonies in America.

3. *(a)* Name two members of Washington's first cabinet who were leaders in different political parties. *(b)* What was the leading principle at issue between these parties?

4. Name three legislative acts affecting slavery. *(b)* Name one judicial decision defining the status of the slave.

5. In whose administration was each of the following acts passed? *(a)* Civil Service Act; *(b)* Interstate Commerce; *(c)* McKinley Bill; *(d)* Dingley Bill?

6. What was: *(a)* The Embargo Act; *(b)* Alien Law; *(c)* Kansas Nebraska Bill; *(d)* Missouri Compromise; (e) Wilmot Proviso?

7. What wars did the following treaties conclude:

    (a) First Treaty of Paris?

    (b) Second Treaty of Paris?

    (c) Treaty of Ghent?

    (d) Treaty of Guadelope Hidalgo?

    (e) Treaty of Portsmouth.

(C. E. October 27, 1905.)

Saying at bottom of Souvenir above:

Let fate do her worst: there are relics of joy. Bright dreams of the past that she cannot destroy: Which come in the night time of sorrow and care, And bring back the features that joy used to wear.

ARITHMETIC.

Note: Answer any five questions and only five; if more than five are answered, credit will be given on the first five answered.

1. Which is the better investment of $4,000.00, a three per cent. bond or a house that rents for $250.00 per year, taxes being $27.50 and annual repairs $35.00?

2. How much will it cost to plaster a room 18 feet long, 15 feet wide and 10 feet high at 37 cents per square yard, allowing 102 square feet for openings?

3. A farmer bought a quarter section of land at $12.00 per acre, which he planted to wheat. The cost of cultivating the land, seed and harvesting was $3.25 per acre. The taxes on the farm were $14.80. How many bushels of wheat per acre will it require to pay the expense of operating the farm and pay 6 per cent. on the original investment; wheat being worth 65 cents per bushel?

4. The insurance on two-thirds the value of a house costs $30.00, the rate being three-fourths of one per cent. What is the value of the house?

5. At $4.75 per cord, what will it cost to fill with wood a shed 34 feet long, 18 feet wide and 10 feet high?

6. Suppose your county superintendent sold John Doe 1,650 lbs. of hay at $13.00 per ton; 2,650 lbs. of coal at $9.50 per ton; 5,120 lbs. of oats at 24 cents per bushel. Make out a bill for above goods, carrying out the amounts for the different items and giving total amount of bill.

7. Plat a congressional township and number the sections. Locate in some one section a farm of 160 acres; one of 80 acres; one of 40 acres. Give the description of each farm according to its location in the section.
(C. E. October 27, 1905.)

Teacher at Golden Glen School No. 2, LaMoure County *(SHSND)*

CIVIL GOVERNMENT.

Note: Answer any five questions and only five; if more than five are answered, credit will be given on the first five answered.

1. *(a)* By whom are U. S. Senators elected? *(b)* How long is their term? *(c)* What qualifications must they possess to be eligible for election? *(d)* What is a copyright? *(e)* A patent?

2. How may the Constitution of North Dakota be amended? *(b)* How does the county superintendent of schools secure his office? *(c)* Who may vote for him? *(d)* How long is his term of office?

3. What sole power has the national House of Representatives in regard to impeachment of U. S. Officials? *(b)* What sole power has the U. S. Senate in impeachment charges? *(c)* Who presides over the trial of the president of the United States on impeachment charges?

4. *(a)* What bodies in North Dakota decide the amount of tax to be raised for the use of the state? *(b)* The county? The city? *(c)* The township? *(d)* The schools?

5. Name a judicial officer *(a)* of the state of North Dakota; *(b)* of a county; *(c)* of a town; *(d)* mention one way in which a bill, vetoed by the governor of North Dakota may become a law. *(e)* What is a city ordinance?

6. What are the duties of: *(a)* The executive department of our own state; *(b)* the legislative; *(c)* the judicial?

7. *(a)* What is a census? *(b)* When was the last national census taken? *(c)* The last North Dakota state census? *(d)* What benefits are derived from a census?
(C. E. October 27, 1905.)

Teacher in School Dist. 65, Barnes Co. *(SHSND)*

PHYSIOLOGY AND HYGIENE.

Note: Answer any five questions and only five; if more than five are answered, credit will be given on the first five answered.

1. Mention three school practices which seem to you unhygienic. Suggest a remedy for each.

2. Name three principal divisions of the brain, and one function of each part.

3. Give three reasons why physical exercise promotes health.

4. What is temperance? In what way may it be taught to fifth grade pupils? Why is such instruction vitally important?

5. What would you do in case one of your pupils severed an artery? Received a severe burn? Should faint? Break a bone?

6. Define: muscle, vein, assimilation, congestion, gland, sprain, tissue.

7. On what grounds is the state justified in requiring the teaching of the injurious effects of the use of narcotics and alcoholic drinks?

(C. E. October 27, 1905.)

Teacher Margaret C. [last name unknown] wrote in 1907 when this photograph was taken (enlargements below), "We are planning to have a basket social to start a library when the new building is finished." Colgan School, Williams County (SHSND)

THEORY AND PRACTICE.

Note: Answer any five questions and only five; if more than five are answered, credit will be given on the first five answered.

1. What books on teaching have you read during the past year? What works of general literature? What benefit did you derive from reading?

2. Do you approve of a monthly written review? Give reasons for your answer.

3. How may good discipline be secured? Why is it that our schools are turning out such poor spellers? What is the chief fault in the teaching of geography? United States history?

4. Why is a course of study necessary? Should all pupils in an ungraded school be compelled to follow the course strictly? Why?

5. How would you impart lessons of cleanliness and morality to pupils whose home surroundings are bad? Why is this sometimes a delicate task?

6. When can a person be said to be well educated?

7. Name two educational journals and three magazines you might use profitably in your school work.

(C. E. October 27, 1905.)

PHYSICS.

Answer all questions.

1. What is a machine? State the law of machines. Define friction.

2. Distinguish between acceleration and velocity. What is meant by the resultant of two forces? Illustrate.

3. Define: adhesion, cohesion, bouyancy. Why will a steel ship float on water?

4. Describe the methods and principles involved in the formation of artificial cold, or ice.

5. Describe the operation of the telephone.

(C. E. October 27, 1905.)

GEOMETRY.

Answer all questions.

1. Define: Theorem, chord, inscribed angle, transversal, and mean proportional. Illustrate.

2. Construction: Circumscribe a circle about a given triangle.

3. Prove that the perpendicular bisectors of the sides of a triangle meet in a point.

4. If any chord is drawn through a fixed point within a circle, the product of its segments is constant in whatever direction the chord is drawn. Demonstrate.

5. Prove the area of a triangle equal to one-half the product of its base and altitude.

(C. E. October 27, 1905.)

ALGEBRA.

1. Factor. *(a)* $4a^2 x^3 -9x$. *(b)* $x^4 +x^2 y^2+y^4$. *(c)* $3x^2 +7x-6$. *(d)* $a^6 -a^4 -a^2 +1$. *(e)* $x^4 -36$.

2. Define equation, coefficient, radical, surd, pure quadratic; and give example of each.

3. What is the meaning of a fractional exponent? Find value of x in the expression $(3x+2)^{2/3}=4$.

4. The sum of two numbers and the difference of their squares are both equal to 9; find the numbers.

5. A picture frame 6x10 inches is surrounded by a frame whose area is 144 square inches. Find the width of the frame.

(C. E. October 27, 1905.)

Olive Richardson (enlargement below) with her students at School No. 1, Dist. 36, Williams Co., c.a. 1903-1913 *(SHSND)*

PSYCHOLOGY.

Answer all questions.

1. Define: Apperception, intuition, prejudice, volition.

2. Distinguish between fancy and imagination. What is the relation of imagination to education?

3. What is meant by interest? What rules should teachers observe in developing interest? Why is cramming bad?

4. Distinguish between inductive and deductive reasoning. Illustrate.

5. Define sensation. What are the conditions of sensation? Is sensation knowledge? Why?

(C. E. October 27, 1905.)

PHYSICAL GEOGRAPHY.

Answer all questions.

1. State the relation of the physical geography of a region to the activities of its people.

2. How is soil formed, and how do you account for the difference in variety and fertility?

3. Give the cause of cyclones. What is their direction of movement in the northern hemisphere?

4. Explain the formation of dew, frost, and hail.

5. Climate, define; state effect of large bodies of water; of forests and vegetation.

(C. E. October 27, 1905.)

Griggs County Teachers' Institute, 1897-1898 *(Porterville Collection, NDIRS)*

Chapter 9

A Teacher in Early Days in Sargent County *

An Old Teacher of Sargent County

For a young girl, still in her teens, because of her burdens and the burdens of others, the sorrow and suffering, she felt hopeless and discouraged. There seemed to be neither justice nor reason in it all.

It was a new country and everything seemed hard for everybody. She did not know then that that was the way in all new countries; that the comforts of civilization must

*Source: The North Dakota Teacher, Vol. 5, No. 1, September, 1925, pp. 13-15.

"Once in the dear, dead days beyond recall,
When on the world the mist began to fall—"

School Teacher and Six Scholars Claimed Victims by Prairie Fire —

The Belfield Times, Thursday,
November 5, 1914, p. 1.

One of the saddest catastrophies that ever occurred in this part of North Dakota, was the prairie fire which swept a large portion of country southwest of this town, claiming as human victims Miss Gladys Hollister, teacher of the Davis school, and six of the scholars.

The fire started about noon today (Friday) by a spark from a threshing engine and, the high wind soon fanned it into a conflagration, a number of farms already being flame-swept.

Miss Hollister first discovered the fire just as the children were assembling after the noon hour. Believing that to remain in the school would result in cremation for them all, she ordered the scholars, eleven in number, to a plowed field north of the schoolhouse. Five heeded her instructions, but the other six became excited and started in a southerly direction in the very path of the fire. Miss Hollister tried to stop them and in a last frantic effort started in pursuit, her intention being to save them at any risk. But the fire demon was merciless in his relentless march, and within three rods of a stubble field overtook the fleeing teacher and children. The heat and smoke was so intense that it is presumed they were overcome immediately, as the bodies were in a small radius when help arrived. The flames claimed for instant death three of the children, the other three living until along in the evening, and the teacher until midnight.

Miss Hollister's parental home is in Mapleton, Ia., where the remains will be shipped for internment in the family plot. She was a young lady of exceptionally high character, her very life being a model of purity. She was in her twenty-first year.

The little ones who met death with their teacher, were as follows:

Ernest Geary, aged 8, a son of C. H. Geary: Irvin and Alfred Menge, aged 10 and 8 respectively, children of William Menge: Rexie Smith, aged 8, a son of Vern Smith: Francis Pike, age 7, and Ruth Olson, age 13, son and stepdaughter of William Pike.

continued on next page

154

be paid for, everyone, by hardships and heartaches, and that life in the older countries was not so hard in some ways.

But this hand-to-hand struggle with nature in her untamed state brought out the strength of the fighter as nothing else could do, as was proven to her later.

By dint of hard work and study this slip of a girl had won permission to teach, and her new joy knew no bounds when at last she began her work and knew that she could help the children and the home folks who needed it so much.

Soon after she had begun her work, one morning she noticed the startled glances of her pupils, as they noticed something out of the window. She followed their glance to find a thick cloud of smoke and fire in the distance, driven by a terrific wind, directly toward them. The children, perhaps seeing the fright in her face, sensed the danger and clung to her. In this supreme test of her stewardship, she closed her eyes a moment and asked for help.

Quickly considering their every possible means of escape, she decided to keep them in the schoolhouse, and as if in answer to her prayer, she saw two men driving, with horses on the run, swaying from side to side as the wagon bounded back and forth in the deep ruts of the Indian trail that passed the schoolhouse. Working like madmen, they jerked the plow from the wagon and just succeeded in running two furrows and getting the back fire started when the wall of flame was upon them. Fire fought fire and again proved the friend as well as the foe of man. The men then fought the side fires as the roaring torrent passed by the fury, the terrible fierceness, the terrific grandeur of its uncontrolled power is beyond the power of words to describe. It left the little group weak and awestruck—this wonderful display of nature's power—and showed them that only in their power to think and judge and use nature's forces were they the masters. They were only renters of power beyond them, for weal or woe. They stood for a few moments and watched the receding fire, hoping that all settlers were protected by firebreaks.

Then there was a short season of rejoicing and the men left for distant fields and the children took up the usual routine—there was no time for "feeling of their feelings" those days.

At noon a woman drove up and told the teacher that the only child of a settler had died during the night and they wished that she would close school so as to attend the burial that afternoon; that she would call on her return, for her and the older pupils.

When she returned and they were getting into the wagon, the woman suggested to the teacher that she take her "singin'" book along, so it was taken. The teacher felt quite sure before they had traveled the four miles that intervened between the schoolhouse and that home, that the boards they were sitting on were hard wood, and ought to be very valuable, but that was a matter of very small importance after they passed over the low range of hills and saw that lone sod house in the blackened valley before them.

There was no other human habitation in sight—all was black—black—except the stones, the buffalo bones, the white curtains at the windows, the geraniums—and—there was the sky, too—one always has the sky on the prairie.

The gloom in that little home was even blacker than the black outside. The very cleanliness of the pine floor, the curtains, the bed and the plants made the little homemade, black covered casket and the drooping form of the mother beside it, express all the more forcefully the concentrated grief of ages. O, the pain of it, the helplessness, the depth of her despair! There had been no doctor as there was no minister. Her illness was unnamed as her future was unexplained. There were no men at home; it was a season when they had all gone back to civilization seeking work to earn money to help them hold their homes. The father had been sent for, and had come just at the last and in time to make a casket for their treasure.

The mother had covered it. The grandmother had gone miles and miles to get a friend who would dare to read a chapter from the Bible and the little teacher must sing. Could she do it? As she looked at the beautiful little form and felt the grief of the stricken mother, could she sing?

She must—she must bring the consolation of those grand old hymns to these stricken ones. Above all this blackness was a blue sky—there was the clean floor, the white curtains, the geraniums—the love of God and the love of man must be

The heads of the entire community are bowed in deepest mourning, and much sympathy is felt for the bereaved and heart-sore families.

Six Little Caskets Tell the Sad Story

Never before has it fallen our lot to record a funeral where life ended with such a sorrowful and heart-rending history as the one held in the opera house Tuesday afternoon over the six little corpses who so tragically and untimely passed to the soothing arms of their Maker last Friday, helpless victims, with their teacher, of the prairie fire which swept across a large stretch of country southwest of town. Words fail us in our effort to express the dark gloom which fell over the city, or the horror stricken faces of our citizens, when the news of the terrible catastrophe reached Belfield.

The life-claiming conflagration started by a spark from a threshing engine northeast of what is know as the Davis school, about fifteen miles southwest of Belfield. It was just as the teacher, Miss Gladys Hollister, was assembling the scholars after the noon hour. The vast clouds of smoke so rapidly nearing the school, grasped as it were, the inmates in a grip of consternation. Fearing that to remain in the building would cost the lives of the little ones—eleven in number—Miss Hollister ordered them to a plowed field outside the path of the fire. However, terror and bewilderment seemed to rob them of their reason, and in a frantic effort to escape, five of the smaller children ran directly in the course of the fire demon. Among them were a brother of Ruth Olson, Francis Pike, and a son of Mr. And Mrs. Vern Smith, Rexie. Ruth's sister love and Miss Hollister's heroic character, called them back from the plowed field which they had already reached, in a last effort to save these two helpless and struggling little boys. But all in vain; they too falling prey to the fury of the blaze.

When help arrived terrible was the destruction which met the eye. Frank Davis and Wm. Pike were the first to reach the horrible scene. The bodies of seven young lives, outstretched in the charred grass, their clothes burned off, three already dead, told of the dreadful vengance of the fire to human life.

Miss Hollister still lived and was conscious when carried to the school, practically remaining so until the Finger of Death touched her cheek at 1:00 the following morning. Thus ended untimely, yet triumphantly, a life from childhood consecrated to "He, who does all

continued on next page

Funeral, 1914, in Belfield Hall for 6 children and teacher, victims of the prairie fire which burned Rock Ridge School No. 11 (SHSND)

united in some way—some time we would understand.

On that deathlike stillness her timid voice began—"Lead Kindly Light, amid the encircling gloom, lead thou me on." As a prayer it fell on the hushed group. Then the man fresh from the plow, after several attempts to speak the first word, read a comforting chapter from the Bible and repeated the Lord's Prayer. The hush that fell on the little group seemed to extend to the great black plain outside through the open doorway, and a ray of comfort must have followed the path of light that fell in across the threshold and the sun shone out, as if in benediction.

There was only the one man besides the father and grandfather, so the older girls and the teacher carried the casket and led the little procession to the hillside, where the father had dug the grave so it could be seen at all times from the window of their home. The friend and grandfather lowered the casket, a psalm was read, the little teacher sang, "Safe in the Arms of Jesus," and the father led the mother away as the grandfather and friend completed the burial.

That empty home! Those blackened fields! Could there be deeper gloom? Could peace come from such desolation? Why must it all be? Yet, in the spring the prairie would be as green as ever; the flowers would all be [blooming].

things well." We call it sad, yet how little we realize the anguish gnawing at the hearts of the aged parents in that Iowa home. Her future was full of promise, and we dare not ask why she was taken from us so suddenly and so severely, unless as flowers are picked before frost finds them, that we may not witness their decay. The remains were taken to her home, Mapleton, Ia., for internment in the family plot in that Silent City, which will, sooner or later, mark for us all the culmination of life's labors. They were accompanied by her sister and brother-in-law, Mr. and Mrs. Robert Gray.

Poor little Ruth! Her's was a quicker ending. While still contending bravely with the smoke and fire, regardless of untold physical tortures, intent only on the rescue of her brother, an Angel came. Her resistance weakened, the body tottered and fell, and with the angel, left her spirit for its reward in that land beyond. We cannot think of Ruth as dead, but, as a flower wafted to a distant shore, where, touched by a Divine hand, is blooming in richer color and sweeter fragrance than those of earth.

The women stayed as long as they dared to help and comfort, but they must be back to do their chores. The grandfather stood with his head bared in the sunset light on the low doorstep and waved his hat to the little group as they took up the trail that led over the hills to their homes. They were hushed again in the presence of a power above and beyond them.

Do you wonder that this young girl began to look upon life as a perplexing problem, and, as they passed the deserted schoolhouse on their way home, wondered what relation she and it held to God's great plan?

An institute! The county was to have its first teachers' institute. Our awkward, shy young girl was there. There were also some brilliant minds, like shooting stars that had strayed away from the beaten paths of learning—come west in search of wealth and health (?) Among them was the instructor, an old gray-headed man, with a love for humanity that kept him young in spite of

continued on next page

his years. He seemed to exhale wisdom as a flower does perfume and our little teacher absorbed it as a flower does dew.

But one thought above all others appealed to her. It was this: "that evil is perverted good," or good turned wrong side up or inside out or upside down, or rather power misdirected through ignorance. She could easily understand how her worst boy in school had the ability to do the most good. Glory! Here was something to get hold of—something to help untangle the snarl humanity was always making for itself. To find this good—to direct it aright—she would look for it—she would help—she was fairly aflame with the inspiration of it—she would prove it!

The little schoolhouse on the blackened plains did not seem so desolate when she returned—it contained the germs of infinite growth, or rather the pupils did, and so did the blackened plains, they would develop together.

So she began to look for the good in everyone—and especially in the "bad" boys and girls. When she found it and let them see it, too, they were so surprised and comforted over it that they tried to let her see more and more of that good side, and people began to turn their best sides toward her as plants follow the sunshine.

Sometimes it was hard to look beyond the "bad" and keep her eyes just on the good. Sometimes public opinion opposed and criticized her because it had not caught the vision she had of the good of God's man so carefully hidden in each heart.

Finally others wanted to know the secret of her success—for she had succeeded beyond her fondest hopes. What spell did she cast over the children to change them so? Was it hypnotism? No, it was simply this, that God is good and more powerful than evil; that the good thoughts will attract good thoughts and must show forth in action.

Make much of the bad boy, a man or a woman, and they instinctively show you, and develop by use, the worst there is in them.

Sometimes it may be necessary that they suffer much before they will let their own nobleness have a chance to show, but you will find the good there some time, some place. The blackened plains and the desolate home cover a good somewhere.

Our little teacher told me that in her search for the gold of good she had found more than she

And those five little boys! How our hearts swell in sympathy as we think of the bereaved ones at home,—the mothers and fathers, the sisters and brothers. And as we observe the falling tears, we offer silent prayer for those whose tears but mark another rent in hearts so sorrow torn. Like a morning glory plucked in the first hour of its bloom, were these little boys called so suddenly from this world in the very springtime of life. Death is a hard master, but at that he fails to rob us of the sweet and precious memories of their young lives that come crowding in. Herewith we give their Christian names and the names of their parents: Irvin and Alfred Menge, children of Mr. and Mrs. William Menge: Francis Pike, son of Mr. and Mrs. William Pike, Mrs. Pike being the mother of Ruth Olson also: Rexie, son of Mr. and Mrs. Vern Smith; Ernest, son of Mr. and Mrs. C. H. Geary.

When found life had already flown from the bodies of Ruth Olson, Ernest Geary, Alfred Menge, the others living several hours.

The six little caskets, swathed in the mysterious silence of death, and a card on which was inscribed, "Memoir to Our Teacher," were placed before the rostrum, where sat Rev. Essig of the German Lutheran church, Rev. Mutshnick of the Presbyterian church, and Rev. Thorpe of the Norwegian Lutheran church. Rev. Thorpe preached in English, Rev. Essig in German, while Rev. Mutshnick read a message of condolence from the teachers of Billings County, and offered the closing prayer.

The number of people who turned out for the services were estimated at 700, the hall accommodating less than half.

In the funeral procession were numbered some seventy rigs, measuring a distance of at least three quarters of a mile.

At the graves Rev. Mutshnick performed the last sad rites over the bodies of Ruth Olson and Francis Pike, Rev. Essig over Irvin and Alfred Menge, and Rev. Thorpe over Rexie Smith and Ernest Geary. And with these sad words closed the early lives of five boys and one girl who, being dead yet speaketh.

May time bring its resignation, and may the shores of eternity that receive their souls surround them with everlasting sunshine and flowers.

continued on next page

When the news of the terrible accident first reached the officers of the school board, they immediately called a meeting and appropriated out of the funds of the district—Fryburg—$75 each for the burial of the pupils and teacher. Mrs. Price collected $52 from the Belfield business men, $30 of which she used for flowers, the balance for the payment of meals for the mourners. Besides the flowers purchased by Mrs. Price, there were many other floral tributes, one of the prettiest being presented by the Belfield school faculty and scholars. The hall was appropriately draped, Mesdames Hilke, Fleming, Geo. Keith, A. S. Ward and Price, and Miss Ellen Thompson, lending their services.

A choir composed of Mesdames Geo. Flint and Ed. Harkins, and Messrs. C. J. Parker and S. S. Ward, sang the hymns of the service, accompanied by Miss Zantow. The Misses Lillian Wheeler, Marvel Ward, Beulah Keith, Lois Chendle, sang "Lead Kindly Light."

As an act of courtesy and an expression of sympathy, the business places in the city were closed during the service, and the schools dismissed for the afternoon.

A. A. Skinner, embalmer in charge of the Bishop & Wiebke undertaking parlors, very commendably directed the funeral, being ably assisted by C. O. Brunsoman, E. P. and Frank Bishop.

The pall bearers were picked from the children of the Belfield school and were as follows:

RUTH OLSON—Olivia Nelson, Hazel Fulton, Beryle McCarty, Margaret Pelissier, Agatha McCabe, Ella Schlevitz.

FRANCIS PIKE—Roy Sharman (?), Merrl Doty, Mike Ruff, George Coutts.

ERNEST GEARY—Walter Cameron, William Kudrna, Albert Thomas, Lester Tickfer.

REXIE SMITH—Leroy Simonson, Lloyd Doty, Schley Schuhrke, Brunell Glass.

IRVIN MENGE—Willie Sylvester, William Schuhrke, Hugh Steffen, John Kudrna.

ALFRED MENGE—Wesley Fleming, Tom Eslick, Frank Christianson, Chester Fuller.

Distant relatives who attended the funeral were: Fred Carlson and wife of Buttzville, N. D., R. Neeb and wife, of Moorhead, the women being daughters of Mrs. Pike; Philander Pike of Fonda, Ia., father of Wm. Pike; Mrs. Lewis Menge, Fall Creek, Wis., mother of Wm. Menge; Carl Lambert, Augusta, Wis., Mrs. Menge's brother; Henry Julian, of Bowman, an uncle of Ruth Olson.

had even hoped to find and that life had yielded its richest stores for her. Her happy face reveals it.

She has asked me to give this to you as her New Year's gift—"Life is reflected in love," and

Deep in our hearts it dwells forever more;
Footsteps may falter, weary grow the way,
Still we can hear it at the close of day;
So till the end, when life's dim shadows fall,
Love will be found the sweetest song of all.

Finally others wanted to know the secret of her success—for she had succeeded beyond her fondest hopes. What spell did she cast over the children to change them so? Was it hypnotism? No, it was simply this, that God is good and more powerful than evil; that the good thoughts will attract good thoughts and must show forth in action.

Rock Ridge School No. 11 near Belfield in Stark County where 6 children and the teacher died in a prairie fire in 1914
(SHSND)

Chapter 10

A Country School Pupil Remembers Country School in the 1930s

Sister M. Patricia Forrest, O.S.F.

REALITY, ACCORDING TO N. SCOTT MOMADAY, is both event and our perception of the event, a perception that is influenced by memory, mood, and personal temperament. Looking back 50 years to the beginning of an eight-year education in one-room rural schools in Red Cross Township (1931-39), I am amused by what my memory surfaces with a little prodding.

Sister M. Patricia Forrest, O.S.F.

A Country School Pupil Remembers — Edwin M. Iszler

From 1926 to 1934 I attended Tanner School No. 1. There were seven other country schools in the area. My first day in school was a slow and long one. I spoke little English and everything was strange. Fortunately, I had older brothers and sisters to depend on. Very few young teachers got jobs in town schools; their first teaching positions were in country schools. My teachers were mostly young, inexperienced, and had little training, only a high school diploma or maybe a college summer session. Most of them had never lived in the country.

We never played pranks on our teachers nor were there any bullies in our school. What I liked most about my favorite teacher was that she was understanding and sympathetic. At that time there was a great deal of misunderstanding and mistrust between town and country people.

School was not boring but exciting. We were glad we had the opportunity to be in school and we were also glad to be relieved of some of the heavy, farm-related, physical labor. We were disciplined by having to stay in at recess, or by being given extra school work, or in severe cases by the yardstick.

One of the things I liked in country school was saying the Pledge of Allegiance. We were given turns to lead it. The subject that gave me the most trouble was Grammar, especially when we had to learn the different parts of speech. Fortunately, our teachers gave us homework to help correct our weaknesses.

Attending country school did make a difference in my upbringing; I developed a much better appreciation of education. I went on to graduate from high school and college.

✍ ✍

I began school in 1930 at the age of five in a tiny one-room school about a mile from our farm. One night in early fall the school burned to the ground. Neighborhood rumor had it that the school was burned by a family who had quarreled with the teacher, but the matter was prudently left uninvestigated. This terminated my first year's education, since the nearest school was now four miles away (Red Cross Township School #1) located about four miles north of Towner beside a gravel highway running north to Willow City.

In September 1931, I began again, often walking the four miles to the school in the morning and home again in the afternoon, During the winter when my parents tried having me board at a neighbor's home a short distance from the school, I became so homesick that I was allowed to stay home during part of December, January, and February, My mother, who had been a rural school teacher, tutored me at home with assignments supplied by the teacher. This partial attendance was pattern for our family from 1931 to 1938.

My memories of the lower grades are happy. One of my earliest school recollections is sitting on a little chair in a semi-circle while the teacher read aloud to us the carrot-stealing escapades of Flopsy, Mopsy, Cottontail, and Peter. A number of phonics lessons later, we were beginning to read for ourselves out of primers with colored pictures. The first story I remember reading for myself was about an old woman who heard a noise. Through several pages, she persisted in going up stairs and down stairs, opening doors to look for it, Finally she opened a cupboard door — and out jumped BOO! Here I must have fallen in love with the rhythm and repetitive patterns in language, for the story is still delightfully with me.

There were four of us in the first grade at Red Cross School # 1 in 1931: Lucille Dugan (Genre), Adrian and Rinehart Dokken, and I. The total enrollment was about 20. Mr. and Mrs. Dokken had come from Norway, and the boys spoke little or no English when they started school. The teacher spoke both English and Norwegian; and the Norwegian children quickly learned to speak and read English. To expedite the process, there was a ground rule: only English was to be spoken on the school ground.

Through the years of grade school there ran a fun-filled rivalry between the Norwegians and the Irish, which consisted chiefly of chanted or shouted banter on the playground: "The Irish and the Dutch don't amount to much — but look out for the Scandinavians!" A boy whose grandfather had come from Ireland observed one day, "If I had a drop of Norwegian blood in me, I'd take it out," "Yes," a quick-witted Norwe-

McHenry County, Deep River School District, Teacher Mrs. Winifred Erdman, ca. 1904 *(SHSND)*

gian replied, "it would be so precious, you'd take it out to look at it," A boy whose father was Norwegian and whose mother was Irish reflected dolefully on his mixed state: "I have just enough Irish in me to be always getting into a fight, and just enough Norwegian to run when I get into it."

These mutual insults remained friendly banter, however. Participation in games was decided on the basis of age and ability, Third through eighth-graders played endless games of kittenball in fall and spring, while the first and second graders were relegated to Farmer in the Dell, Drop the Handkerchief, Red Rover, and several other running games. During the winter nearly everyone skied. In the spring we practiced for the annual Play Day, where rural school children from a number of schools met to compete in broad jumping, high jumping, potato races, and so forth. (By the upper grades, I could usually clear a barbed wire fence by taking a running jump at it.)

The teachers were almost all young women — and nearly every fall brought a new one, many of them just out of Minot State Teachers' College. Apparently they needed a year or two of experience before applying for a town school, Yet I think they did reasonably well. During the 1930's North Dakota had a detailed course of study; and by faithfully following it, the teachers succeeded in giving us the basics of the three R's and the content subjects. I remember our health book in the lower grades as something almost as marvelous as Cinderella, a real incentive to daydreaming. During the depression it pictured what for me was a fantasy world, a shining, porcelained world

Sister M. Patricia Forrest, O.S.F.

A Country School Pupil
Remembers —
Esther Olafson Rousseau

My parents Alf and Mina Olafson, though 60 miles from a railroad on the bleak North Dakota prairies, were very interested in their children getting an education. My paternal grandfather was a teacher and choir director and my maternal grandfather was a Lutheran minister in Laerdal, Norway.

When there were a sufficient number of children in the Halliday community Father and Mr. Comstock organized the Jule School District about 1908. The district was named after Sam Jule who came to the area in 1883. He lived in a dug out, hunted and trapped, became a blacksmith, shod horses, and kept wheels and plow shares in repair in this area. When the railroad came through in 1914 he ran the Rough and Ready Restaurant in a box car.

The school board decided on the best, a wooden building for their children. The lumber for the school was hauled from Taylor, 120 miles round trip by horse and wagon. It was a tedious and grueling trip for the men while the women were home with all the responsibility of those days.

A beautiful white school house was built with a cloak room on each side and a platform with the teacher's desk between. The windows were on one side so the light came over the left shoulder. There was a Primer and one reader for each grade. What a contrast to the numerous primers and first grade books our son Phil had when he entered the first grade with Mrs. Sullivan in Tacoma, Washington.

The teachers were very dedicated to their work, they often had only an eighth grade education but they had passed a teacher's examination and received a certificate to teach. They were held in high esteem in the community and rightly so.

The school was just a little over a mile from home. The first year my sister Margaret enrolled and when the snow was deep and the weather cold Dad would put her on his back, jump on his skis and over the beautiful white expanse they traveled.

The following year Marian, 11 months younger, enrolled. When the snow was many feet deep and if the wind was whistling around every corner a box was put on the stone boat, a horse hide robe thrown over the top and Dad would stand on the back and pilot us to school.

continued on next page

where boys and girls lived in city homes complete with sinks and bathtubs, something as yet unseen in the ranch homes in our area.

My best teacher was my seventh-grade teacher, Martha Rossing, the daughter of the Lutheran minister at Bergen, North Dakota. She seemed a little older than most of the others and was highly organized. She taught history and geography in considerable detail, opening windows on new worlds. Her brother was a Lutheran missionary on the island of Madagascar; and that year I developed an interest in Madagascar and Africa. Miss Rossing also brought a number of books with her; and when we had finished our assignments, we could read edifying novels. More importantly, she was kind, considerate of each youngster, and genuinely concerned that we learn as much as possible. I still have a note from her, dated February 18, 1938. She writes in part:

> We miss you at school. But Spring is coming now, so we'll soon see you again, too. . . . Today, for the first time since Christmas, we were all outside to play in the snow. The boys teased me into trying to ski, so I had a few hearty tumbles. But I was gallant about them! . . . We haven't covered as much work in 7th grade as we should have as the attendance (not counting you) has been irregular. . . . Our Valentine party was small. Only four were present that day. I guess we'll have to do something some other time to make up for that — when everyone can be there. With best wishes to all, Martha Rossing.

Martha Rossing, like most of my other teachers, took some time each day to read aloud to us from interesting stories — in spite of a crowded schedule that sometimes included all courses for all grades. This daily story time fed our imaginations in a TV-less world.

When I was in the intermediate grades, I had an overpowering determination to get to school as many days each year as possible. But at 7 a.m. it was often difficult to assess the day's weather. One balmy spring morning when I was about in the fourth grade, I stubbornly insisted upon going to school although my father warned that the weather signs portended a blizzard. By noon the blizzard struck in a fury of wind and driving snow. The teacher decided to let us start out for home, I had the farthest to go and I was walking alone. I knew that I could stay with a neighbor family, but I was intent upon getting home. Mile after

These were sometimes very scary rides as the horses were very spirited because of the cold and the good care Dad gave them.

The fall of 1910 was a time I had longed for since my sisters entered school. Up to this time I had few book friends, among them the Norwegian Bible, hymn book, and some books Grandpa Bing had sent from Norway. There was the *Decorah Posten* which was a Norwegian paper published in Iowa. The *Sears Roebuck Catalog* was the best source of reading.

Fall days were often beautiful and I was decked out in a clean dress, new shoes, my Karo lunch pail, and a five cent tablet and pencil.

Being shy I wanted to sit with Margaret but I suppose she thought at six I should be on my own, she pushed me aside. I sidled in with Marian and she took me under her wing until I was enrolled.

I was given a beautiful precious primer. My arithmetic class was called to the recitation bench. Miss Libby asked if I could count. I stood up and recited "en to tre fire fem sex, etc.," real proudly until I heard snickers. I was so embarrassed I broke into tears. I think I understood English but couldn't speak it. My parents were now loyal citizens and said we must speak English but they still had a strong love for their Mother tongue.

For some years we had Norwegian bible school in the summer taught by a student pastor, also by Enoch Nordal. We three oldest children were confirmed in the Norwegian language. At times I resented this when I first went to English bible class and when in my last year of college my English teacher said I had a horrible accent and must get into a corrective class. When I did this my teacher told me to be proud of my Norse accent as we were the melting pot. When I heard Lawrence Welk speak I wondered if he was right.

Recess was full of wonders. The big kids played Annie Over, Pom Pom Pull Away, Last Couple Out, and Tree Deep. There were advantages of not having the modern elaborate equipment of today as it made for inventive minds always seeking new games. Soon we were playing Ring Around A Rosy and tag games. There was usually one in the school wealthy enough to have a baseball. There was hop-scotch and a game played with a cut-up

continued on next page

mile I plodded through the drifting snow along the gravel highway. Our farm was a mile off the highway, and I wasn't sure if I could make my way along the drifted dirt roads for the last mile. Besides, it was getting colder and darker, and the swirling snow was blinding. Suddenly a bulky form loomed through the swirls of snow. My father had come to meet me, carrying an extra overcoat. Bundled in that, I followed him across the fields for the last mile. It says much for his devotion to his oldest child that he didn't even say, "I told you so."

(Porterville Collection, NDIRS)

When I was in the eighth grade, we got a second school for our side of the township: Red Cross School No. 2. The building had been an old church, and it was simply moved in and set up on the open prairie. The enrollment was about 12 youngsters from three or four families. To have a school within a mile and a half of home seemed a real luxury.

There were only two of us in the eighth grade — both ambitious, competitive girls. While the teacher conducted classes for the first and second graders, we worked on our own. Having finished reading all the required books listed in the North Dakota Course of Study by January, we began reading high school literature. With honest delight, we read Tennyson's *Idylls of the King*. (When I saw "Camelot" in Washington, D.C., in the early 1960's, I was profoundly disappointed. The characters were not as romantically lovely as I had imagined them — and Morgan le Fey, who lived in my imagination as a mysterious wizardess of considerable charm, was only a grotesque caricature on the stage.)

broom stick. Some mothers made bean bags; beans were a common staple of the day.

After recess we lined up at the water pail. The water was hauled to school by Walter Christensen in a cream can. There was the good old dipper. I guess we believed in sharing inasmuch as we shared each other's germs, but we seemed no worse for it because we seemed to be a healthy lot.

Going home was a thrill. In the fall my feet felt like prisoners in shoes as I had gone barefoot all summer. When I was out of sight of school, off came my shoes. It was a thrill to feel the hot rough ground on my toughened feet.

Now the friendly meadow larks were getting their families together for a move to a warmer clime.

The golden rod was yellow and made a beautiful bouquet for my hard working mother who was home with my two younger brothers. Marian was a good baby tender. I would rather be out with the chickens. Often we would see the wily coyote running through the tall grass blending so perfectly with the landscape.

A fire break was plowed around the school every fall to protect it against the dreaded prairie fire. These horrible fires would travel with the speed of a terrible wind across sun dried prairies. There ranchers were the fire department and they kept a wagon loaded with barrels of water, gunny sacks, and a hand plow. Whenever the terrible tang of smoke or an unearthly glow was seen on the hori-

continued on next page

Williams County, ND, F.W. Dingler, Teacher

(Martha P. Tatem Collection, SHSND)

It was a good thing that we had literature to warm our hearts in 1938-39 because our feet and hands were often freezing. The temperature fell to about 36 degrees below zero for most of January. The school room, heated only by a wood- burning cast-iron stove, was drafty and cold. Dressed in snowsuits, we sat around the stove with our feet up on the iron rail circling the bottom of the fire box — and classes went on as usual.

Mrs. Pompoo, our teacher that year, was a valiant woman who waged an unrelenting battle against ignorance, bad behavior, and germs. She firmly believed that any misconduct must be "nipped in the bud." One of my younger sisters was kept an hour zon horses were hitched quickly to the wagon and they drove with all speed to help.

Winter brought a different life. We now must wear itchy long underwear, heavy overshoes to go through snow, warm coats, caps, mittens and scarves. Often our hands and feet would be so cold the nails would ache. We called this "nagle spret" in Norwegian. Often our cheeks or nose would be frozen white. The teacher had a pail of snow and would put snow on them to thaw them out. In extreme weather the school house would be cold and we would leave our top clothes on and huddle around the stove and have our classes there. Many times our home-made bread and meat was frozen. Winter also brought snowmen, snow fights, snow forts and many fun games like Fox and Geese.

Christmas was such a festive and joyous time. There was always a Christmas program and beautiful Christmas songs and lovely new dresses. Dear Mother would work all night making dresses for three girls. As I think of it now, those early women were the Madonnas of the Prairies. Then there was a sack of candy for each pupil. Sometimes there was a Santa Claus but we were well versed in the fact that we were celebrating the birth of the Christ Child.

I suppose the drastic change in seasons kept life from being boring where there was so much, yet so little. Spring came and everyone and everything seemed to rejoice.

The sun was warm, days lengthened, the kerosene lamps were not used as much, the snow melted and little rivulets ran down the hills. Oh, the joy and rapture of making little paper boats and sailing them. Heavy coats and underwear were shed. We were like butterflies coming out of their cocoons. The meadowlarks came back with

their song "See the pretty girls petty coat." The gophers and prairie dogs were back to greet us after sleeping all winter. The rabbits now changed their beautiful white winter coats for the drab brown.

It was always a race to see who could find the first crocus or pasqueflower, a delicate bluish lavender flower with a furry green cap to keep it warm. This little flower and the friendly meadowlark are two of my fond memories of the Dakotas.

School was a joy to me and I was sad when the term ended. My first grade library consisted of three little books. My favorite was *Peter Rabbit*. I drooled over it, read it many times. The last time I took it home I planned to keep it for good. I had it wrapped and hid under a stone on the hill for a few days. It was such a dear story about Flopsy, Mopsy, Cottontail and Peter. With stern parents and the prying eyes of two sisters and two brothers, I reluctantly took it back.

There was one thing about vacation. I could run barefooted. The feet were tender at first from being trapped in shoes all winter. Marian and I could now put strings on the Russian thistles and tumbleweeds. What wonderful play horses they made as the wind took them over the hills as fast as our tanned legs would let them.

The one room rural school has gone the way of the buffalo, the prairie dog, and the wolves on the prairies. The little white buildings were important links in my life. I attended them, taught in them, and during the dust storm days in Dunn County I had the heart breaking privilege of overseeing 108 rural schools as county superintendent.

When I see a schoolhouse now I think what secrets they could tell. Many children and adults wore down their thresholds. The walls could tell of

continued on next page

after school because she refused to make her molding-clay igloo according to the teacher's specifications. Daily Mrs. Pompoo insisted that we wash our hands in hot water laced with lysol before our hot lunch (usually a potato baked on top of the stove).

We took our art projects, including the clay igloos whitened with chalk dust, to a school festival in Towner in the spring. This was also a declamation contest, where we recited the long poems we had memorized from the North Dakota poetry book. This book had poems for reading and memorization for each grade. (Another of my happy memories is sitting on the schoolhouse steps year after year memorizing poems. In the fourth grade, I especially liked Longfellow's "Psalm of Life.")

Our rural school houses were used for elections, for neighborhood dances, and for basket socials The entire family attended the dances, where our parents taught us how to waltz, polka, fox trot, and square dance. When I was in the eighth grade, my high school girl friend's boy friend invited me to dance with him — probably at her suggestion. As I had danced only with my parents and with other girls up to that time, this seemed a golden moment of growing up.

voices of happy children, services of religious groups, baptisms, confirmation communions, and funeral services. Then there were political meetings, basket socials, and dances.

Some still stand as a landmark used as a polling place, otherwise frequented only by mice. Some have been sold, converted to granaries or homes. This is progress. Big yellow buses now take children to more progressive and elegant schools.

Since students don't get exercise walking to and from school, elaborate gymnasiums are provided for exercise. No good Mother Earth to soften the jar as they run. Buses take them to nature areas. What better way to study then to discover the bird nest, the busy ant hills, and the hawk getting lunch for his babies by pouncing on a baby rabbit, on walks to school.

Sometimes I think I was cheated; sometimes I think I was blessed with my early experiences.

☙ ✍

(Carrie Busby Collection, NDIRS)

Every year, too, we had a Christmas program: plays, songs, poems. By the eighth grade, we were becoming more innovative. That year we had an angelic chorus appear out of blue crepe paper clouds near the ceiling as a special stage effect for "Angels We Have Heard on High." The secret: standing on piled up tables behind a curtain and sticking our heads — and wings — out of suspended crepe paper.

Looking back, I am grateful for those eight formative, hurry-burly years. I had no problem in adjusting from the rural grade schools in Red Cross Township to the public high school in Towner. I had acquired a love of literature and history, a sense of being rooted in the prairies, and an interest in almost every kind of learning. I had gained respect and affection for the neighborliness of a Norwegian Lutheran community — and a lifelong love of good coffee.

☙ ✍

Chapter 11

The Young Citizens League

Warren A. Henke

ALEXIS DE TOCQUEVILLE, the shrewdest foreign observer of the American scene, noted in the 1830s that

In no country in the world has the principle of association been more successfully used, or more unsparingly applied to a multitude of different objects, than in America. . . . Americans of all ages, all stations in life, and all types of dispositions are forever forming associations. There are not only commercial and industrial associations in which all take part, but others of a thousand different types — religious, moral, serious, futile, very general and very limited, immensely large and very minute. . . . Finally, if they want to proclaim a truth or propagate some feeling by the encouragement of a great example, they form an association[1]

At his inaugural on January 20, 1961, President John F. Kennedy offered the following advice: "And so, my fellow Americans, ask not what your country can do for

Clarence Miller, a Slope County delegate, tells of his experience at the 1940 YCL Convention

Source: *Slope County Post*,
May 16, 1940, p. 1.

*S*aturday morning we got up feeling quite well considering the amount of sleep we had. There certainly was a lot of noise in the hotel all night.

First we had a nice breakfast at one of the cafes. After our breakfast we drove to the penitentiary and there a guard lead us through the various rooms and cell blocks. We were also shown where the twine was made and the road signs. Each of us were given an address plate for our car.

From the penitentiary we drove to the Fort Lincoln airport where we had the good fortune to see the twenty-two passenger Northwest airline plane land, stay for five minutes, and then take off for the trip to the west coast.

We then went to the capitol for the morning meeting where each county responded to roll call by giving an entertainment number. Charles Lien introduced the Slope County delegates over the loud speaking system and Doris Johnson gave a reading. After the meeting we went through the museum and Roosevelt's cabin before lunch. We spent some time and money in the ten cent store before packing to leave for home. Just before leaving Bismarck, we drove back to Fort Lincoln, then went to look over the fire engines in the fire hall, and noted other places of interest.

We boys were really sleepy so we slept all the way home.

We all enjoyed the trip very much and wish to thank every person who helped make this trip for Charles Lien, Doris Johnson and me. We want to thank Mrs. Brown* especially.

*Clara D. Brown, long time county superintendent of schools for Slope County, was a pioneer and articulate supporter of the YCL movement.

❧❧

Michael Miles Guhin, Superintendent of Schools, Brown County, South Dakota, 1910-1914 *(South Dakota Historical Society)*

you; ask what you can do for your country." But long before the youthful president put forward his suggestion, young citizens on the northern Great Plains began practicing that philosophy when they joined an organization common to the country school experience. Teaching school in Minnesota in the early 1900s, Anna Shelland Williams concluded that merely teaching *about* democratic ideas of citizenship to elementary school children without *demonstrating* those activities was unsatisfactory. What was needed was an education tool whereby students would not only apply those ideas but also actively perform the role of citizen. About 1912 she prepared *The Little Citizens League,* a bulletin issued by the Minnesota Department of Public Instruction that explored the feasibility of organizing school children for the practice of citizenship. It outlined carefully the structure of a Little Citizens League, thereby originating the idea of a Young Citizens League (YCL). Included in the release were a model constitution, by-laws, creed, and pledge which read as follows: "I hereby pledge my active devotion to my country; by a study of its ideals, by care of my body, and in actually doing something each day to aid my country's cause." Mamie Thompson wrote the little citizens' creed: "I am a Little Citizen of the United States and I believe in my country, my school and my flag. I believe that I can serve my country best by attending school every day, and by endeavoring to become intelligent, honest and efficient. I believe that my country gives to me the same rights and privileges that she can give to anyone, and that it is my duty to cultivate my talents and to enrich my life in order that I may better serve her interests. I believe that my flag stands for honor, truth and justice in all things, and that God is with us."[2]

When a copy of *The Little Citizens League* came to the office of Michael Miles Guhin, superintendent of schools of Brown County, South Dakota, he became intrigued with the possibility of establishing leagues among the school children of his county. He began his experiment by ordering about 100 copies of the bulletin. Discussing the possibilities of such an organization with a few of his strongest teachers, he gave each a copy, and waited. Some reactions to the idea were positive and enthusiastic. Soon he received a few requests seeking permission to organize leagues. Meanwhile, Guhin and his "remarkable girl Friday," Lucille Trott, decided that the word "Little" would not appeal to students in the grammar grades, who at that time were a bit older than average

Ottomenia Jorgenson, a Slope County delegate, tells of her experience at the 1939 YCL Convention.

Source: *Slope County Post*, May 11, 1939, p. 5.

What an exciting time we had last week. Four young citizens of Slope county were given the honor and pleasure of being able to attend the YCL convention at Bismarck on May 5 and 6. We were graciously chaperoned by our County Superintendent, Mrs. Clara D. Brown. While in Bismarck we visited many places of interest such as the following: early Friday morning we visited the museum in the Memorial Building. We saw many species of birds, animals, flowers, and insects. There were many Indian relics and many other things too numerous to mention. Just north and a little west is the state capitol. This is a beautiful structure. We all enjoyed riding up the elevator and walking down thirty-flights of stairs. We enjoyed looking at all the rooms especially the Chamber of the House of Representatives.

The place that gives you a queer feeling is the penitentiary. All occupants were busy doing the duties to which they had been assigned.

Another interesting sight we saw was the soldiers practicing target shooting at Fort Lincoln. At the KFYR broadcasting studios many fascinating things drew our attention. For instance the machines and records. We were also shown how NBC and the process of short wave was carried on.

The place in which I was most interested was the State Training School. Here the boys are assigned certain duties which they are to do for a certain length of time. As, for instance, a certain number of boys are appointed each week to milk cows.

We also visited the Burleigh county court house while in Bismarck, and drove around through the residential district. As we had visited all points of interest in our capital city, we began our way home. A large keg caught our eye between Mandan and Bismarck. Here we stopped and were given a treat by Mrs. Brown.

We all enjoyed the trip and can thank Mrs. Brown for her kindness and patience. If anyone has the chance to go with Mrs. Brown don't miss it. I can assure you that you will enjoy every minute of it.

✍ ✍

---

grammar school children. They decided to call their proposed organization the Young Citizens League. The first YCL was established in 1912. Its value as an educational tool became so well established there that by 1915 forty-three leagues had been organized. League work languished temporarily in the county, but organizing leagues was given new impetus when Lucille Trott became Brown County superintendent; she was aided materially by a Miss McArdle, the county nurse. Thereafter, the YCL made remarkable progress; at the close of Trott's term of office in 1923 about one-half of the schools of Brown County had organized leagues. By 1924 the number of leagues in South Dakota increased to 842. The next year the idea was adopted as a state-wide project by the county superintendents who organized a state organization. By 1935 South Dakota's 4,737 chapters had a total membership of 72,300 children.[3]

William
Marks
Wemett
(NDIRS)

Professor William Marks Wemett, head of the department of history and social science, State Teachers College, Valley City, meeting with several county superintendents at Valley City on February 2, 1927, introduced the movement into North Dakota by organizing the Young Citizens League of North Dakota. Established on a small scale in Stutsman, Griggs, Barnes, and Dickey counties, invitations were extended to other county superintendents to join the league and promote the work among their schools.

The league was a manifestation of John Dewey's discussion of the purpose of education that focused attention on the development of young children and that declared that education is "to give the young the things they need in order to develop in an orderly, sequential way into members of society." Based somewhat on the successful

Jeanne Mack on KFYR from State YCL Convention

Source: North Dakota, State Historical Society of North Dakota, MSS 10529, Young Citizen's League, Slope County, ND, Chapter Records, 1934-1954.

As early as 1937 KFYR radio aired segments of the state YCL convention. On May 2, 1941 Jeanne Mack, a Sand Creek School student and vice-president of the Slope County YCL, greeted KFYR listeners.

Hello Radio Audience and especially Slope County listeners: The afternoon session of this state YCL convention closed just a few minutes ago. Tomorrow morning we meet again. This evening directly after this broadcast we attend the annual state YCL banquet. It is a wonderful experience to be one of this large group of grade boys and girls.

I would like to take just a few minutes and pass a few remarks on the letters "Y", "C", and "L".

"Y" is for young — well, we are young in years. We are all grade students and how grand to have this organization with a definite purpose and well planned way of helping us to become good young citizens.

The word citizens takes care of the letter "C". I am sure I am quite safe in saying that 99% of us are natural born citizens and proud we are to learn to serve our county to the best of our ability.

The "L" stands for league. Leagued together in this great work of becoming useful, well trained young citizens means one thing. When we are old citizens — long after our grade and high school years are past — our rules of good citizenship will always be with us because we are learning by doing and then rules become habits.

We young citizens are happy that the older citizens take such an active interest in our welfare and we hope we will always be deserving of the time and effort given for us. I thank you.

South Dakota league its stated purpose was: "to assist in giving to the grade children of North Dakota the best possible instruction and training in good citizenship by directing them in the study of the vital problems of American life and government, and by helping them to take part in and assume responsibility for the proper solution of these problems." School children became members of the YCL by organizing local chapters in one-room schools or in rooms of a graded school. Local chapters elected their officers, conducted regular meetings, developed projects, and produced public programs to raise funds to improve the school and its equipment. Acting as a service club for that school and community they were designed to do for country boys and girls what Boy and Girl Scout organizations did for villages and cities. Sponsored through the efforts of Wemett and the county superintendents of North Dakota, the organization became a function of the Department of Public Instruction (DPI) in 1935, through the interest of state Superintendent Arthur E. Thompson. Because of declining rural school enrollments, decreasing rural populations, and a restructuring of elementary classroom programs the state superintendent, M. F. Peterson, would place the YCL under the supervision of the Director of Elementary Education in 1976.[4]

By 1943 about 200,000 young citizens in 14,000 schools in more than five states had joined a YCL chapter. To maintain momentum and a reasonable uniform policy and type of training, leaders of the movement met on August 14, 1943, at Bismarck, North Dakota, and organized temporarily The Young Citizens League of America. A permanent national organization was formed in Pierre, South Dakota, shortly thereafter and incorporated under the laws of that state. Professor Wemett was selected president; its board of directors held its first meeting at Hot Springs, South Dakota on July 8, 1944.[5]

Both Wemett and Guhin recognized the desirability and necessity of securing funds from the private sector to sponsor a national organization. As early as January 1936 Wemett had written Dr. Max Mason, president of the Rockefeller Foundation, requesting "information concerning the possibility of securing financial assistance in developing The Young Citizens League." Noting that "We believe that we have been fortunate enough to hit upon the most practical method of training children in the habits that make for good citizenship," he told Mason that it had been tested in the schools of the two Dakotas for fifteen years, that the organization was composed of 7,000 schools with a membership of 125,000, and that "The idea is to give children the right

What the YCL Did For One School —
Anna A Braun, Dickinson, Stark County

*S*chool was a dull, uninteresting place livened now and then by an occasional outburst of disorderliness. The children did not care about their work; they did what they were told with neither interest nor enthusiasm. For a moment their interest would be aroused by a new project or a change in the program but with no lasting result. The possibilities of what the YCL might do for the life of the school room and the welfare of the children had been suggested to me. A YCL manual was secured from the County Superintendent's Office, and after reading it carefully the subject was presented to the school.

We talked about the YCL during an opening period and the children were interested and eager to read the information in the booklet. Madge, one of the eighth grade girls, was especially impressed. She talked about what the YCL had done in other schools and what we could do if we had an organization. Soon others began to express a desire to organize a League. It seemed wise to work through Madge. She is a natural leader and liked by all the children. They asked when we might organize and a time was set. The children chose a chairman and elected officers. They made many blunders for they were not familiar with the rules and had

no experience in business meetings but after the election, the rules were carefully explained and discussed and we were ready for our first meeting.

The president, Madge had been selected for the office, called the first real meeting of the League in October. Tho timid, she was well prepared. The children sat in breathless quiet while she said, "The meeting will please come to order. Stand and repeat the pledge." The children rose and gave the Flag Salute. The president passed copies of the YCL Pledge and the children read it in unison. They were asked to learn it for the next meeting.

The presiding officer explained that each child should say "present" as his name was called by the secretary who read the roll after which he took his seat and recorded the minutes of the meeting.

President Madge had appointed a Recommendation Committee of three to decide what our League could do, first in school; second, at home. The chairman of the committee read a report: "We find that we need a lunch-box shelf, a reading table, an extra chair, and a sand table in our school. We ought to clean the yard and move the small ash pile to the big one over by the fence. At home, we can obey our League Home Rules." (Our Honor

continued on next page

attitude toward their fellow beings and fix those attitudes into habits through self activity and responsibility." He explained that state money could not be used to sponsor the national organization and that local county superintendents had "to object to a membership fee because of the opposition of some disinterested parents." Moreover, the movement had "become too large for our officers to manage in their spare time and at their own expense. . . . " Wemett wondered "whether there might be some foundation or patriotic organization that would finance this service to the extent of about $10,000 a year, sufficient to maintain an office and a full-time secretary." He asked Mason if he could suggest possible sponsors, concluding that "the movement should not be capitalized upon or drawn into any partisan faction."[6]

On the last day of January 1936 Guhin wrote Wemett: "I think it would be wonderful if we could get someone to sponsor the Y.C. L. financially — without any ulterior motive. My nephew is going to Chicago next month and will confer with my cousin, Leo Sheridan, who happens to be in touch with the 'millionaire class.' Possibly he may suggest someone who may be interested in furthering good citizenship." Guhin also told Wemett he was willing to go to Kansas, at his expense, to "boost the Y.C.L."[7] Those initial efforts to secure private funding for the YCL were unsuccessful.

Germany moved into the Rhineland that same year Wemett wrote to Mason; Austria was invaded and annexed in March 1938. Adolph Hitler's invasion of Czechoslovakia on March 15, 1939, prompted the United States State Department to denounce Germany's "wanton lawlessness." And two days after Hitler invaded Poland on

Rules are copied from the laws of the Boy Scout Organization).

President Madge thanked the chairman and asked for "some talks about the report." The discussion was orderly and lively, consisting of ways and means by which they could obtain the various things. Each speaker rose and addressed the president as "Miss President." When the speaker sat down the president said "Thank you," calling the name of the speaker.

It was decided to make the lunch-box shelf first. Two of the older boys offered to bring the necessary materials.

Two Standing Committees were appointed—Physical Training and Health and Sanitation. The Physical Training Committee was instructed to clean up the yard and make plans for a sand table. The Committee on Health and Sanitation was asked to weigh and measure each child and place the data on the Health Crusader's Chart. The ten Health Rules were used as a basis for a YCL race to Health Land. "This" remarked the chairman, "is to be a friendly race to see who is the healthiest citizen in our school." All committees were instructed to consult with the Adviser.

President Madge had arranged for two speakers; a girl from the sixth grade gave a talk on doing a kindness each day. An eighth grade pupil spoke on what he would like to do when he became a man. Both talks showed thoughtful preparation.

The president asked for someone to make a motion to adjourn with singing "Dakota Land" after which she asked the teacher to take charge.

The children had been given only a general idea of what to do. The details were their own. During the entire meeting the children were quiet and orderly and deeply interested. They were beginning to realize their responsibility for doing many things and when they went back to their work it was with a more willing and a much happier attitude. We have had several meetings, each one better than the one before. Two brothers brought a six inch board, hammer, nails, and a saw and put up the lunch-box shelf in the cloak hall. A girl brought an unused chair from home, and the boys fastened the legs with wire so it no longer wobbles. The boys brought shovels, pails, and a wagon and moved the small ash pile during the noon and recess periods. The boys also put legs on an old school house door they found behind the coal shed. This was carried into the school room and the girls washed the top and covered the legs with crepe paper. It serves very well for a reading and supply table.

We are starting a harmonica band and have made plans for a sand table; and are working on some special programs.

The children have a common interest in school which has made the daily activities full of meaning. They are happy, alert and industrious because of the surroundings which they have helped make pleasant. They attend many of the civic meetings of the community for they wish to bring new ideas to our league meetings.

Every parent was present on Visiting Day this year. They show a renewed interest in the children and the activities of our school. The YCL seems to be the tie which binds together the school and the home.

One parent said he was glad we had the "Home Rules" because his boys worked better at home. A mother said she enjoyed the way they worked together because there were no more quarrels among the children.

The school is under constant observation and is a never failing topic of interest. The YCL is an interesting venture for the community as well as for the classroom. It arouses interest, promotes friendly feeling and brings ready, willing cooperation between the home and the school.

Source: *North Dakota Teacher*,
April, 1932, pp. 13, 22.

September 1, 1939, Great Britain and France declared war on Germany; the Second World War had begun.

In 1940 the YCL received nationwide attention in articles in two widely read magazines, *Good Housekeeping* and *The Saturday Evening Post.* Writing for *Good Housekeeping,* Gretta Palmer worried about the fate of democracy in her article, "Learning to Live." "If democracy is to last, we must have millions upon millions of men and women who are educated in matters pertaining to government. And if we don't have them the voters will elect scoundrels and crackpots, who will lead them into tragedy and social conflict....Americanism may not be strong in your section of the world in the coming years. Graft will intrude into politics, and the voters will make unwise decisions at the polls. 'Isms' from Europe will win many converts among those who have never learned to value democracy, or to demand that it be made to work. Public-spirited citizens will be few, and a grasping selfishness will prevail in business, industry, and trade unions."[8]

Palmer thought that rather than focusing on the attitudes of "voters-in-the-making," those individuals in their late teens and early twenties who were "finished products," more attention should be given "the boys and girls in the hair-ribbon and marble-shooting stage." Those young citizens were "not yet set in a mold of completed personality." "What are we doing in their formative years," she asked, "to make them wish to save democracy? How are we aiding them in learning to live?"[9]

In her effort to find out she consulted numerous people interested in preserving democracy to try "to define the things that tomorrow's citizens will need to carry on our American way of life....We agreed that they must have two possessions if the future is to be safely entrusted to their hands: They must have knowledge. They must have character to enable them to use their knowledge." Palmer was not worried about the ignorance of future voters but was concerned about the matter of character. Noting that contemporary schoolbooks had "religious emphasis in less than 5 percent of their text" and that "religion, which formerly molded the characters of young Americans and gave them a strong sense of responsibility toward their state, appears to be declining in its influence when we need it most," Palmer praised the trend toward "character education" appearing in public and private schools and told her readers about programs and "outstanding teachers" who had realized that mere book learning was not enough for good citizenship. It had to be undergirded with some guidance in morality.[10]

One of the more notable and farsighted programs, with 4,000 chapters, was the South Dakota YCL. It gave youngsters practice in self-rule and believed "that right social attitudes were a part of what one ought to take away from school." Palmer noted that at the state convention at Pierre, YCL problems were discussed "with strictly parliamentary procedure," that "delegates have platform poise their elders might envy," and that "debate is good-natured, and just about the best training in citizenship that any state gives its young." Palmer told her readers that if their children attended schools where character education was largely ignored democracy would be jeopardized. Every community in America could and should develop an excellent character-education program. "If the women and mothers of that town are good enough citizens to insist upon it," she said, "every town will!"[11]

A Dunn County, North Dakota, Y. C. L. Meeting

Source: *The Young Citizen*, Spring, 1940, p. 17.

Approximately one hundred-twenty boys and girls gathered for the Y. C. L. Pep Meeting at Manning, November 3rd. The young citizens very ably took care of the various activities of the Meet.

Edward Wolf, the County President first led the group in the Salute to the Flag and the Y. C. L. Pledge. It was decided at the business meeting that since this was the 50th year of our statehood, we would hold a North Dakota Scrap Book Contest and have a County Banquet in the spring.

The result of the election showed Edward Semerad, President; Delores Dinehart, Vice President and Frances Roshau, Secretary for the coming year. The retiring officers were Edward Wolf; Georginia Kadrmas and Vernon Judt.

Edward Semerad and Edward Wolf chose sides and a most interesting and educational Memory Quiz on North Dakota was held. The sides called themselves the "Elephants" and "Giraffes." The contest was very close with the gong sounding but seldom. At the close, the score keeper showed the 'Elephanes' one point in the lead. Whistles were awarded to the winners.

After an hour of various games and singing, apples were served and the young citizens went merrily homeward having gleaned much through actual doing. It is hoped that every school in the county will organize a Young Citizens League, carry out its activities, and send delegates to the Spring Banquet. The dues per year are 25c per league. This is used to defray expenses to the State Convention in Bismarck.

YCL members
buying
defense
stamps, ND
(Young
Citizen
League
Records,
A484,
381505,
Box 1
SHSND)

Reflecting on his belief that children were the most unemployed members of American society, Farnsworth Crowder, in an article for *The Saturday Evening Post*, concluded that: "How to bridge the frightening gap that steadily widens between the child and the grown-up worlds has become the American school's No. 1 problem. Teachers' colleges, schools and school systems are having their go at it. The shelves of books written on the subject talk about 'participation.' 'How to get their fingers in the pie' would be more expressive."

Crowder acknowledged that there were many answers; however, he wanted to call his readers' attention to only one experiment. "That it is so little known is surprising," he said. "I have questioned educators — renowned ones, at that — who never heard of it. Yet this particular experiment in 'participation' has been going on for more than twenty-five years. It takes in the elementary-school system of an entire state. It involves more than 4000 schools and annually touches more than 50,000 children. It is supported by legislative appropriation and is directed by a permanent secretariat of educators. It is one of the most suggestive and significant efforts being made anywhere in American education to keep children alive to adult responsibilities."[12]

The experiment Crowder wrote about was Michael Miles Guhin's Young Citizens League of South Dakota. Crowder had characterized him in 1912 as "an impatient young superintendent of schools in Brown County, South Dakota," sitting "in his office, wondering what was lacking in the routines of memorizing facts, reading textbooks and solving hypothetical problems. What did such exercises, so largely academic and secondhand, contribute to the development in children of social responsibility, of acquaintance with real and immediate problems? They contributed, young Guhin felt, very little. They made his pupils literate, and helped toward making them scholars, but they did not do a great deal toward making self-reliant, judicious citizens." Crowder lauded Guhin for not writing a book or resigning his office to enroll in a graduate program to compose a Ph.D. thesis to solve this dilemma. He commended him for doing "what he could with the materials at hand. He did not dream of setting the world of pedagogy afire, he thought of trying an experiment in Brown County." In organizing the Young Citizens League Guhin "became an unsuspecting Columbus in the field of progressive education."[13]

Leaders of the movement had visions of transforming their local efforts into a viable national movement. Wemett wrote George Kienholz of Pierre, South Dakota, who had gained a considerable reputation as a result of his work with crippled children, that ". . . you are the one man who ought to be the executive director of the Young Citizens' League of America. . . . and I am wondering if you wouldn't enjoy rounding out with the unusual and very very fine social service redord (sic) that you have made by establishing a great Y. C. L. movement throughout this country on a basis as large and full and fine as it deserves. I would rather work with you in such a movement than anybody else I know, and I think we would both get a real bang out of working it out together."[14]

Of major concern to Wemett was financing such a movement. "I am sick and tired and also humiliated," he told Kienholz, "by the philosophy that an organization such as ours should be conducted on a missionary basis. It will never be what it should be until it is placed upon a sound financial basis and pays good salaries commensurate with those of the Red Cross and the Boy scouts. At present we don't even rank with the consolidated drives."[15] The organization never gained such a fiscal foundation.

After forming the national organization in 1943, leaders of the movement issued a circular to county superintendents, concluding that "we need only a simple, inexpensive organization, just enough to keep the various states working along the same line, leaving all supervision to each county superintendent as at present. We do need to maintain a unity of purpose and method as far as the movement may extend and sufficient financial support to pay a part-time secretary and the cost of some printing and postage." To solve the problem of financing the organization's program the leadership suggested every league affiliate with the national YCL and subscribe to its official magazine, *The Young Citizen*, at one dollar a year. "There is a swell profit in the magazine which, with the full cooperation of the leagues, should yield sufficient income." It also promised that "the editors of The Young Citizen will make every effort to make it a truly interstate magazine. This is all we will ask of the schools. If more funds are necessary, they will be raised from the public." Wemett also suggested each league seek out a prominent member of the community to subscribe to the magazine and sponsor its activities. Another suggestion was to persuade a merchant or a group of businessmen in the county seat to act as sponsor for the entire county and have them send the magazine to all county leagues as a worthy advertising plan.[16]

During the period August 23, 1943 to August 23, 1946, solicitations in Barnes County, $496, and two annual grants from the North Dakota War Chest, totaling $13,803.28, provided initial monetary support for the organization. Grants from the War Chest were made to maintain the president's office in North Dakota "and through that office to get the Young Citizens League back into good condition after the slump of the depression and war years." Eighty-five percent of the funds were to be spent to benefit North Dakota's children, the remainder was to "be used to cooperate with other states in keeping the YCL movement from dissolving into diverse groups and purposes." The State Teachers College at Valley City generously provided office space.[17]

Young Citizen's League Vacation School For Teachers

Source: *YOUNG CITIZEN'S LEAGUE VACATION SCHOOL*, For Teachers, North Dakota State University, Institute for Regional Studies, MSS 449, Box 3, Folder 8.

In the spring of 1941, Mr. Wemett, the Senior President of the Y.C.L. of North Dakota, had a vision. His idea was to promote a Y.C.L. vacation school where teachers would be able to combine personal improvement in extra-curricular activities with a pleasant vacation at a low cost. He thought that courses should be offered in five activities; namely, athletics, music, handicraft, nature study and art, Y.C.L. management, speaking and personality.

As a fitting setting for this vacation school he chose Cross Lake Park, North of Brainerd, Minnesota, and made the necessary arrangements for accommodating those who would choose to take advantage of this opportunity.

Let us see how this vision materialized.

Saturday morning, August second, and several North Dakota cars filled to capacity with passengers and luggage, sped east along the highways with a single destination in view—Cross Lake Park, Minnesota, and the first Young Citizen's League vacation school. It was to be a combination of work and pleasure, and all of the occupants were looking forward with great anticipation. That afternoon all arrived at Brainerd, Minnesota, sooner or later and then went north twenty-five miles to Cross Lake Park

continued on next page

Resort. There they were given the cottages which were to be their homes for the following two weeks.

On Monday the entire group met to decide upon the courses which they were interested in taking and the time schedule. There were twelve teachers who had come to take the courses. It was decided that the courses to be offered would be: Nature Study and Art, Y.C.L. Management, Music, Swimming, and Sports. The classes were to begin at 8:00 o'clock in the morning with Nature Study and Art, followed by Y.C.L. Management, and Music in the morning, and Swimming and Sports in the afternoon.

Regular classes began on Tuesday morning. The first class was Nature Study and Art. These were alternated to give the best arrangement for each.

The first lesson in Nature Study was a discussion of birds. A morning hike for the purpose of observing birds followed. The girls discovered birds that they had not noticed before. An interest in birds was aroused and nearly every day after that some person reported new observations on birds that she had made. A study of trees followed. On the hike for observing trees, an interest in stones was aroused incidentally. Many facts regarding stones were discussed, and some of the girls started a nice collection to take home with them.

Our first venture in Art work was soap carving. Each of the girls obtained a bar of ordinary laundry soap. Then with jack knives, finger-nail files, and some simple patterns, they started their designs. The next piece of work undertaken was sand painting. In this the girls learned how to color the sand and then how to apply it to their designs. The last project was spatterwork. The stencil for this had already been cut, but each of the girls experimented with actually applying the paint. Considering that these projects were new to all of them, some of the girls did some very unusual and excellent work.

Besides actually doing the things already mentioned, the girls obtained many new ideas in handicraft and art through discussions and demonstrations. They learned how to make durable and practical covers for books using masonite; and processes of making egg shell vases, of doing block printing, and metal and cork work were carefully explained using many appropriate illustrations to give the girls an idea of how the finished work should look.

The second class of the day was Y.C.L. Management. This was approached from the point of view of helping one who had not had any experience in

continued on next page

"By 1946 the most completely organized states were South Dakota and North Dakota. Wemett calculated that with 2,415 leagues North Dakota was about 82 percent organized."

Under Wemett's leadership the organization actively promoted its goal. College students provided clerical help for 50 cents an hour, later increased to 60 cents. A field service was established to promote the organization and during the first three years of his presidency Wemett spent 241 days in such service. Other field workers traveled through the country, district conferences for county superintendents were held, rural departments of the state teachers' colleges supported the program, and several county superintendents helped instruct teachers in other counties in YCL work. Promoting the league was exhausting work; it was also rewarding. By 1946 the most completely organized states were South Dakota and North Dakota. Wemett calculated that with 2,415 leagues North Dakota was about 82 percent organized. Colorado had about 1,000 leagues and the movement had county-wide organizations in Minnesota and Kansas.[18]

Wemett's promotional activities extended into the far reaches of the country. In 1932 Anne Raymond, an Associate in the School Service Division of the Cleanliness Institute headquartered in New York, told him of its interest in the movement. To promote the YCL she suggested it run a competition in which local chapters competed to develop "the most interesting satire on a serious subject" that would show progress in improving certain habits among league members. The League could sponsor a six or eight-week publicity campaign promoting "Better Habits of Personal Appearance and Health." Raymond was willing to forward, at no cost, a quantity of such a satire, The Strange Case of Mr. Smith, developed by a Junior High School in Louisville, Kentucky, along with mimeo-

176

conducting a Y.C.L. The material in the handbook was carefully discussed. Then the group organized as a school would and considered and practiced the essentials for conducting a meeting properly. General discussions on material for programs, ways of raising money, projects and how to carry them out, material for teaching citizenship, and appropriate songs and poems were carried out. From these the girls gained much information and a great deal of inspiration for carrying on the work of the Young Citizens League.

The class in Music followed. The classes for the first week were devoted to directing group singing. This was very helpful. It was something that could be used by the teachers in their own schools. The second week was spent on the fundamentals of the tonette. Some of the girls learned how to play several short selections by the end of the week.

In the afternoon everyone went out for swimming. A few of the girls had had some lessons before but most of them were beginners. The first thing that was necessary was to overcome fear of the water. After the first two or three lessons, all had more confidence so that they would try to float and to swim. Nearly every girl learned how to float both face down and on her back and also to swim a few strokes. All regretted that they would not have access to swimming facilities after leaving so that they might practice what they had learned.

The day was finished with sports of various kinds—tennis, badminton, horseshoe, and softball were all given consideration. One girl was inspired to make a badminton set of her own from discarded materials that she found around the camp.

The girls had two hours at noon and the evenings free to do whatever they chose.

The place that was chosen for the camp was ideal. It was located between two lakes, Cross Lake, and Pleasant Lake. The cabins were comfortable and well furnished. There was excellent fishing, and each cabin had a boat so that the girls could go boating whenever they chose. The girls especially appreciated the many lakes and beautiful evergreens. On the nearby lakes were located some of the most beautiful and exclusive summer resorts in the United States. Among the interesting places that could be visited that were not far distant were a paper mill, an open iron mine, the tame fish garden, and a lookout tower. During the last week of our stay at Cross Lake Resort, Daniel Boone, third, and his son, Daniel fourth, with the rest of the family were there. They were from Tennessee, and we found them to be a very interesting family.

Upon talking over the vacation school with those who were there it was found that very one felt that it had been really worthwhile. They had come to learn something about extra-curricular activities, and they were taking many new ideas and much inspiration back home; they had expected to have a delightful vacation, and it had been most enjoyable.

As in most things, the girls who applied themselves derived the greatest benefits. Nevertheless, after taking all things into consideration, all felt that the vacation school had been a great success and hoped that it might be continued.

graphed sheets to supply clubs in North Dakota. The only expense to the state YCL would be the general covering letter accompanying the promotion.[19]

In April 1950 Principal J. E. Beasley of the Rosemont Graded School in South Carolina informed Wemett that it was qualified to receive its charter and that it planned to have the mayor of Charleston present the document. In December of that year Nebraska's Superintendent of Public Instruction Otto G. Ruff informed Wemett that his state was involved in developing a new program of citizenship for elementary schools. He requested a list of the names of the twenty-two states in which the league was active and wanted to know the extent of their involvement.[20]

In his efforts to establish the YCL in Arizona, Wemett had an ardent, well connected, and professional supporter. Ken Dale, Phoenix College, had a cadre of day and night school students on his campus in the fall of 1952 to "spearhead the organization throughout the state." The group planned to use the impetus of the 1952 general election to arouse enthusiasm for the league. Dale told Wemett: "Frankly, I think this [YCL] is the biggest thing you have done in your life." He advised Wemett that "down here in this area we have lots of colored and Spanish-American students. We can establish a chapter in every parochial school we can

"Frankly, I think this [YCL] is the biggest thing you have done in your life."

Y. C. L. PRAYER

Dear God, there are so many things
    I ought to do and be,
But please just help me do what's right
    So the YCL is proud of me.

MORNING PRAYER

Be with me, Lord, as here I pray,
And keep me by thy side today.
Please make me gentle, pure and true
And kind in all I say and do,
Honest in every word and deed,
And quick to help when others need.
    Amen.

A CHILD'S GRACE

Thank you for the world so sweet.
Thank you for the food we eat.
Thank you for the birds that sing.
Thank you, God, for everything.
    —Author Unknown

GRACE

Be present at our table, Lord
Be here and everywhere adored
These mercies bless and grant that we
May feast in fellowship with Thee.

A CHILD'S GRACE

"Thou are great and Thou art good,
And we thank Thee for this food;
By Thy hand will we be fed,
Give us, Lord, our daily bread."
    Amen

Source: North Dakota, Department of Public Instruction, *The Young Citizens League Manual*, September, 1955, p. 28.

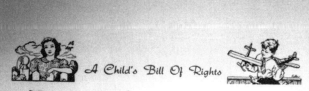

"A Child's Bill of Rights by W.M. Wemett, President of the Young Citizens League of America *(NDIRS)*

service." Furthermore, he said county superintendents would follow the lead of the Phoenix system; the elementary superintendents he talked with were "all the way from lukewarm to enthusiastic."[21]

Dale urged Wemett to attend the Arizona teacher's convention. "Come on down with him [John West, president of the University of North Dakota], Bill, and we will have some fun. We will go to the Rancho Grande in Nogales and take over the joint for the weekend. I already have 15 rooms reserved. . . ." The break and the change of scene for Wemett would center on the aftermath of the general election, the teacher's convention, the game of the year between the University of Arizona and Arizona State College, and a bullfight in Nogales. Refreshments were already waiting at the Rancho Grande. "If Eisenhower wins overwhelmingly, we will send a Republican senator from Arizona to Washington and re-elect our Republican governor. If that happens, we will tear the roof off the Rancho Grande the eighth. I might even fight that bull in Nogales myself. Come on down." It is unknown if Wemett accepted Dale's invitation.[22]

The organization had also secured the endorsement of three of the country's prominent citizens.

(ND Young Citizens League Records, A 484, 381505, Box 1 SHSND)

- Father E. J. Flanagan, Founder and Director of Boys Town, Nebraska: "In these times every effort is made to teach our boys to accept responsibility and to foster good citizenship in our youth who tomorrow become the backbone of our nation. At Boys Town every effort is made to teach our boys to accept responsibility, to serve their community, and to become better citizens. The work being accomplished by the Young Citizens League is a step in the right direction. My congratulations!"

- J. Edgar Hoover, Director of the Federal Bureau of Investigation: "The work of organizations in educating young people in real Americanism is sorely needed today. Without such training in good citizenship it is difficult to successfully combat crime and un-Americanism. I hope that the activities of the Young Citizens League will continue to be most successful."

- William Allen White, Emporia, Kansas, best known newspaper editor in the United States: "I have just looked over the Young Citizens League Personal Growth leaflet. I have read it with great interest. It seems to me that it has something that every young person in this country should read and ponder."[23]

In 1949 the organization was still struggling to secure funding from the private sector. One YCL supporter, Hub Peterson of Valley City, solicited his friends for support. He wrote Christensen & Company of Watford City: "Here is a matter which requires our serious attention....Do you know about The Young Citizens League, and what it is doing? It is a real story. This organization is training 35,000 North Dakota children in careful driving, sobriety, fire and accident prevention, conservation, loyalty to American ideals, personal responsibility, cooperation, proper conduct, etc. This is being done at a cost of less than 10 cents per child per year." "It is a movement we morticians have long advocated," Peterson said. "Here it is all set up and doing a fine job." Peterson stated that Wemett continued working for the movement through the years, "entirely without compensation," that the organization was rapidly spreading to other states, and that what was needed was an annual budget of $3,000 for postage, office supplies, and a full-time stenographer. If 300 business firms or professionals each donated $10, that amount trained 100 youngsters for a year, that goal could be reached. Noting that "they are doing all the work for nothing, and asking us for $10," Peterson asked, "Isn't that fair enough?" He urged the addressee not to lay the letter aside as just another request for money.[24] Despite such pleas, apparently nearly

A letter to *The Young Citizen*

Source: *The Young Citizen*, Spring, 1941, p. 21.

We too have a Y. C. L. in our school, which has been organized for eight years.

We have eighteen members in our league. Our league is called the Morning Glory Y. C. L. In our county there are several Y. C. L.'s. Each spring we hold a convention at which every league is present.

We think the Y. C. L. is very interesting. We all get a lot of pleasure out of the meetings we hold twice a month. Every month we elect officers and every two weeks we appoint committees. Every child has a duty which they take care of. We do our best to keep our schoolroom neat and attractive, we also do our best to keep garbage and scraps off our playgrounds. The required dues for our Y. C. L. are five cents from each family each month.

Every fall our league sponsors a program at which we raise money for the following year. With the money we pay our phone bill, buy material to make presents for unfortunate children. We also make presents for our fathers and mothers at Christmas time and on Mother's Day.

Each year the Delamere Community Club gives our Y. C. L. $5 which we repay by furnishing an evening's entertainment in the spring. We will have this program on Friday, March 21st. At this entertainment Arlene Ostern (one of our Y. C. L. members) will give a long reading about the Y. C. L., where it started and what the leagues do.

Two years ago we organized a Junior Red Cross which the Y. C. L. supported until, from our Red Cross penny dues, the organization could support itself.

At all our Y. C. L. meetings we repeat our Y. C. L. pledge which every member has memorized.

Will you send us a copy of *The Young Citizen*. We like to know what members of the Y. C. L. are doing in other states.

Kathryn Johnson, DeLamere, North Dakota.

all in the private sector thought such letters were just that and efforts to secure private funding of YCL activities failed.

The organizational structure of the YCL was hierarchic. Below the state organization local chapters organized into a Junior County Y. C. L. that held fall rallies and spring conventions. The Senior Y. C. L., formed by local teachers involved in the program, managed the work of local chapters, under the supervision of the county superintendent. The most important unit of the organization it suggested projects to schools, planned rallies and county conventions, decided what part the county would play at the state convention, and acted as the YCL's principal promoter in persuading other schools to join the movement.

"To help, Uncle Sam, one another, our school, our home, and our community."

Most likely, President Kennedy had no knowledge of the YCL. If he had, and if it had been well-known, influential, and ubiquitous it may have been invited to participate in his inaugural festivities. In any case, he would have voiced approval and made much of its motto: "To help, Uncle Sam, one another, our school, our home, and our community." Clearly, John Dewey would have agreed that it strove "to give the young the things they need in order to develop in an orderly, sequential way into members of society." Both would have agreed with the psychology underlying the organization: "It seeks (1) to give the child a proper attitude toward his fellows and (2) to make that attitude permanent by forming good habits. This is done best (3) when he is young (4) by his own activity and (5) by giving him responsibility. (6) He thus learns to be governed by the forces within him, instead of having to be governed by police, courts and jails. (7) At the same time he is taught to respect our government, its laws and its flag, and later (8) is made an intelligent citizen by a study of how the government works and the reasons for it."[25]

Leaders of the movement particularized its psychology into six major benefits received by the child:

- A Child Learns to Govern Himself. Consideration must be given to actions in relation to the rights of others; fellow students will judge conduct in terms of "being a good citizen."

- A Child Learns to Assume Responsibility. Elective offices and committee work in YCL chapters encompass duties and require judgment, tact, and courtesy.

- A Child Learns How to Conduct a Meeting. Learning correct parliamentary procedures is a mark of being a good citizen.

- A Child Develops Personality. Reticent, taciturn, or diffident children learn through YCL work to develop confidence in themselves, to become leaders, and to conduct a meeting, give a report, or speak in public with ease.

- A Child Develops His Talents. YCL programs enable students to gain confidence and give them an opportunity to play instruments, speak, sing, demonstrate projects and show other skills and abilities.

- A Child Becomes Courteous, Tactful and Considerate. Through the courtesy committee students learn social manners and skills: receiving and welcoming school visitors, making introductions, and writing various kinds of social and business letters.[26]

A Good Citizen — Richard Skaufel, Grade 3, Griggs County, North Dakota

I can be a good citizen by doing many things. I am only a boy but I can be a helper. I want to begin now so that I shall know how when I grow up.

I can always be happy and cheerful. When Mother needs an errand boy I know I can help her. I can be sure to hang up all my clothes and I can always put away my playthings when I am through playing with them. I shall try never to ask my mother, father, or teacher to do anything for me I can do myself.

Source: *The Young Citizen*, Spring, 1940, p. 15.

Not just another organization for the teacher to supervise, an established YCL chapter benefited both school and teacher. Discipline became easier because the child's attitude toward the school changed. It was no longer just the teacher's school, but the pupils' school too. Good conduct was something to be proud of; an athletic committee could insist that younger students had their turn at using athletic equipment; and YCLs might discipline their own members thereby developing attitudes of good citizenship in working and playing with others.

Although organizers emphasized that neither the teacher nor the school should organize a chapter for the purpose of doing janitor work, they believed that it would be easier to keep schoolhouses and grounds clean and orderly if one were organized. Pupils would take pride in the appearance of their school. Furthermore, courteous students and clean and orderly schoolhouses and grounds would make a favorable impression on parents when they visited school. By giving programs chapters could earn money to purchase items for the school and enhance the school setting — books, a new flag, musical instruments to start a band, sheet music to start a YCL chorus, athletic equipment to start a baseball team, individual drinking cups, or new curtains.

An official request from the YCL fostered community spirit and cooperation by bringing patrons together to complete projects. Pioneers in the movement saw it "not something for a weak teacher to lean upon." Rather, for an intelligent one, it had many direct personal benefits: county and state conventions provided contacts with her col-

YCL
Convention,
1941, House
Chambers,
North Dakota
State Capitol

*(ND Young
Citizens
League
Records,
A 484,
381505,
Box 1,
SHSND)*

leagues and broadened her outlook, the probability of a better recommendation, possibilities for promotion, a chance to make a more significant contribution to the community, and more effective classroom management and organization.[27]

Upon joining a local chapter students took the Young Citizens League Pledge: "I hereby pledge my active devotion to my country by a study of its ideals and by a constant interest in the general welfare of my state and nation. I shall strive to do something each day to improve the standard of my home, my school, and my community, and thereby endeavor to promote better citizenship."

The organization's Code of Ethics promulgated six cardinal principles: Patriotism, Duty, Courtesy, Good Health, Sportsmanship, Truth and Reliability. Its march song pledged allegiance to America and declared that a patriot's creed demanded that to best serve the country's need young citizens must develop clean hearts, minds, and bodies. And like the nation's founders who wrote the United States Constitution and defended it in the ratification process, the leaders of the YCL respected religion and believed that moral citizens who believed in God benefited democracy. The national organization put forward A Child's Bill Of Rights that declared, among other rights, that children "have a right to be taught to go to church where I can sing hymns and pray and worship God." It also encouraged prayer.[28]

Founders of the organization realized the power of ritual. At appropriate times YCLers conducted the Y. C. L. Candlelight Service. It bore resemblance to particular rituals of fraternal organizations. Values of the organization were communicated and affirmed as defined in its Code of Ethics. During the service the ceremonial speaker stated the purpose of the organization and lit a red candle that signified the six cardinal principles of the Code. Six Outstanding Young Citizens, each in turn, then lit a white candle from the red and affirmed a specific principle. At that point, with six white candles surrounding the red, the Young Citizens, in unison, recited the Y. C. L. Pledge. Next, flagbearers brought the Colors forward and the ceremony closed by singing either the Y. C. L. March Song or the Star Spangled Banner.[29]

All of these aspects became integral parts of local YCL chapter meetings and county and state conventions. After the organization was introduced into North Dakota in 1927 Wemett's promotional efforts were successful, resulting in a significant increase in the number of leagues and total membership. By 1942-1943 the number of YCLs numbered 2,321 with a total membership of 32,194. After World War II, in 1945-1946, the number of leagues increased to 2,415 with a total membership of 34,269. In 1950 the number of leagues had decreased to 2,260; membership dropped to 30,555. A decade later there were only 1,596 chapters, but statewide membership increased to 33,151 members. Thereafter the organization began to suffer significant decline.[30]

Individual league names reflected, among other categories, geographical locations, the country's work ethic, and its patriotism. For example, in Rolette County which began YCL work as early as 1932, leaguers named their units Pleasant Valley YCL, Wildwood YCL, Busy Bee YCL, Uncle Sam's Helpers, Old Glory YCL, and George Washington YCL. Each league discussed and chose yearly projects that it might carry out for the benefit of their group, school, or community. Union YCL in Rolette County purchased blackboard paint and treated the school's blackboards in 1934. The next year it bought a set of New American Song Books. Two years later the league paid for a ball and bat and in 1938 acquired a scale so that their monthly weight gain or loss could be recorded. In 1940 the league produced a program, sponsored a pie social, raffled off a blanket, and purchased library books.[31] Elsewhere, leagues bought such items as sash curtains, radios, and hot lunch equipment, and built overshoe and rubber racks, trellises, and sand boxes.[32]

YCL County conventions had been held in Stutsman and Dickey counties as early as 1928. The first state assembly was held November 14-15, 1930, in the house chamber of the capitol building in Bismarck; thereafter the event was held there in early May of each year. At that convention, thirty-eight regularly elected delegates represented ten counties: Barnes, 8; Benson, 2; Dickey, 5; Golden Valley, 3; Griggs, 2; LaMoure, 4; Sioux, 2; Stutsman, 8; and Wells 4. Featured at the first day's session was a twenty-one piece YCL band from Glover, conducted by a Miss Bostrop. The Patterson Hotel served a banquet to 85 guests on Friday; in all, about 120 people attended the convention. The first YCL junior state officers, elected unanimously for the year 1930-31 by the delegates were: Boyd Chamley, Griggs County, president; Billy Finch, Stutsman County, vice-president; and Evelyn Holms, Secretary.[33]

One of the turning points in the YCL's history occurred in 1949 when the gender gap ended; Janis Brooks, Sharon, Steele County, was elected the first girl to serve as state junior YCL president. Neither the 24-hour measles, which resulted in her catching a little cold, could deter her from presiding over the 1950 convention, nor

A Country School Teacher Remembers — Elizabeth Ahrlin Fedje

I always wanted to teach school, and my father encouraged me, but he had no funds left over from his $100 a month check to help me; the money was used to support his family of five. My uncle and Aunt Lydia helped me often with transportation when I attended my last two years of high school in Forman, North Dakota and I worked in private homes earning room and board for four years in both Forman and Ellendale when I attended school. My first year of teaching was in Ransom Township in Sargent County in 1928-1929. My salary was $75 a month, plus an extra $5 for doing janitor work.

The county superintendent visited the rural schools unannounced and spent the whole day taking notes and checking on the pupils' work and recitations. I admit I was fearful of the first visit because it was my first year of teaching. I was 18 years old and had doubts about the methods I was using. In Normal School I received lots of theory but so very little practical help to use in the classroom.

Generally the standard exams given to the seventh and eighth graders were very difficult, so for several weeks before the test I would drill the class on old exam questions; the class would get an idea of what would be expected. It must have worked because 2 of the 3 in the class scored 95 and 98 on their finals.

We heard of the Ku Klux Klan in the 1920s. I remember visiting my sister-in-law to be in Fargo in 1929, my very first trip to that big city. A big convention of the Klan was going on. It scared me no end to see all those white-sheeted people marching and burning a large cross, and delivering their inflammatory talks. I hope never to witness again such a display of anti-Semitic, anti-black, and anti-equality sentiments.

A Country School Teacher Remembers — Earl N. Shearer

The date was September 22, 1930; just one day earlier I had become 18 years of age and qualified as a rural school teacher. Most of the 21 students arrived early on the opening day by horse-drawn dilapidated vehicles from distant farms in the hill country of Stutsman County. Some students walked, carrying a half-gallon metal "karo" syrup pail filled with food to be consumed or traded for more delectable items possessed by other students.

My attention focused immediately on the exchange of conversation by the seven "eighth graders" who claimed to "boss the school." Listening carefully, they were recounting incidents that occurred during the previous term of seven months when three "women teachers" tried to "discipline and teach." Wow, I thought, *three different teachers in seven months!!* No small wonder the school board decided to hire a "man teacher." Would I survive to complete the contract that I had signed? My inward stress began to grow in multiples. I was less than a year older than one of the students, if the information in the teacher's register was correct. Could I control and teach? I was uncertain but challenged by what I had overheard.

At nine o'clock I rang the hand bell and the students were assigned desks. For more than one hour I talked to the students concerning many subjects such as order, discipline, honesty, fairness, citizenship, law, rules in the home, and rules at the school. I asked questions of the students and they responded very well except for one first grader that spoke only Polish. I walked slowly up and down the rows of desks among the students repeating their names, giving a compliment whenever possible on new clothing, shoes, and well groomed hair. Farm boys always carried pocket knives, of which they were proud. I asked to see theirs and I showed them mine. In case any were lost on the school grounds we wanted them returned to the rightful owners.

Suddenly, it was recess time. I brought out some new playground materials and we all went out for recess. Afterwards a fifth grader confided that this was the first time he could remember that any teacher had played games with the students at noon or recess. I was more determined than ever, to be interested in student interests.

Four o'clock finally came—I was exhausted physically—and the most important day was now history. From then on I was confident I could cope with stressful school related situations.

≫ ≪

could a blinding snowstorm and poor roads prevent delegates from thirty-four counties from attending it. Driving 15 miles on a tractor, one father guaranteed that his daughter would accompany her group's trip to the capital city. Along with Edyth Lange, Sterling, Burleigh County, state vice-president, and Phyllis Strand, Brocket, Ramsey County, the first all-girl slate of officers led the convention.[34] Highlighting the opening session was the first state officials' reception, held in Governor Fred G. Aandahl's office. Even the supreme court recessed to greet the youngsters. Of special interest to the convention was an address by Miss Lois Gratz, a field consultant of the Midcentury White House Conference on Children and Youth. Edythe Lange was the toastmistress at the convention banquet; delegates furnished their own entertainment.[35]

Another landmark in the league's history occurred at the 1952 convention when once again an all-girl slate of candidates was elected: Bernice Belohlavek, Morton County, president; Judith Berg, Walsh County, vice-president; and Linda Baltzer, Logan County, secretary. All were 12-year-old seventh graders attending one-room schools. With 135 delegates representing 47 of the state's 53 counties it was the largest convention, to date, in the league's history. Fargo's invitation to host the 1953 convention was rejected; holding the convention in the state capital had become traditional for the league.[36] Girls won election to the highest junior league offices again in 1953: Lois Bell, Dickey County, president; Marlys Schmidt, Nelson County, vice-president; and Marilyn Kelly, Richland County, treasurer.[37]

Convention attendance had increased during the Great Depression: 24 counties sent delegates in 1936, 731 people attended the banquet; two years later 32 counties were in attendance, the Patterson Hotel served 951 persons at the banquet. In 1940 about 1,200 boys and girls from 32 counties attended the state convention. The following year 37 counties were represented at the convention. Because of the large number attending the previous convention official delegates and visitors had to be limited to seventh and eighth grade students. The Patterson charged children 50 cents and adults one dollar for accommodations, 50 cents a plate for the banquet.

Delegates to the YCL Convention, 1946, North Dakota State Capitol

(ND Young Citizens League Records, A 484, 381505, Box 1, SHSND)

After a break during the war years, 1942-45, the league met again in Bismarck in 1946. During the next decade attendance at the convention increased again, in 1956 and 1957 all fifty-three of the state's counties sent delegates. Thereafter, attendance began to drop.[38]

The growth of the YCL during the latter 1930s, the 1940s and 1950s is attributable, to a large degree, to the leadership and dedication of one of Wemett's strongest supporters, Lorene Evans York. In 1954 the Bismarck Tribune told its readers that "all worthwhile activities succeed because some people give them a little more than the routine support. For Mrs. York, the YCL and its members are quite special. The combination of zestful young people who think seriously of themselves as future voters, and devoted, conscientious adult leaders has made the Young Citizens League a real force for good in North Dakota." As one of its pioneers, York served as its state executive director for many years; she also served as director of certification for the DPI for three decades. Addressed as "Mrs. Y. C. L." by an enthusiastic leaguer at a county convention the sobrique endured. Primarily because of her work with the league the Administrative Women in Education named her the "Woman of the Year" in 1952.[39] No person of her stature, enthusiasm, commitment, and dedication to the YCL seems to have replaced her in the DPI.

Attending a YCL state convention, preferably as a delegate, was a memorable experience for a young citizen. It was educational, entertaining, an effective tool to teach good citizenship, an excursion for country-school pupils to visit a "big city," and a two-day economic boon for merchants in the state capital. Few, if any, of the young conventioneers realized that many of them were getting a taste of their future life-style, working in urban centers where the sights, sounds, and smells were vastly different from rural and small-town environments.

It was the culmination of the league's yearly activities. Young citizens demonstrated talents by providing entertainment, showed adeptness at social skills while introducing major speakers and meeting various government officials at receptions, illustrated expertise in parliamentary procedure as they conducted and participated in the business part of the meeting and the election of officers, and displayed proficiency when conducting the Candlelight Service. County delegations reported on activities and local projects, resolutions were debated, and next year's state-wide project was

The unveiling of the YCL marker at the International Peace Garden, September 9, 1950

(The Young Citizen, February 1951)

approved. Those endeavors united the widely dispersed chapters and gave focus to the league's educational activities.

In 1937 leaguers had studied "Safety on the Highways" and "Conservation of Wildlife in North Dakota." A decade later they were focusing on safety education, parliamentary procedure, beautification of school grounds, famous paintings, the Garrison Dam, and international correspondence. A highlight of the 1948 convention, in a special Arbor Day ceremony in recognition of the League's 20th Anniversary as a state organization, was the planting of an American elm, the state tree, near the statue of Sakakawea on the capitol grounds. Dedicated to the Young Citizens of North Dakota the exercises were presided over by the YCL's retiring president, Dale Pleasance of Pembina County, and Attorney General Nels G. Johnson, representing Governor Fred G. Aandahl.

Some 35,000 children in North Dakota's grade schools contributed their pennies to purchase a marker that was dedicated to the Young Citizens of Canada and the United States. Dedicatory ceremonies were held September 9, 1950 at the International Peace Garden. Taking part in the exercises were Donald G. McKenzie of Winnipeg, president of the International Peace Gardens and other dignitaries from North Dakota and Manitoba. The marker, carved from North Dakota granite by Hynek Rybnicek of Mandan, was unveiled by Jay Johnson of Mylo, North Dakota, state president of the YCL and Miss Heather Stewart of Deloraine, Manitoba. The inscription on the marker reads as follows:

UNDER GOD
LET CHILD LOVE CHILD
AND STRIFE WILL CEASE.
DEDICATED
TO THE YOUNG CITIZENS
OF
CANADA AND THE
UNITED STATES.

The theme during the state's Seventy-fifth Anniversary of statehood, 1964, was "North Dakota, Today and Tomorrow." And for 1996-97 the YCL chose the theme, "Nature Awareness Through History, Culture and Art." Members were asked to question parents, grandparents, and elders about changes in foods eaten or plants grown over their lifetime, to discover the origins of plants native to their area, to grow foods and study gardening techniques from other cultures, to explore different works of arts, music, and writing for plant images and references, and to examine a range of plant products.[40]

A Country School Teacher Remembers — Vicki Bjornson

Parents in the Manning School District, located approximately 17 miles southeast of Bismarck, realize how important it is for their children to have the same benefits as children in larger school districts. They also realize that there are benefits to rural schooling, so when the old Manning School burned down in 1980, they rebuilt. The school is a modern structure equipped with electric heat, electric lights, carpet, ample chalkboards, and indoor plumbing. Parents are responsible for their children's transportation to and from school.

Each morning a student raises the American flag. The school day begins at 9:00 a.m. when the teacher rings the brass hand bell. The bell was salvaged from the ashes of the old school and restored. Classes begin after the Pledge of Allegiance.

The school has an adequate collection of library books and magazines. The Burleigh County Bookmobile visits once a month. Each child may check out as many as ten books. These are kept on a special shelf so that everyone may share. Audio-visual materials are also available from the library and the Burleigh County Superintendent's office. There are also reference materials, globes and wall maps for the children's use. There is also an Apple IIe computer with a printer in the classroom. There are a variety of disks and every student knows how to use the equipment. Students enjoy Science. In 1986 the school participated in the Scientist-in-Resident Program. They have also attended the Turtle Mountain Environmental Learning Center at Lake Metigoshe.

Recess activities vary with the seasons. In the spring everyone practices for Play Day. Many of the students belong to the Manning/Telfer Bas-

continued on next page

The YCL convention was an economic boon for certain capital city merchants. A reporter for the *Bismarck Capital* told readers that

Mothers and Stomachs — Are First Concern of YCL

Mothers and stomachs formed the chief concern of the Young Citizens Leaguers of North Dakota on Saturday during the annual state convention of the YCL in Bismarck.

Here are some of the facts and incidents discovered by an inquiring reporter 'round about town.

The Patterson Hotel restaurants had served more than 500 orders of hamburgers, ice cream and coca cola at 6:30 o'clock Saturday morning — for BREAKFAST.

Both the Grand Pacific and Patterson hotels reported that every leaguer was out of his room and on the street by 5:30.

Ice cream cone consumption at all restaurants was way above normal.

The Grand Pacific restaurant reported Milk Shakes, Malted Milks and hamburgers popular.

Woolworth's lunch counter was swamped when they opened at 7 and a full crew of clerks was given an emergency call to open the store proper at 8. The store manager reported the second largest day in the store's history, the bulk of the shopping being done from 8 to 9:30. The most popular items were gifts for Mothers Day, toys, and ice cream sandwiches.

Scott's were equally swamped, with hamburgers and frosted malteds the favorites on the menu.

Both movie houses were packed Friday night after the YCL banquet (at which 950 were served) was rushed through in an hour and 15 minutes so that the first show could be made. Chief other diversions were the museum at the Capitol and riding the elevators in the Capitol tower.

Best YCL remarks: "Gee, you can get central without ringing on those hotel telephones."

Addressed to a capital elevator operator as the doors opened on the third floor: "Does it cost anything?"[41]

ketball Team. There is a girls' and a boys' division. They compete against other rural schools during basketball season. Parents recently poured a cement slab and put up a basketball hoop for the children.

All the students help in publishing a monthly newspaper, *Prairie Rose News*. There is a music teacher who comes out twice a week.

Young Citizens League (YCL) is a very big part of rural school. All of the students are members. They learn how to conduct a business meeting, hold an office, take notes, and speak in front of an audience. They also do things that will, as stated in the YCL Creed, "improve the standards of our home, our school, and our community," and thereby endeavor to promote better citizenship. In addition to local meetings, the students also attend the Burleigh County YCL Convention and the North Dakota YCL Convention in Bismarck each spring. Rural students compete in the Spelling Bee, Mathcounts, and Academic Olympics.

The Burleigh County Multi-District Special Education unit and the Burleigh County Nursing Services are available for the Manning School District. Eileen Mack, Burleigh County Superinten-

dent and her assistant, a former Manning School student and teacher, Cheryl Helm, are also very important to the success of rural schools. County teachers appreciate the in-service training, available materials, and the help they receive from the county office.

The teacher attends the school board meetings. Parents visit the teacher often and work together to make the school a good place for their children. Any successful school district must have a positive working relationship between the superintendent, the school board, the parents, the teacher, and the students. There is a certain closeness in a rural setting.

At the end of the day students help the teacher put the classroom in order for the next day. Everyone is assigned a new task each week. A student takes down the flag and has someone help to fold it correctly.

One student said that what she liked about country school was, "That it can be busy and peaceful at the same time."

Throughout the years the capital city welcomed and praised the activities and behavior of the YCLers. In 1937 the Capitol displayed the letters YCL in colored lights as a special tribute to visiting members of the organization. Radio station KFYR aired part of the program. The next year Donald Enger, the 13-year old state junior president from Dickey County, representing 16,000 YCL members, told a standing-room only crowd in the House chamber of the state capitol that: "I understand that this is one of the best behaved conventions that comes to Bismarck." The *Bismarck Capital* agreed. "There wasn't a store keeper, a hotel clerk, a restaurant proprietor," it told its readership, "that didn't say this week that he had never seen a 'nicer bunch of kids' than the Young Citizens who took over the city Friday night and Saturday morning. Even for a city the size of Bismarck, the assimilation of 1,200 youngsters in one bunch is noticeable, and might well present a problem, but not the Young Citizens. They came, they enjoyed themselves, they behaved like ladies and gentlemen and all Bismarck is looking forward to next year when they can come again." In 1950 the *Bismarck Tribune* told its readers that "No group that meets in Bismarck is more important than this one. It is almost trite to say so, but trite or not it is a fact that in them grows North Dakota's future."[42]

The next year the YCL received its most superlative endorsement. Among the visitors who packed the galleries of the house chambers at the capitol at the opening session of the league convention was Representative C. G. "Gus" Fristad, R-Morton County. The orderliness of the session and the "glowing list of activities" reported by the various county delegations so impressed him that he wrote the following note to M. F. Peterson, superintendent of public instruction, who read it to the convention: "Congratulations to the YCL, the most intelligent delegation I have seen in these chambers." Three years later the Bismarck Tribune in an editorial echoed that thought: "Those for whom the chamber was constructed — the lawmakers who convene there every two years — would probably be the first to argue that today's sessions are apt to be far more orderly and logical in some respects than many legislative assemblages are."[43]

Since 1930, with the exception of the war years, 1942-1945, the capital city had hosted the state YCL convention, an organization described as "the only unique character building program ever developed on a statewide basis in the elementary schools."[44] Forty-four counties sent delegates in 1965; in 1973, when the YCL met in conjunction with the State Spelling Bee, only nineteen counties were represented. In 1975 delegates and visitors from sixteen counties attended the convention; a decade later nine counties participated. With only four counties participating and a handful of visitors attending the 1996 meeting, delegates decided to put the 1997 state convention on "hold."[45] At this writing the continued existence of a statewide organization is in doubt.

There are various reasons for its decline. In 1985 the DPI concluded that some county superintendents lacked experience with the YCL and others did not want the extra work. There was also a misunderstanding that it was extracurricular. What was needed to breathe new life into the organization was in service training for principals and teachers, an updated manual, and also more of them. While its long-range goal called for an active YCL organization in each county, the department intended to double the organization's membership in the near future.[46] Detailed plans to reach those goals, however, were never developed; the department was unwilling to commit personnel, money, or time to reach the objectives it established for itself. At this writing they remain unrealized.

Cover of brochure for Y.C.L. Vacation School for Teachers *(NDIRS)*

Founded primarily to teach citizenship and build character in rural school settings, various other forces were at work to weaken the organization. Better roads, decreasing rural school enrollments, continued consolidation and school reorganization, the restructuring of elementary classroom programs, along with the weakened power and influence of county superintendents also contributed to the organization's decline. No visionary in the movement during the last few decades emerged to promote adapting the organization to an urban setting.

Another problem, adequate financial support of the organization, recognized early on by Wemett, was never resolved. There are no specific county or DPI funds earmarked for the promotion and operation of the organization. The state provides staff support that is meager at best.

As a professional educator, Wemett, who died in 1965, would most likely have supported contemporary Mathcounts, Spelling Bees, Science and History Fairs, and the Close Up Foundation. However, he would, in all probability, tell today's educational leaders and patrons that one is first born a citizen; only at a later date does one become a mathematician, scientist, historian, or politician or choose a different calling. He would, undoubtedly, acknowledge that citizens, indeed, may shirk their civic responsibilities during their life span. However, he would argue that nationals do not give up their citizenship lightly and would reaffirm that citizenship training and character building are essential to elementary educational programs.

A Country School Teacher Remembers — Clara Bakke Olson

I never forget my teaching days in North Dakota, and I often reminisce those experiences. I loved my work as a teacher both good and bad days, and appreciate having had the opportunity to serve as a teacher.

I finished high school in 1919 and went to 6 weeks of summer school at the Agricultural College [North Dakota State University] in Fargo. After finishing I was offered a contract to teach a rural school in my home community. I should never have accepted it.

My first day was frustrating! The older pupils helped distribute books. They knew the grades the children were in. After all were settled, I called each grade up to the front of the room. Not much was accomplished but we did get acquainted. The day went fast. I prepared a temporary or trial program so the pupils would know what books to study the next day. I later changed it as I saw fit. Books were scarce. There were very few library books; I had to make the best of what I had.

I had 23 pupils, 6 boys and 17 girls. They were all easy to handle except a 15 year old, overgrown boy. A real "bully" and tough to handle. I had gone to school with him, and he came mainly to make life miserable for me which he succeeded in doing. He would come in the morning and glare at me with an evil look. No "good morning." At recess time he caused trouble on the school ground, and had the smaller ones crying. If I disciplined him he would make some nasty remark. At times he would throw big blocks of wood on top of the roof and it sounded like a bombardment. Talking to him, only made matters worse, so I tried to put up with him. Talking to his folks didn't help, they were rather strange and unfriendly.

I struggled through the 7-month term, but was on the verge of a nervous breakdown. I couldn't eat my noon lunch, and when the pupils went home I put my head on the desk and cried. After a crying

spell, I had to sweep the floor, carry water from an outside well to fill a fountain for the next day, take down the flag, and split wood for the fire the next morning. By then I was both physically and mentally exhausted. My frustrations were eased somewhat, thanks to a thoughtful mother who came to get me so I didn't have to walk home 2 1/2 miles. At night I took home a couple of books such as history or arithmetic so I could keep a jump ahead of the eighth graders. In the winter my dad took me to school when it was stormy and cold and also came for me.

My mother knew it was hard for me, but she kept encouraging me and told me that the term would soon end.

My second year I was hired to teach in a 2-room school near Walcott. Then, for several years I taught in town schools. However, teachers were getting more plentiful and better qualified. Their qualifications entitled them to schools in preference to lesser qualified teachers so I had to return to teaching a rural school.

The big problem I faced during this term was at my rooming place. The man of the house, also president of the school board, became very attentive and tried to date me. He tried several ways to get me interested, but I told him off and had to be on guard at all times. I always locked my bedroom door at night. His wife didn't pay any attention to his whims; apparently she was used to them. One night his wife and children, an eighth-grade girl and a fourth grade boy, went upstairs to bed and so did I. As I was sitting on my bed about to remove my shoes, I heard a thud against the outside wall of my room. I quickly jumped up, turned the light down, and looked out the window. There I caught the "rat." He had put a long ladder up against the window to "see what he could see." He saw me and

continued on next page

Established in 1970 the national Close Up Foundation is "committed to the belief that informed civic participation is essential to a responsive government and a healthy community." Its efforts to "help citizens of all ages, abilities, and backgrounds prepare for a lifetime of effective citizenship" is reflected in its slogan "Education For Democracy."[47] For 70 years the YCL, now in danger of dying out, was indeed educating for democracy, only in a different setting.

After printing the YCL pledge and noting that "'Courtesy, cooperation, patriotism' were watchwords urged upon the YCL" at the 1938 convention, the *Bismarck Capital* asked: "How can we go wrong on a program like that?"[48] Teachers, parents, all North Dakotans need to address that query once again — today.

Endnotes

1. Alexis de Tocqueville, *Democracy in America: The Republic of the United States of America and its Political Institutions* (New York: Barnes, 1877) Part I, p. 204; *Democracy in America*, ed. J. P. Mayer and Max Lerner (New York: Harper and Row, 1966), p. 485. Fraternal orders satisfied social needs in the United States; they reached their zenith about 1925. By that date there were some 800 distinct orders organized into tens of thousands of local lodges with about 35 million members. The voluntary association, however, is perhaps the major institution in American culture for maintaining or reforming American society. The *Encyclopedia of Associations*, Vol. I: *National Organizations of the United States*, 5th ed. (Detroit: 1968) lists over 12,000 active associations on nearly 1,000 double-columned pages.

2. The Young Citizen's League of America, *Y. C. L. Manual*, n.d., p. 31; *The Young Citizen*, January, 1936, p. 1; South Dakota, South Dakota Historical Society (SDHS), Vertical File, Young Citizens League, *Helps in Organizing and Conducting A Young Citizens League*. Much teaching in American society is "ideational"—teaching ideas *about* activities, not demonstrating activities.

3. *Y. C. L. Manual*, n.d., p. 31; North Dakota, Department of Public Instruction (DPI), The Young Citizens League, *How to Organize and Conduct a Chapter of the Young Citizens League*, 1935, p. 32; SDHS, Vertical File, Young Citizens League; Farnsworth Crowder, "Their Fingers In The Pie," *The Saturday Evening Post*, October 26, 1940, pp. 39,43-44, 46. Two sources (DPI, *The Young Citizens League of North Dakota*, August, 1928, p. 3; *Ibid.*, *The Young Citizens League Manual*, July, 1931, p. 15) state that Guhin took up the idea in 1910. He thought Garden Prairie No. 26-4 , Brown County, taught by Miss Ethel Cocking, was the first school in South Dakota to organize a YCL .She was dubious of this honor. Guhin is certain that among the first in the state to sponsor a YCL were: D. C. Mills, teacher, Podoll School, Shelby Township; E. C. Giffen, principal of the Verdon two-room school, Garden Prairie Township; Herbert Melcher, teacher, rural school in Highland Township; and Mrs. Myrtle Lathrop, rural school teacher, Gem Township. The first two YCL county conventions in South Dakota were held in the spring of 1926 in Brown County and in Potter County. The first state convention was held at Pierre in 1927.

4. *The Young Citizens League of North Dakota*, August, 1928, pp. 2-3; John Dewey, *Education Today* (New York: G. P. Putnam's Sons, 1940) p. 269; *The Young Citizen*, May, 1936, p. 1; W. M. Wemett to Dr. Max Mason, president of the Rockefeller Foundation, January 16, 1936, North Dakota State University, Institute for Regional Studies (IRS), MSS 449, Box 1, Folder 3; DPI, *The Young Citizens League Manual*, October, 1976; *The North Dakota Teacher*, March, 1928, p. 18. Wemett, considered the founder of the YCL in North Dakota, was head of the history and social science department at Valley City State Teachers College. Born in Hemlock, New York, February 10, 1884, he received a degree from Syracuse University, moved to Valley City in 1910, and taught at the college until 1954. He died September 29, 1965. He was elected the League's first president; other officers: vice-president, Harriet E. Perry, county superintendent of Stutsman County; secretary-treasurer, Nell Cooper, county superintendent of Barnes County.

climbed down as fast as he could; he grabbed the ladder and ran. It was a nice moonlit night so I could see it all. I was furious, but at the same time it struck me as being funny. I laughed so hard that I was afraid his wife would hear me and come in to see what was so funny. I didn't see him the next morning.

I was given a raise and asked to renew my contract for the coming year. Of course the answer was "No! Never again!"

A rural school can be very frustrating, nerve-racking, and also lonely. A teacher needs contact with other teachers and other interests outside of school. There is no one to talk to and you can't discuss your troubles with a colleague. You sit there alone and look at carved old desks, slivery dusty floors, and four uninteresting walls, badly in need of paint to cheer up the place. I would think to myself, "Is the struggle for $75 a month or $525 for the term worth it?"

I don't think that a rural school is good for either the teacher or the pupils. Too much work for the teacher and too many subjects to teach . A teacher can't do justice to her job. Pupils don't get what they should out of school, especially when all grades had to be taught.

A Country School Teacher Remembers —
Erling Nicolai Rolfsrud

*N*one of my pupils came to school that day. My common sense and my family had insisted no parent would allow a child to set out in that furious below-zero wind.

But, warmly clad, my back to the north wind, I had walked the mile and a half to the school house that morning. I had not been able to shake from my mind the remote possibility that one of my seven pupils might come—and not find Teacher at school.

Replenished with clumps of lignite coal, the old jacketed stove kept me reasonably warm. At times the wall of north windows shuddered against the winds, yet I felt an almost cozy contentment.

Why not stay through the day and write? Pursue this ambition that ever held me?

By late afternoon, the wind had whipped the snow into a blizzard. Reluctantly, I quit the writing, knowing that I must reach home before dark.

I "banked" the stove, then dressed for the hike into the wind and shifting walls of snow. I walked only a short way from the schoolhouse and realized I would freeze my face. To the schoolhouse I returned, wondering what protection I could muster.

One west window had a cretonne curtain. I pulled this off its rod and wrapped it about my head after cutting two slits so I could see out.

Again I started homeward, hunching into the wind. Most of the way I could follow a barbed-wire fence.

Fear did not trouble me. Youth that I was, I felt a strange exultation in besting the storm.

A mile down the road, the home of one of my pupils stood close by. I stopped there to warm for the final half mile.

The mother there had known me since childhood. "Oh, Erling, Erling," she fondly scolded, "don't you know better than to go to school on a terrible day like this?"

She examined me carefully, and she had to admit that my cretonne-curtain mask had saved my face from harm.

5. *Y. C. L. Manual*, pp. 11-12,15, 31-32; *We Want You To Know*, IRS, MSS 449, Box 3, Folder 8. Colorado and Minnesota established chapters in the early 1930s. The former held a state convention in Denver in 1939 and by the mid-1940s had more than a thousand leagues. Four counties in Minnesota were completely organized by that time and one county in Kansas. Wemett was elected president of the national organization. Local leagues were urged to affiliate with it. For $2 local chapters received membership in the national organization, a subscription to the official magazine, *The Young Citizen*, a national charter, *The Y. C. L. Code of Ethics*, ready for framing, and support from the national organization.

6. W. M. Wemett to Dr. Max Mason, January 16, 1936, IRS, MSS 449, Box 1, Folder 3. At this writing no response from Mason has surfaced.

7. *Ibid.*

8.. Gretta Palmer, "Learning To Live," *Good Housekeeping*, April 1940, pp. 34, 153.

9. *Ibid.*, p. 34.

10. *Ibid.*, pp. 34-35.

11. *Ibid.*, pp. 35, 153. One "character education" program cited by Palmer was developed by Dr. Charles B. Glenn of Birmingham, Alabama. It focused on a different slogan over a twelve-year cycle: "Character Through Health, Sportsmanship, Work, Beauty, Thrift, Courtesy, Nature Study, The Worthy Use Of Leisure, Service, Wonder, Cooperation, Self-Reliance." Other efforts named were the activities of the National Honor Society and the Pathfinders of America, and the New York City schools' *Character Story Readers*.

12. Crowder, pp. 39,43-44, 46.

13. *Ibid.*, p. 39.

14. IRS, MSS 449, Box 1, Folder 4.

15. *Ibid.*

16. *Ibid.* The first state edition of *The Young Citizen* was published in 1929 with Mrs. Aileen Erickson Klawiter as editor; the first edition of the *Young Citizen* appeared as a national publication in January 1936, *The Young Citizen*, January, 1936, p. 9.

17. North Dakota, State Historical Society of North Dakota (SHSND), North Dakota Young Citizens League Records, *Audit and Report, The Young Citizens League of America*, A-484, 381505, Box 1, Folder Finances.

18. *Ibid.* Field staff received a per diem of $15, actual hotel expenses, and 5 cents per mile. Wemett received $2,260, an average of $9.38 per day for his work. He billed the organization for only two-thirds of the days spent in the field during his vacation time and "off" days at the college. He taught extra classes if he missed any college work and took no compensation for his office work. Other members of the field staff included Philimine Berglund, Clara Brown, Leila Ewen, Ray Fearing, John Headlely, Charles Johnson, Erich Selke, A. E. Thompson, Lena Vangstad, Lorene York. At the close of the 1928 school year South Dakota had chartered about 4,218 YCL chapters. Minnesota, Minnesota Historical Society (MHS), La Qui Parle County Superintendent of Schools Records, 128. C. 12. 1B, *Helps in Organizing and Conducting A Young Citizens League*, p. 4.

19. Ann Raymond to W. M. Wemett, May 19, 1932, MSS, 449, Box 1, Folder 3. The Cleanliness Institute was founded by the Association of American Soap & Glycerine Producers, Inc.

20. J. E. Beasley to W. M. Wemett, April 14, 1950, MSS 449, Box 1, Folder 5; Otto G. Ruff to W. M. Wemett, December 20, 1950, MSS 449, Box 1, Folder 5.

21. Ken Dale to W. M. Wemett, October 23, 1952, MSS 449, Box 1, Folder 5. Dale was the Director of Commercial Teacher Education at Arizona State College during the summer session of 1951 and was planning to teach at University of Arizona at its 1953 summer session. Grady Gammage, president of Arizona State College was a friend of University of North Dakota's President John West and Professor Selke of that institution.

*T*he mention of the early school board brings a little sour note. Yes, they were unfair. If the board member had a daughter who needed a job, she got it. I've known some school board clerks who didn't present other applications to the rest of the board. The clerk just merely said he had only one application or that he had another, but it was someone that he knew wasn't qualified. You couldn't bargain for wage increases. In the early years hiring and firing was done by a select few, which I believe was very unfair in most cases. After New School District No. 8. in Williams County was organized in 1950 this problem never came up. We had better buildings, equipment, books, and school board relations. We got away from local school boards and unfair practices. We could ask for a raise if we felt we were entitled to it without fear of losing our job. However, I never asked for a raise but I got a raise anyway. The school board visited once a year and all they did was ask if I needed or wanted anything. I never asked for anything that I didn't need.

✍✍

22. *Ibid.* There is no indication of the success or failure of Arizona's effort to organize the YCL in the Wemett material.

23. MHS, Scott County Superintendent of Schools Miscellaneous Records, 69. D. 10. 7B, *The Young Citizens League of America. What? Why?*, p. 6.

24. MSS 449, Box 1, Folder 4.

25. *Y. C. L. Manual*, p. 4.

26. DPI, *The Young Citizens League Manual*, September, 1955, p. 7; *Y. C. L. Manual*, pp. 5-6.

27. *Ibid.*, pp. 8-9; *Y. C. L. Manual*, pp. 5-8.

28. *The Young Citizens League Manual*, September, 1955, pp. 27-30; IRS, MSS 449, Box 3, Folder 8. The following prayers were included in the 1955 *Manual*: Y. C. L. Prayer, Morning Prayer, two versions of A Child's Grace, and Grace.

29. *The Young Citizens League Manual*, September, 1955, pp. 33-34.

30. DPI, Form 32, n.d., n. p.; *21st Biennial Report*, 1950, p. 77; *26th Biennial Report*, 1960, p.234.

31. North Dakota Young Citizens League Records, Rolette County, 370105.32, 10527, Box 1.

32. SDHS, Vertical File, Young Citizens League, "Helps in Organizing and Conducting A Young Citizens League."

33. *The Young Citizen League Manual*, July, 1931, p. 16.

34. *Bismarck Tribune*, May 7, 1949, pp. 1,3; May 5, 1950, pp. 1,3.

35. *Ibid.*, May 5, 1950, pp. 1,3.

36. *Ibid.* May 3, 1952, p. 3.

37. *Ibid.*, May 2, 1953, p. 1.

A Country School Teacher Rembmers — Jessie Schade

Living on a not-too-productive farm in the extreme southwestern part of North Dakota, we all had to work very hard physically at a very early age. We had enough plain farm food to eat but my clothes were always "hand-me-downs." I was very much aware of the "better things" other kids had. When I was a sophomore in high school one of my teachers had a fur coat. I fell in love with this teacher, but more so her fur coat. That was the ultimate in fine clothes. I felt that the only way I could ever afford such an expensive garment was to become a teacher.

Toward spring of my senior year each of us had a conference with the school superintendent. When I told him that I had plans to become a teacher, he pointed out several reasons why I should not. "There are too many rural teachers in the area now. You'll simply marry some farmer and that will be the end of your career." He urged me to enter nurses training. It was cheaper than getting a teaching degree.

My parents somehow managed to send me to Dickinson Normal School for one year. My counselor was right. It was difficult to find a teaching position in 1927 and 1928. However, the county superintendent of Bowman County suggested I teach in my home district. This I did not want to do. I wanted to get away from that area. There was no other opening, however, so I signed my first contract to teach in the same school I had attended for eight years, in Medicine Hills School District.

38. SHSND, YCL Manuscript Collection, A 484-381505, Box 1; Young Citizens League Files 1986, 1988,1992, Series No. 31690, Box No. 3, Box 4; DPI, "Address The Group—P.E.O.," n.d. . The address was given either by State Superintendent Arthur E. Thompson or Mrs. Lorene York. Counties usually sent three official delegates and alternates, one from the sixth, seventh, and eighth grades.

39. *Bismarck Tribune*, May 6, 1954, p. 4; *Pioneer Women Teachers of North Dakota*, pp. 55-56. Coming to North Dakota from Des Moines, Iowa, as a child, Lorene Evans attended a country school in Dunn County, completed high school in Dickinson, taught in Halliday for two years, attended Moorhead Teachers College and received a two-year diploma in 1920. She taught in Idaho and Washington, married Carroll York, and was widowed when her husband was killed in an auto-train accident. In 1929 she ran for county superintendent of Dunn County and left that position when she was appointed director of certification in the DPI in 1935; she retired from that position June 30, 1965.

40. *Bismarck Tribune*, May 8, 1937, p. 1; May 3, 1947, pp. 1,3; *The Young Citizen*, February, 1951, n.p.; *Bismarck Tribune*, May 8, 1948, p. 1; North Dakota Young Citizens League Records, A 484 381505 Box 1; DPI, 1996 State YCL Convention, YCL Theme for 1996-1007.

41. *Bismarck Capital*, May 10, 1938, p. 1.

42. *Bismarck Tribune, May 7, 1937, p. 1; May 5, 1950, p. 4; May 5, 1951, p. 1; May 6, 1954, p.4; Bismarck Capital, May 10, 1938, p. 2.*

43. *Ibid.*

44. Nellie R. Swanson and Eleanor C. Bryson, eds., *Pioneer Women Teachers of North Dakota* (Minot: *Ward County Independent*, 1965), p. 55.

45. YCL Manuscript Collection, Box 1; DPI, *The Biennial Report*, 1985, p. 45; *State YCL Convention Delegates, 1996; Young Citizen's League Manual*, 1987, p. 14. Burleigh, Ransom, Slope, and Williams counties sent official delegations. The president of the YCL for 1995-1996, who presided over the meetings, was Luke Storer, a sixth grader from Cando Elementary School in Towner County. His league was specifically organized so that he could meet the requirement that state officers be members of a local league. Because there were so few organized counties in attendance, selecting state officers became somewhat complicated: under present rules counties are not eligible to hold the same state office for two consecutive terms, no one person can hold a state office for more than one term and only state delegates in grades 5-7 may be elected to hold state offices.

46. *The Biennial Report*, 1985, p. 46.

47. *Close Up Foundation*, Brochure. The DPI got involved with the program in 1983 and sponsors and supports the high school program for students in grades 10 through 12.

48. *Bismarck Capital*, May 10, 1938, p. 2.

Y.C.L.
March Song

WORDS BY
MAJ. JOSEPH M. HANSON
YANKTON, S.D.

MUSIC BY
RICHARD BROUGHTON
SIOUX FALLS, S.D.

PRICE 25¢

SPECIAL PRICES ON ONE HUNDRED OR MORE COPIES

PUBLISHED BY
THE YOUNG CITIZENS LEAGUE
PIERRE, SOUTH DAKOTA.

2

Y. C. L. March Song

Words by
Maj. JOSEPH MILLS HANSON
Yankton S.D.

Music by
RICHARD E. BROUGHTON
Sioux Falls, S. D.

INTRO
Tempo di Marcia

O,
In

up from ev-'ry val-ley And down from ev-ry crest, We come, thy loy-al
all the winds of heav-en, There breathes a patriot's creed, Clean hearts and minds and

child-ren, By all thy fa-vors blest, To pledge our firm al-le-giance, A-
bo-dies, Serve best our coun-try's need, That creed we hold A-mer-i-ca, En-

mer-i-ca to thee, Thy guar-dians of to-mor-row, By moun-tain, plain and sea.
shrined in heart and soul; A deep-er sense of du-ty And bet-ter lives our goal.

The contest to secure a suitable song for the Young Citizens League was made possible by two South Dakota citizens. { *Fifty Dollars in gold for words - Mr. Guy H. Harvey, Yankton, S.D.* { *Fifty Dollars in gold for music - Mr. W. R. Larson, Sioux Falls, S.D.*

Chapter 12

Report of Committee on Salaries and Social Status of Teachers *

Webster Merrifield

REPORT.

The committee on teachers' salaries appointed by your president a year ago begs to submit the following report:

Shortly after our appointment we submitted the following series of questions to all state superintendents of public instruction and to all county superintendents, city superintendents and high school principals in this state:

1. What is approximately the average of wages per month (a) for male teachers, (b) for female teachers, in the common or graded schools in your state, county or city?

2. What is approximately the average of wages per month (a) for male teachers, (b) for female teachers in the high schools in your state, county or city?

3. What is approximately the average salary paid to principals of high schools in your state, county or city?

4. What, in your judgment, are the causes of low wages or salaries for teachers in your state, county or city so far as they exist?

5. What remedies can you suggest for these lower wages?

From most of these persons we received replies, and upon these replies and such supplementary information as is contained in recent reports of Commissioner Harris of the U. S. Bureau of Education, the annual reports of the U. S. Commissioner Of Labor and the report of the U. S. Industrial Commission, the report of your committee is largely based. The first points to be determined in the investigation were these: First, are the wages of teachers in this country and in the most civilized countries of Europe lower than those paid in other occupations calling for equal ability, character and training as does the occupation of the teacher; second, are the wages paid to

A Country School Teacher Remembers — Pearl Wick

One year the process of my being rehired was very interesting. Near the end of the school term the school board made the following offer: $125 per month if I did not attend summer school or $140 per month if I took a 12-week course at Valley City Teachers College. The contract, however, would not be issued until the end of summer school.

When I arrived home after summer school the president and one member of the board came to see me. They informed me that a single girl who just graduated from college had applied for the position and agreed to teach for $125. They would, however, give me the contract if I agreed to teach for the same amount.

I said, "No, a single girl needs the position. I would not think of depriving a single girl of a job." My husband and I lived on a farm, so our financial problems were fewer than hers, or so we thought.

Three days later the same men came to our door. "We came to hire a teacher," said the president. I replied, "Oh, didn't Miss X accept the offer?" "Mrs. Wick, we have a confession to make. No one applied! We thought by telling you what we did you would teach for $125." Graciously, I hope, I accepted their offer. I really enjoyed teaching that school. My wages were $140 per month.

teachers generally in this country lower than those paid to teachers in other countries of corresponding civilization; and, third, are the wages of teachers in North Dakota lower than those received by teachers of the same grade in other sections of the country? Unless your committee should succeed in establishing the affirmative of at least one of these questions there would seem to be no such thing as a problem of teachers' salaries. Your committee believes that it has been measurably successful in establishing the affirmative of all three of the questions propounded. That it has succeeded in ascertaining the reason of this condition and especially an adequate remedy for it, your committee feels by no means sanguine. Let us consider briefly the question of the relative remuneration of the teacher and of other employees, skilled and unskilled. The advance sheets of Commissioner Harris' forthcoming report give the average monthly salary of men teachers in North Dakota as $42.70; of women teachers as

*Source:** North Dakota Department of Public Instruction, *Ninth Biennial Report*, 1906, pp. 37-51. Webster Merrifield, the "father of the state high school system," was a Yale graduate in classical languages and president of the University of North Dakota from 1891 to 1909. Together with Walter L. Stockwell, state superintendent of public instruction from 1903 to 1911; Edwin J. Taylor, deputy superintendent for Stockwell and then state superintendent from 1911 to 1917; and Neil C. Macdonald, state inspector of rural and graded schools under Taylor and state superintendent in 1917 and 1918 this foursome was outspoken in telling North Dakotans about the weakness of their schools. State aid, larger school districts with the county as the basic unit, better trained teachers, and school consolidation were among the many reforms they recommended during the Progressive Era.

Male teacher and his charges in the early twentieth century in North Dakota *(Hulstrand Collection, NDIRS)*

$37.14. How do these wages compare with those received by reliable, unskilled laborers in this state? At the State University there are employed four men janitors, two teamsters and two firemen who are paid $45 per month each, or $2.30 more than the average man teacher in this state receives. There are employed one assistant engineer who is paid $55 a month and one engineer, a young man twenty-one years old, without a high school education, but unusually intelligent and reliable, who is paid $90 per month through the year. Even at the above wages it is exceedingly difficult to get and keep good men. Your committee is told by farmers that they have to pay $40 to $45 per month (board being commuted into its equivalent money value) oftener the latter than the former wage, for farm laborers throughout the year. There is this consideration in favor of the common laborer even at this figure, that his wages continue through twelve months, while those of the teacher run only nine months with little likelihood of his being able to get employment during most of the summer vacation, even if that time were not devoted, as it usually is and ought always to be, to needed rest and professional improvement.

How do the wages of our women teachers compare with those of unskilled female labor in this state? In most North Dakota towns good household help commands an average of $4.50 a week and a home — the equivalent, say, of $35 per month. The domestic servant's wage, like that of the male common laborer, extends through the twelve months of the year, while that of the women teacher runs through nine months at most and often through only five or six months of the year, with no opportunity for earning during the long vacation. Indeed, if the woman teacher were to go to domestic service (practically the only remunerative occupation open to her in North Dakota) as soon as her school closes, the chances are overwhelmingly that she would fail, as she ought, to secure another school — not, however, for the reason that she ought so to fail, namely, that she would be neither physically nor mentally equipped for her school when it opened, but because in most communities she would be thought to have lowered herself socially by going into domestic service. Moreover, it is to be observed that the wages given above for this state namely, $42.70 for men teachers and $37.14 for women teachers, are not the average of wages paid in the common schools merely, but the average paid in all schools of the state, including the high schools.

To recapitulate, the man teacher receives in North Dakota an average yearly salary as much less than $384, (nine months at $42.70 per month), and the woman teacher an average yearly salary as much less than $334 as their average school year is less than nine full months. Probably $300 per year for men teachers and $260 for women teachers would be a liberal estimate in this state. As against these figures, the average teamster, fireman, janitor and farm laborer receives in this state a yearly salary of $540 and the average domestic servant a yearly salary of $420. To repeat, the man teacher in North Dakota receives $300 a year; the average day laborer, $540; the average woman teacher receives $260, the average domestic servant $420. In other words, the man teacher in North Dakota receives 55 per cent as high real wages as the common laborer and the woman teacher 62 per cent as high real wages as the domestic servant. If we compare the teacher's wage in this state with other occupations requiring similar — certainly not superior — intelligence and training as that of the teacher, we shall find the odds against the teacher even greater. Your committee sent letters to the proprietors of two of the largest department stores in this state asking for a statement of wages paid to their salesmen and saleswomen. From one of these proprietors we received the following reply: "I estimate the average wage of experienced saleswomen at $75 per month and that of salesladies at $50. These figures do not apply to heads of departments. The experienced woman in the office earns $60 per month. Beginners are paid on the average $20 per month. These are generally boys or girls living with their parents, to whom the store is a business school. Department managers are paid from $100 to $125 per month." From the other proprietor we received the following reply: "We pay our clerks by the week, the average salary for men clerks being $13.03 and for lady clerks $8.43 per week. The salaries for the men range from $5 to $30 per week and from $5 to $18 per week for women according to ability and experience." Similar letters addressed to the general managers of the Great Northern and Northern Pacific railroads brought the following responses: The Great Northern answered through its comptroller as follows: "I beg to advise that there are employed by this company in the city of Grand Forks (in the superintendent's and agent's offices) thirty-five men, including all of the employees from superintendent

A Country School Teacher Remembers — Alma Rognlie Ronning

I was born on a farm in Eldon Township in Benson County. I attended country school the first five years of grade school. In September 1924 I received a Second Grade Elementary Certificate after completing a teacher's training course. It was valid for two years and qualified the holder to teach in any of the first eight grades of the public schools in the state. It was difficult to get a job in those days because teachers were plentiful. A year went by before I signed my first contract to teach in Aurora School District No. 38 in Benson County in School No. 1, also known as the Stony Lake School. The term was for 8 months, beginning October 5, 1925 and ending May 26, 1926. My salary was $80 a month.

I attended Mayville State Normal School [Mayville State University] after I finished my first year of teaching. I was granted a First Grade Elementary Certificate on August 20, 1926. It was valid for three years and entitled me to teach in the ninth grade in schools doing not over one year of high school work. I continued to attend summer school there from 1927 to 1932, except for one year, 1931. I received another First Grade Elementary Certificate in the meantime, issued September 11, 1929 that was valid for three years. I had by that time completed two years of college and was graduated August 5, 1932, receiving a Standard Diploma and a Second Grade Professional Certificate that was valid for three years. After 18 months of successful teaching I received my Second Grade Life Professional Certificate on June 28, 1935. What a proud day that was for me, after struggling with teaching during the winter, having only two weeks of vacation, and then attending summer school for 12 weeks each summer for 6 years to get it!

to office boy. Their salaries average $75.15 per month. In the city of Fargo we have at the station eight men, the average salary per month being $65. This includes salary of the station agent and all of his employees." The Northern Pacific replied through its Auditor of Disbursements that the general average of pay for general, office clerks in North Dakota is about $63 per month and for agents $60 per month, all but one of their employees being men or boys. Similar inquiries addressed to the proper sources of information brought the statement that the Presbyterian church in the state at large pays its pastors salaries averaging $875 and in Pembina Presbytery, $1,065; that the Catholic church pays its priests an average salary of $1,000, and that the Methodist

A Country School Teacher Remembers — Margaret Sturlaugson

*I*n the fall of 1930 I applied for my first school. The president of the school district was hesitant in signing me up because I had no experience. However, his father who was also a member of the board said, "Somewhere these poor things have to start." I could have kissed him for that remark. I signed a contract for $70 a month to teach 19 pupils in all eight grades for an 8-month term at Sunnyside District No. 69 in Pembina County.

church pays its pastors an average salary of $943, the parsonage in all cases being an addition to the salary paid. To recapitulate, we find that men teachers in this state receive, on the most favorable showing, that is, on the supposition that all schools run the full nine months, on the average $384 per year and the women teachers $334 per year, while men clerks in stores receive an average of $788.78 per year and women clerks an average of $519.18 per year, that clerks in railroad offices from office boy to superintendent receive an average salary of $817.56 per year and station agents an average of $720; and that the priests and pastors in the Catholic, Methodist and Presbyterian churches in this state receive an average salary of $939.33 and parsonage together with fees and perquisites from baptisms, marriage, funerals,

etc. Principals of high schools and teachers in high schools fare better, of course, than teachers in the common schools, but the average gross salary of all superintendents in classified high schools in this state last year was $1,266; of men teachers in high schools was $702.50, and of women teachers, $578.08. Certainly, in point of average ability, training and experience, these superintendents, principals and teachers are quite the equal of the department manager; or floor walkers in mercantile establishments in this state who receive from $1,200 to $1,500 a year. In view of the statistics which have been quoted and which have been derived from the highest sources and earn fully verified, it may safely be stated as a general proposition that teachers in North Dakota are paid in real wages not to exceed from 50 per cent to 70 per cent as much as persons employed in other occupations requiring an equal degree of native ability, education and experience. His shorter hours of labor per day or week may be alleged as a consideration in favor of the teacher. The answer to this allegation is that the time spent by the teacher in the class room is no criterion of the length of his real working day. For the faithful teacher there are always lessons to be carefully prepared and even for the most careless and indifferent teacher there are records to be kept and weekly or monthly reports to be made out. What teacher in this hearing believes that he or she gives fewer hours per week to the work of teaching and the duties incident thereto than the average business man or clerk or the average typewriter, stenographer or bookkeeper in the same community give to their respective occupations? It is

Ring School, Grand River Township, Bowman County *(Bowman County Collection, SHSND)*

well known that superintendents and school boards often insist that the teacher shall not, in justice to her work, go into so-called society, i. e., attend social functions in the evening during the working part of the week. Is the business man, the clerk, the bookkeeper or stenographer so debarred? Again, it is alleged that the teacher is paid a lower money wage because of the long summer vacation, but it is the community and not the teacher who asks for this vacation, and there are few teachers who would not be glad to obtain remunerative work in summer schools if such were offered.

In every occupation save that of the teacher a short working year, as in the case of masons and builders, is made an excuse if not a reason, for charging an abnormal wage while the season lasts. The teacher as well as the mason must eat and be housed twelve months in the year and must make his working year earn enough to pay for such food and shelter or enter some other occupation where it will do so. Because the teaching vocation does not at present pay such a wage, the man teacher, particularly if he be mature and experienced and

Barnes County School District 46 (Collection 77-80, SHSND)

has a family dependent upon him, leaves teaching to women who are dependent upon their own efforts for a living and who must take such occupation as they can get or to young girls who are glad to relieve their parents of part of the burden of their support while waiting for an eligible offer of marriage, or to school girls who are dependent upon their own efforts for education and whose meager earnings during four or five months of the year enable them to keep in school the other seven.

So much for North Dakota. If we turn to other states we shall find the same general condition prevailing there, oftentimes in an aggravated form. Instead of a single state let us take as a basis for comparison, as being less open to error, each of the traditional subdivisions of the United States namely, the New England States, the Middle States, the Southern States the Central States and Pacific States. The following table is compiled from the U. S. census report for 1900 and from Commissioner Harris' report for the same year:

Section	Black-smiths	Carpenters	Foremen in Machine Shops*	Painters	Machinists	+All Below	Men Teachers
New England	$67.17	$58.33	$82.53	$73.66	$58.50	$49.83	$57.75
Middle states	65.00	56.33	97.50	52.00	60.66	45.50	50.10
Southern states	71.50	56.33	91.00	——	58.50	45.50	49.32
Central states	71.50	56.33	91.00	——	58.50	45.50	49.32
Pacific states	80.16	——	——	——	78.00	60.66	62.36
AVERAGE	$69.76	$55.75	$90.27	$62.83	$63.26	$48.62	$48.77
*Foremen in machine shops. +All other occupations including those in which women are engaged.							

It appears from the above table that in all sections of the United States the man teacher receives a lower wage per month than blacksmiths carpenters, foremen in machine shops and machinists, and practically the same wage as the average employee in

Form 17.

Original (For School Clerk) for Teacher

TEACHER'S CONTRACT

STATE OF NORTH DAKOTA,

County of __Mountrail__ } ss.

__Banner__ School District No.__12__

THIS AGREEMENT, Made and entered into this __11__ day of __June__ A. D. 1936, between __Mrs. Ralph Lee__, a duly qualified teacher, of __Mountrail__ County, State of North Dakota, and the School Board of __Banner School Dist.__ School District No. __12__ County of __Mountrail__ State of North Dakota.

WITNESSETH: That the said __Mrs. Ralph Lee__ is to teach School No.__1__ in said School District for a term of __8__ months, beginning on the __7th__ day of __Sept.__ A. D. 1936, for which services truly rendered the School Board of said School District agrees to pay said __Mrs. Ralph Lee__ at the expiration of each month of service the sum of __fifty ($50.00)__ Dollars. Provided that five percent may be retained until said Mrs. Lee has completed the term.

Provided, That the salary of the last month in the term shall not be paid until the term report shall be made, filed with and be approved by the County Superintendent of Schools, as provided by Section 1381, Compiled Laws of 1913.

PROVIDED FURTHER, That the school may be discontinued at any time, as provided by Sec. 1189, as amended by the Session Laws of 1931, and that no compensation shall be received by said teacher from the date of such discontinuance. __One__ per cent of her salary at the end of each month and remit same to the county treasurer as required by law. See Sec. 1506, Compiled Laws of 1913.

†FURTHER PROVIDED That all janitor work is to be done by Mrs. Ralph Lee and the above salary covers same. Holiday vacation is to be six weeks, except that if tax collection warrant the term will be nine months instead of eight and the holiday vacation will be only two weeks.

By Order of the District School Board

Florence C. Lee — Teacher.

Thomas Elton — President.

Hugh Miller — Clerk.

NOTE—This Contract must be made and signed in triplicate before school begins, and one copy delivered to the teacher, one copy filed with the Clerk of the District School Board, and one copy filed with the County Superintendent.

NOTE—If teacher is to do janitor work, same should be provided for in the Contract.

*If teacher is not a member of Fund, strike out this provision. One who became a teacher in the public schools after Jan. 1, 1914, must pay this assessment.

†Board may here insert any other provision deemed advisable.

A Teacher Contract from 1936 (Courtesy of Florence C. Lee)

"all other occupations." If we take the yearly instead of the monthly wage for comparison we shall find that in no section does the man teacher receive so much as 70 per cent of the average wage of all workers in all other occupations than that of the teacher, and that in the country as a whole, even on the untenable assumption that the average school year is nine months, the man teacher receives only 57 per cent as high a yearly wage as that of the average employee in all other occupations. As a matter of fact, Commissioner Harris' report for 1900 (See Vol. 1, p. 717) gives $342.36 as the average annual salary of men teachers in the United States for 1900. Using this as a basis we find that the average yearly salary of men teachers in this country is only 41.7 per cent of the average yearly salary of blacksmiths, carpenters, foremen in machine shops, machinists and painters. Strange as these figures may seem, they are based upon the official reports of U. S. Commissioner of Education, W.T. Norris, and of the U.S. census report for 1900. Is it any wonder that men will not go into teaching in the lower grades of school except as a makeshift, and that, in all grades but the college, the man who prepares himself for teaching as a life calling (we believe that teaching is nowhere regarded as a profession) is almost as extinct as the dodo? So much for teaching in the lower grades. If we turn to the higher grades of teaching, as in our colleges and normal schools, the condition is but little better. Men in these positions are, almost without exception, college graduates and have had on the average a far more elaborate preparation in the way of training for their chosen calling than the average doctor or lawyer. The salaries of men teachers in our North Dakota colleges and normal schools vary from $600 a year to $3,000 — the largest salary paid to any man teacher or educational executive in this state. How does this compare with the income of lawyers and doctors in North Dakota? How many lawyers or doctors of experience and of fair reputation and character are in receipt of an income as low as $600 per year? Who does not believe that at least two score men in each profession in this state have an income in excess of $3,000? Your committee knows at least a dozen of each who are related to have incomes in excess of $10,000 each and one is said to have an income of from $30,000 to $40,000 a year, or from three to four times that of the highest paid man engaged in educational work in the United States. Commissioner Harris, as is well known, receives a salary of only $3,500 a year as against $5,000 each received by the Commissioner of Patents and of Pensions and $4,000 received by the Commissioner of Indian Affairs. Twice in the last ten years a member of our committee has signed petitions to congress for the increase of Commissioner Harris' salary but in both instances congress turned this petition down, sympathizing, apparently, with that member of our own legislature who, some years ago, moved that the salary of professors in our State University be lowered to $1,200 a year, adding by way of justification that, in his opinion, no school teacher ever yet earned even that salary. Some years ago a gentleman known to a member of your committee was talking with Col. Parker of the Parker House in Boston, when Colonel Parker volunteered the information that his chef, or chief cook, received $10,000 a year. Upon the other gentleman's remarking that that was more than President Eliot of Harvard received, Colonel Parker replied — "He's worth more."

If we turn to European countries we shall find the salary of teachers still low — in some cases even lower, as represented in dollars and cents, than in this country: but we shall find that, as compared with the income received by salaried employees in other occupations and particularly in the government service, the teacher occupies relatively a much more favorable position both as regards income and social standing than he does in the United States. In Germany, the country which in many respects leads the world in education, teachers constitute a professional body with life tenure and old age pension and are accorded a social standing similar to that of the clergy. The average salary of teachers throughout the empire below the grade of principals or superintendents of secondary schools is about $360 a year, to which, however, must be added an allowance sufficient to cover house rent and fuel. In Germany nearly all teachers are men and the great majority of them are men with families. When it is considered that the cost of living in Germany outside the great cities and away from the beaten track of tourists is probably one-half less than in the United States, it is obvious that the real salary of the teacher there is relatively much higher than in this country. Germany provides an old age pension for all her teachers as she does for all her employee in the civil service. In Prussia this amounts to 25 per cent after twenty years' service, 50 per cent after thirty years', 75 per cent after forty years, and full salary after fifty years. "To maintain the pension fund the state requires all teachers to pay an annual premium into the pension fund rated at 1 per cent of a salary of $400, at 11/2 per cent of salaries from

A Country School Teacher Remembers — Frances Armstrong

From the time I was a little girl I was interested in teaching, probably because two of my sisters became teachers before me. My training to become a teacher was rather piece-meal. I took a teacher training in high school and after graduation I was issued a Second Grade Elementary Certificate that was good for three years; I renewed it by attending summer school. After teaching for four years I enrolled at Jamestown College, spent one year there and then returned to teaching. In 1927 I decided that I wanted my Life Certificate so I wouldn't have to renew my credential every three years. I attended Valley City Normal School for one year and upon graduation received my Standard Certificate and also a Special Certificate in Commerce.

I taught in Bloom School in Stutsman County for eight years and another two years in Woodbury Township before I received my Standard Certificate. Then I taught the intermediate room in Cleveland, North Dakota for three years. After I was married in 1931 I taught only one full year in the next twenty years, but I did substitute work in seven or eight schools, some rural and some in small towns. In 1951 I finished the year in the primary room at Buchanan, North Dakota. The school board asked me to take the school for the next year and I continued teaching there for six years after which I became Deputy County Superintendent for Stutsman County for six years.

My starting salary in Bloom School was $60 per month; I received an increase to $75, then to $90, another to $100, and the last year there I received $115 per month. During my eight years at this school I never had a contract. It was my home school and the school board would just ask if I was coming back the next year and told me what the salary was to be. Nothing was said about duties other than teaching. My beginning salary in Cleveland was $130 per month; I received a $5 raise the next year. When I returned to teaching after twenty years I received $225 per month; the last year I received $300 per month.

One interesting thing about my first years of teaching was that the pupils who were in the sixth, seventh, and eighth grades had been my schoolmates when I was in the grades.

The schools I taught in didn't have much equipment. We did have a large jar for drinking water and either the teacher or one of the pupils

continued on page 207

$400 to $1,000, and at 2 per cent on all higher salaries," but as a matter of fact many cities and communes pay the premium as an addition to the salary. In France teachers are regarded as in the government civil service and receive from the government a guarantee of a minimum salary ranging from $200 to $400 for men and from $200 to $350 for women, together with house rent and fuel, or their money equivalent.

Section	Blacksmiths	Carpenters	Foremen in Machine Shops	Machinists	Painters	Men Teachers
Germany	$318.24	$327.60	$471.12	$309.00	$333.84	$358.00
France	330.72	352.56	——	330.62	340.08	300.00
England	430.56	499.20	758.16	452.41	414.84	615.00

It appears from this table that in Germany the average teacher's wage in elementary schools is 100.1 per cent of the average yearly wage of blacksmiths, carpenters, foremen in machine shops, machinists and painters; that in France the average yearly wage of teachers in elementary schools is 88. 6 per cent of the average wage of employees in the same five occupations, and in England, 120 per cent; that in all three of these countries the teacher receives on the average 101.2 per cent as high a yearly wage as do employees in the five occupations named, while in the United States he receives only 41.7 per cent as much. In other words the teacher in Germany receives a real yearly wage 2.4 times as great as that of the teacher in the United States; the teacher in France, a real yearly wage 2.8 times as great. This difference, of course, is partly accounted for by the fact that the school year is longer and therefore the yearly wage greater in each of these countries than in the United States, but chiefly by the fact that the standard of requirements for teachers is far higher and popular appreciation of the service rendered by the teacher far greater in these three leading countries of Europe than in our own. As Professor Munsterberg of Harvard observes "America is the only country in the world which gives over the teaching of its youth to the lowest bidder."

Our second question, whether the wages paid to teachers generally in this country are lower than those paid to teachers in other countries of corresponding civilization has already been answered for Germany, France and England, the three foremost countries, if not the three countries of highest civilization in Europe. In Austria the average wage of teachers is but a trifle under $350 a year, and in the Netherlands is about the same. The country of high civilization in Europe which pays the lowest salaries to teachers is Switzerland, where only eleven per cent of the teachers receive as much as $400 a year. It has been characteristic of democracies in all times to place a low money value upon the services of its public servants. Tabulating for purposes of comparison the salaries paid to all elementary teachers in the countries of highest civilization, we find as follows:

Great Britain (elementary teachers)	$520.00 per annum
Germany (elementary teachers)	358.00 per annum
Austria (elementary teachers)	350.00 per annum
Holland (elementary teachers)	348.00 per annum
United States (elementary and secondary)	312.44 per annum
France (elementary teachers)	300.00 per annum

In this table the United States stands, apparently, next to the foot, but when it is borne in mind that in all the other countries named the teacher enjoys a permanent tenure, an old age pension, beginning usually after twenty years' service and amounting to full salary after fifty years' service: that he possesses a social standing far superior to that which he possesses in this country; that he is given, as a rule, in all European countries, house rent, fuel and garden in addition to his money salary, and that the purchasing power of money in all European countries is from a third to a half greater than in the United States, we are forced to the conviction that the American teacher is the poorest paid teacher in the civilized world.

Let us see now, how the North Dakota teacher fares as compared with teachers in other sections of the United States. As already stated, the advance sheets of Commissioner Harris' report give the average wages of men teachers in North Dakota as $42.70, of women teachers as $37.14, the average of the two being $39.92. The following table shows how teachers' salaries in North Dakota compare with those of other sections of the United States. Inasmuch as the census year of 1900 has been used generally in our comparisons heretofore, we will take Commissioner Harris' report for that year rather than for the year 1902, the last year reported.

AVERAGE MONTHLY SALARIES OF TEACHERS

	Men	Women
United States	$46.53	$38.93
North Atlantic division	56.70	41.34
South Atlantic division	28.48	25.73
South Central division	37.49	30.89
North Central division	49.04	39.22
Western division	58.77	50.05
North Dakota	41.72	36.80

It appears from the above table that men teachers in North Dakota are paid a lower money salary than men teachers are paid in any of the five divisions of the United States, except the South Atlantic and South Central divisions; that women teachers also are paid a lower salary than in any

brought water. Each child had his own folding drinking cup. There were no workbooks or other aids to help the teacher, but we did have a globe and wall maps. Along with various textbooks that was all the equipment we had. Items the Bloom district provided, that other rural schools did not, were tablets and pencils. The teacher was given permission to go to the store and buy these and charge them to the school district.

In all the years I taught I never had many discipline problems. Once in a while a child was caught cheating in spelling or whispering when they weren't supposed to, but there were never any big problems and "no bullies."

Many of the school buildings were just one room buildings with a hallway for the entrance that was used as a cloakroom, washroom, and place to keep the lunch pails; toilets were usually buildings back of the school. The main room had a coal heater in one end that burned soft coal or lignite that had to be carried in from an outdoor coal shed. However, I was fortunate. The first three years our school was a school of this type, but the stove was a jacket stove. The building had a coal shed attached so you didn't have to go out of doors to get the fuel. The district always burned hard coal that was so much nicer to handle, the fire kept overnight and the temperature was more even. After three years in the old school a new building was constructed; it was one of the nicest rural schools in the county. It was built on a foundation. There was a large cloakroom for the boys and a large one for the girls, a library room to store the books and a large main room with hardwood floors and slate blackboards. There was a full concrete basement. In the center was a large furnace. One corner of the basement was partitioned off for a coal bin and another part had indoor toilets.

It was the teacher's duty to start the fires and to keep them banked at night so the school would be easy to warm in the morning. Each night the floor was swept and the blackboards cleaned. We usually used sweeping compound to keep the dust down. I don't know if we were expected to scrub the schoolhouse or not but several of us teachers did. We would have the children who drove to school bring a five gallon can of water that we would put on the register to keep warm. At last recess we would dismiss school. The little ones would clean the erasers, the next older cleaned the boards and dusted the desks, and the older ones and the teacher got down on their knees and scrubbed the floors.

continued on next page

The schoolhouse was used for dances on weekends. For recreation we attended dances, card parties, and just neighborhood parties, although the first year I taught in Cleveland my contract stated that I could not attend dances on school nights.

The first time a parent came to visit me occurred one evening when a father came to tell me that I couldn't keep his son after school. Not many parents visited school and only one school board visited in all the years I taught.

In the rural schools I taught in one of the board members usually asked if I wished to come back the next year; that was all there was to hiring. The last year I taught in Cleveland the president of the school board said they wanted me to come back the next year, but they weren't hiring married teachers. Since I was getting married I couldn't accept.

One of the greatest changes I found when I returned to teaching after many years was the use of workbooks. They were a great help to the teacher and also were good for the pupils, unless they were used excessively. Another change appeared in mathematics textbooks. Back in the early days problems dealt with such things as paper hanging, lumbering, finding the capacity of cisterns, or making partial financial payments; today, those kinds of problems are not mentioned.

I think children in a country school learned to study and to depend upon themselves more than children in larger systems; but they didn't get as much individual attention as children in city schools. Most of the rural pupils did well in the basic subjects, but they didn't have any of the outside activities that city children were able to take part in.

other division except the two named; that men teachers receive on the average $7.32 a month less than the average salary paid to men teachers in the North Central division of states as a whole — the group to which North Central division of states as a whole — the group to which North Dakota belongs — and $4.81 per month less than the average paid to all male teachers in the United States; that women teachers in North Dakota receive on the average $2.42 per month less than the salary paid to women teachers in the North Central division of states as a whole, and $2.13 less than is paid on the average to women teachers throughout the United States. Of course, in considering the real wages in one section of a country as compared with those in another, the relative value of money or cost of living in the two countries or sections must be taken into account. There are, unfortunately, no reliable statistics showing the relative cost of living in different parts of the United States. After all, living for any given community is more a matter of standards of living than of the actual cost of commodities. Five hundred dollars in many a charming New England village would go farther than five thousand dollars in Washington or New York City, not because provisions are so much higher in Washington or New York than in New England, but because the standard of living is far higher. Man is well off almost anywhere when he can afford to live as well as his neighbor does — when his occupation yields as good an income as theirs, assuming both to be equally safe and respectable. If we ascertain the ratio which the yearly wage of the man teacher in each main division of the United States bears to the average wage in all other occupations in the same division, and compare this ratio with that which the average wage of the teacher in North Dakota bears to the average wage in all other occupations in the Central Division of states, in which North Dakota is classified by the U. S. Industrial Commission, we shall ascertain with sufficient approximation the relative actual advantage or disadvantage which the man teacher in North Dakota labors under as compared with his fellow teachers in each of the other chief divisions of the country. It thus appears that, using 100 per cent as the standard, the man teacher in North Dakota is 48 per cent as well off as regards his yearly salary as the average worker in "all other" occupations in the same territorial division: that he is 6 per cent better off than the average man teacher in the south, 19 per cent worse off than his fellow teacher in New England, 12 per cent worse off than his fellow in the Middle States, 9 per cent worse off than his fellow in the Central States, 19 per cent worse off than his fellow on the Pacific coast, 7 per cent worse off than his fellow teacher in the country at large, and 58 per cent worse off than the average male teacher in England, France and Germany.

To recapitulate, in answering the question how teachers' wages in this country and in European countries compare with the wages paid in other occupations of the blacksmith, carpenter, foreman in machine shops, machinist and painter as a basis, we find that Germany pays her teachers a one per cent higher wage than the average wage of the several occupations named; that France pays her teachers 11.4 per cent less than the average paid in these occupations; that England pays her teachers 20 per cent more than the average in these occupations, and that the United States pays her teachers 58.3 per cent less than the average wage paid in these occupations in the United States. We find, therefore, that in money wage alone the United States pays her teachers less than any other leading country of high civilization except France, and that in real wages it is probable that she pays her teachers not much more than half the wages paid in those countries. We find further that North Dakota pays her teachers on the average $7.23 a month less than the average of the other states of the north central section of states to which North Dakota belongs; lower wages, indeed, than any other state in that section except South Dakota, in which the average of wages is a little lower even than in North Dakota; that North Dakota pays her men teachers $4.82 a month less than the average paid to men teachers throughout the United States, and her women teachers $2.13 a month less than is paid on the average to women teachers throughout the United States.

Let us now turn to a consideration of the causes of this deplorable condition and its possible remedies.In the circular letter sent by your committee to state superintendents and to county superintendents, city superintendents, principals and others in this state, was the following question: "What in your

Sod School District, Lincoln School No. 4, 1908-1909 (Burke Co. Collection 32 BK/13-6, SHSND)

The United States pays her teachers 58.3 per cent less than the average wage paid in these occupations in the United States. We find, therefore, that in money wage alone the United States pays her teachers less than any other leading country of high civilization except France, and that in real wages it is probable that she pays her teachers not much more than half the wages paid in those countries.

judgment, are the causes of low wages or salaries for teachers in your state as far as they exist?" The replies received have been classified as follows, the numerals opposite each assigned cause indicating the number assigning that as the cause of the prevailing low teachers' salaries:

Lack of funds · 30

Plenty of teachers who will underbid the good teachers · · · · · · 25

Lack of appreciation of good teachers by school boards · · · · · · 17

Too low standard of qualification for teachers · · · · · · · · · 11

Wages fixed by custom · 11

Lack of ability of officers to discriminate between teachers · · · · 9

Supply of teachers greater than the demand · · · · · · · · · · · 9

Too many young, inexperienced teachers of poor ability · · · · · · 9

Teachers get all they are worth · · · · · · · · · · · · · · · · · · 8

Desire to keep the tax rate down · · · · · · · · · · · · · · · · · · 8

Teachers are satisfied with present wages · · · · · · · · · · · · · 8

Teaching used as a stepping stone · · · · · · · · · · · · · · · · · 7

Indifference and unwillingness to pay higher wages · · · · · · · · 7

Too great competition · 6

No concerted demand for higher wages · · · · · · · · · · · · · · 6

Failure of boards to realize the importance of higher wages · · · · 5

Low standard of certification · 4

Resident teachers will teach for less to be at home · · · · · · · · 4

The mercenary spirit of the school board and taxpayers · · · · · · 4

Many teachers come from eastern states which pay small wages · · 4

Lack of power to compel recognition of rights · · · · · · · · · · · 4

Lack of interest on part of parents · · · · · · · · · · · · · · · · · 3

Teachers employed thru political influence
who are not properly trained · · · · · · · · · · · · · · · · · 2

The cause assigned by the largest number answering, namely thirty, is "lack of funds." Let us analyze briefly this reply. It is presumed that by "lack of funds" is meant a lack of available resources in the form of acquired wealth. There is probably no state in the union in which the individual taxpayer on the average receives a larger proportion of his income in the form of cash than does the taxpayer of North Dakota. A "lack of funds," therefore, cannot mean a lack of ready money but must mean a lack of wealth, implying that, if wages be lower in North Dakota than in most other states, it is because North Dakota is poorer than most other states.

The true index of a state's wealth is its per capita wealth. North Dakota's assessed valuation for 1900 was $117,204,485. Its population according to the census of 1900

German School on Wild Rice River, Richland County (SHSND)

was 319,145. This gives a per capita valuation for purposes of taxation of $367, the fraction of a dollar being disregarded. For the same year and determined in the same manner, Iowa's per capita valuation was $250 and that of Kansas $246. It is understood , of course, that a state's assessed valuation is no true index of its real wealth. The assessed valuation of the several states, however, probably gives a fair indication of their relative wealth and in the total absence of statistics as to the real wealth of the several states must be accepted for present purposes. Now if "lack of funds" be the cause of low teachers' wages in North Dakota, such wages should be lower in Iowa than in North Dakota and still lower in Kansas, but what are the facts?

While the wages of men teachers in North Dakota for 1902 were $42.70, corresponding wages in Iowa for the same year were $43.66, and for Kansas, $44.24. In both states teachers are better paid than in North Dakota in proportion to the per capita wealth of the state as indicated in their respective assessed valuations, but wages are the higher in that state in which the assessed valuation is the lower. The per capita

wealth of South Dakota in 1900 was $431 as against $367 in North Dakota, but teachers' wages in South Dakota average $3.75 per month lower than in North Dakota. It would thus appear that there is no necessary connection between the wealth of a state as indicated in its per capita assessed valuation and the rate of wages paid to its teachers.

It is generally true that agricultural communities pay much lower wages than manufacturing communities. The farmer is traditionally conservative in the matter of salaries for public servants. He has, as a rule, to which there are, fortunately, many exceptions, particularly in our own state, a much less keen appreciation of the value of efficient service than has the business man in the city and has a correspondingly less keen appreciation of the economy of paying such salaries as will command the most efficient service. Statistics show that on the average the teacher in town schools commands a salary nearly 40 percent higher in this country than the rural teacher.

Let us now consider the "lack of funds," as the alleged cause of the prevailing low salaries for teachers in North Dakota, from another point of view. There is the implication, certainly, that the taxpayer in this state is poor and cannot afford to pay teachers higher wages than they at present receive, and consequently that teachers ought not to ask more than they are already getting. But why should all the altruism fall to the lot of the teacher? As is shown by the report of the U. S. Industrial Commission, the miller, the carpenter, the blacksmith and other artisans command a larger wage in North Dakota where teachers' wages are low than they do in Massachusetts where teachers' wages are high. If the North Dakota tax payer wishes a chimney built, he must pay a mason a 50 percent higher wage to do it than the tax payer in Massachusetts has to pay. If he is not willing to pay the wage he must go without the chimney or hire a quack mason whose chimney will fall down, very likely, before the year is over. Is the latter not the thing which the tax payer too often does in North Dakota in the matter of education? Does he not, with lamentable frequency, turn down the skilled teacher and hire the quack in his place and would it not go far toward solving the whole problem of teachers' wages if the work of the quack teacher fell down as quickly, or at least as visibly, as does the work of the quack mason or the quack carpenter? In

Blooming Prairie School Picnic at the home of its first teacher, Martha Berg, Blooming Prairie Township, near Ambrose, ND in Divide County (*Divide Co. Collection 32 DR/46, SHSND*)

A Country School Teacher Remembers — O. A. Parks

Teaching school seemed to come quite naturally for me. My father, paternal grandfathers, and an elder brother had been teachers for more than a century. My farm home was the lodging place for the teacher of our home school during most of the years I attended elementary school.

Parental influence and home environment developed a desire to be a contributor to society in a wholesome manner. As a result I had the desire to devote myself to a life of service at an early age. Teaching was one of the available avenues. I have never regretted my choice.

My first days as a substitute teacher occurred before I attended college. During my college years, I continued to be called on to substitute for rural teachers. My college years were interrupted by years of teaching, getting married, and starting a family. I completed a two-year Standard III Curriculum in 1937. I taught rural school for two years in McLean County. One year back in college gave me a Commercial Special Certificate that qualified me, according to the State Department of Public Instruction, to teach in North Dakota high schools in commercial courses. In the years that followed, I taught each year, took correspondence courses, and attended summer sessions until I had completed a B.S. degree and an M.S. degree in Business Administration. During my teaching career I moved "up the ladder" from classroom teacher, to part-time coaching, to high school principal, to junior college in a business department, and to administrative assistant to a college president for ten years.

✐✐

this difference between the work of the teacher and the artisan is there not contained the whole problem in a nut shell?

Socrates, meeting Callias, the son of Hipponicus, one day in ancient Athens, said to his enlightened townsman: "Callias, if your two sons were foals or calves, there would be no difficulty in finding someone to put over them. We should hire a trainer of horses, or a farmer, probably, who would improve and perfect them in their own proper virtue and excellence; but as they are human beings, whom are you thinking of putting over them?" In ancient Athens as in North Dakota today, everyone conceded that an expert was needed to train a foal, but when it comes to training the human mind, does not the North Dakota taxpayer fall into the error which Socrates ironically attributes to the democrat of ancient Athens of supposing that an expert is not needed?

Your committee might take up seriatim each of the other causes assigned for the prevailing low standard of wages paid in North Dakota and in the country as a whole, but upon analysis it would be found that, altho variously phrased, each of the other reasons assigned practically resolves itself into the one already hinted at above, viz., lack of appreciation of the importance of good teaching on the part of school boards and taxpayers and lack of ability on the part of these same to distinguish between good teaching and bad. If the wastefulness of poor teaching could be shown in as tangible and convincing a form as can the wastefulness of poor carpentry, poor masonry and poor blacksmithing, the teachers' wages should go up a hundred percent in North Dakota in the next twelve months.

We have in North Dakota a state board to pass upon the qualifications of barbers. If the candidate for the practice of the "tonsorial art" cannot pass the examination, he is summarily rejected; but in many cases candidates for the practice of the divine art of training the human mind are allowed to teach on permits even tho they cannot pass the merely nominal test imposed as a safeguard to the calling of the teacher in North Dakota. "Thus (and we are quoting one of the great names in American scholarship and one of the brightest ornaments to the teaching profession in this country—David Starr Jordan) the ranks of our teachers become filled with those who know nothing and have no care to know, with those who use the office of teacher while seeking marriage or an opening in a law office; with those who pay more for dead birds on their hats than for all the books they read, reckless of the fact that every bird killed wantonly leaves this world a little less worth living in; with those who know more of palmistry than of psychology, of euchre or the two-step than of the art of training children."

Your committee is well aware of the plea put forth by county superintendents that if the standard of qualifications for teachers is raised, many schools will go untaught, and of the further plea that if the state superintendent rejects too many candidates he will offend influential voters and thereby endanger his re-election to office. Your committee would

Your committee would not be too hard upon the superintendent; it recognizes to the full the fact that the would-be reformer in politics must, first of all, look out for his official head else he will in all probability lose the opportunity to effect any reform at all. He, too, is human and ought not to be blamed too severely if he thinks sometimes of his salary and of those who are dependent upon it for a living. After all, the superintendent, tho he do his best, is but a feeble stop-gap to the flood of ignorance and cupidity which must be dried up at its source if we would save from its devastating effects the fair field which it is the province of the worthy teacher to cultivate.

not be too hard upon the superintendent; it recognizes to the full the fact that the would-be reformer in politics must, first of all, look out for his official head else he will in all probability lose the opportunity to effect any reform at all. He, too, is human and ought not to be blamed too severely if he thinks sometimes of his salary and of those who are dependent upon it for a living. After all, the superintendent, tho he do his best, is but a feeble stop-gap to the flood of ignorance and cupidity which must be dried up at its source if we would save from its devastating effects the fair field which it is the province of the worthy teacher to cultivate.

As to the other plea that unless the standard of qualifications for teachers be kept low many schools will remain untaught, it were a thousand times better, in the judgment of your committee, that a part of the youth of our state should go wholly untaught for a time, so far as schools are concerned, than that all should remain poorly taught. It is not, in the judgment of your committee, evident that North Dakota would be worse governed or our jails or penitentiary more crowded if 10 percent of the youth of North Dakota who now learn merely to read and write, should remain entirely illiterate until the supply of teachers shall meet the demand with such a higher standard of qualifications for teaching as would command an average teachers' wage of $60 per month in this state as against the present average wage of $39.92.

Official "Permit to Teach" issued to Wm. H. Gierke in Dickey County in 1911 *(from collection of Warren A. Henke)*

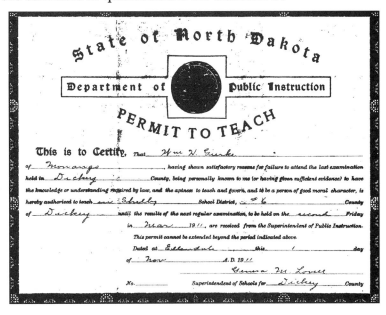

Tis brings us to — it anticipates, indeed — our next topic, viz., the remedy for the prevailing low average of teacher's salaries in this country and particularly in North Dakota. Your committee, in the circular which it sent out to superintendents, principals and others invited suggestions as to the appropriate remedy for the low average salary of teachers' salaries so far as it exists. Following is a classification of the replies received, the numeral opposite in each case indicating the number so replying:

Higher standard of qualification	58
More enthusiasm for education and good teachers	18
A teachers' union	14
Appreciation on part of boards of importance of higher wages	12
Concerted action but not unionism	9
Consolidation of rural schools	7
Concerted demand for higher wages	7
Agitation	6
Arouse public sentiment by brochures and newspaper reports	5
Greater permanency of positions	5
Realization of the expense to which a teacher is put	5
Teachers should give better service	5
Time and expansion	5
More state aid	4
Compulsory attendance at teachers' training school, after certification has been granted	3
Professional or expert supervision of teachers	3
Special taxes	2
An indirect tax	2
Not enough good teachers to go around	2
More conservative use of permit	2
Legislation	2
More normal schools	1
Better facilities for training teachers and harder exams	1
Better training schools	1
Kick	1
Efforts of high school board on behalf of teachers	1

Of the 182 replies received, 104 suggest a more enlightened public sentiment in regard to the importance of education and of good schools, or a higher standard of qualifications on the part of the teacher, one or both.

Of the 182 replies received, 104 suggest a more enlightened public sentiment in regard to the importance of education and of good schools, or a higher standard of qualifications on the part of the teacher, one or both. Of the other remedies suggested, the one by far the most frequently given is a teachers' union or at least concerted action with or without a union. Nearly 80 per cent of the replies suggest, directly or indirectly, consciously or unconsciously, a limitation of the supply of teachers as the proper remedy for the prevailing low average of teachers' wages.

A higher standard of qualifications for teachers would limit the supply of teachers and so raise wages. An increased demand for good schools and a more general appreciation of what a good school is would do the same thing by eliminating the supply of inefficient teachers. A concerted demand for better wages on the part of teachers thru some form of unionism would perhaps work to the same end, tho just how, it is difficult to see, unless teachers are prepared to enforce their demands by a strike if need be, backed up by the picketing of "scab" teachers and perhaps by mob violence. It is assumed that teachers desire better wages only as the result of a higher professional standard and a quickened appreciation of their services on the part of the tax paying public, while it is universally understood outside of labor unions themselves that labor unionism acts not as an incentive to the most efficient labor but as a protection to the most inefficient; that it does not tolerate a graduated scale of wages according to efficiency but demands a horizontal scale sufficient to afford a "living wage" to the most inefficient labor in the union. It is to be feared that union of teachers in North Dakota, while it might serve in some slight measure to advance wages, would be chiefly instrumental in perpetuating the present low standard of qualification on the part of teachers.

Something can be done by associations of citizens interested in better schools. For example, a woman living in a suburban town along the lakeside north of Chicago recently told the writer that the members of the federation of women's clubs in her town had, in the last year, by pressure brought to bear upon the local school board, succeeded in having the salary of the principal of their recently established high school raised from $2,000 to $2,500 a year. Such efforts, however, will always be more or less sporadic and spasmodic.

To secure results that shall be general and permanent there must be a systematic and persistently maintained campaign of education of the tax paying public by our state and county educational associations, our federations of women's clubs, the newspaper press and all other available agencies. Perhaps the most immediately tangible results can be secured if this and similar associations shall give to our state superintendent and our county superintendents assurances of their

A Country School Teacher Remembers — Francis Bloom

My father suggested that I might want to become a teacher. The Boyingtons are a family of teachers and I think his dream was to have me become one. I once considered becoming a beauty shop operator, but was discouraged in this by my father. I loved teaching. It was always a challenge to me and something I never regretted doing. It was so rewarding. I feel so great when former students stop to see me. Some of them now have grandchildren.

I had two years of college education before I started teaching and I attended summer school and participated in workshops periodically thereafter.

My favorite school was probably in Cleary Township, Burke County, near Battle View in North Dakota. I also taught for four years in Pleasant View School in Thoreson Township, also in Burke County. I got married then, but I also agreed to teach in Ivanhoe Township in Renville County in 1955, when that district was unable to get a teacher.

I had a very good school board that first year. One time I told them, "I have to have newer books." Somehow they got them for me. When I started teaching in the Grubb School in Cleary my salary was $55 a month. When I asked for a raise to $100.00 a month my last year there, the president of the board, John Grubb, said, "You're crazy," and he walked away; however, I did get the raise.

My first day of school was an education in itself. School started March 23, 1941 and the area had received a heavy snowfall. I had walked about a mile and a half to the school that was located in the hills along Highway 50. When I arrived I was very wet and tired, but I did start a fire in a temperamental stove that I knew nothing about. I was reasonably ready for my students when a family of five students walked in. Among them was a girl whom no one had told me about. She was about nineteen years old and in the eighth grade. She wasn't much younger than I was and she immediately let me know it. She also felt she knew as much as I did. Maybe she did.

All subjects the state course of study required were taught during a typical school day. School began at 9:00 a.m., followed by the morning recess at 10:15 a.m. Students enjoyed an hour lunch break at noon and another recess at 2:15 p.m., and were dismissed at 4:00 p.m. All the students brought their own lunches and drink-

continued on next page

ing water and I carried water for washing hands and other needs. During the lunch break I always supervised the playground and the students and I usually played baseball.

I had ten students in this school and loved them all; they were such a good bunch of "kids" and I can't recall ever having a discipline problem. I taught every grade except the seventh. Everyone helped one another; we seemed to have time in school to study our lessons so I was never too enthusiastic about homework, except for studying the multiplication tables and spelling words. My first grader could do most things my third grade girl could do. I think my sixth grade girls could probably have passed the eighth grade state exams. And an eighth grade boy, the brother of the 19 year-old student, was the first boy to ever pass the state exams and to pass the eighth grade in that school. He was proud, his parents were proud, but probably not as proud as I was. I think my relationship with the children and the parents was very good. My first term was indeed a learning and rewarding experience for me.

In my second school I had a first grader who spoke only Norwegian and I spoke only English. He learned English quickly.

We had two outdoor toilets. These were quite good ones and I scrubbed them thoroughly once a week. Of course my first chore after school was sweeping and dusting my classroom and every Friday I dismissed school at 3:30 p.m. and scrubbed the floor.

My school was used for church meetings and other activities and as long as various groups left it clean they could use it.

I boarded at the Willard Grubb farm. My room and board cost me $15 a month when I was getting $55 a month. I was accepted as one of the family. I often baby-sat for them and sometimes helped with ironing and other household chores. In turn, they took me with them everywhere and were generally very good to me. I was paid by warrant and had to find someone to drive me to get the warrant and then to drive me to a bank that would purchase it from me.

I was never lonely. The Grubb's "hired man" escorted me to dances and shows in Columbus and Powers Lake. It was a good community and everyone made me a part of it. I later married the "hired man"!

I think the one thing that the community might have objected to would have been if I had been either a smoker or a drinker. Nothing was ever said, but I'm sure I would have been chastised if I had done a lot or even a little of either.

continued on next page

united support in all efforts made by them to eliminate the incompetent teacher thru the medium of teachers' examinations and thru the denying, except in the rarest instances, all permits to teachers who have failed to pass a satisfactory examination. If this be done, some schools will be closed, it is true, but, as was said in olden times, it will be far better for North Dakota educationally, now and hereafter, that she enter into life halt or maimed as regards the number of her open school houses rather than, having some teacher, however incompetent, weak or frivolous, in every school house in the state, to be cast indefinitely into the hell fire of a half paid teaching class in all her schools, with the consequent permanent intellectual and spiritual impoverishment of teacher, pupil and community alike. If this be done, some communities will become antagonistic and some voters will threaten retaliation at the next election or at the next state or county convention. But if our state and county associations, with all whom they can influence, will stand squarely and aggressively behind our state superintendent and county superintendents in their efforts to elevate the schools of North Dakota, such antagonism and such threats may safely be disregarded.

The path of duty is, far oftener than is generally thought, the path of expediency as well as the path of honor. The teachers' labor, like all labor, is an economic commodity. Its price, in the long run, like the prices of all commodities, is determined by the inexorable law of supply and demand. The demand for teachers in North Dakota will continue to increase as the state develops, but for a given year it is practically a fixed quantity.

The only way, therefore, to raise teachers' wages at a given time is to diminish the supply of teachers, and the only way to do this is to lessen the number of available teachers by raising the standard of teachers' qualifications. The standard generally for certificated teachers in this country as compared with that of England, of France and of Germany is disgracefully low. The minimum requirement for elementary teachers in all these countries may be roughly given as the equivalent of graduation from one of our state normal schools. As a matter of fact, all these countries require a certain minimum of professional training in addition to a good academic education. A mere first-class teachers' certificate in North Dakota would not entitle a teacher to teach a single elementary school in England, France or Germany. Suppose, however, that even a first-class teachers' certificate, as defined in our statutes, were imposed as a minimum requirement for teaching in every district school in North Dakota, does any one here believe that teachers' wages in this state would not go up by leaps and bounds? Do not the above statements, which have been carefully verified, contain in a nutshell the whole problem of teachers' salaries and its solution?

Your committee does not forget that it was charged with the duty of inquiring into the social status of the teacher as well as into teachers' salaries. This is a matter upon which statistics throw little light. It is a matter rather of personal observation and opinion. The social standing of the American elementary school teacher is far better than that of the English teacher in elementary schools. Daughters of clergymen and other professional men in England are considered to have compromised their social position if they engage in teaching in the lower grades of schools. This is doubtless due to the fact that in England very few, although an increasing number, of well-to-do parents send their children to the board or voluntary schools, whereas in the United States it is the rule for well-to-do parents to send their children to the public schools. On the other hand, the social standing of the principal teachers in English secondary schools, particularly of the head masters in these schools, and, above all, of the head masters in the so-called great "public" schools of England like Eton, Harrow and Winchester, is far higher than in similar schools in this country. The head masters of Eton and Harrow are said to receive six thousand pounds, i.e., $30,000, each annually. They are clergymen in the Church of England and stand next in order of promotion to bishoprics, which not only pay salaries running from $50,000 to $75,000 a year, but carry with them the title of lords spiritual of the realm with membership in the British House of Lords. University Professors, too, enjoy a social prestige practically unknown to university professors in this country. Many of the chairs in English universities and, until their recent overhauling, in the Scotch universities also, are upon foundations which yield as high as $25,000 a year. So intrenched in the doctrine of vested interests in English law, that professorship or livings which, as the result of fortunate investments hundreds of

This particular school had a summer program and one memorable event occurred during the middle of the summer program. I asked the fathers for planks and nail kegs and the mothers for sheets so we could construct a stage. The fathers helped me build the stage, I hung the sheets for stage curtains, and we had a program. I wanted blue lights for one part of the program so we put blue cellophane around gas lanterns. When the lanterns were lit all the cellophane melted. While everyone around was real "shook-up" one little girl sat in a small rocker with her doll and never stopped rocking or singing *Skeeters Am a Humin.*

When County Superintendent Mabel Wahlun visited my school she stayed all day. She made suggestions as I taught my classes. She was very helpful and thorough. There were very few visits by the school board or the parents, however.

The president of the board visited me when it was time to renew our contracts. If we said yes, we got a contract. In Thoreson Township I got a letter asking if I were interested in a contract for the next year. I was never fired. When I wished to leave a school I just told the board orally that I was no longer going to teach.

During my career my teaching methods changed most noticeably in the teaching of reading. I started out teaching phonetically. Then, that seemed to be out so I tried teaching sight reading. I thought it was a total disaster and went back to teaching phonics. I also switched from traditional math to modern math, but later used a combination of the two that worked well for me.

My memories of teaching in rural schools are mostly positive.

One day while teaching a class I fainted, really fainted on the floor! When I came to I was lying on the floor. All the windows and doors were open and every child except one was sitting in his or her desk. One fifth grade boy had gone to a farm nearby for help. Interestingly, we had studied emergency procedures earlier in the year.

I can't say that I think too much was wrong with the country school. My former students have done reasonably well, maybe in spite of me not because of me. I'm quite proud of their records. I went to a rural school and I've never felt cheated. I think it provided a reasonably good education.

✍✍

217

Webster Merrifield

"No, the American is not anxious for the money itself; but money is to him the measure of success, and therefore the career needs the backing of money to raise it to social respect and attractiveness, and to win over the finest minds."

years ago, now yield a princely income, are allowed to remain the perquisite of individual professors or rectors although the college or church to which they are attached may be burdened with debt. All the great English and Scottish universities, as is well known, send representatives to parliament and the Lord-Rectorship of any of them, although a purely titular office, is an honor coveted even by prime ministers. In France and Germany teachers in elementary schools — particularly men teachers — are accorded the same social recognition as other members of the civil service. They are required to be men of high character and of high scholastic attainments. Their tenure is permanent, and, as a rule, they spend their lives in the community where they begin to teach. They enter, therefore, into the social life of the community in a way which is impossible to the American elementary or secondary teacher, who rarely spend three years in the same community and who is regarded by the neighborhood as more or less of an adventurer. As is well known, the German university professor and even the private docent occupies a rarely enviable position in the German social life. Both in France and Germany there are few avenues to social prestige comparable to high scholarship. Mere wealth carries with it no such prestige. The nearest analogy, doubtless, is noble birth. The small social prestige accorded to scholarship in this country is, it is believed, quite as much as the small salary it commands, responsible for the generally low average of scholarship prevailing here. Apropos of this Prof. Munsterberg of Harvard, in his "American Traits," speaks as follows:

> I well remember a long conversation I had with one of the best English scholars, who came over here to lecture when I had been only a short time in the country and was without experience in American academic affairs. We spoke about the disappointingly low level of American scholarship, and he said: "America will not have first-class scholarship, in the sense in which Germany or England has it, till every professor in the leading universities has at least ten thousand dollars salary and the best scholars receive twenty-five thousand dollars." I was distinctly shocked, and called it a pessimistic and materialistic view. But he insisted: "No, the American is not anxious for the money itself; but money is to him the measure of success, and therefore the career needs the backing of money to raise it to social respect and attractiveness, and to win over the finest minds." My English acquaintance did not convince me at that time, but the years have convinced me, the years which have brought me into contact with hundreds of students and instructors in the whole land; the years in which I have watched the development of some of the finest students, who hesitated long whether to follow their inclination toward scholarship, and who finally went into law or into business for the sake of the social premiums.

Is not the pith of the whole matter contained in the sentence which Prof. Munsterberg quotes — "No, the American is not anxious for the money itself; but money is to him the measure of success, and therefore the career needs the backing of money to raise it to social respect and attractiveness, and to win over the finest minds?" It is lamentable that it should be so, but, it being so, will the social status of the teacher in this country ever be equal to that of the successful banker, merchant, lawyer or doctor till his income is approximately as great as theirs? In European countries scholarship is respected and even reverenced by all classes in the community, but it is not so in America.

218

In conclusion, if it be the desire of the Association that this agitation end in something more substantial than talk, your committee would urgently recommend that this association lend its united effort to securing the passage this winter of a law repealing the present provision in regard to teachers' certificates and providing that after 1907 no third grade certificates be issued and no permits except to teachers holding a first grade certificate from another state; that after 1908 no second grade certificate be issued and that after 1910 the requirements for a first grade certificate be the equivalent of graduation from a normal school or from a high school with a certain modicum of professional training. This latter requirement is already in force in all our important town schools. In a purely agricultural state like ours there is no good reason why the children of the farmer should not be as well taught as those of the banker or merchant who live off the farmer. It is believed by your committee that the step proposed would be indefinitely more effective than any other yet proposed in bringing about that great desideratum in this state, the general consolidation of our rural schools. This proposal will doubtless be considered visionary by many. But, if it had not been for the world's visionaries we should to all intents and purposes be living today in the eleventh century instead of in the twentieth.

In the school-marm's car, ca. 1916 at Lakeview School No. 1, Lallie Township, Benson County *(Benson Co. Collection 32 BE/11-8, SHSND)*

Respectfully submitted,

PRESIDENT WEBSTER MERRIFIELD, Chairman
SENATOR JOHN L. CASHEL, Grafton
JUDGE C.F. TEMPLETON, Grand Forks
SUPT. ROBT. S. DEWAR, Devils Lake
SUPT. WILLIAM MOORE, Bismarck
SUPT. W.G. CROCKER, Lisbon
PROF. THOMAS GROSVENOR, Mayville

This proposal [the consolidation of our schools] will doubtless be considered visionary by many. But, if it had not been for the world's visionaries we should to all intents and purposes be living today in the eleventh century instead of in the twentieth.

Chapter 13

Paying the Teachers

FROM THE EARLIEST DAYS OF SETTLEMENT OF DAKOTA to the waning years of the twentieth century, adequate pay for teachers has been a topic of discussion among the citizens of the sparsely-populated, rural state. Among all those engaged in teaching the state's young people, country school teachers have always been paid the least. In a profession dominated by women, men were always paid considerably more.

The statistical information on the following pages compiled by Dan Rylance and the staff of the E.B. Robinson Department of Special Collections, Chester Fritz Library, University of North Dakota in 1981 is something of an economic history of the state in numbers and a social history in its evidence of the value placed on primary education by different geographical regions of the state.

There are hundreds of personal stories behind the numbers, stories yet to be published by some of those 6,556 women teachers who received nearly 50 percent less in 1936 than their sisters who taught in 1926. In 1936 women taught for an average salary of $64.87 while men received an average of $93.44; in 1926 women were paid an average of $109.45 and men $143.53. When World War II ended and men returned in 1946, the distance between the average salaries of men and women was an historic record — women received only 66 percent of what men were paid. By 1952, it had become a little better, for the state average salary for women at $229.20 a month was 74 percent of that paid men, $313.96. But it was still below the average percentage from 1894 to 1952, 78 percent.

There are stories in comparisons of the county averages and the relative numbers of men and women teaching in each of the 53 counties in selected years from 1894 to 1952. In 1894, for example, when women teachers outnumbered men in the state nearly two to one, there were 49 men and only 15 women teaching in McIntosh County, but they were paid an average of 95 percent of what men were paid. In Mercer County that year, women actually averaged a greater salary than that paid men (see bottom of table on page 227). Historically, the most equitable of counties in terms of paying teachers in the period of the study were Billings, Oliver, Sheridan, Sioux and McIntosh (see chart on page 228), but they were also the counties who paid the lowest average salaries in the state (see chart on page 229). Those counties with the greatest disparity between men and womens' salaries paid the highest average salaries in the state.

Among those with greatest historic inequity was Grand Forks County, home of the University of North Dakota, where women teachers averaged but 68 percent of the salaries paid men.

Among those with greatest historic inequity was Grand Forks County, home of the University of North Dakota, where women teachers averaged but 68 percent of the salaries paid men. Most curious are differences between neighboring counties in the western part of the state: Golden Valley had the worst record in equal pay, Billings the best.

The numbers on the tables on pages 222-227 and the charts and maps on pages 228 and 229 represent the livelihood of more than 7,000 teachers in most of the years of the study, a number which rose dramatically from about 2,700 in 1894 to nearly 7,000 in 1915 and changed little in the fifty years thereafter. One teacher's thirty-six-year career is offered in detail on pages 230-231, Anna Bakken Carlson who taught from 1928 to 1970. Details of her contracts tell the story of one of the 7,000 who taught: waiting for her pay in the 1930s, paying for electricity if she used more than $1.50 worth in 1952, teaching all eight grades, agreeing to do janitorial work.

Teachers' pay in North Dakota, when compared to national averages paid to teachers elsewhere in the nation and the world and to average salaries of professionals with similar education and training has continued to decline in purchasing power in the years since 1952.

What Dr. Webster Merrifield bemoaned over ninety years ago remains a major problem in North Dakota, where citizens expect the best for much less than what teachers deserve.

❧❧

Average Monthly Salaries of Public School Teachers in North Dakota by Selected Years

COUNTY	1894				1906				
	Average Salary Men	Average Salary Women	Percent of workforce women	Percent of mens' salary paid women	Average Salary Men	Average Salary Women	Percent of mens' salary paid women	Percent increase from 1894 for men	Percent increase from 1894 for women
Adams									
Barnes	$38.55	$35.23	68%	91%	$60.00	$48.90	82%	56%	39%
Benson	$35.98	$33.05	62%	92%	$49.12	$45.65	93%	37%	38%
Billings	$40.00	$37.50	50%	94%	$58.33	$47.92	82%	46%	28%
Bottineau	$42.55	$36.55	74%	86%	$54.33	$45.55	84%	28%	25%
Bowman									
Burke									
Burleigh	$77.50	$34.33	95%	44%	$53.18	$44.27	83%	-31%	29%
Cass	$47.98	$45.41	72%	95%	$68.53	$49.47	72%	43%	9%
Cavalier	$40.14	$33.87	57%	84%	$53.75	$43.82	82%	34%	29%
Dickey	$40.65	$32.02	73%	79%	$50.77	$43.47	86%	25%	36%
Divide									
Dunn									
Eddy	$46.25	$31.72	91%	69%	$45.00	$43.00	96%	-3%	36%
Emmons	$31.61	$32.33	65%	102%	$40.00	$40.00	100%	27%	24%
Foster	$43.40	$35.00	71%	81%	$54.95	$46.93	85%	27%	34%
Golden Valley									
Grand Forks	$45.00	$39.50	64%	88%	$69.83	$44.63	64%	55%	13%
Grant									
Griggs	$39.31	$35.25	69%	90%	$51.28	$46.78	91%	30%	33%
Hettinger									
Kidder	$51.11	$31.76	76%	62%	$46.00	$46.00	100%	-10%	45%
LaMoure	$41.50	$37.22	63%	90%	$53.32	$43.30	81%	28%	16%
Logan	$36.58	$32.98	50%	90%	$36.76	$36.64	100%	0%	11%
McHenry					$46.41	$44.75	96%		
McIntosh	$31.53	$29.87	23%	95%	$34.33	$33.35	97%	9%	12%
McKenzie					$50.00	$43.66	87%		
McLean	$38.16	$35.36	83%	93%					
Mercer	$30.00	$33.12	56%	110%	$43.50	$42.26	97%	45%	28%
Morton	$51.90	$38.08	88%	73%	$49.50	$47.86	97%	-5%	26%
Mountrail									
Nelson	$38.77	$34.76	64%	90%	$52.80	$44.46	84%	36%	28%
Oliver	$35.00	$34.74	80%	99%	$41.90	$41.90	100%	20%	21%
Pembina	$47.50	$36.00	54%	76%	$67.19	$46.23	69%	41%	28%
Pierce	$35.00	$34.74	80%	99%	$46.95	$44.54	95%	34%	28%
Ramsey	$41.51	$35.73	62%	86%	$51.78	$42.18	81%	25%	18%
Ransom	$46.19	$35.43	68%	77%	$56.81	$45.00	79%	23%	27%
Renville									
Richland	$36.98	$35.10	57%	95%	$55.13	$43.55	79%	49%	24%
Rollette	$39.70	$33.75	86%	85%	$52.00	$46.70	90%	31%	38%
Sargeant	$36.89	$34.63	57%	94%	$50.34	$45.15	90%	36%	30%
Sheridan									
Sioux									
Slope									
Stark	$49.59	$38.33	77%	77%	$50.40	$44.90	89%	2%	17%
Steele	$38.76	$36.99	64%	95%	$51.96	$47.54	91%	34%	29%
Stutsman	$45.24	$35.83	90%	79%	$54.74	$45.17	83%	21%	26%
Towner	$42.95	$36.01	76%	84%	$51.18	$47.72	93%	19%	33%
Traill	$44.72	$42.32	67%	95%	$66.48	$47.60	72%	49%	12%
Walsh	$44.06	$37.52	63%	85%	$53.70	$44.39	83%	22%	18%
Ward	$50.82	$34.00	79%	67%	$48.50	$42.40	87%	-5%	25%
Wells	$41.12	$34.00	64%	83%	$52.75	$46.48	88%	28%	37%
Williams	$50.00	$39.16	80%	78%	$45.85	$49.30	108%	-8%	26%
Average	**$42.49**	**$35.51**	**69%**	**86%**	**$51.78**	**$44.70**	**88%**	**24%**	**26%**

Compiled by Dan Rylance and the staff of the E.B. Robinson Department of Special Collections, Chester Fritz Library, University of North Dakota, March 1981

Average Monthly Salaries of Public School Teachers in North Dakota by Selected Years

COUNTY	1915 Average Salary Men	Average Salary Women	Percent of mens' salary paid women	Percent increase from 1906 for men	Percent increase from 1906 for women	1926 Average Salary Men	Average Salary Women	Percent of mens' salary paid women	Percent increase from 1915 for men	Percent increase from 1915 for women
Adams	$60.36	$54.32	90%			$138.26	$106.55	77%	129%	96%
Barnes	$102.39	$59.68	58%	71%	22%	$178.58	$120.92	68%	74%	103%
Benson	$82.75	$61.54	74%	68%	35%	$154.60	$102.50	66%	87%	67%
Billings	$56.67	$61.69	109%	-3%	29%	$103.25	$115.00	111%	82%	86%
Bottineau	$102.67	$66.61	65%	89%	46%	$163.69	$102.54	63%	59%	54%
Bowman	$73.63	$57.93	79%			$159.00	$114.00	72%	116%	97%
Burke	$78.65	$57.27	73%			$163.96	$108.35	66%	108%	89%
Burleigh	$64.85	$55.65	86%	22%	26%	$148.14	$121.82	82%	128%	119%
Cass	$93.83	$58.10	62%	37%	17%	$212.45	$143.73	68%	126%	147%
Cavalier	$80.05	$55.72	70%	49%	27%	$171.31	$118.30	69%	114%	112%
Dickey	$70.82	$56.95	80%	39%	31%	$152.26	$110.29	72%	115%	94%
Divide	$74.50	$60.08	81%			$131.87	$110.02	83%	77%	83%
Dunn	$56.87	$55.36	97%			$139.79	$104.09	74%	146%	88%
Eddy	$84.30	$56.93	68%	87%	32%	$153.24	$108.17	71%	82%	90%
Emmons	$58.41	$53.32	91%	46%	33%	$103.08	$96.29	93%	76%	81%
Foster	$78.75	$63.20	80%	43%	35%	$156.80	$113.64	72%	99%	80%
Golden Valley	$110.00	$58.88	54%			$145.77	$111.99	77%	33%	90%
Grand Forks	$114.25	$64.50	56%	64%	45%	$190.94	$132.97	70%	67%	106%
Grant						$120.62	$102.85	85%		
Griggs	$104.00	$55.00	53%	103%	18%	$151.69	$116.29	77%	46%	111%
Hettinger	$61.66	$58.00	94%			$127.53	$109.41	86%	107%	89%
Kidder	$59.92	$53.59	89%	30%	17%	$131.50	$103.33	79%	119%	93%
LaMoure	$78.54	$59.40	76%	47%	37%	$145.02	$105.04	72%	85%	77%
Logan	$49.39	$47.47	96%	34%	30%	$96.10	$90.49	94%	95%	91%
McHenry	$71.22	$64.07	90%	53%	43%	$144.99	$113.18	78%	104%	77%
McIntosh	$47.65	$46.82	98%	39%	40%	$89.21	$101.66	114%	87%	117%
McKenzie	$66.50	$59.14	89%	33%	35%	$109.17	$98.71	90%	64%	67%
McLean	$70.57	$55.03	78%			$117.30	$106.59	91%	66%	94%
Mercer	$56.30	$56.71	101%	29%	34%	$107.12	$106.52	99%	90%	88%
Morton	$53.38	$55.88	105%	8%	17%	$133.21	$104.64	79%	150%	87%
Mountrail	$59.01	$57.66	98%			$128.27	$105.20	82%	117%	82%
Nelson	$78.64	$61.69	78%	49%	39%	$156.07	$104.40	67%	98%	69%
Oliver	$56.65	$55.48	98%	35%	32%	$83.77	$100.48	120%	48%	81%
Pembina	$96.31	$52.82	55%	43%	14%	$159.82	$102.34	64%	66%	94%
Pierce	$64.83	$55.76	86%	38%	25%	$110.45	$102.69	93%	70%	84%
Ramsey	$91.22	$60.86	67%	76%	44%	$193.50	$122.68	63%	112%	102%
Ransom	$83.34	$59.23	71%	47%	32%	$166.62	$114.30	69%	100%	93%
Renville	$74.98	$58.69	78%			$158.81	$111.64	70%	112%	90%
Richland	$75.00	$52.77	70%	36%	21%	$162.54	$102.40	63%	117%	94%
Rollette	$64.57	$58.65	91%	24%	26%	$139.13	$113.02	81%	115%	93%
Sargeant	$93.88	$56.84	61%	86%	26%	$133.33	$98.01	74%	42%	72%
Sheridan	$53.94	$54.50	101%			$81.10	$105.98	131%	50%	94%
Sioux	$56.25	$50.50	90%			$100.33	$101.89	102%	78%	102%
Slope	$65.00	$55.21	85%			$137.61	$93.72	68%	112%	70%
Stark	$68.72	$55.91	81%	36%	25%	$132.51	$117.71	89%	93%	111%
Steele	$82.19	$59.17	72%	58%	24%	$157.01	$108.80	69%	91%	84%
Stutsman	$68.21	$55.89	82%	25%	24%	$158.18	$116.20	73%	132%	108%
Towner	$79.04	$63.17	80%	54%	32%	$188.73	$117.53	62%	139%	86%
Traill	$107.72	$59.65	55%	62%	25%	$163.56	$113.13	69%	52%	90%
Walsh	$82.27	$53.21	65%	53%	20%	$172.28	$109.15	63%	109%	105%
Ward	$81.34	$55.30	68%	68%	30%	$181.02	$122.58	68%	123%	122%
Wells	$71.99	$55.88	78%	36%	20%	$159.56	$104.63	66%	122%	87%
Williams	$75.66	$60.45	80%	65%	23%	$142.50	$112.50	79%	88%	86%
Average	**$74.88**	**$57.27**	**79%**	**48%**	**29%**	**$143.53**	**$109.45**	**79%**	**95%**	**92%**

		1936				1946				
Average Monthly Salaries of Public School Teachers in North Dakota by Selected Years										
COUNTY	Average Salary Men	Average Salary Women	Percent of mens' salary paid women	Percent increase from 1926 for men	Percent increase from 1926 for women	Average Salary Men	Average Salary Women	Percent of mens' salary paid women	Percent increase from 1936 for men	Percent increase from 1936 for women
Adams	$98.10	$67.63	69%	-29%	-37%	$245.48	$153.79	63%	150%	127%
Barnes	$114.19	$74.98	66%	-36%	-38%	$243.97	$148.90	61%	114%	99%
Benson	$98.01	$70.34	72%	-37%	-31%	$172.50	$143.16	83%	76%	104%
Billings	$52.03	$53.22	102%	-50%	-54%	$111.21	$152.25	137%	114%	186%
Bottineau	$97.72	$63.09	65%	-40%	-38%	$231.66	$152.93	66%	137%	142%
Bowman	$85.54	$64.55	75%	-46%	-43%	$303.70	$148.41	49%	255%	130%
Burke	$94.80	$62.59	66%	-42%	-42%	$267.36	$148.19	55%	182%	137%
Burleigh	$83.37	$59.42	71%	-44%	-51%	$234.93	$146.89	63%	182%	147%
Cass	$159.97	$107.34	67%	-25%	-25%	$270.08	$172.47	64%	69%	61%
Cavalier	$103.37	$59.73	58%	-40%	-50%	$244.53	$139.07	57%	137%	133%
Dickey	$87.70	$61.57	70%	-42%	-44%	$183.88	$133.08	72%	110%	116%
Divide	$88.29	$61.71	70%	-33%	-44%	$246.28	$130.80	53%	179%	112%
Dunn	$75.23	$55.64	74%	-46%	-47%	$192.84	$132.89	69%	156%	139%
Eddy	$93.04	$68.04	73%	-39%	-37%	$240.44	$140.01	58%	158%	106%
Emmons	$68.48	$58.49	85%	-34%	-39%	$176.65	$124.66	71%	158%	113%
Foster	$102.28	$76.07	74%	-35%	-33%	$249.20	$149.40	60%	144%	96%
Golden Valley	$112.17	$69.64	62%	-23%	-38%	$262.68	$131.73	50%	134%	89%
Grand Forks	$143.22	$91.92	64%	-25%	-31%	$266.02	$162.51	61%	86%	77%
Grant	$71.37	$56.88	80%	-41%	-45%	$188.00	$140.78	75%	163%	148%
Griggs	$96.92	$68.96	71%	-36%	-41%	$225.00	$140.63	63%	132%	104%
Hettinger	$91.54	$61.51	67%	-28%	-44%	$201.56	$139.86	69%	120%	127%
Kidder	$72.48	$55.42	76%	-45%	-46%	$198.85	$93.53	47%	174%	69%
LaMoure	$99.44	$67.76	68%	-31%	-35%	$205.71	$146.17	71%	107%	116%
Logan	$64.12	$49.09	77%	-33%	-46%	$147.63	$123.30	84%	130%	151%
McHenry	$82.48	$57.46	70%	-43%	-49%	$215.71	$151.96	70%	162%	164%
McIntosh	$61.53	$52.24	85%	-31%	-40%	$169.11	$107.01	75%	175%	144%
McKenzie	$91.15	$63.62	70%	-17%	-36%	$214.32	$130.85	61%	135%	106%
McLean	$91.62	$59.01	64%	-22%	-45%	$230.52	$143.38	62%	152%	143%
Mercer	$73.33	$58.52	80%	-32%	-45%	$215.91	$141.01	65%	194%	141%
Morton	$90.83	$67.85	75%	-32%	-35%	$214.86	$140.58	65%	137%	107%
Mountrail	$87.84	$56.95	65%	-32%	-46%	$238.03	$147.03	62%	171%	158%
Nelson	$100.28	$63.61	63%	-36%	-39%	$278.39	$144.29	52%	178%	127%
Oliver	$60.45	$52.26	86%	-28%	-48%	$151.32	$130.70	86%	150%	150%
Pembina	$71.92	$55.46	77%	-55%	-46%	$249.66	$156.39	63%	247%	182%
Pierce	$107.73	$66.92	62%	-2%	-35%	$234.80	$140.31	60%	118%	110%
Ramsey	$124.16	$78.53	63%	-36%	-36%	$236.00	$155.98	66%	90%	99%
Ransom	$101.68	$69.33	68%	-39%	-39%	$214.74	$134.06	62%	111%	93%
Renville	$111.45	$63.98	57%	-30%	-43%	$229.79	$153.55	67%	106%	140%
Richland	$116.64	$66.92	57%	-28%	-35%	$244.02	$136.18	56%	109%	103%
Rollette	$88.04	$61.96	70%	-37%	-45%	$236.69	$151.13	64%	169%	144%
Sargeant	$109.11	$64.13	59%	-18%	-35%	$256.11	$132.52	52%	135%	107%
Sheridan	$71.26	$56.32	79%	-12%	-47%	$206.60	$133.03	64%	190%	136%
Sioux	$67.42	$58.30	86%	-33%	-43%	$134.77	$122.94	91%	100%	111%
Slope	$86.33	$58.61	68%	-37%	-37%	$249.78	$140.62	56%	189%	140%
Stark	$75.39	$59.21	79%	-43%	-50%	$188.34	$130.07	69%	150%	120%
Steele	$120.38	$64.33	53%	-23%	-41%	$214.50	$145.74	68%	78%	127%
Stutsman	$80.50	$77.96	97%	-49%	-33%	$229.95	$147.05	64%	186%	89%
Towner	$108.20	$70.63	65%	-43%	-40%	$259.84	$156.95	60%	140%	122%
Traill	$108.35	$70.12	65%	-34%	-38%	$244.51	$140.17	57%	126%	100%
Walsh	$92.84	$61.48	66%	-46%	-44%	$227.87	$141.71	62%	145%	130%
Ward	$94.16	$77.98	83%	-48%	-36%	$237.08	$162.85	69%	152%	109%
Wells	$105.89	$63.55	60%	-34%	-39%	$236.78	$145.29	61%	124%	129%
Williams	$118.07	$75.15	64%	-17%	-33%	$228.31	$151.82	66%	93%	102%
Average	**$93.44**	**$64.87**	**71%**	**-34%**	**-41%**	**$222.62**	**$142.10**	**66%**	**143%**	**122%**

Average Monthly Salaries for Men and Women Teachers in North Dakota in 1952

Statistical Information for 1952 with percentages of increase from 1948 and 1936 and average percentage of mens' salaries paid women from 1894-1952

COUNTY	Number of Men	Average Salary Men	Number of Women	Average Salary Women	Percent of workforce women	Percent of mens' salary paid women	Percent increase from 1946 for men	Percent increase from 1946 for women	% increase from 1936 for combined	Historic average paid women
Adams	22	$321.99	50	$234.95	69%	73%	31%	53%	256%	74%
Barnes	52	$323.06	125	$236.61	71%	73%	32%	59%	210%	71%
Benson	29	$338.65	81	$223.73	74%	66%	96%	56%	230%	78%
Billings	9	$239.50	27	$213.29	75%	89%	115%	40%	315%	103%
Bottineau	47	$331.79	107	$242.34	69%	73%	43%	58%	284%	72%
Bowman	14	$232.84	40	$237.20	74%	102%	-23%	60%	239%	75%
Burke	27	$341.19	73	$231.66	73%	68%	28%	56%	275%	66%
Burleigh	51	$328.46	154	$264.93	75%	81%	40%	80%	345%	73%
Cass	125	$403.85	312	$307.55	71%	76%	50%	78%	184%	72%
Cavalier	47	$296.15	129	$214.87	73%	73%	21%	55%	245%	70%
Dickey	28	$304.07	94	$209.00	77%	69%	65%	57%	243%	76%
Divide	28	$311.79	50	$233.49	64%	75%	27%	79%	284%	72%
Dunn	34	$257.77	82	$207.40	71%	80%	34%	56%	267%	79%
Eddy	18	$346.06	53	$225.56	75%	65%	44%	61%	240%	71%
Emmons	42	$249.74	99	$194.52	70%	78%	41%	56%	247%	89%
Foster	21	$326.76	57	$223.74	73%	68%	31%	50%	202%	75%
Golden Valley	11	$359.74	37	$223.74	77%	62%	37%	70%	230%	61%
Grand Forks	82	$383.81	212	$276.69	72%	72%	44%	70%	193%	68%
Grant	34	$271.76	91	$211.22	73%	78%	45%	50%	272%	79%
Griggs	23	$297.04	55	$222.23	71%	75%	32%	58%	223%	74%
Hettinger	25	$287.71	81	$234.08	76%	81%	43%	67%	266%	80%
Kidder	35	$264.83	72	$209.95	67%	79%	33%	124%	282%	76%
LaMoure	41	$313.98	106	$212.89	72%	68%	53%	46%	225%	75%
Logan	30	$238.17	84	$183.86	74%	77%	61%	49%	271%	88%
McHenry	53	$328.87	132	$230.68	71%	70%	52%	52%	312%	79%
McIntosh	53	$272.82	88	$202.74	62%	74%	61%	59%	320%	91%
McKenzie	24	$304.78	91	$233.05	79%	76%	42%	78%	269%	79%
McLean	53	$342.81	149	$245.82	74%	72%	49%	71%	317%	77%
Mercer	38	$292.24	97	$214.58	72%	73%	35%	52%	280%	89%
Morton	46	$312.30	152	$229.63	77%	74%	45%	63%	242%	81%
Mountrail	35	$328.93	110	$238.36	76%	72%	38%	62%	321%	76%
Nelson	37	$330.50	80	$228.11	68%	69%	19%	58%	259%	72%
Oliver	17	$227.37	40	$194.72	70%	86%	50%	49%	278%	97%
Pembina	50	$339.16	113	$234.09	69%	69%	36%	50%	353%	67%
Pierce	21	$338.24	95	$218.70	82%	65%	44%	56%	234%	80%
Ramsey	50	$343.01	130	$255.54	72%	74%	45%	64%	220%	72%
Ransom	36	$337.31	82	$234.44	69%	70%	57%	75%	237%	71%
Renville	26	$331.78	47	$241.67	64%	73%	44%	57%	259%	69%
Richland	35	$351.35	159	$220.89	82%	63%	44%	62%	224%	69%
Rollette	21	$342.02	64	$252.22	75%	74%	45%	67%	299%	79%
Sargeant	26	$320.46	76	$210.13	75%	66%	25%	59%	221%	71%
Sheridan	26	$258.49	62	$209.47	70%	81%	25%	57%	276%	91%
Sioux	5	$251.93	31	$222.84	86%	88%	87%	81%	276%	91%
Slope	5	$294.69	35	$201.00	88%	68%	18%	43%	231%	69%
Stark	43	$366.70	133	$246.16	76%	67%	95%	89%	339%	79%
Steele	20	$318.39	56	$225.51	74%	71%	48%	55%	244%	74%
Stutsman	63	$302.59	180	$223.79	74%	74%	32%	52%	211%	79%
Towner	28	$329.09	51	$229.07	65%	70%	27%	46%	235%	74%
Traill	28	$341.14	106	$226.23	79%	66%	40%	61%	224%	68%
Walsh	38	$341.45	144	$236.21	79%	69%	50%	67%	289%	70%
Ward	100	$346.35	209	$277.75	68%	80%	46%	71%	269%	75%
Wells	37	$320.92	97	$226.85	72%	71%	36%	56%	255%	72%
Williams	45	$353.32	137	$262.08	75%	74%	55%	73%	240%	78%
Average		**$313.96**		**$229.20**	**73%**	**74%**	**44%**	**62%**	**260%**	

225

Summary of Percentages of Men Teachers' Salaries Paid Women Teachers with Numbers of Men and Women Teachers for Selected Years

COUNTY	1894 Number of Men	1894 Number of Women	1894 Percent of workforce women	1894 Percent of mens' salary paid women	1906 Percent of mens' salary paid women	1915 Number of Men	1915 Number of Women	1915 Percent of workforce women	1915 Percent of mens' salary paid women	1936 Number of Men	1936 Number of Women	1936 Percent of workforce women	1936 Percent of mens' salary paid women	1946 Percent of mens' salary paid women	1952 Number of Men	1952 Number of Women	1952 Percent of workforce women	1952 Percent of mens' salary paid women	Historic average paid women
Adams						16	56	78%	90%	17	71	81%	69%	63%	22	50	69%	73%	74%
Barnes	51	106	68%	91%	82%	27	198	88%	58%	53	164	76%	66%	61%	52	125	71%	73%	71%
Benson	18	29	62%	92%	93%	33	129	80%	74%	37	119	76%	72%	83%	29	81	74%	66%	78%
Billings	1	1	50%	94%	82%	17	29	63%	109%	11	44	80%	102%	137%	9	27	75%	89%	103%
Bottineau	8	23	74%	86%	84%	48	209	81%	65%	41	160	80%	65%	66%	47	107	69%	73%	72%
Bowman						11	71	87%	79%	18	56	76%	75%	49%	14	40	74%	102%	75%
Burke						17	140	89%	73%	29	102	78%	66%	55%	27	73	73%	68%	66%
Burleigh	3	57	95%	44%	83%	13	137	91%	86%	29	160	85%	71%	63%	51	154	75%	81%	73%
Cass	81	205	72%	95%	72%	38	288	88%	62%	93	373	80%	67%	64%	125	312	71%	76%	72%
Cavalier	34	45	57%	84%	82%	32	220	87%	70%	42	164	80%	58%	57%	47	129	73%	73%	70%
Dickey	32	87	73%	79%	86%	19	120	86%	80%	32	115	78%	70%	72%	28	94	77%	69%	76%
Divide						12	113	90%	81%	31	98	76%	70%	53%	28	50	64%	75%	72%
Dunn						24	72	75%	97%	39	119	75%	74%	69%	34	82	71%	80%	79%
Eddy	2	21	91%	69%	96%	6	71	92%	68%	21	50	70%	73%	58%	18	53	75%	65%	71%
Emmons	22	41	65%	102%	100%	54	111	67%	91%	42	137	77%	85%	71%	42	99	70%	78%	89%
Foster	7	17	71%	81%	85%	16	60	79%	80%	24	64	73%	74%	60%	21	57	73%	68%	75%
Golden Valley						8	79	91%	54%	13	59	82%	62%	50%	11	37	77%	62%	61%
Grand Forks	83	146	64%	88%	64%	34	254	88%	56%	71	216	75%	64%	61%	82	212	72%	72%	68%
Grant										45	106	70%	80%	75%	34	91	73%	78%	79%
Griggs	19	42	69%	90%	91%	7	86	92%	53%	22	69	76%	71%	63%	23	55	71%	75%	74%
Hettinger						25	79	76%	94%	24	98	80%	67%	69%	25	81	76%	81%	80%
Kidder	4	13	76%	62%	100%	18	99	85%	89%	29	89	75%	76%	47%	35	72	67%	79%	76%
LaMoure	28	47	63%	90%	81%	34	125	79%	76%	33	132	80%	68%	71%	41	106	72%	68%	75%
Logan	8	8	50%	90%	100%	34	80	70%	96%	39	97	71%	77%	84%	30	84	74%	77%	88%
McHenry	49	15	23%	95%	96%	46	197	81%	90%	44	160	78%	70%	70%	53	132	71%	70%	79%
McIntosh	3	15	83%	93%	97%	49	77	61%	98%	37	116	76%	85%	75%	53	88	62%	74%	91%
McKenzie						23	114	83%	89%	20	135	87%	70%	61%	24	91	79%	76%	79%
McLean	4	5	56%	110%	87%	29	188	87%	78%	44	196	82%	64%	62%	53	149	74%	72%	77%
Mercer	6	43	88%	73%	97%	36	55	60%	101%	30	92	75%	80%	65%	38	97	72%	73%	89%
Morton	15	49	77%		97%	91	275	75%	105%	48	180	79%	75%	65%	46	152	77%	74%	81%
Mountrail						26	154	86%	98%	28	149	84%	65%	62%	35	110	76%	72%	76%
Nelson	28	49	64%	90%	84%	32	112	78%	78%	34	106	76%	63%	52%	37	80	68%	69%	72%
Oliver	1	4	80%	99%	100%	8	55	87%	98%	14	49	78%	86%	86%	17	40	70%	86%	97%
Pembina	74	88	54%	76%	69%	15	165	92%	55%	37	149	80%	77%	63%	50	113	69%	69%	67%
Pierce	1	4	80%	99%	95%	22	126	85%	86%	14	98	88%	62%	60%	21	95	82%	65%	80%
Ramsey	30	49	62%	86%	81%	22	161	88%	67%	35	144	80%	63%	66%	50	130	72%	74%	72%
Ransom	35	74	68%	77%	79%	18	103	85%	71%	40	94	70%	68%	62%	36	82	69%	70%	71%

Summary of Percentages of Men Teachers' Salaries Paid Women Teachers with Numbers of Men and Women Teachers for Selected Years

COUNTY	1894 Number of Men	1894 Number of Women	1894 Percent of workforce women	1894 Percent of mens' salary paid women	1906 Percent of mens' salary paid women	1915 Number of Men	1915 Number of Women	1915 Percent of workforce women	1915 Percent of mens' salary paid women	1936 Number of Men	1936 Number of Women	1936 Percent of workforce women	1936 Percent of mens' salary paid women	1946 Percent of mens' salary paid women	1952 Number of Men	1952 Number of Women	1952 Percent of workforce women	1952 Percent of mens' salary paid women	Historic average paid women
Renville						18	109	86%	78%	25	72	74%	57%	67%	26	47	64%	73%	69%
Richland	84	110	57%	95%	79%	26	220	89%	70%	41	196	83%	57%	56%	35	159	82%	63%	69%
Rollette	4	24	86%	85%	90%	20	96	83%	91%	23	64	74%	70%	64%	21	64	75%	74%	79%
Sargeant	48	64	57%	94%	90%	8	110	93%	61%	26	90	78%	59%	52%	26	76	75%	66%	71%
Sheridan						26	77	75%	101%	24	84	78%	79%	64%	26	62	70%	81%	91%
Sioux						2	5	71%	90%	13	47	78%	86%	91%	5	31	86%	88%	91%
Slope						9	61	87%	85%	14	54	79%	68%	56%	5	35	88%	68%	69%
Stark	10	33	77%	77%	89%	46	115	71%	81%	40	139	78%	79%	69%	43	133	76%	67%	79%
Steele	28	50	64%	95%	91%	13	89	87%	72%	15	85	85%	53%	68%	20	56	74%	71%	74%
Stutsman	9	79	90%	79%	83%	42	213	84%	82%	72	226	76%	97%	64%	63	180	74%	74%	79%
Towner	6	19	76%	84%	93%	18	94	84%	80%	21	74	78%	65%	60%	28	51	65%	70%	74%
Traill	50	100	67%	95%	72%	12	133	92%	55%	27	120	82%	65%	57%	28	106	79%	66%	68%
Walsh	67	115	63%	85%	83%	36	226	86%	65%	35	188	84%	66%	62%	38	144	79%	69%	70%
Ward	4	15	79%	67%	87%	35	318	90%	68%	66	263	80%	83%	69%	100	209	68%	80%	75%
Wells	10	18	64%	83%	88%	33	122	79%	78%	29	133	82%	60%	61%	37	97	72%	71%	72%
Williams	1	4	80%	78%	108%	25	168	87%	80%	47	191	80%	64%	66%	45	137	75%	74%	78%
Total	953	1865	66%	86%	88%	1329	6764	84%	79%	1778	6556	79%	71%	66%	1934	5217	73%	74%	78%
Maximum County Average			95%	110%	108%			93%	109%			88%	102%	137%			88%	102%	
(county)			Burleigh	Mercer	Williams			Sargeant	Billings			Pierce	Billings	Sioux			Slope	Bowman	
Minimum County Average			23%	44%	64%			60%	53%			70%	53%	47%			62%	62%	

The Country School Teacher

Are We Using Her Fair?
by a Farmer's Wife

*I*t has always been a task to keep a school teacher in our neighborhood, and I have been wondering if the fault lies with the teacher or with us. Are we not too insistent that she concur with what we think is right, and leave her own opinions entirely out of the matter?

Do we expect her to manage our children or do we intend for our children to manage her. If she corrects them should we put in our oar in favor of the child.

We know that we must correct our children when they are home, then how can we expect a teacher to get along with ours and about a dozen other children without using the same methods? The school teacher is neither an angel nor the opposite; she is a very human being, and wants to do what is right, and she appreciates constructive criticism, as well as praise; but for us to find fault indiscriminately is neither fair nor just.

When your child comes home with a long tale of woe, do not "fly all to pieces" and condemn the teacher without a hearing.

Remember, children are prone to exaggerate, and what to them seems to be a mountain may prove to be a mole hill, and a small one at that.

I have always pitied the little country school teacher from the bottom of my heart.

In many cases she is among strangers, far from home and mother, and in a neighborhood which she fears may prove hostile to her. From the woman who writes her a letter of complaint everyday, to the mother who says: "It must be so, for Johnnie wouldn't lie," she has a hard life indeed, and when to this is added a salary

continued on next page

which a scrub-woman would refuse with scorn, surely there is but little inducement held out to the teachers of our country schools, and I wonder that so many are willing to undertake the task.

But in many cases it is a labor of love, with no thought of the hardships to be endured, nor the sacrifices to be made. I shall never forget the words of one of these dear girls when I asked her why she had not sought a better paid vocation than teaching is at present:

"I love my work, and I want to see each and every one of my boys and girls grow into a noble young man and womanhood."

"I feel that in this way I may partly repay the debt I owe to those noble women who once made the path of knowledge less thorny for my feet to tread."

Source: *Bismarck Tribune*, October 2, 1920, p. 4.

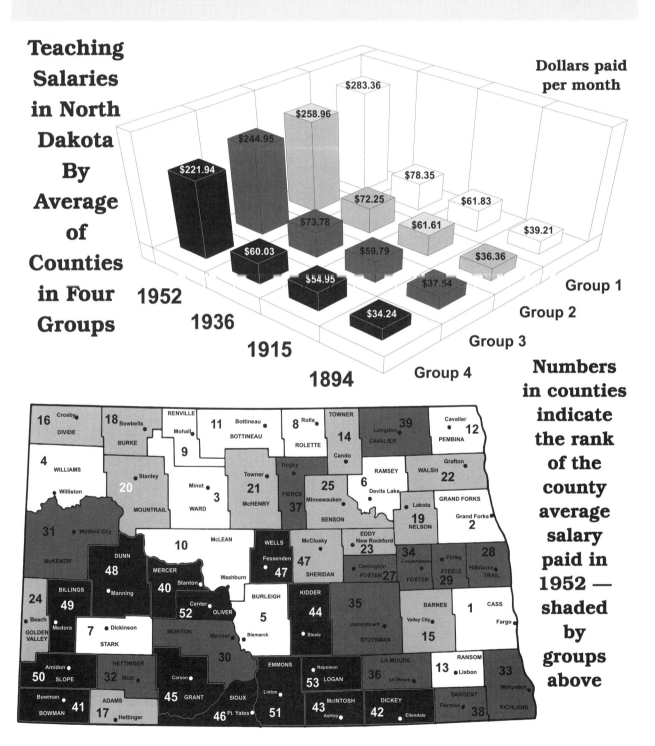

Teaching Salaries in North Dakota By Average of Counties in Four Groups

Dollars paid per month

Numbers in counties indicate the rank of the county average salary paid in 1952 — shaded by groups above

Average Teaching Salaries for Men and Women in North Dakota

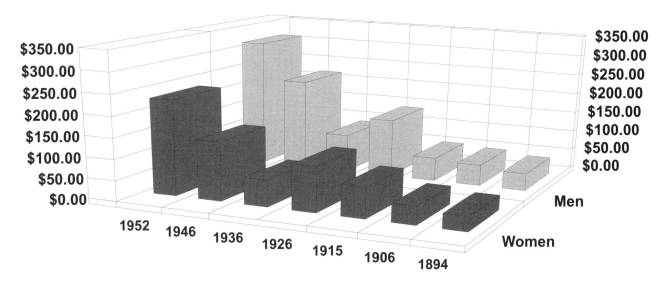

Historic Average of Percentage of Men Teachers' Salaries Paid Women Teachers in North Dakota, 1894-1952

91-103%   81-90%   71-80%   60-70%

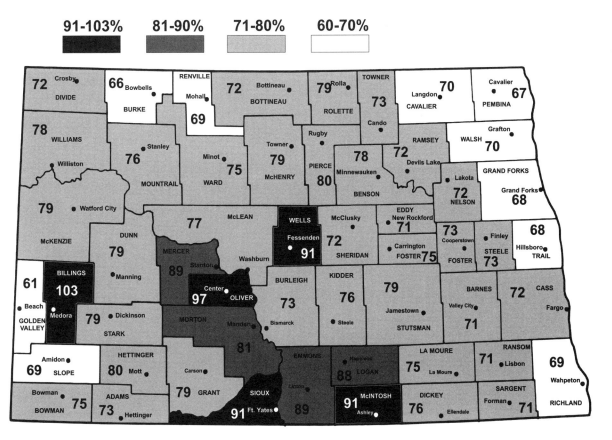

Anna Bakken Carlson's Contracts

ANNA BAKKEN CARLSON was born to Andrew Bakken and Beret Anna Tornes Bakken May 11, 1908. Her father was born in Rissa, Norway on June 16, 1878; her mother in Romsdal, Norway. She married Roimen Carlson; two children, Mildred and Loretta, were born of that union. Her special interests included art, sports, music, and gardening. Active in the Lutheran church she also served for a time as secretary of the local Republican Women's Club. During her 36-year teaching career she taught three generations of students, including one sister, five nephews, two daughters, and three grandchildren. Her education included three years of college at Valley City State University. She was issued a Second Grade Professional Life Certificate in January 1954.

Significant changes in the state's educational system are reflected in the standard provisions found in her contracts during her 36-year teaching career. It took the state almost 75 years to mandate a 180-day school term. Beginning in 1890 common schools were to be in session not less than four months; however, if the average attendance was fifteen or more, schools were in session not less than six months. In 1903 the school term was lengthened to six months; in 1911 to seven months, in 1947 to eight months, in 1959 to 175 days, and in 1963 to 180 days. Also, beginning in 1890 schools could be closed if average attendance for ten consecutive days was less than four students. In 1939 the number of students in the guidelines was increased to six. The state also protected itself through a provision which denied a teacher compensation from the date a school was closed.

Anna B. Carlson in 1996, age 88 (*Anna B. Carlson*)

Carlson spent most of her career teaching country schools. Another standard provision declared that her last month's salary would not be paid until her term reports were filed and approved by the county superintendent of schools. Beginning in 1958 one more provision in her contract said that her first month's salary would not be paid until she furnished evidence of a valid teacher's certificate.

In 1913 the state established a pension plan for its teachers, membership was optional until January 1, 1914. Standard contract provisions referred to legal contributions required by the system. Her 1950 contract noted that a teacher could apply seven years of out-of-state public school teaching to the plan. Two years later her contract stipulated that to qualify for increased benefits under the 1947 pension law a teacher had to teach at least one year after July 1, 1947.

After World War II teachers became more militant and her contracts reflected further changes in the educational environment, brought about by negotiating with school boards and lobbying the legislature. The 1948 contract noted that it continued in effect for the next school term unless she was notified prior to April 15 that her services were not required, in 1954 the notice had to be in writing. The teacher had to accept the contract in fifteen days. In 1958 the notification date was extended to May 1, and the contract had to be accepted in 30 days. Also in 1948, a provision made it difficult to break a contract. The provision indicated that in the event of a breach of contract on the part of a teacher the superintendent of public instruction *shall* suspend the teacher's certificate for a period not to exceed one year during which it *shall* be unlawful for the teacher to receive payment for teaching in public schools in the state. In 1960 a hearing had to be held before suspension took place.

An important fringe benefit was added to Carlson's contract in 1959. Her contract noted that she was granted five days sick leave, cumulative to twenty; in 1968 she was granted ten days, cumulative to thirty.

Williams Co. School No. 1, School District 63, May 1914, Teacher Ella Petterson
(Martha P. Tatem Collection, SHSND)

Anna Bakken Carlson's Salaries, Terms, Places Taught, and Restrictions During Her 36-Year Teaching Career

Year	County	School District	Term	Monthly Salary	Provided that . . .
1928	Logan	German No.6 School No. 1	7 month, Sept. 15	$80.00	Salary includes janitorial work; last month's salary withheld until term reports filed and approved; school may be discontinued at any time, no compensation if discontinued.
1929	Logan	Cokato No. 5 School No. 1	7 month, Sept. 30	$85.00	Same as 1928
1930	Logan	Cokato No. 5 School No. 1	7 month, Sept. 29	$85.00	Same as 1928
1931	Logan	Cokato No. 5 School No. 3	7 month, Sept. 28	$75.00	Same as 1928; teach school on regular school hours from 9 a.m. to 4 p.m.
1932	Logan	Cokato No. 5 School No. 3	7 month, Oct. 3	$45.00	Same as 1931; time schedule deleted
1933	Logan	Glendale No. 28 School No. 4	7 month, Sept. 18	$45.00	Same as 1928; teacher agrees to wait for her salary till funds are collected
1937	Logan	Glendale No. 28 School No. 2	6 month, 15 days, Sept. 30	$55.00	Same as 1928
1941	Logan	Cokato No. 5 School No.3	7 month, Oct. 6	$65.00	Same as 1928
1943	Kidder	Grant No. 38 School No. 3	7 month, Oct. 18	$120.00	Same as 1928
1944	Logan	Glendale No. 28 School No. 4	8 month, Sept. 11	$110.00	Same as 1928; hold the 7th and 8th grade examination in May
1945	Logan	Glendale No. 28 School No. 4	8 month, Sept. 10	$125.00	Same as 1928
1946	Logan	Cokato No. 5 School No. 3	8 month, Sept. 9	$140.00	Same as 1928
1947	Logan	Cokato No. 5 School No. 3	8 month, Sept. 8	$150.00	Same as 1928; teach all grades from first to eight; paid at the end of each month
1948	Logan	Cokato No. 5 School No. 3	8 month, Sept. 7	$175.00	Same as 1928 without janitorial work clause; continuing contract unless teacher is notified; teacher certificate revoked if contract breached
1949	Logan	Cokato No. 5 School No. 3	8 month, Sept. 5	$175.00	Same as 1948; paid at end of each school month
1950	Logan	Cokato No. 5 School No. 3	8 month, Sept. 4	$175.00	Same as 1949; includes janitorial work clause
1951	Logan	Cokato No. 5 School No. 3	8 month, Sept. 3	$190.00	Same as 1950; janitorial work clause excluded
1952	McKenzie	Grail No. 1 Kinning	9 month, Sept. 1	$297.50 for 10 months	The teacher do the janitor work. If the school house is used as a teacherage the teacher shall pay for any electric current used in excess of the minimum of $1.50 per month which is paid by the district. If electric current is used for cooking hot lunches the teacher shall make arrangements with the patrons for paying the bill. Tenth payment to be made when the teacher's final report has been approved by the county superintendent of schools.
1953	McKenzie	Grail No. 1 Kinning	9 month, Sept. 7	$306.50 for 10 months	Same as 1952
1954	Logan	Cokato No. 5 School No. 3	8 month, Sept. 13	$250.00	Receive salary at end of every month
1955	Logan	Cokato No. 5 School No. 3	9 month, Sept. 5	$250.00	Same as 1954
1956	Logan	Cokato No. 5 School No. 3	9 month, Sept. 3	$250.00	Teacher to do the janitorial work; last check received when reports accepted
1957	Logan	Cokato No. 5 School No. 3	9 month, Sept. 3	$300.00	Teacher to do the janitorial work
1958	Logan	Cokato No. 5 School No. 3	9 month, Sept. 2	$315.00	Teacher to do the janitorial work
1959	Logan	Cokato No. 5	9 month, Sept. 7	$325.00	Teacher to do the janitorial work
1960	Logan	Starky No. 26	9 month, Sept. 7	$370.00	Teacher to do the janitorial work; 10% of salary withheld until end of term
1961	Logan	Foster No. 2	9 month, 1 week, Aug. 28	$3750.00 per year	Teach 5th Grade; other duties as directed by the Supt. of Schools; 3 % social security deduction; pay in 9 or 12 month installments
1962	Logan	Foster No. 2	9 month, Sept. 4	$3900.00 per year	Teach 5th Grade; other duties as directed by the Supt. of Schools; in classroom from 8:30 a.m. until 4:30 p.m., social security deduction on the full salary; pay in 9 or 12 month installments
1963	Logan	Foster No. 2	9 month, 1 week, Sept. 3	$3900.00 per year	Same as 1962; must return contract by April 8, 1963
1964	Logan	Foster No. 2	9 month, 1 week, Aug. 31	$3850.00 per year	Same as 1963 without return of contract clause
1965	Logan	Foster No. 2	9 month, 1 week, Sept. 7	$3900.00 per year	Same as 1964; $50.00 extra compensation allowed if teacher receives 4 quarter hours of summer school training, or its equivalent in work related to teach field; social security deduction at legal rate
1966	Logan	Foster No. 2	9 month, 1 week, Sept. 6	$3950.00 per year	Same as 1965
1967	Logan	Foster No. 2	9 month, 1 week, Sept. 5	$4250.00 per year	Same as 1966
1968	Logan	Foster No. 2	9 month, 1 week, Sept. 3	$4550.00 per year	Same as 1967; further that no income in salary above the 1967-1968 school year, unless teacher produces evidence of receiving 5 semester hours of college credit within the last 5 years; transcript of credits must be on file in the office of the superintendent
1969	Logan	Foster No. 2	9 month, 1 week, Sept. 2	$5280.00 per year	Teach 5th & 6th grade English; may be assigned extra curricular duties by the superintendent; in room from 8:30 a.m. until 4:30 p.m. on school days; deductions from salary according to existing laws; increase in salary provision remained in effect; extra pay, ($440) for teaching basic skills under Title I
1970	Logan	Foster No. 2	9 month, 1 week, Aug. 26	$5412.00 per year	Teach 5th & 6th grade English and Spelling; may be assigned extra curricular duties by the superintendent; in room from 8:30 a.m. until 4:00 p.m. on school days; increase in salary provision remained in effect

Chapter 14

It Wasn't All Bad

Ben Walsh

A COMEDIAN ONCE DEFINED A COUNTRY SCHOOL as a building built for the purpose of depriving a child of an education.

While I concede that there is much truth in this glib statement, I cannot agree in its entirety. I clearly recognize the disadvantages and shortcomings of such a school, yet it also had its positive side. Let me tell you about such a school I once attended as a small boy not long after the turn of the century — when Teddy Roosevelt was in the White House and Babe Ruth was in short pants.

It stood alone on a breezy knoll miles from the nearest town in Wells County, surrounded on all sides by farm land. It was the typical school build-

North Dakota Journal of Education, May, 1972, pp. 10-13.
Benedict Walsh, born in 1899, retired from farming in 1977. He was born on his parents' homestead the year after they settled north of Harvey. His parents came from Canada in 1886.

Tumbling Around These Prairies

by Robert Cory

Source: *Minot Daily News*, October 21, 1950, p. 5.

We should have a law, I think, that would require some properly constituted authority tear down and erase from the blackboard of Nature, every old, abandoned schoolhouse.

It is just bad outdoor housekeeping, that's all, to leave one standing.

The little old schoolhouse stood for something in its day, just as the settler's claim shack did. It still stands for something where it has been improved to meet the needs of the times and where no better building is justified. But it was not built to be a monument, and indeed it makes a poor one.

Schoolhouses should not be made to look like monuments, anyhow. They should be supremely useful, according to the best standards of the times for which they were intended. They ought, also, to be beautiful, with all the beauty that can be embodied in simplicity. Each one ought to represent and demonstrate the best in construction that the building industry knows in the way of techniques to meet the specific needs of a particular community in a particular place and in keeping with its climate. But they should not be built to last forever. Foreseeable need should govern, with due regard for the type of economy on which the community is based. And probably no schoolhouse should ever be built on a plan that does not lend itself to addition or alteration. These things about a schoolhouse we should have learned by now; along with the fact that any building in disuse is an eyesore.

Steadily in the past 5 years, while the fruits of agriculture have brought decent returns, from land units of ample size, our farmsteads have been improved. Houses and barns and granaries have been remodeled, or new ones built. The change is in the direction of better appearance and more substantial usefulness. Old ramshackles have been removed. Many old, run-down sets of buildings have vanished. The occupied farmsteads have become neater, cleaner, healthier looking places.

Even the villages are looking up, altho the streamlining remains far from complete. The villages, more than anything, would benefit from a law, or an unwritten convention, that every unused building had to be razed. The transition is hopeful. It is a sign of life and awakened realism. Whether you speak of a family farm, or a village, or a scattered neighborhood,

continued on next page

ing of the locality and of that era—a one room structure with four windows on each side. Well back behind it stood the two toilets, wisely and discreetly separated by the coal shed, all under one roof. Also in the background and to one side, stood a small barn, built to shelter the horses of pupils who lived too far from the school to walk.

Most one room school houses actually consisted of two rooms — an entrance and a main room and this one was no exception. The entrance, or cloak room was, as the name implies, just a small room where the wraps and overshoes were left. It also contained a shelf where our drinking water was kept. Beside the pail, on the same shelf, stood a wash basin, but to my knowledge it was never used.

The other room, the big one, was of course the school room where we worked and studied when we were not out at play. This big room contained all of the equipment deemed necessary for a school those days.

In my memory they still exist — the big stove in the center of the room, that kept us warm (at least on one side) during the long winter months — the bell, the broom, the books, the out-of-date globe and the "coal scuttle" piled high with lignite. There were the desks—little ones for the little kids, big ones for the big pupils, bearing the carved initials of boys long since men. They were perhaps more skilled with the knife than with the pen. They had left their mark before going forth to carve their way in the world, helped perhaps, by the smattering of education they acquired in the humble building.

There were the usual maps and pictures found in the schoolhouses of that day, including a picture of our president, Theodore Roosevelt. He squinted down upon us with his weak eyes, from high above the blackboard. Our knowledge of him was very limited. In our innocent ignorance we only knew that he was our president, that he could ride a horse, that he carried a big stick and that he lived in a white house in Washington, D. C. — wherever that was.

Along one end of the room was a small library. Yes, a library in a country school shortly after the turn of the century! It was put there through the efforts of some long forgotten teacher who had the recognition is coming that it vitiates all efforts toward wholesome living for the occupants of any rural establishment to let themselves sit among the idle ghosts of the past.

Tearing down deserted schoolhouses would be recognizing this as fact. It would be like hauling away from the farm all the worn-out binders and plows and tractors that used to sit, like ghosts, on the perimeter of a neglected farmstead.

Then, if eventually, the community produces a new crop of youngsters, let them ride to learning in a new and more suitable machine.

Which brings me to a suggestion worth considering, if you are a school officer in one of those far-flung reorganized districts, like the one in Williams County.

To serve remote areas, where small, one-room or two-room schools are the only practical solution for elementary grades, wouldn't it be well for the district to own one or two semi-portable schoolhouses?

They could be neat, compact and modern, made of substantial materials, possibly of metal construction like some of the new automotive service stations. In that case, they could be dismantled easily and put up again where needed.

In that way, the educational serving station could be moved to whatever locality had the most children within reach.

And along with the movable schoolhouse, either attached or separate, the district should own a couple of movable housing units for teachers. I'm not thinking of trailers, but again of readily assembled or dismantled prefabricated dwellings, comfortable in every respect.

Equipment of this kind would help make rural education respectable, as well as shifty.

After one has admitted that there is more to the problem of elementary education than buildings, the fact remains that in a climate like ours, the little white crackerbox schoolhouse no more deserves to survive than its contemporary, the claim shack.

We still have in service, in not very remote parts of North Dakota, buildings of a type that might be satisfactory housing for rural pupils in the backwoodsy mildness of the Ozarks.

A rural school in North Dakota, unless it is of necessity the semi-portable type, should be an establishment that is roomy, comfortable, well-heated, attractive to the eye, and adaptable to a variety of community uses. In quality of construction and in comfort, it should be equal to the best private housing in the community, not worse in these respects than the poorest home.

There is no reason at all worth a snap of the fingers why the children of the wide, open spaces should have to go to a school where they huddle in pioneer dinginess.

At least part of the blame for the fact that many rural youngsters grow up with an urge to get away from the farm, without doubt, must be laid at the door of the unimaginative kind of school housing that their father have been satisfied to send them to.

The late Dean J. V. Breitwieser of the University of North Dakota, writing about what the rural school could be, once indulged in this bit of dreaming:

"The schoolhouse, where one or two teachers serve, should be on an attractive plot of ground, larger than a cramped city lot. Trees and shrubbery should surround the building but not be too close so as to obstruct lighting. The grounds and grove should be so well maintained that they will attract neighborhood picnics.

"A comfortable teacherage should be provided, so the teacher and his or her family become a part of the community life.

"A library at the school should serve the adults as well as the children.

"The individual development, group type of organization should be maintained, rather than the lock-step grade type of city organization.

continued on next page

tried (and failed) to bring a little of the outside world into our lives. Like the wash basin in the entrance, I never saw it used.

The interior of the building had been vandalized from time to time during the years, but unlike today's vicious destruction of property, it consisted only of throwing a few books on the floor, or making a few senseless scribblings on the blackboard.

Of course there was nothing modern about the building according to today's standards. Water for drinking was carried from the nearest farm home in an open pail, generally by some of the older pupils during the noon recess. This provided water for the afternoon and the next forenoon, all of which was well and good during the mild weather months. However, when winter arrived and the icy blasts came roaring in,

"The larger consolidated type of school should be developed wherever feasible. This kind of school should be surrounded by a small experimental demonstration farm supervised by a skilled agriculturist. Here an auditorium for meetings should always be available. . . . Some members of the teaching staff should be on hand at this educational community center all the time. . .

"Examples of many progressive, successful rural and consolidated schools are available, but many more are needed to take the place of the cheap, dreary imitations of city schools that are all too common."

He went on to say that as a new rural culture takes shape, it will be an outgrowth of the new science and arts of agriculture. It will not be satisfied to transplant city ways to farm life. "What is needed," he said, "is the development of the country in its own way, so that comfort, rewards, recreation and culture in rural communities will have a pleasant flavor of their own."

fresh and fierce, out of Manitoba, it was a different story. The weather-wise children of the prairie knew what would happen to a pail of water left overnight in a country schoolhouse in a Dakota winter. Therefore, during the winter months there was no water carried and the pupils simply went without—something they were used to doing many times and in many ways, during their young lives.

These pupils were, of course, all farm children. Most of them were the offspring of struggling farm parents, living and farming land in the neighborhood. The lot of these children was far from easy. They were born into hard work and hardship. There were no checks in the mailbox. They learned, while still very young, that what they wanted they must first earn, or do without. They shared with their parents, both the work and the responsibility. Maturity came early. Boys were men at fifteen, for there is nothing that develops maturity like a combination of work and responsibility. Although they were destined never to have an education, they nevertheless learned much by attending that shabby little school. They learned as much on the playground as in the schoolroom, by contact and association.

These young people were being raised in an era and a locale where complete indifference prevailed toward education by parents. Children old enough to work were allowed to go to school only after the farm work was done for the season. After the last bundle was threshed and the last furrow turned, they could go to school, if they so desired. In most cases the young boy or girl wished to go, not that he or she valued education any more than the

Guest at Mary Guthrie's School after 4:00 pm, Norge, N.D., July 19, 1910 *(Divide Co. Collection WD/8-12, SHSND)*

parents, but because the pupil wished to join in the fun games at school. Even in winter they knew they must do the farm chores before and after school—or they could stay at home, no one cared. In these modern times when education is considered as being of utmost importance, the young person of today may find it difficult to believe that little more than a half century ago parents raised large families of near-illiterate children, without a qualm of conscience.

Unlike most people of that neighborhood, my parents believed strongly in education and as a result my father served on the school board much of the time. Each autumn as the date from the opening of the school term drew near, he would ready the schoolhouse. After he had seen that a teacher was hired, the necessary books, etc. in their places, coal and kindling in the shed and the floor scrubbed, he would hitch his driving mare to the buggy and drive around the neighborhood spreading the sad tidings that school would open next Monday morning.

Early School, Divide County (Divide Co. Collection DV/5-1, SHSND)

Now, if there was anything that those neighbors did not want to hear, especially at that time of the year, it was the word "school," coming as it did in the heart of the threshing season. School was for "lazy people." As a result many an irate mother poured forth her wrath (sometimes in a strange and foreign tongue) upon this meddlesome neighbor who was forever trying to educate her children. Only little children too small to pitch a bundle, swing a shovel, or milk a cow, showed up at school at that season of the year. Likely there were laws then governing the education of the children, but if there were, they didn't penetrate the farming communities.

The teachers of those days were for the most part young, single women and could be divided into three categories. One group intended making teaching a career and was teaching a country school only as a stepping stone to something higher. Another group came to the country to teach only because they could find no better job available at the time. The third group came looking solely for romance and adventure and often found it.

Although a teacher's wages were low, her status in the neighborhood was high. And although she was not highly educated by today's standards, she was better educated than the farmfolk of the community at that time.

Because of that fact, she received much honor and respect. She was always in great demand at a country dance or other gathering. At a basket social her basket invariably sold the highest and many a humble farm hand paid what amounted to nearly a month's wages for the fleeting pleasure of eating supper with the school marm.

A country school teacher's tasks were many and diverse. Her pupils ranged in number between 10 and 25, and in many sizes and ages, from the little first grader, who many times spoke no English, to the "educated" boy or girl in the sixth or seventh grade.

Although her status was high from the beginning, her value as a teacher was not fully determined until after the night of the Christmas program.

Although her status was high from the beginning, her value as a teacher was not fully determined until after the night of the Christmas program. On that night the teacher who passed out the biggest sacks of candy, the largest oranges and the reddest apples was judged the best teacher—not only by the pupils but the parents as well. Her chance of being rehired often depended upon her generosity that night.

Our noon lunch consisted mainly of bread and butter or bread and syrup, with sometimes an apple in the winter time to lubricate the esophagus—although I doubt if anyone of us knew that we possessed such a thing. This simple meal was carried in syrup pails—the standard dinner bucket of those days. Perhaps, somewhere in the world, the modern lunch bucket had been invented and was in use, but if it was, we were none the wiser. Each child carried his own pail and although they all might seem identical to a stranger, nevertheless each pupil knew his own and could pick it out from all of the others, by some uncanny means.

"Modernizing the Old Rural School," Lake View District, Benson County, Lallie Township #1, 1917-1918 *(SHSND)*

Most country schoolhouses had a smell and ours was no exception. However, the smell might differ from school to school, from season to season, from day to day, or even from hour to hour. I knew ours did. When school opened in the fall it smelled, both inside and out, of the rodents that had made their home and raised their young unmolested under the building. That was only a passing smell. Later on, however, when the weather grew cold with the approach of winter and a fire was kept burning in the big stove, the interior took on a permanent smell of coal dust, coal smoke, food and feet.

There was another smell that ebbed and flowed with the time of day, and with the season. The farm boys of those days did the morning and evening farm chores in the same clothes in which they came to school. When the severe winter began in earnest and the morning and evening temperatures, both inside and outside of the building, were far below zero, we huddled in a circle around the big stove, not unlike little chickens around a mother hen. When the lignite got "well lit" and the great stove began "putting out" with blistering heat, the interior of the building took on an aroma suggestive of the Chicago stockyards.

Like many other reminders of our past, the country school has nearly disappeared from the scene. Many of the buildings have been converted to granaries to help house the ever-present surplus of grain that has plagued the American farmer for so many years. Others have been moved away and placed on exhibition at museums, so that future generations may see how and where their forefathers acquired their meager education. I believe they should be viewed with the reverence and respect that they deserve. It was these humble little buildings, scattered over the desolate prairies, that brought the first gleam of enlightenment to the child of the isolated farms of a half century ago.

It was in one of these little structures that many a country child learned the English language (in its simplest form, of course). It was there, too, that he or she learned the "three R's" (again in the simplest form). It was because of the meager education gained in these humble settings that it became possible for a country boy or girl to face the world and to compete, with a better chance of success, than had he not attended school at all. Although they are gone, what finer tribute can we pay them than to say that when they were needed they were there!

Many a senior citizen of today, as he sits alone with his thoughts and watches the jet age world speed by, may think of the slower and quieter life of his youth. And perhaps, if his memory serves him well that day, he may see, once again, through the mists and shadows of time, the shabby little building where he first learned to read and for a moment he is a boy again.

His old eyes may light once more with the mischievous gleam of youth and he may give vent to a chuckle or two, as he recalls some boyish prank that he and his mates played on a teacher long since gone to her reward.

It wasn't the best, but it wasn't all bad, either.

My Feelings for My Rural School

by Irene Jacobson

A King

A one-roomed school with a rickety frame
And furnishings scarcely worthy, of name;
Yet I'm proud of it all in my own stern way;
For here I am king over all I survey!

This one little room is my castle so fair;
Tho it's furnished so poorly I give not a care;
For I am the ruler of all just the same;
I'm king of the castle, lord of the domain!

Twelve farm children that come to my school
Study their lessons, adhere to each rule
And I love them all in my own queer way,
For again I am king over all I survey!

They are my subjects so loyal and so true,
Doing quite well all I bid them to do;
Obeying me implicitly in most everything
As tho bowing down reverently, hailing me king!

Early Morton County School (*Brown Collection, SHSND*)

Chapter 15

The School Lunch Bucket

Francis Wold

IT'S HARD FOR MANY OF US TO BELIEVE that the school lunch pail is fast following the kerosene lamp and the buttonhook into oblivion. The advent of hot-lunch programs in school across the state has retired most lunch pails from circulation, and has freed mothers from the unloved task of trying to come up with something different to put in them.

"It took me two weeks after they started serving hot meals at school to realize that I really didn't have to make sandwiches every morning," one mother recalls.

Source: Francis Wold, *Prairie Scrapbook*
(Washburn: Borlaug Publishing Company, May, 1982), pp. 38-39.

"Every day after I put the coffee on to perk I'd reach for the lunch pails and a loaf of bread, only to remember that I was all through with that chore."

Another mother recalls that the worst part about packing lunches was that no two children would settle for eating the same kind of sandwich. "One would eat nothing but peanut butter and jelly," she remembers, "and the other couldn't even stand to smell peanut

Noon lunch in a Morton County School in the 1930s *(SHSND)*

butter, let alone eat it." After years of eating cold lunches, most children gave any kind of a sandwich a less than enthusiastic reception. "Yet what else can you put in a lunch pail?" their exasperated mothers would sigh.

Fruit, carrot sticks and milk were supposed to help assure a balanced diet in the school lunch, but often mothers learned (usually by accident) that these had been traded off for store-bought marshmallow cookies, bubble gum, or soda pop. For some reason, whatever was in another person's lunch pail always was better than the contents of your own bucket.

Potato chips, brownies with thick chocolate icing, dill pickles, chocolate chip cookies, doughnuts, and chocolate milk were most children's idea of the perfect lunch.

Older people who as children carried lunches in tin syrup pails or "Cut Plug" tobacco boxes with wire handles as they walked across snow-covered fields to country schoolhouses have memories of scantier noon meals. Doubled slices of home-made bread were usually all that was in the pail, and during the winter when the cows were dry, the bread was often bare of butter. Salted lard sometimes took the place of butter, but syrup or jelly was the rule. Sometimes a piece of roast meat with the bread would make a sandwich, or a fried chicken leg or piece of sausage would be included, but this was not every-day fare. An occasional oatmeal or sugar cookie was a real treat.

The contents of the lunch pails many times were half-frozen by noon, both from the walk to school and from sitting in the frigid school room for several hours.

In cold weather potatoes were often brought to be roasted in the ashes of the potbellied heater — the first and only hot school lunch that many children ever knew.

In later years, a small kerosene stove was sometimes bought for the school, and at noon the teacher would heat up a kettle of soup or some stew that was sent by families in turn. Hot cocoa brewed on one of these little stoves was delicious and satisfying beyond belief.

A few country schools are still in operation in North Dakota (one or two in our own area) so some children still carry lunch pails, and some mothers still automatically reach for the bread box when they enter the kitchen in the morning. However,

241

School Teacher, Williston, skiing to school ca. 1903-1913 (Martha P. Tatem Collection, SHSND)

most youngsters now eat hot lunches prepared from nutritionally balanced menus, and most mothers can forget the nagging question, "What have I got to put in the kids' lunch pails?"

Of course, the youngsters complain about the hot lunches just the way they used to complain about the contents of their lunch pails — except for the days when there's pizza or Sloppy Joes—but you can't win every day!

🖎🖎

A Country School Teacher Remembers — Mary McDaniel

As a young 17-year-old teacher with a teaching certificate from Valley City State Teachers College, I had stars in my eyes and the high ideals of a beginner. I knew nothing of rural life or rural schools so here I was with one of those lignite monsters with a jacket around it. I struggled through the fall days but when Jack Frost settled down to business, I struggled with that stove. One morning I thought I had a fire going. I shut off the damper and settled into teaching my first classes of the day. Our routine was upset with a terrific explosion. The stove pipe fell down. The stove puffed smoke and sparks, soot covered everything, and we all exited rapidly. Bless the understanding board members who comforted the tearful teacher. The laughing pupils were given the day off and several neighborhood ladies volunteered to help clean up the mess. Later in the day one of the board members gave me a few pointers on how to build and regulate fires; believe it or not, I became a master of heating a country schoolhouse.

Several other incidents may also fall into the believe it or not category. I taught two different terms in a school where everyone was related and each pupil had head lice. Patrons believed the situation was normal. Imagine giving a student individual help with a problem and watching head lice frolic from hair to hair. One winter day I was skating with my 45 pupils on ponds near the school. The county superintendent arrived for a surprise visit to an empty building. He spent the remainder of the day with us; I did get a good report. We did manage to have hot lunches at school. Potatoes were baked in a pan in the furnace. Cocoa was made on a kerosene stove and a kettle of water holding fruit jars of soup or stew was put on the furnace ventilator to heat. By noon hot lunch was ready.

🖎🖎

We did manage to have hot lunches at school. Potatoes were baked in a pan in the furnace. Cocoa was made on a kerosene stove and a kettle of water holding fruit jars of soup or stew was put on the furnace ventilator to heat. By noon hot lunch was ready.

Chapter 16

Disappearing School Barns

Francis Wold

The two men — one middle-aged, the other in his late teens — tossed a last few weathered boards on top of the towering truckload of old lumber that stood at the rear of the rural school yard.

"Well, I guess that about finishes the job," said the older man, as he wiped the back of his canvas-gloved hand across his sweaty forehead.

"Yeah, this is the last load, and I'm mighty glad of it," the other replied as he squatted in the shade of the truck box. "This has been a tougher job than I figured. That old barn was really built—it would have stood for another 50 years."

Source: Francis Wold, *Prairie Scrapbook*
(Washburn: Borlaug Publishing Company, May, 1982), pp. 40-46.

A Country School Teacher Remembers — Margaret Trautman

This was February 1933, my third year of teaching a one-room rural school near Cleveland. I was 19 years old. It had been blizzarding for three days, high winds, heavy snowfall, and falling temperatures. Perhaps the thermometer read 30 degrees below zero, I don't recall. The 3-day blizzard had blown on eastward, snarling traffic and chilling everyone and everything that dared to be out. On the fourth day the wind was calm. In North Dakota, the world looked beautiful, but huge drifts blocked roads and barnyards. I decided to go to school. I arose early because I was anxious to be on my way. Being the teacher, I felt so responsible to be at school early and have the fire started before any pupils arrived.

I stayed at my parent's place, 2 miles from the school. Normally, I walked to school as did most of my pupils, but that morning I decided to ride Sally, our riding horse. That was my first mistake. Because of the drifted road, she labored through the piled snow at a walk. In just a short distance, my feet began to sting, although I had on knee-high leather boots, warm stockings, and jeans. I kept my hands warm by swinging my arms and putting my hands under my armpits alternately.

One more mile to go! Sally faced into the wind. I could see the school house and the idea of a warm fire was with me. But I could also see the drifts of snow on the road and into the school yard. As I left home, my father told me. "Put Sally in the school barn when you get there. She'll be sweated up." So my first thought was to care for the horse.

As I approached the school buildings, I saw the huge 6 foot drifts in front of the doors. There was no shovel. I managed to get inside the school house and pick up the dustpan. I tried to break the drift in front of the school barn because Sally was my first concern. By this time my feet and legs were blocks of ice. I gave up as the dustpan bent and broke. I tied Sally to the flag pole that was out of the wind.

To my dismay, someone had been in the school during the blizzard. They had burned all my carefully prepared supply of fuel, the paper, the wood, and even the coal! In those days, school houses were never locked. I tried to start a fire with the few scraps of paper and a few shavings of wood left in a cardboard box. I managed to get a small flame going. Again, I tried to get to the coal bin, which was in a building out-

"I kinda hated to be the one to tear it down," the first man said slowly. "After all, I used to stable my horses here years ago when I was a school kid, and it just doesn't seem right that I should be the one to wreck it."

The young fellow reflected for a few moments. "I know what you mean, Dad, but if you didn't do it, someone else would. There was a lot of sound wood in that old building, and with the price of lumber what it is, you made a good buy."

His father did not answer, but gazed morosely at the bare brown area in the tangled grass where the old barn had stood. Soon, he knew, the encroaching grass would move relentlessly inward, and next year a thriving crop of pig weeds would be the only sign that a building once occupied the spot. For some reason, the tree-like weeds flourished on abandoned building sites. It hurt him to think that their tall stalks rattling in the wind would play the death dirge for the old landmark.

Embarrassed by such an unwonted flight of fancy, he moved briskly toward the truck. "Well, the chores won't get done at this rate. Your ma will be wonderin' what happened to us." He glanced over his shoulder and noticed how solitary the schoolhouse looked without the length of the barn bulking behind it. "It just don't seem right," he murmured as he climbed into the cab.

All over North Dakota the school barns are disappearing. They are succumbing to the ravages of time, weather and neglect; they are being converted to other uses; or, as in this case, they are being sold for the lumber they contain. Their disappearance is marked with regret by the many men and women whose school day memories center around the old barns to an extent hard to explain to the children of a newer generation.

In their day, the barns were an indispensable part of the educational program. Most of the families lived some distance from the school—in many cases too far for the youngsters to walk, especially in cold weather. The only form of transportation was by horseback, or by a horse-drawn vehicle. Where there were only very young children attending school, the father would bring them in the morning and call for them when classes were dismissed; but as soon as the oldest child reached

continued on next page

an age where he could be trusted to drive a team, he would take over the chore, stabling his horses in the school barn during the day.

Big families were the rule, and by the time the oldest child was ready to begin driving, there would probably be three or four younger ones to go. The gentlest team on the place was always the "school team."

Hitched to a bob sled in winter, to a spring wagon or old buggy in spring or fall, the team plodded off countless patient miles between home and school.

In cold weather, the younger children, snugly scarved, mittened and covered up with heavy quilts or horse-hide robes, huddled in straw piled into the bed of the sled with their feet against bricks warmed in the oven of the family range. The driver had no such protection, and many were the frozen fingers, toes and noses suffered by those plucky children. They were jealous of their responsibility, however, and showed a sturdy self-reliance that would have done credit to most adults.

When the young drivers and charges arrived at the school the little ones piled out and into the warmth radiating from the huge tin-jacketed heater which stood in the center of the room. But the drivers must pilot their teams to the barn and unhitch with fingers so numb from cold that it was hard to manage the snaps and buckles.

Then the horses were guided inside to their own particular stalls, where they drowsed the day away, rousing only to munch at the hay which their small guardians had brought along for them.

The barn at our consolidated school, thought larger than most, was typical of those in the area in that it was well built and tight, and the horses were comfortable in even the bitterest weather.

Each driver took care of his own team, and each was responsible for keeping his own stall

side. I had no luck—and by then my tiny fire went out. I don't remember crying, but I do know I was worried about my horse.

Then I heard a team and bobsled coming. The nearest neighbors, the Jacob Martin family, were bringing the children to school. Immediately the two oldest boys broke through the drifts to get coal and wood from the shed. They helped me get a fire going, but I was, oh, so cold by then. My legs and feet and hands were swollen. We stayed at the school long enough to see if other pupils came. By that time the wind was coming up and the weather was getting blustery. We bundled into the bobsled, tying Sally behind and set off to their home.

Mrs. Martin was a hard-working woman of German descent. She helped me get my boots and stockings off. She brought a pan of kerosene to put my feet in, to thaw out the frost. She wrapped me in a warm feather quilt until I finally quit shaking. In early afternoon the boys took me home.

My legs and feet were badly swollen and began to blister the next day. My hands would ache at times. The iron stirrups on the saddle left marks across my feet and insteps for a long time even tho' I had worn leather boots.

The next morning the raging wind and storm were upon us again. It was Monday of the next week before school was back in session. Thanks to that kind housewife I was able to walk the two miles, wearing my dad's 4-buckle overshoes. I had learned that if I had walked that morning I would have kept reasonably warm by exercise. I wouldn't have worried about the horse. By walking I did not break through the drifts as the horse did, but could walk over the crusted top.

I prepared an old cardboard box, in the back entry, with scraps of paper, wood, and coal, even a tin container with matches in it. I concealed it under some old desks and a broken pail, so never again would I be unprepared for just such an emergency. [At Parshall, February 15, 1936, the temperature dropped to 60 degrees below zero, the coldest temperature on record in North Dakota.]

☙ ✍

clean—except for the girls. Boys, with unusual gallantry (or what was more likely, under orders from home), took turns cleaning stalls for the feminine drivers. Many a staid, middle-aged matron, when asked how she met her husband, will reply with a nostalgic gleam in her eye, "Oh, he used to take care of my team and clean my stall when we were both seventh graders." Budding romances among the pupils were usually first evident when a boy bashfully offered to "hitch up" for a girl, or when he chivalrously fed her team as well as his own.

Our barn was originally built to hold 28 horses, but as new families moved into the community swelling the school attendance and increasing the number of horses to be stabled, it was enlarged by three double stalls. Stalls were assigned to families on a permanent basis, with possession remaining the same from year to year. Many of the pupils in attendance at that time can close their eyes today and name off the families whose horses occupied each stall down the long length of the barn. They can name not only the families, but also the horses.

"Let's see—Andersons drove Babe and Nell—or was it Belle?" "Belle was the big bay with the three white feet, but she went lame the winter of the big ice storm, and

then they put old June in with Babe. They had the third stall from the front on the north side."

"That's right! And remember how Jim Johnson and his little brother rode bareback on that old sway-backed roan? Her name was June, too."

In listening to these reminiscences one can't help thinking that every family in the country must have had horses named Babe and June. One of my friends bears an everlasting grudge against her parents for christening her June. "Every time I walked down the aisle at school someone would whisper 'Whoa, June!' or 'Back up, June!'" she says. "You would have thought my parents would have had more sense."

The barns are larger than the schools — above, Barnes Co. School District No 55, below, Barn on homestead in Foster Co. with Pleasant Valley School in background *(SHSND)*

As such times as Christmas programs, literary socials and community dances, the capacity of the barn would be taxed to its limits. Riding horses might be shoehorned into already occupied double stalls, or teams would be split and stabled separately wherever room could be found.

On such occasions, if the weather was cold, the barn would fill with steam from so many animals. The horses would be covered with frost when they entered, and as this melted it contributed to the steamy atmosphere. At times the fog was so thick that the rays of the kerosene lanterns were powerless to penetrate it, and drivers were forced to grope their way from stall to stall.

One classic tale in our community concerns the night a team was actually lost in the barn. It was a bitterly cold night—about 26 degrees below zero—but a large crowd had braved the frigid weather for a dance in the school. The barn filled quickly, and late arrivals were hard put to find places for their horses.

One of the last to drive in was Johnny Ennis and his girlfriend, proudly riding in a brand new cutter behind a team of spanking roans. Steam hung so thick around the stalls that it was hard to see clearly, but Johnny, with the help of a couple of his friends, managed to squeeze the roans in, one far to the rear of the building with a team of blacks, the other near the middle with two ponies.

The dance lasted till early morning, and when the weary crowd emerged into the arctic air it was so cold that their breath billowed before them in huge clouds. In the barn, the fog hung thicker than any of London's best. Confusion ensued as drivers sought to find their horses, and then tried blindly to lead them to the door.

Poor Johnny was utterly unable to locate either of his roans, though he twice made his way up and down the murky length of the barn. As he was about to grope his way back again, he heard someone call his name.

"Hey, Johnny!" a voice called. "Somebody says the Riley boys untied your team and turned them loose—you better ride home with us."

Bitterly cursing his Irish rivals, Johnny found his girl and rode home crowded ingloriously into a bobsled full of sleepy youngsters.

As soon as the frost-bitten sun peered cautiously above the horizon Johnny and two of his buddies were galloping over the countryside looking for the lost team. Two hours of hard riding failed to show any sign of the roans, and the boys were wondering where to look next when they saw a neighbor coming toward them.

"Hey, Johnny!" he yelled as soon as he was within earshot. "I found your team!" Something seemed to be tickling him, and he couldn't wait to tell what it was. "Guess where your horses are, Johnny! They're right where you left them—tied up in the barn!"

The neighbor had gone to the barn early to look for a missing saddle blanket, and there standing forlornly in their separate stalls, were the two roans, whickering hungrily. To this day Johnny is apt to hear the question, "Lost any teams lately?"

The big barn served as a center of recreation for the school children. The long stringers and cobwebby rafters of the building were a constant temptation to lively youngsters, and wild games of "tag" with overtones of Tarzan took place every recess.

The barns dominate the school grounds *(Porterville Collection, NDIRS)*

The upper reaches swarmed with boys jumping from rafter to rafter, swinging and chinning themselves, and daring each other to even more reckless feats of aerial acrobatics.

These gymnastics came to a sudden halt one winter day when Billy Sundahl lost his balance and fell in the gutter directly behind a young pinto pony. The startled pony kicked Billy on the side of the head and knocked him senseless. Luckily the blow was a glancing one, and Billy's head was protected by his heavy cap, so he came around in a few minutes with a headache and a huge purple lump the only after effects. However, the resulting scare to the teacher and parents stopped the exploits among the rafters—at least for that term of school.

In nice weather, when many children walked to school—often for several miles—the partly empty barn was a wonderful location for Hide and Seek, or Follow the Leader.

The long, low building also served as a perfect base for a bitterly competitive game of Annie Over that continued on a more-or-less permanent basis throughout the year. This was no sissy game of "catch" for small youngsters, but a dog-eat-dog, do-or-die affair that allowed no quarter given or taken. Little kids were not allowed to play, and only the hardiest girls were tolerated in the line-up.

A Country School Teacher
Remembers —
Irene Theige Lill

I remember the winter of 1935 the highway had been blocked for a month. No snowplow had even been out! I was so homesick. When a beautiful weekend finally came, I walked about 15 miles to Harvey where my family lived. It took me about 5 1/2 hours to pick my way over crusted snow. One time I sat down to rest, but when I heard the coyotes howling in the distance I didn't sit any longer. I had heard that one really shouldn't sit down if you were tired because you could fall asleep and freeze to death.

My opening exercises depended on what was most important at the time. If we were preparing for the Young Citizens League convention, time was spent on our special songs. Other exercises included choral readings of poetry we all had learned, *September,* or *October's Bright Blue Weather,* for example. Sometimes, memory gems we had learned were recalled or maybe we spent time getting the meaning of a new one which had been put on the board. At times an oral book report was ready and was scheduled for that day or we might have picture study. Occasionally we just talked because I knew some one was sad. I would ask, "Is anyone sad this morning?" A hand would go up. I recall one time a grandmother had died. The event gave the child a chance to talk about it. Other children would recall sad moments too. By the time we were through talking, the child was consoled and felt the empathy of his classmates. Now they were more ready to go to work.

Many stratagems were used in lobbing the ball over the roof—a hard, high pitch that sailed half way across the yard might be followed by a gentle roller that would tumble slowly down the splintery shingles. Similar devices were resorted to in order to creep up on opponents after a successful catch. Sometimes a wild, concentrated rush around one end of the barn was the best policy; another time a divided, sneak attack would yield the most victims. Rod Peterson had the best arm for a hard, long delivery, while Lettty Gunderson was always in demand for her fleetness of foot in the chase—even if she did suffer the handicap of being female.

At times the boys declared the barn to be a male stronghold, and made it unofficially off limits to any one in skirts. On such occasions many a surreptitious cigarette made the rounds despite dire warnings from home regarding the danger of fire where there was so much hay and straw.

The area behind the barn was the traditional area where disputes were settled by hand-to-hand combat—and this was not confined exclusively to boys. Not long ago I was having coffee with a neighbor, a lady who is five times a grandmother and a pillar of our rural church, when for the first time I noticed a small, curving scar on her still shapely ankle. Out of idle curiosity I asked her how she received it.

"Oh, that!" she replied rather sheepishly. "That dates back to my days in country school. Josie Peterson and I were having a hair-pulling match out behind the barn, and that mark shows were she kicked me with her copper-toed shoe." Then she continued with an unmatronly glint in her eye, "But I got even with her! When she was saddling their old mare, Bess, to ride home that evening I sneaked a cocklebur under the saddle. When Josie tried to get on, that old mare pitched her end-over-apple-cart into a big snowbank, and everyone saw the printing on her flour-sack bloomers."

My friend stopped to wipe the wicked tears from her eyes at the memory of Josie's black stockinged legs waving from the depths of a snowdrift. "She knew darned well I did it," she laughed. "But she never could prove a thing."

It was usually the boys, however, who repaired "out back of the barn" to settle affairs on the field of honor, and black eyes and bloody noses were every-day consequences.

Once a hulking bully had been making life miserable for the small boys in school until some of the older lads decided to take a hand. Two of them forced the protesting aggressor to accompany them "out back" where six of his victims were waiting.

The little fellows stood prepared for battle, with fists clenched, sleeves rolled up, feet braced apart, and faces grim with determination. At a signal from one of the older boys the bantams swarmed all over their tormentor, punching, kicking, pulling hair, even hitting one another in their enthusiasm. It was soon finished—the bully dropped to his knees, protecting his head with his arms, and with blood streaming from his nose he tearfully promised "never to pick on the little guys again."

A smaller barn on the grounds of a later country school *(Porterville Collection, NDIRS)*

The increased use of the automobile marked the beginning of the end for the school barns. Even after most farmers bought cars, the barns were still used during the winter months when roads were bad, but better roads and more efficient snow-removing equipment soon made even this limited use unnecessary. Progress had its way, and the barns began to disappear.

Today, consolidation and reorganization of school districts are closing many of our rural schools, and huge buses transport pupils for miles to centrally located buildings. It is not unusual to see one of our little white school houses being converted into a township hall, a home, or a granary. They may soon follow the barns into limbo.

Only the usual crop of weeds marks the site of our old barn today. Two years ago it was moved to an adjoining farm to be used as a sheep shed. The square schoolhouse has a forlorn look as it stands lonesomely in the center of the neglected yard, its usefulness ended by a reorganization plan which sends its former pupils to a nearby village.

Once, in a nostalgic mood, I attempted to show a group of neighborhood youngsters how to play Annie Over by throwing the ball over our garage. After a few tries our young son snorted contemptuously, "That game is for the birds! You musta been hard up for something to do when you were a kid, Ma, to waste your time on that!"

I seethed at my inability to communicate to him the fun, thrills and excitement that were ours as we stood craning our necks for a glimpse of the ball, listening for the warning cry, and careening wildly back and forth around the friendly old barn.

Perhaps we were "hard up for something to do," but if so, we never knew it. Our social contacts were limited mostly to school, and the work and recreation that centered around the barn were important to us. Perhaps we knew a freedom that our children miss in a day of organized recreation and planned activities.

Be that as it may, it is with an almost physical pang that we read in our local weekly that another school barn is being wrecked for its lumber, or that the tottery old barn in Lignite District finally blew down in last week's wind storm. But maybe it's just as well. In an age of jet planes, supersonic missiles, and flights to the moon, there isn't much time for fretting over relics of a slower era. And the old barns won't really disappear as long as somewhere someone remembers the layout of the stalls, or thrills to the echo of Annie Over!

Chapter 17

Telling the Teacher

Lists of Instructions from the Turn of the Century

From the earliest days of statehood, lawmakers and the state Department of Public Instruction sent teachers lists of suggestions and directions on how to teach and what to teach.

Many of these directives were highly moral in tone and most didactic. Moreover, they stressed good citizenship and personal morality much more than content: the object of education in the 1890s and early 1900s was to turn out *good* human beings as opposed to *clever* people, in the language of the 1894 suggestions.

The first list of instructions comes from Dakota Territory days, 1872. While the list of nine emphasizes personal conduct and duties, the lists of 1894 and 1900 concentrate on how to turn students into better people. Curiously, none of these early lists address the content of the lessons.

Instructions to Teachers
Dakota Territory
September, 1872

1. Teachers will fill lamps, clean chimneys and trim wicks daily.

2. Each teacher will bring a scuttle of coal and a bucket of water for the day's use.

3. Make your pens carefully. You may whittle nibs for the individual tastes of the children.

4.   Men teachers may take one evening each week for courting purposes or two evenings a week if they go to church regularly.

5. After ten hours in school, the teacher should spend the remaining time reading the Bible or other good books.

6. Women teachers who marry or engage in other unseemly conduct will be dismissed.

7. Every teacher should lay aside from his pay a goodly sum for his declining years so that he will not become a burden on society.

8. Any teacher who smokes, uses liquor in any form, frequents a pool or public hall, or gets shaved in a barber shop will give good reason for suspecting his worth, intentions, integrity and honesty.

9. The teacher who performs his labors faithfully and without fault for five years will be given an increase of 25 cents a week in his pay providing the Board of Education approves.

Source: *South Dakota Historical Society*

SUGGESTIONS TO TEACHERS.*

1. Study the course until perfectly familiar with its requirements.

2. Do not *press* pupils into classes with which they cannot do good work.

3. Do not be in a hurry to change the classification made by your predecessor, but wait until you are thoroughly familiar with the needs of the school.

4. Classify the pupils in that grade in which he has most of his work.

5. Encourage and assist pupils in every way possible to bring up the work in which they are most deficient.

*Source: North Dakota, Department of Public Instruction, *Manual of the Elementary Course of Study for the Common District Schools of North Dakota*, 1894, pp. 154-156.

A Country School Teacher Remembers — Ruby Sybella Burns

My first position was teaching Valley School No. 3 in Kidder County in 1917; my pay was $55 a month. That first day of teaching was one hard to forget. The school was new and clean, but rather bare. There were desks for the children and one for the teacher; blackboards, chalk, and class books were available, but no reference books, no dictionary, and no flag. There were 18 children as frightened as their teacher. Nine of them could not speak English. I got the names of the children from the older ones. I made a chart of letters, wrote short sentences on the blackboard, assigned work for the older ones, then worked with the first grade. The day was over sooner than I expected, we put in a full day.

I made out a program that evening that I followed closely the first week. The second week a new program was needed because I had to include the eighth grade. A 16 year old girl entered school. She was very helpful and a good student; she completed the work in March. Final exams were given in March and again in May. She didn't tell her parents she had completed her work in March; she continued to come to school until her birthday in April.

The children did all their lessons in school, no homework. Most of the parents didn't speak English; they couldn't help their children.

My first boarding place was about half a mile from school with the only English speaking family in the area. Their house was small, but much better than some others in the district. They had three children; the youngest was 18 months old; the other two were 4 and 7 years old. There were no modern conveniences, no reading material; however, there was an old phonograph and a few old worn out records. I spent a lot of time with the children.

My room was very small and cold; furnishings included a single cot, my trunk, dresser and one chair. The mattress was so thin I could not keep warm until I got some newspapers and put them between the springs and mattress. A hailstorm had destroyed their crops that year; there wasn't money for frills. However, the meals were good, but very ordinary. The family had a car so transportation was available. Sometimes on Saturdays I would help with the work. It was better than sitting and waiting for Monday morning.

Only one of my boarding places had electricity, used only for light. Baths were taken in a wash basin and the water would cool very quickly. A bath had to be done in a hurry.

I would not say life was too lonely. During my first year of teaching a young man in the area took me places. He had a team of driving horses and a top buggy. There were no dances or social gatherings. The second year there were card parties and I often stayed overnight with a family of young folks who lived near the school. The other years there were parties and dances.

Religion never bothered me. When in a community I attended whatever church was convenient. The first year I found myself at an Evangelical church, the second at a Lutheran, then a Methodist and last a Catholic church.

6. Do not attempt to do *too much* at once, but carefully and considerately accomplish the work.

7. Endeavor to set a good example in all things.

8. Never overlook a fault; to do so is unjust to the children, since you will, no doubt, soon have to correct them for a repetition of it.

9. Spare no pains to investigate the truth of every charge; and if you cannot satisfy yourself, make no decision. Leave it for the future to develop.

10. Do strict justice and avoid favoritism.

11. Always prepare for your lesson by previous study. Never attempt to teach what you do not *thoroughly* know.

12. Try to bring forward the dull and backward children; the quick intellects will come on without your special notice.

13. Teach thoroughly and do not try to get on too fast. Remember that you are laying the foundation for the future life of the pupil.

14. Attend strictly to the personal neatness and cleanliness of your pupils.

15. Attend to the cleanliness and neatness of the school room, and to order and neatness of the playground.

16. Do not attempt to give undue attention to the older to the neglect of the younger pupils. Such a course would be fatal to the general advancement of the school.

17. Strive to cultivate a spirit of true politeness in your dealings and associations with all your pupils. Remember that children cannot be properly educated until they catch the charm that makes the lady and gentleman.

18. Take every opportunity for moral training. Consider that it is better to make children *good* than *clever.*

19. Constantly seek improvement and endeavor to increase your stock of learning. Remember that your character, education, and ability to instruct constitute your stock in trade.

20. Tell *little* and *develop much.* Teach your pupils to *think.* It is what a pupil *does for himself* that benefits him.

21. School government should be as much as possible *self-government*; and the school-room restraint, the *self-restraint* of pupils. The end sought is best attained through occupation. The teacher then should endeavor to provide pupils with constant employment, so varied in character as to be always interesting.

22. It may be assumed, in regard to government, that to be well taught a school must be well governed. The requisites for good order and good government are as follows:

    1. Self-government on the part of the teacher and a careful preparation for the work in hand.
    2. Comfort as a condition of the pupils.
    3. Occupation for all at all times.
    4. Pure air.
    5. Cleanliness.
    6. Earnestness, love for the work, love for, and an understanding of, child nature, on the part of the teacher.

A Country School Teacher Remembers — Laura Grafsgaard

When I cam home from my first day in school in Glenvil, Nebraska in September 1914, my mother told me later that I had said to her, "Mom, when I get big I want to be a teacher." I liked my teacher, Miss Taylor, I liked to learn the new things in school, and I liked to play with the other children my age. Teaching was the only profession I ever cared about. I tried office work one summer after I had taught one year, but found it very boring.

I always thought that one very important thing for a teacher to do is to give each child a feeling of worth for what he is capable of doing. He must not be ridiculed or shouted at, but told in a nice and friendly, but serious way, how certain things must be done, in school work as well as on the playground. A teacher is a person who teaches without shouting at a child who tries, but fails. A teacher tries to make a child feel that he can do the things he thinks he cannot do.

I never stayed more than two years in a rural one-room school. It seemed to me that after teaching youngsters from the same family for that long somehow there was trouble the third year.

A Country School Teacher Remembers — Pearl Skor

*I*n the fall of 1923 I was asked to finish the term in school No. 3 in Dolphin School District No. 17 in Divide County. The teacher that had signed the contract for the school year had decided to get married and in those days no school board would hire a married woman. I had no training what so ever but I was eager to learn and I did like children. I took a teacher's examination and Bertha Tweed, the county superintendent, gave me a permit to teach. The school term started on October 23, 1923 and was to last seven months. My salary was $75 a month and I was to do the janitor work.

I have good reason for remembering Bertha Tweed. She was a kind, tactful person ready to help an inexperienced teacher as I surely was. Among my pupils were two first graders. A little boy who couldn't speak English, and a very shy little girl who would not get out of her desk or say a word. One morning an aunt, who was visiting at the little girl's home, brought her to school, and proceeded to give me a lecture on neglecting her niece, I tried to explain but she would not listen. Shortly after the lady left Bertha Tweed came to visit. She saw how upset I was and soon I found

myself telling her the whole story. She immediately went to work on the little girl. She was very kind but firm in having my first grade come to the front of the room for their lessons. Miss Tweed stayed all day with me giving helpful suggestions in all of the grades.

When school was dismissed for the day she had the little girl tell what she had learned that day in school so she could tell her mother when she got home. I was to do this every day until the little girl gained confidence in herself. The little girl went home happy and so did I.

What was it really like? I guess I would have to say that while I was not really qualified to teach that first year, I started on a permit, I was not qualified to keep the schoolhouse clean and warm either. In the spring a board member told me I had used 11 tons of coal that year. Eleven tons of coal that I had carried into the schoolhouse from the coal shed which was several feet from the schoolhouse. I wonder how many "tons" of ashes I carried out each morning.

MAXIMS OF PURITY.*

1. Bring up a child in the way he should go, and when he is old he will not depart from it—*Proverbs.*

2. Children have more need of models than of critics.—*Joubert.*

3. The least and most imperceptible impressions received in our childhood may have consequences very important and of a long duration.—*John Locke.*

4. In bringing up a child, think of its old age.—*Joubert.*

5. The scenes of childhood are the memories of future years.—*Choules.*

6. Circumstances form character; but, like petrifying matters, they harden while they form.—*Landor.*

7. But whoso shall offend one of these little ones which believe in me, it were better for him that a millstone were hanged about his neck, and that he were drowned in the depths of the sea.—*Matthew XVIII, 6.*

8. Custom may lead into many errors; but it justifies none.—*Fielding.*

9. Perish discretion, when it interferes with duty.—*More.*

10. Wherever the speech is corrupted, so also is the mind.—*Seneca.*

*Source: North Dakota, Department of Public Instruction, *Manual of the Elementary Course of Study for the Common District Schools of North Dakota*, 1894, pp. 158-159.

11. Youth is like virgin parchment, capable of any inscription.—*Massinger.*

12. Zeal for the public good is the characteristic of a man of honor and a gentleman; and must take the place of pleasures, profits, and all other gratifications.—*Steele.*

13. Wisdom sits with children round her knees.—*Wordsworth.*

14. Such as thy words are, such will thy affections be; such thy deeds as thy affections; such thy life as thy deeds.—*Socrates.*

15. Vice is contagious, and there is no trusting the *sound* and the *sick* together.—*South.*

16. Be not deceived; evil communications corrupt good manners.—*New Testament.*

17. Virtue never dwelt long with filth.—*Rumford.*

18. Men resemble the gods in nothing so much as in doing good to their fellow creatures.—*Cicero.*

19. Behavior is a mirror in which everyone shows his image.—*Goethe.*

20. Grows pure by being purely shown upon, or foul through contact close with foulness.—

21. Moral beauty is the basis of all true beauty.—*Cousin.*

22. Virtue is the beauty, and vice the deformity of the soul.—*Socrates.*

(Porterville Collection, NDIRS)

Wisdom sits with children round her knees. —
Wordsworth

A Country School Teacher Remembers — Thelma Mallatt Aune

June, 1924 I graduated from Washburn High School. That fall I began teaching in a one room country school in the Iowa District, north of Wilton; I had obtained my teaching certificate by taking a teaching course and by doing practice teaching during my senior year. I started with six pupils, but during the term a widower and his five children moved into the community. In those days we did not have wall maps, encyclopedias, or library books, so the children had very little chance for outside reading. Few parents subscribed to magazines or newspapers.

I received $40 per month for a seven-month school term and had to pay $1 a day for room and board. I taught only one term at the school; however, while teaching at this school I met my future husband, Edwin Aune, whom I married in 1929.

The county superintendent or his assistant would visit each school once during the term. I was very nervous about the first visit but should not have been because he was one of my high school teachers and he gave me some good pointers.

I boarded with a family who lived about a mile from the school; I shared a room with their ten year old daughter. We walked to school each day. Most of the students walked except for two families who used horse-drawn vehicles.

In the winter the mailman used a horse and sleigh and usually came by the school about the time school was out. He would wait until I "banked" the fire and would give us a ride home. We had to do our own janitor work so I would have to go early in the morning to do the sweeping and get the school warm before the children arrived.

We had a Christmas program and had to use kerosene lanterns for lights. At this particular school we had a program the last day of school. That evening they allowed the young people in the community to have a dance in the school because it had been sold to a neighbor to use on his farm. The community built a new school about two miles southeast of the old one.

Town schools had a nine-month school term. A family from Washburn moved into the Ingersol District two months before the term was over; they wanted their three children to finish the school term, but a new school could not be started unless there were four pupils. A nearby German family had a son who would be able to begin school that fall. The authorities let him start in the spring in order to meet the requirement. I stayed at their home those two months and walked to school with him. It was a long walk. We all carried our lunches and drinking water in syrup pails. I

continued on next page

MORALS AND MANNERS.
MORAL ELEMENTS IN THE SCHOOL.*

1. The discipline of a good school affords a valuable moral training, this being especially true when desired results are secured by an appeal to high and worthy motives, and by conscientious training in the cardinal virtues of truthfulness, kindness, and justice.

2. All good teaching has a potent moral element.

3. The several branches of study taught in school have a valuable moral element, this being especially true of literature, history, natural science, and music.

4. Back of all effective instruction in duty there must be a true life. *The one vital condition of effective moral instruction is character in the teacher.* If he would make his pupils truthful, gentle, kind, and just, his own life must daily exhibit these virtues.

*Source: North Dakota, Department of Public Instruction, *Course of Study for the Common Schools of North Dakota, Circular No. 5*, 1900, pp. 136-139. The material was taken verbatim from *White's School Management*, by special permission from The American Book Company.

MORAL LESSONS IN THE
SCHOOL PROGRAM.

F INSTRUCTION BE A VALUABLE ELEMENT IN MORAL training, it should have an assigned place in the weekly program, and thus received its due share of attention. It is not meant that all moral instruction should thus be regulated, but that incidental instruction should be supplemented by instruction of a more progressive and systematic character. It is not a question of choice between incidental and regular instruction, but each should be faithfully used, the one supplementing the other.

1. **Cleanliness and Neatness.** 1. Body, face, hands, hair, nails, etc. 2. Clothing, shoes, etc. 3. Books, slates, desk, etc. 4. Everything used or done.

2. **Politeness (Children).** 1. At school. 2. At home. 3. At the table. 4. To guests or visitors. 5. On the street. 6. In company.

3. **Gentleness:**—1. In speech. 2. In manner. 3. Rude and boisterous conduct to be avoided. 4. Patience, when misjudged. 5. Docility, when instructed.

just loved to open my lunch pail because it always had those delicious German baked goodies in it. More families moved into the community that summer and I was hired to teach the next term. I stayed with a family who lived closer to the school. They would take us and come and get us in bad weather.

One of my students at this school was a sixteen year old boy who stayed with a family and helped with the farm work. They let him come to school for a short time that winter. He said he was in the second grade, but he couldn't even do first grade work. He was there such a short time that I left him in the second grade. He was always drawing pictures; he was very good at it. He was very cooperative and I felt so sorry for him.

This was the only school district I taught in that furnished paper, pencils, and chalk. The district also supported an active PTA. All the schools in the district would meet once a month at different schools for their PTA meeting. After the program and meeting food was served and the patrons socialized.

The next fall I taught in another school, southeast of Underwood on Highway 83. I instructed thirteen students in all grades. It was a lot of work, but I enjoyed it because the people in the community were very nice and cooperative. We had a Christmas program and a program and wiener roast on the last day of school. The whole community turned out.

The next year I started to teach a school northeast of Washburn, but had to give it up because of medical considerations.

After I married, I was asked to substitute for two weeks at the Conkling School west of Washburn and then asked to finish out the term. I was paid $70 a month and had to pay $1 a day for room and board. I had four students, two girls in the seventh or eighth grade and two girls in the middle grades. Another family had a girl who would start school the next fall; they let her come for a couple of months in the spring. The two older girls in school liked to tease her. One noon they told her that the Methodist church was the best. She said: "No, the Swedish Lutheran was better." They argued for a while and she said: "Well, I guess Jesus was a Swede." That ended the argument and we all had a good laugh. She also came to school one morning and told me that her aunt had a new baby. To show interest, I asked her if it was a boy or a girl and she replied: "Oh, it's a Swede."

During my teaching career airplanes weren't very common so when one would fly over the school we would all go out and watch it and then return to the classroom for a discussion about planes. Two activities that were conducted on a regular basis, however, were saying the pledge to the flag every morning and holding fire drills at appropriate times.

I enjoyed the teaching but did not enjoy walking in the winter and wading through snow banks. Roads were not kept cleared in those days. Some days the fire in the stove would go out during the night and the school would be cold in the morning; I didn't enjoy that either.

When my certificate expired I left teaching and decided to become a full-fledged homemaker.

✍✍

A Country School Teacher Remembers — Verna Ellsworth

One day the school board president visited class; he was interested in seeing what each child was doing. I had been allowed to order only one workbook for each of the pupils in the first two grades. One boy slipped his workbook into his desk, I suppose because he didn't want to be watched. I was reprimanded because 1 person out of 17 was not studying. I kept all my pupils busy the rest of the 42 years I taught.

I bought my own hectograph and used it for primary units of study. I always subscribed to the *Grade Teacher* or *Instructor*. I paid for the *Weekly Reader* and *Current Events* myself. I was allowed to order some construction paper and chalk. At Big Bend School the Flasher school superintendent had sold sets of library books to the school

board, convincing them that teachers would buy only books they wanted to read and that his collections were for all the grades. I rather resented that as I would have chosen more books that were suitable for the lower grades. I felt they needed to read more. I generally had boxes of books sent from the State Library.

At one of the places I boarded the man of the house was an atheist, but when he was outside his wife and I listened to religious services on the radio. He was the dictatorial type and always insisted the Germans were right in World War I; he was for Bruno Hauptmann in the Lindbergh kidnapping case.

✍ ✍

4. **Kindness to Others:**—1. To parents. 2. To brothers and sisters. 3. To other members of the family, and friends. 4. To the aged and infirm. 5. To the unfortunate. 6. To the helpless and needy. 7. The Golden Rule.

Forms—(1) Sympathy; (2) deference and consideration; (3) helpfulness; (4) charity; (5) no cruelty or injustice.

(Porterville Collection, NDIRS)

5. **Kindness to Animals**:— 1. To those that serve us. 2. To those that do not harm us—the killing of birds. 3. The killing of those that do us harm. 4. The killing of animals for food. 5. Cruelty to any animal wrong.

6. **Love:**—1. For parents. 2. For brothers and sisters. 3. For other members of family, and friends. 4. For teachers, and all benefactors. 5. For one's neighbors— "Thou shalt love thy neighbor as thy self." 6. For God.

7. **Truthfulness:**—1. In words and action—"Without truth there can be no other virtue" 2. Keeping one's work—promises to do wrong. 3. Distinction between a lie and an untruth. 4. Telling what one does *not know to be true*. 5. Prevarication and exaggeration. 6. The giving of a wrong impression, a form of falsehood. 7. Telling falsehoods for fun.

8. **Fidelity to Duty**:—1. To parents—to assist, comfort, etc. 2. To brothers and sisters—older to assist, etc., younger. 3. To the poor and unfortunate. 4. To the wronged and oppressed. 5. Duty of God.

9. **Obedience:**—1. To parents. 2. To teachers and others in authority. 3. To law. 4. To conscience. 5. To God.

Nature—(1) Prompt; (2) cheerful; (3) implicit; (4) faithful.

10. **Nobility:**—1. Manliness. 2. Magnanimity and generosity. 3. Self-denial and self-sacrifice for others. 4. Bravery in helping or saving others. 5. Confession of injury done another.

11. **Respect and Reverence**: —1. For parents. 2. For teachers. 3. For the aged. 4. For those who have done distinguished service. 5. For those in civil authority.

12. **Gratitude and Thankfulness:**—1. To parents. 2. To all benefactors. 3. To God, the giver of all good.

13. **Forgiveness:**—1. Of those who confess their fault. 2. Of those who have wronged us. 3. Of our enemies. 4. Generosity in dealing with the faults of others.

14. **Confession:—1.** Of wrong done another, manly and noble. 2. Denial of faults— "The denial of a fault doubles it." 3. Frankness and candor.

15. **Honesty**:—1. In keeping one's word. 2. In school and out of school. 3. In little things. 4. Cheating, ignoble and base. 5. "Honesty is the best policy." 6. Honesty is right.

16. **Honor**:—1. To honor one's self; i.e., to be worthy of honor. 2. To honor one's family. 3. To honor one's friends. 4. To honor one's home. 5. To honor one's country.

17. **Courage**:—1. True courage—daring to do right and to defend the right. 2. False—daring to do or to defend the wrong. 3. In bearing unjust censure or unpopularity. 4. In danger or misfortune. 5. Heroism.

18. **Humility**:—1. True greatness—not blind to one's own faults. 2. Modesty becoming to the young. 3. Avoidance of pride and vanity. 4. Self-conceit, a sign of self-deception. 5. True humility, not servility or time-serving.

A Teacher's Creed — Edwin Osgood Grover

I believe in boys and girls, the men and women of a great tomorrow; that whatsoever the boy soweth the man shall reap. I believe in the curse of ignorance, in the efficacy of schools, in the dignity of teaching, and in the joy of serving another. I believe in the wisdom as revealed in human lives, as well as in the pages of a printed book; in lessons taught not so much by precept as by example; in ability to work with the hands as well as think with the head; in everything that makes life large and lovely. I believe in beauty in the schoolroom, in the home, in daily life, in out of doors. I believe in laughter, in love, in all ideals and distant hope that lure us on. I believe that every hour of every day we receive a just reward for all we are and all we do. I believe in the present and its opportunities, in the future and its promises, and in the divine joy of living. Amen.

Source: North Dakota, Department of Public Instruction, *Rural School Management*, 1923, p. 12.

Unknown
school
*(Col.
239/154,
SHSND)*

19. **Self-respect**:—1. Not self-conceit—based on conscious moral worth. 2. Not self-admiration. 3. Resulting in personal dignity. 4. Distinction between self-love and selfishness. 5. "Be not wise in your own conceit."

20. **Self-control**:—1. Control of temper. 2. Anger, when right. 3. Avoidance of hasty words—"Think twice before you speak." 4. Self-restraint when tempted. 5. Self-restraint under provocation—"Bear and forbear." 6. Rule your own spirit.

21. **Prudence**:—1. In speech and action. 2. When one may be misunderstood. 3. Respect for the options of others. 4. "Judge not that ye be not judged."

22. **Good Name**:—1. Gaining a good name when young. 2. Keeping a good name. 3. Keeping good company. 4. Reputation and character.

23. **Good Manners** (*Youth.)*—1. At home. 2. In school. 3. In company. 4. When a visitor or a guest. 5. In public assemblies. 6. Salutations on the street. 7. Politeness to strangers. 8. Trifling in serious matters, to be avoided.

24. **Health**:—1. Duty to preserve health. 2. Habits that impair health, foolish as well as sinful. 3. The sowing of "wild oats"—"What a man sows, that shall he also reap." 4. The body never forgets or forgives its abuse. 5. An observance of the laws of health, a duty.

25. **Temperance**:—1. Moderation in the indulgence of appetite in things not harmful. 2. Total abstinence from that which is injurious. 3. Dangers in the use of alcoholic liquors. 4. Courage to resist social temptation to indulgence. 5. Injurious effects of tobacco on growing boys. 6. Cigarette smoking by boys a serious evil.

26. **Evil Habits**:—1. Those that injure health. 2. That destroy reputation. 3. That dishonor one's self and family. 4. That waste money. 5. That take away self-control. 6. That incur needless risks, as gambling. 7. That are offensive to others, etc.

27. **Bad Language**:—1. Profanity, foolish and wicked. 2. Obscenity, base and offensive. 3. Defiling books or other things with obscene words and characters, a gross offense. 4. The use of slang, vulgar and impolite.

28. **Evil Speaking**:—1. Slander a serious offense. 2. Tale bearing to injure another. 3. Repeating evil which one has heard without knowing that it is true. 4. "Thou shalt not bear false witness against thy neighbor."

29. **Industry**:—1. Labor a duty and a privilege. 2. Right use of time. 3. Manual labor honorable. 4. Self-support gives manly independence. 5. Avoidance of unnecessary debt. 6. When begging is right. 7. An opportunity to earn a living by labor, due every one.

30. **Economy**:—1. Saving in early life means competency and comfort in old age. 2. Duty to save a part of one's earnings—"Lay up something for a rainy day." 3. Extravagance wrong—"A spendthrift in youth, a poor man in old age." 4. The hoarding of money needed for comfort or culture or charity, wrong. 5. Charity— "No man liveth unto himself."

31. **Patriotism**:—1. Love of country. 2. Reverence for its flag. 3. Respect for its rulers. 4. Its defense when necessary. 5. Regard for its honor and good name.

32. **Civil Duties**:—1. Obedience to law. 2. Fidelity in office—bribers. 3. Honor in taking an oath—perjury. 4. Duty involved in the ballot—buying or selling votes. 5. Dignity and honor of citizenship, etc.

A Country School Teacher Remembers — Catherine Lee Fitzgerald

I taught in country schools for 15 years and can say I really enjoyed it for the most part. I taught the "home" school my first year and had 15 pupils, including my brother. That situation may not have been all that good for the children because I knew them all quite well; however, they cooperated very well and were so helpful. I especially appreciated the help the older boys gave me, cutting wood, carrying in the coal, and taking out the ashes.

It was "heavenly" when in 1954 the patrons and school board of the school I taught installed an oil burning heater before the term began. What a pleasant change! No more wood to split, or coal to carry, or ashes to carry out and clean up. We were never so modern as to have indoor plumbing while I taught country school, but we made do with the "little houses" in back of the schoolhouse.

The children were deprived of extra-curricular activities such as music, art, and athletics; but on the whole I think the country school child fared pretty well. They learned from one another by listening to lessons of other classes and probably knew their older classmates' lessons better than theirs. The teacher took a little more time to give individual help to those who needed it and especially to the timid child who had trouble adjusting to a group. I remember a little first grade boy who would not speak above a whisper for the first two months of school, but then did well. He was alone in his grade, and the second child in the family.

Economy

1. Saving in early life means competency and comfort in old age.

2. Duty to save a part of one's earnings— "Lay up something for a rainy day."

3. Extravagance wrong— "A spendthrift in youth, a poor man in old age."

4. The hoarding of money needed for comfort or culture or charity, wrong.

5. Charity— "No man liveth unto himself."

Chapter 18

The Story of the Wohlk Boys and Hazel Miner

Five Students Die in Blizzards

AN AWFUL TRAGEDY*

THE STORM WHICH SWEPT THE STATE MONDAY AND TUESDAY
[March 15-16, 1920] with a fury equaled only by storms recalled by
pioneers will long be remembered by Ryder and vicinity. As farmers and townspeople
were safely within their homes and at their firesides they were unaware of the fact that
four little boys were pitting endurance and pluck against the storm which in blinding
gale put the average blizzards of North Dakota into the flurry [sic] class.

Editor's Note: Beginning Sunday , March 14, 1920 about 10:00 p.m., a light rain began to fall. It
quickly turned to snow and became the storm that took the lives of the five country school students in
North Dakota. The storm eventually covered both Dakotas, Montana, Minnesota, Wisconsin and Iowa. The
high winds and an eight-inch snow fall stopped rail service at Bismarck on March 15th. Only one telephone
line was functioning between Fargo and the Twin Cities, and wires were down between Fargo and Devils
Lake. There were other deaths in North Dakota as a result of the storm: Charles Hutchins, north of Doug-
las; the twelve-year-old son of Matt Yashenko, who lived five miles south of Ruso; "Chicken Pete" Johnson,
a well known Minot character, was found dead in his dug-out on South Hill; and an unsung heroine, Mrs.
Andrew Whitehead, was found frozen to death in a wagon three miles from Fort Totten — she saved her
four-year-old son by shedding some of her own clothing to bundle him in blankets.

The four boys, Adolph, Ernest, Soren and Herman Wohlk, ages respectively 14, 12, 10, 9, left Monday for home after school in an open sleigh. The distance to drive was about two miles. While they were on their way the father Gust Wohlk hitched up a team to go and meet them. The horses refused to face the blinding storm so he was obliged to unhitch and put the horses in the barn. Mr. Wohlk now concluded that since the teacher had board and lodging at the schoolhouse their boys would surely stay over night when those gloomy forebodings cast the parents into gloom concerning the children. The father calmed the anxious mother with the assurance that God would take care of their little ones. Clinging to the hope that the little ones were safe and warm within the schoolhouse they trusted all was well till morning.

Gus Wohlk and five of his seven sons. The oldest four died in the blizzard in March 1920 *(photograph and funeral announcement courtesy of Gorlyn Wohlk)*

In the meanwhile the boys got stuck with the rig about ¾ mile from home in a slough in the road which had during the terrific storm become filled with snow. It seems that after attempting to have the horses plunge thru the horses became exhausted and were unable to rise. The two oldest boy[s] [got] out of the sleigh, unhitched the horses and sought to get them out but the horses only turned their backs on the weather and refused to move and in this position they remained until found the next day. Too wet and exhausted to crawl back into the sleigh Ernest aged twelve sank into the snow and fell asleep. Adolph the oldest evidently realizing the desperate danger struck out for home.

Reaching the lane that leads from the road to the house Adolph was obliged to face the blinding hurricane. Unable to do this he turned and attempted to back against the weather the short distance of 15 rods left. Overcome by exhaustion and the storm he fell face forward. Attempting to rise he must have lost consciousness in this crouching attitude he remained until found the next forenoon. The two brothers in the sleigh were huddled together. The older one from the marks on his face must have been weeping. But ten years old he realized the danger. He had then covered his younger brother and thus with his body he sheltered Herman's face and breast. The youngest dozed into the icy sleep. His features remained in calm repose as if dreaming. This shelter offered by the shelter of Soren kept him alive until his father found him but his soul left the frozen body while the father took them home.

Adolph lived but two hours after being brought home. He never gained consciousness.

The little boys were devoted to one another. They were members of the St. John Lutheran Sunday School. Not only

*Source: *Ryder News*, March 25, 1920, p. 1.

Editor's Note: The boys' father, Gus Wohlk, was born in Schleswig-Holstein, Germany, May 26, 1870. Once the personal bodyguard to Field Marshal Von Hindenburg he came to the United States at age 24, settling in Breckenridge, Minnesota. In 1910 he homesteaded south of Ryder in Hiddenwood Township in McLean County.

IN LOVING REMEMBRANCE OF

Adolph Wohlk, Aged 14.
Ernest Wohlk, Aged 13.
Sorn Wohlk, Aged 10.
Herman Wohlk, Aged 9.
Died March 16, 1920.

Gone but not forgotten

Four little angels now on high,
They hand in hand together roam,
Four links now bind us to the sky,
Four fingers beckon us to come.
Lord give us strength our loss to bear,
And lead us in the Heavenly way,
Oh! may we meet our children there,
In realms of everlasting day.

Copyright 1906 by H. F. Wendell, Leipsic, Ohio.

the pastor and congregation from whose midst these little ones have left the village of Ryder the community and countryside extend to these grief stricken parents their sincerest sympathy.

The funeral services were held the following Saturday, at the Lutheran church of Ryder. Rev. T. S. Stockdal officiated.

These children were the only ones present at school that day.

⋐ ⋑

THE STORY OF HAZEL MINER

HAZEL MINER IS THE LEGENDARY HEROINE of North Dakota's country schools. The story of how she spread her coat and lay above her younger brother and sister after their sled turned over in a coulee in a blizzard was commemorated in a song by the state's Centennial Troubadour, Chuck Suchy in 1989. Oliver County, her home, erected a monument to her memory on the Court House grounds in Center after her sacrifice, for Hazel Miner froze to death, but her brother and sister lived.

Forty-three years after the event, her brother Emmett recalled the events for a reporter from the *Bismarck Tribune* (March 16, 1963):

Brother She Saved Recalls
How Hazel Miner Met Death

Emmet Miner, Bismarck, painting contractor who lives today because of his older sister's heroism, Saturday recalled the blizzard of 43 years ago that took Hazel Miner's life.

"She had us sing songs and holler a lot to keep us from falling asleep," he said, describing the long hours during which Hazel and he and a smaller sister lay in their overturned sled.

The three spent part of one day, and entire night and well into the afternoon of the next day before a search party found them.

Hazel was dead by that time, and Emmett, then 11, and the younger sister, Meredith, 9, were badly frozen. Emmett and Meredith were taken to a nearby farm house where they were put to bed and their frost-bitten limbs rubbed to restore circulation.

He recalled that the day the blizzard started was not particularly cold, maybe about 15 above zero. But the storm came up fast and visibility was quickly zero in the part of Oliver County where they lived.

"Our dad rode a horse to the schoolhouse from our farm

ABOVE IS A ROUGH MAP, based upon Emmett Miner's recollections, showing how Hazel Miner and her younger sister and brother became lost in a storm while trying to return to their Oliver County home from school March 15, 1920. Figure 1 indicates the gate through which they should have started home. Figure 2, the gate they did use and the route they followed. Figure 3 indicates where they had trouble crossing a ravine, and Figure 4 indicates the route followed by their father down the ravine in search for them. At Figure 5, they attempted to turn through a gate, but were blocked by a big drift of snow, and Figure 6 shows where their sled tipped and Hazel died while protecting the others from the cold. Figure 7 indicates nearby haystacks where they might have found protection and Figure 8 the farmhouse nearby where they heard a dog, alarmed by their nearness, barking through the night.

(which was a couple of miles north of the school) to see that we got home all right," recalled Emmett Miner.

The father, said Emmett, told his children to head their horse north and wait for him while he got his saddle horse from the school barn. But somehow the horse pulling the sled — a small, two-runner "jumper" with a little cab built onto it — got headed in the wrong direction, and left the schoolyard through the south gate instead of the north.

"Dad lost us right there. He thought we'd started home, and started riding home to catch up with us." Of course he never did. Others have reported that the father reached the schoolhouse just after his children left.

Hazel Miner, Emmett and Meredith were now headed in the easterly direction through the blinding storm when they should have been headed north, as Emmett recalls it. At one point, he says, he saw some telephone wires and knew they were going in the wrong direction. So they veered to the north.

But pretty soon they slanted down the steep sides of a coulee and at the bottom the horse and sled wallowed in deep mushy snow. A tug came loose, and Hazel stepped out to rehook it. She was wearing one-buckle overshoes, Emmett remembers, and she broke through the snow crust and became wet almost to her waist. But they got the tug hooked up again and started out once more. And once again they drifted away from home instead of toward it. Part of the time one of them led the horse.

Finally, as they tried to turn near the bottom of another coulee the sled tipped.

Hazel D.
Miner at
age 15
(SHSND)

"It wouldn't have been so bad but the sled had been standing by the barn, and the range horses had torn the canvas, so there was no way to keep the cold wind out." says Emmett.

Meanwhile their father and others were searching for them. The father, says Emmett, waded for several miles down the long deep coulee they were crossing when the tug had come unhooked. But they had crossed before he got there. When night came, searchers had to give up until morning.

"All night long, we could hear a dog barking not far away," says Emmett. "But nobody came. The old horse stood there all night long, hitched to our tipped-over jumper. His nose and eyes froze shut, and he banged his head against the sled once in a while, but he never tried to move away."

Emmett says that Hazel did not remove her coat to put it over the smaller children but opened it to share its warmth with them."She sort of fell on us, and her open coat helped cover us."

He recalls that the next day it was discovered that only a few yards from the overturned sled were two or three haystacks that mght have provided good shelter.

The day they left the school was March 15, 1920. The day they were found was March 16. Today a monument stands at Center to Hazel Miner. Meredith lives now at Chewelah, Wash., near Spokane.

LOST IN BLIZZARD
Three Children Of William Miner
Lost In Storm On Way
From School

Source: *The Center Republican*
March 18, 1920

*H*azel Miner, the 16 year old daughter of Mr. and Mrs. William Miner, perished in the blizzard which swept this part of state Monday and Tuesday while attempting to make it home from school.

Monday afternoon, Mr. Miner who lives about two and one half miles north of the consolidated school, which lies 5 miles east of this place, started out on horseback to escort his children home from school.

continued on next page

The three children, Hazel, aged sixteen, Emmett, aged eleven, and Meredith, not quite 9 years old, were accustomed to drive back and forth from school in a light covered sleigh. Upon arriving at the tool house Mr. Miner hitched up the horse to the cutter and told the children to wait until he could get his saddle horse from the schoolhouse barn only a few rods away. When he returned he found the children had already started for home. Passing through the north gate of the schoolhouse yard they disappeared in the storm, and for twenty-five hours were exposed to the bitter elements. The father, hoping to overtake his children, hurried on but soon realized that they had lost their way. He then went home, noti-

continued on next page

HAZEL D. MINER

Source: Obituary exactly as it appeared in
The Center Republican

Hazel Dulcie Miner was born at Sanger, April fourth, 1904, and perished in the blizzard on Tuesday, March 16, 1920, while making a successful attempt to preserve the lives of her brother Emmett and sister Murdith.

With the exception of about two years spent at Staples, Minn., her life was lived in Oliver county.

Hers was a quiet, retiring, loving disposition. She did not seem greatly to care for gaiety but possessed a sunny cheerful nature. She was a great lover of children who never hesitated to bring their troubles to her and found her always a helpful, sympathizing friend.

Hazel would have finished the eighth grade this year and hoped to enroll in the Bismarck high school next fall.

A large concourse of people gathered at the M.E. church for the last sad rites of the girl whose memory they will ever hold dear.

Rev. Madsen preached a very impressive sermon from the text "Greater love hath no man than that he layeth down his life for his friend" and from the scripture "he saved others, himself he cannot save."

In graphic terms he pictured the sacrificial life and death of our Savior and drew a comparison. Here and there are occasionally people who by their acts and lives endeavor to imitate Him.

The choir sang "Rock of Ages," "Face to Face" and "Some Day the Silver Cord Will Break."

Monument to Hazel Miner in Center, North Dakota:
"In Memory
of
HAZEL MINER
April 11, 1904
March 16, 1920
To the dead a tribute
To the living a memory
To posterity an inspiration
THE STORY OF HER LIFE AND OF HER HEROIC TRAGIC DEATH IS RECORDED IN THE ARCHIVES OF OLIVER COUNTY ON PAGES 130-131, BOOK H, MISC. RECORDS STRANGER READ IT."
(Photograph by Warren A. Henke)

fied his wife what had happened, and started out in search of the lost ones.

The alarm was quickly given over the phones, several searching parties were soon out on the prairies where they remained until it became so dark and perilous that the search had to be given over until daylight Tuesday morning.

At nine o'clock Tuesday morning word came to Center that no trace had yet been found of the missing ones and request was sent in for more help. A party of fourteen men volunteered for service. After some delay in securing a team C.S. Sorensen agreed to make the attempt.

The others in the party were Rev. C.B. Madsen, W.H. Rappuhn, Ernest Wick, Henry Cordes, Jr., L.D. Monson, Jimmie Maher, Roy Light, Paul Wolff, Myron Simon, Harry Potter, Harry Clark, Gus Mantz and E.F. Mutchler.

Teams were changed at the W.H. Herrington farm, and the party pushed on to the schoolhouse and teacherage. After a light lunch the south half of section fifteen was gone over without result. This land lies north and east of the schoolhouse. A conference was then held at the Tom McCrea buildings a mile or more east. While this conference was being held with numerous parties most of whom had been out since daylight, Gus Mantz and a few men who had been with him came in and reported that they believed they had struck the trail a short distance to the northeast. Investigation proved the trail to be that made by a single horse and sled. This track led to the west line of T. Stark's pasture when it turned south on the section line and again east where all signs were obliterated. Immediately about thirty men some on foot, others on horseback, and several bobsleds stretching out for a distance of half a mile or more started east and south where in a coulee a mile south of T. Starks the upset sled with horse still attached was found.

With breathless haste we hurried to the rig and will never forget the sight that met our eyes.

Hazel the oldest daughter had placed two blankets underneath the smaller ones, one over them, and had lain down to her last sleep without covering of any kind save the clothing she had on.

Lifting the cover Emmett and his little sister were found to be still alive. They were lifted carefully into the waiting sleds, taken to Mr. Stark's home and tenderly cared for.

Whether the children did not understand their father's injunction to wait for him or whether the horse started off by himself is not known. The horse was a very gentle one and was driven without out a bridle and had not stirred after the tip over and had remained in her tracks evidently since early Monday evening until two o'clock Tuesday afternoon. Any movement would have spilled the precious human freight in the snow.

Harry Clark and Dave Monson remained in the country that night to help care for the children.

Funeral arrangements of the daughter will be announced later.

This community extends its sympathy to the bereaved parents in their sad affliction.

From the position of her body holding down the cover over her little brother and sister, to keep them from freezing, and from the story told by little Emmett, it is known that Hazel died a heroine sacrificing her life to save them.

[The story told by young Emmett] is substantially as follows:

Papa told us to wait for him but the horse started off and we could not hold her. After a while we got into an awful place, the tugs came unhooked, Hazel got out and hooked them up, she got into the water, she said oh, my! I am wet clear to the waist and my shoes are full of water. (This must have been in the coulee just north of the J.C. Wilson place, the children having passed within 200 feet of the house but could not see it.) When Hazel got the horse hitched up she led the horse until she was tired out then I helped her. When we tipped over Hazel was thrown out over the dash board, Hazel then fastened the robe over the back of the sled to keep out the wind. The robe kept blowing down and Hazel kept putting it up until she got so she couldn't put it up any more. Then she covered us up with the robe and lay down on top of it, I told Hazel to get in under the covers too but she said she had to keep us children warm and she wouldn't do it. She kept talking to us telling us not to go to sleep and told us to keep moving our feet so they wouldn't freeze. She kept punching us and told us to punch each other to keep awake. I tried to get out to put the cover over Hazel but I could not move because she was lying on the cover.

The snow would get in around our feet so we couldn't move them, then Hazel would break the crust for us. After a while she could not break the crust any more. She just lay still and groaned. After a while she stopped groaning, I thought she must be dead, then I kept talking to Meredith so she wouldn't go to sleep.

The funeral service of Hazel Miner will be held at the home Friday at ten thirty A.M. and at the M.E. church in Center at one o'clock. Rev. Madsen officiating.

✍✍

Editor's Note: Spelling and punctuation has been changed in the article above to improve clarity.

The Story of Hazel Miner

Centennial Troubadour Chuck Suchy, 1989

Wings on snow, a fate not chose,
morning finds a dove so froze.
Who too soon thought the spring arrived,
in warmth below love survived.

Up in Oliver County, on the North Dakota plain,
lived a farmer's daughter, Hazel Miner was her name.
She was soon to come in bloom, a prairie rose of spring,
she'd never seen the young-girl-dreams her sixteenth year would bring.

A nineteen-twenty mid-March storm caused school to let out early
so each child could reach their farm before the blizzard's fury.
With her brother, sister bundled tight, Hazel hitched the sleigh,
but in the night of blinding white, she somehow lost her way.

For half a day they plodded on, then darkness and desparation,
Hazel put the young ones down and lay her body o're them.
Through the night she gave them songs and stories to sustain,
near the dawn, her strength all gone, three by sleep were claimed.

Hush a bye, don't you cry, cold is like a sorrow,
Sing a song, it won't be long, you'll be warm tomorrow.

Silent song, paling wind,
storm at end, again begin
not all to soar the winds aloft.
Stiffened wings, feathers soft.

The next day the searchers came, found the horse still standin'
it's eyes and nose frozen closed, no duty more demandin'.
They lifted Hazel from the snow, only limp her hair.
With sadness, joy, the girl and boy alive beneath her there.

"Going to School in the Frozen North," 1921 — on the way to Shields
School, from four miles in the country, Eva Dilley on right
(Grant Co., Col GT/14a-3, SHSND)

A Country School Teacher Remembers — Evelyn Lonning Conitz

I began my teaching career in 1949-1950 in
Little Heart District No. 4 near St. Anthony, North
Dakota. The major incentive that brought me to a
life-time career in teaching was a project in the
late 1940s sponsored by the Delta Kappa Gamma
Society in which high school girls could observe
teachers in the Mandan-Bismarck area.

I boarded with the George and Julia Wetsch
family and their three children. Mrs. Wetsch gave
me a private room, did my washing and ironing
and provided all the meals for $45 per month. Mr.
Wetsch took the children and me to school each
day and started the fire if necessary.

Winter was severe for everyone during my first
year of teaching. Mr. Wetsch would haul us to
school each day in a sleigh pulled by two horses,
after the snow became so deep that using his Ford
car became impossible. We had to use that mode
of travel for several weeks until the day before
Good Friday. The children and I snuggled under a
huge quilt in the back of the sleigh and many
times I would look out from under the covers and
see a worried look on his face as he wondered if
the horses knew which way to go in the raging

blizzards. We had so many storms that year.
Sometimes we would get to school and have to
turn right around and return home because of a
bad storm. On the return trip the horses would
know the way and keep to the trail that had been
built up during the winter drive every day. When
we arrived at the house there were often many
stranded motorists there; they could no longer
continue their trip to Flasher or Mandan. The
road was gravel and often got blocked with snow
easily. Mrs. Wetsch saw to it that she always had
extra food and bedding on hand, to feed and
house as many as 12 extra guests sometimes. The
house had no upstairs or basement so the huge
living room served as a haven for the stranded
people. There was no electricity or telephone service in 1949-1950 in the St. Anthony area. During
blizzards we kept in touch with the outside world
by listening to the Wetsch's battery-powered radio, often weak because of continued use. Ca-
nasta was the card game of that time and so we
played cards many wintry evenings.

Chapter 19

One Day at a Country School *

Isabel Wolf Werner

MY FIRST DAY OF SCHOOL DECIDED FOR ME WHAT I WAS TO become as it opened to me the most wonderful world I had ever known, and to the last day of my career the school room never lost its charm.

A typical school day required a teacher to be a good disciplinarian, a custodian, recreational director, nurse, musician and cook. She also had to possess a fine character including cleanliness and good manners. The ringing of a hand bell summoned ages six through fourteen to stack their dinner pails and hang their coats in the long narrow cloakroom. Nearly all stopped at the crock belly-shaped water container. It had been filled with water obtained from the well on the ground but there was no ice.

*Isabel Wolf Werner taught elementary grades for thirty-one years. She taught country school in Oliver County from 1939 to 1945. She comments on a typical school day. The sketches are by Elvera Hintz, a student of Isabel Wolf Werner.

The fifteen minutes of opening exercises varied after we recited the Pledge of Allegiance to the Flag. I might read from a book — *Black Beauty*, *Beautiful Joe*, a *Bobbsey Twin* book, etc. If a birthday child was in our midst we'd sing the birthday song and explain and present each of the handmade cards. (Wallpaper catalogs were widely used as art sources.) Each student would share a current event. A group of students could dramatize a scene from a book or story. Poems could be recited. (All my students enjoyed memorizing.) We might play a game on a wall map by placing a pin on the location named. (The first and second graders were sharp doing this.) Other ideas — riddles about people, places, and things; mental arithmetic such as "6x2+12 -3="; going to the playstore in our room to choose items, to give payment, and to receive right change (We had a play store stocked with empty cartons and play money, but no calculator.)

Other favorite choices were games such as Teakettle. A student would give a sentence substituting the word teakettle for a synonym. For example: "A big black *teakettle* was in the park." The person answering would pronounce "bear," spell it, and spell its synonym. Another game for all was "I'm going on a trip with Aunt Jemima. I'll take along a toothbrush." Each student had to repeat the previous sentences with all the articles named in right order and add one of his own. This trained the memory of all.

Next we'd have the reading block for one hour. The seventh and eighth grades would have literature. At 10:30 there would be fifteen minutes of supervised play. Often the students would prefer to remain in for teacher help at this time if the outdoor weather was unfavorable.

After recess we'd have arithmetic skills. Groups would be combined. Spelling and penmanship were stressed in all content subjects. However, I usually tried to have a fifteen minute session for spelling for all grades. This usually consisted of work in their workbooks. The pronunciation and definition of words were cared for with the reading.

In my second school we received a government grant of potatoes, onions, carrots, etc., so the soup I had prepared before school had simmered all morning in a big iron kettle resting on a flat platform at the top of the potbelly stove and was ready to be doled out after the hands were washed. Our noon hour was just one half hour, but if we were really excited in our involvement in a softball game or whatever we might run over some time. After all, counting scores was arithmetic too.

The first ten minutes after noon we would continue the opening exercises we didn't finish in the morning. The next thirty-five or forty minutes there would be more

"Playing Hide and Seek" — The large square rock in the school yard served as home base. *(Drawing by Elvera Hintz)*

Elvera Hintz
81

271

A Country School Teacher Remembers — Anna M. Gallagher

My desire to become a teacher grew over the years. I admired teachers, enjoyed going to school, loved to read, and liked to help others with their math problems. Probably the one incident that helped make up my mind happened in the sixth grade. I had been unfairly treated by the teacher when he gave me a D in mathematics on my report card, every month, in spite of my perfect daily papers. I was a very shy withdrawn child and could not complain or fight back to the teacher. Then and there I made the decision and decided I would always help children who had problems. This incident unconsciously affected my teaching children who had learning disabilities. I was drawn to them.

As a teacher I urged achievement in all areas. When some pupils questioned the necessity of studying certain material, I stopped to explain the why and wherefore of it. At times discussions arose which were prompted by pupils who questioned the need of a particular study. A funny thing happened the first week in a fourth grade history class. I introduced the text that included a series of stories about people. They sat there not too interested because it was dull. While I was explaining the meaning of history a boy yelled suddenly, "You make it sound as if it really happened." The comment caught me by surprise. I said, "Of course it did. What did you think?" Then they told me they thought these were just stories someone made up. No one had ever explained to them that they were true.

I never chose to stay more than two years in a school. I guess it was a local custom. I taught two years in a school in Rolette County and then went back to it about seven years later.

The most notable changes in country schools that occurred during my teaching career were improvements in school buildings, more up-to-date and better textbooks, and having permission to order supplies needed which in early days was denied either because of lack of funds or not understanding our needs. Salaries also began to increase.

One incident that comes to mind happened in April 1941. It had rained and a spring blizzard set in, not really serious but nasty. Children from one family living two miles away walked to school barefooted because they had no more shoes. But they were happy and wanted to come. They were the only ones that came. We had a good day.

continued on next page

reading for the first four grades. The fourth grade would have geography or history. For twenty minutes the fifth, sixth, and seventh grades would have a geography unit. These units would be alternated for three years. The eighth grade would have fifteen minutes for history.

At two o'clock they would go out for fifteen minutes of supervised play. In the spring play stressed races of various kinds, high and broad jumps, throwing the discus, etc. These sports prepared them to compete with the other schools in the district on Field Day usually held in mid-May.

At 2:15 the seventh grade would alternate health and agriculture for fifteen minutes. They would have county examinations in both of these subjects at the end of the year.

For fifteen minutes the first three grades would have a reading lesson stressing social studies, science, or language. This would be followed by the same subjects for grades four, five, and six. The last fifteen minutes the seventh and eighth grades would have citizenship three days and history two days. On Friday I usually tried to use the last half hour for art projects, picture study, choral reading, storytelling, Junior Red Cross, a map game, or a baseball spelling game in which all grades participated — fun games which involved penmanship as well as correct spelling, usage and so on.

In favorable weather mothers frequently walked to school to visit. Rarely did I have mothers to help, but they would observe a unit on arithmetic problems so they could help their offspring.

To give me more time to help the upper grades, I had them take turns conducting some of the lower grade drills. This allowed two classes to go on at the same time.

One of my favorite lesson plans was to choose a unit that would involve all grades according to their abilities. For example, "Building a House" would involve study about kinds of soil, digging a basement, area, perimeter, volume, interior decorating, architecture, paint, wallpaper, buying lumber, building furniture according to scale, choice of shingles, siding, landscaping, sanitation, health conditions, location according to climate, topography, etc. The culmination of the unit would be the display of a cardboard house, with a hanged roof, made according to scale. Each room

"Enjoying the Ride Home" — The artist says "this is another scene of the fun we had when someone came with the team. Sometimes one of the kids would tie his sled behind and catch a fast ride home. A couple of kids were lucky and had horses to ride." (Drawing by Elvera Hintz)

would be painted and/or papered, carpeted and furnished. The first grade would provide numerous huge reading sheets having sentences they printed after they formulated them. The second grade might recite the poems: "My Shadow," "The Swing," "The Violet," "Come Little Leaves," and read from charts they prepared. Thus each grade had an opportunity to contribute. In addition to learning new vocabulary, mathematics, language, comprehensive reading, critical reading, and new study habits, a unit such as this developed character and citizenship training.

After dismissal students were engaged doing their chores: erasing the blackboards, washing the boards, cleaning erasers, spreading sweeping compound on the floor, bringing the water for washing hands the next day, dusting when necessary, taking the flag down from the pole, making sure small kindling was carried for a fire if needed the next morning, and any other task that was required.

Sometimes students would remain voluntarily (or by teacher's invitation) for help if the days weren't too short. After the departure of all the scholars I would sweep the floor, split more kindling, and make sure I had chunks of coal in readiness for the following day. Often helpful fathers (or older brothers) would stop and get enough fuel ready for a week or two or three.

The mile journey home on foot to my boarding place was a welcome relief if my load of books and papers was not too burdensome.

❧ ❧

I think the country school system was a good system. In a rural school a child was an individual who received help when needed. There was a one-to-one contact. The child was made to feel important. The rural family life style helped much. Every child had an equal chance.

I think the country school system was a good system. In a rural school a child was an individual who received help when needed. There was a one-to-one contact. The child was made to feel important. The rural family life style helped much. Every child had an equal chance. Although I had to teach many classes a day, other children in the room benefited by listening. What was wrong was a lack of money and in some cases school boards and parents had old fashioned ideas about what was needed. School boards sometimes hired unqualified teachers, teachers who couldn't do the job.

❧ ❧

One Room School

Centennial Troubadour Chuck Suchy, 1987

Wind playin'tag with the tattered flag
raised in the cool of the morn.
A gatherin' scene of hopes and dreams
in the next generation born.

Like grain that is grown, seeds of knowledge were sown
deep in the sod, rich and cool.
Now wheat amber waves as plows stir the graves
of the white little one room schools.

   A B C, one two three
   Far back to the golden rule,
   I often turn to lessons learned
   in a white little one room school.

Given the means to imagine scenes
of the world far beyond those doors,
We'd carry those tales like cold-lunch pails
home to our evenin' chores.

Tauntings, laughs, first-loves' epitaphs
carved in the desk top cruel.
Like boots round the stove, young minds unfroze
in a white little one room school.

   A B C . . .

Give thanks and praise for noble days
of knowing those old vestibules
That harbored ships long launched from their slips
from white little one room schools.

   A B C, one two three, far back to the golden rule
   Often I turn to lessons learned in a white little one room school.

Offin I tern to lessins lernd in a wite littel wun room skool. (ps. 1997)

Recess

above,
Bennett
School,
Calisthenics,
1926
(SHSND)

center-left,
New Play-
ground Equip-
ment at One-
room School,
McLean County
(SHSND)

center-right,
School Play-
ground c.a.
1903-1913,
Williams County
(Martha P.
Tatem Collec-
tion, SHSND)

Left, School
Playground c.a.
1903-1913,
Williams County
(Martha P.
Tatem Collec-
tion, SHSND)

275

Chapter 20

Cost of a Country School

*S*TILL IN OPERATION IN 1997, Sweet Briar No. 17 is an art deco building where six boys and five girls attended classes in the 1996-97 school year, including one kindergarten student who came for 90 days.

The cost of educating the eleven youngsters for the 1996-97 school year was $64,681.06, including tuition paid for students from the district to attend high school at $20,252.62 and a special education assessment of $6,915.98. The elementary school costs were $31,979.13, including $2,907.20 paid for instructing the kindergarten student and the rest for elementary instruction. The teacher was paid a salary

Source: North Dakota, Morton County, Superintendent of Schools, Sweet Briar No. 17, *Records.*

*Sweet Briar
School
District No.
17
(1981
photograph
by Warren A.
Henke)*

of $20,148.66 and $2,643.37 in benefits. It cost $3,677.61 to maintain the physical plant. The school board costs totaled $610.74; business services $854.54.

The Financial Statement issued by the Treasurer for 1912-1913 discloses a total expenditure of $943.40 for educating 22 students in School No. 1 for the Spring Session (April 14 - July 3, 1913), 12 students in School No. 2 for the same session (April 7 - June 27, 1913), and 12 students for the Fall Session at School No. 2 (September 1 - December 19, 1912).

The report form provided by the State of North Dakota listed "male" and "female" teachers separately: Joseph E. O'Connell received $165 for teaching the Spring Session at School No. 1 ($55/month). The official report incorrectly lists $655 paid female teachers. There was only one who received $55/month for teaching both ses-

A Country School Teacher Remembers — Alvin M. Tschosik

A one-room rural school is being built in Emmons County this summer—1988.

In 1955 there were 41 school districts and 89 one-room rural schools operating in Emmons County. With the reorganization and annexation of school districts in the 1950s and 1960s the number of districts was reduced to nine with no one-room rural schools in Emmons County. Two of the districts, namely Glanavon and Union, have not operated a school in their respective districts since 1960.

In the past, students, both elementary and high school, from Glanavon and Union districts in Emmons County, have been educated in Pollock, South Dakota, which is located approximately three miles south of the North Dakota border. An agreement has been signed annually by the chief school officers of North Dakota and South Dakota for the education of these students. The distance to Pollock is much shorter than to schools in North Dakota.

A law (Senate Bill 2044) was passed by the 1987 North Dakota Legislature, which requires school districts to either operate a grade school or merge with one that does. To remain independent Glanavon School District is seeking annexation to Union School District. (Petitions are at present filed in the Emmons County Superintendent's office —1988)

Union School District is building a one-room school, constructed of wooden material with modern conveniences. It will begin operation in September 1988 with approximately 13 elementary students living in the Glanavon and Union area. Bus transportation will be provided for these students.

For the first time in 40 years, Emmons County will have a new one-room rural school.

Financial Statement

BONDS

1. Amount of bonds outstanding July 1, 1912 .... $..............
2. Amount of bonds issued during the year .... $..............
3. Total amount of bonds issued and outstanding .... $..............
4. Amount of bonds redeemed during the year .... $..............
5. Balance of bonds outstanding June 30, 1913 .... $..............
   Average rate of interest on all bonds outstanding ....per cent. $..............

WARRANTS

A. Total amount of warrants outstanding July 1, 1912 .... $..............
1. Amount issued during the year in payment of (a) Schoolhouses, $............
   (b) Sites, $.............. (c) Permanent Improvements, $ *89.90*
   Total .... $ *89.91*

   (NOTE.—Include under the above all outbuildings, fences, wells and other permanent improvements, and desks, tables, chairs, stoves, blackboards and other permanent furnishings of like nature.)

2. Amount issued during year in payment of apparatus, fixtures, libraries, etc., Total .... $..............

   (NOTE.—Library books, maps, charts, standard dictionary, etc., not including fuel, crayons, erasers, etc., for temporary use.)

3. Amount issued during the year in payment of teachers' wages (a) male, $ *165* (b) female, $ *655*
   Total .... $ *720*
4. Amount issued during the year in payment of services and expenses of school officers .... $ *78.35*
5. Amount issued for interest on bonds, $............; warrants, $............
   Total .... $..............

   (NOTE.—Warrant should be issued at end of the year for all interest paid.)

6. Amount paid in payment of Tuition to other School Districts .... $..............
7. Amount paid for transportation of pupils .... $..............
8. Amount paid for in payment of incidental expenses .... $..............
9. Amount issued for redemption of bonds .... $..............
10. Amount issued for purposes not before mentioned ...... *66.35* $ *55.15*
11. Grand total amount of warrants issued for all purposes during the year........ $ *943.40*

    (NOTE.—Sum of Items 1 to 10.)

12. Total amount of warrants issued and outstanding July 1, 1912 ...... $..............

    (Sum of Item A and Item 11.)

13. Total amount of warrants redeemed by County and District Treasurer between July 1, 1912, and June 30, 1913, inclusive .... $ *943.40*
14. Balance of warrants outstanding June 30, 1913 .... $..............

INDEBTEDNESS

1. Amount of interest on warrants outstanding, June 30, 1913 .... $..............
2. Total indebtedness of District June 30, 1913 .... $..............

   (NOTE.—Add Item No. 5 of Bonds, No. 14 of Warrants, and No. 1 of Indebtedness.)

3. Increase of Indebtedness during the year .... $..............
4. Decrease of Indebtedness during the year .... $..............

CASH

1. Amount of school money in hands of District Treasurer, June 30, 1913........... $ *982.10*

Former country schools in North Dakota have become country clubs, bars, township meeting halls, homes, granaries, and a rest stop for travelers as this one maintained by the Rocks and Rills Homemaker's Club in 1981
(Photograph by Warren A. Henke)

sions, and if the total of $720 is correct, she was paid for ten months at $55/month. The District spent $89.90 on improving its plant, $78.35 for administrative services, and $66.35 for "purposes not before mentioned." At the end of the year, the District had $982.10 in the bank.

The following table offers a summary of the cost of educating youngsters at Sweet Briar No. 17 in grades one through eight in 1912-13 and 84 years later in 1996-97:

1912-1913 — Total	$ 943.40	Total # Students	34	Per Student/per month cost — 1912-1913
Percent/Salaries	76 %	Total Student Months (# times months of term)	106	$ 8.90
Teachers' Monthly Salary	$ 55.00			
1912-13 Salary in 1997 Dollars	$ 890.00			
1912-13 Budget in 1997 Dollars	$15,265.93	Cost/per student/month in 1997 Dollars		$144.02
Based upon $1.00 in 1913 having buying power of $16.18 in 1997				
1996-1997 — Total for Grades 1-8	$34,605.26	Total # Students	10	Per Student/per month cost — 1996-1997
Percent/Salaries	66%	Total Student Months (# times months of term)	90	$384.50
Teachers' Monthly Salary	$ 2,532.44	Real salary increase of 284% over 84 years; cost per student/month increased 267 percent.		

A country school in 1997 costs more than twice as much to operate as it did in 1913 in comparable dollars; in this case four times as much because the 1913 Sweet Briar District #17 operated two schools.

Chapter 21

The Center of the Universe

Everett C. Albers

THEY'RE GONE NOW, THOSE TWO BUILDINGS ACROSS THE PASTURE to the west of the farm where I grew up in Hannover Township, Oliver County, North Dakota. A half-century ago, I stood as a six-year-old by the flag pole that divided the "little school" from the "big school."

That September morning in 1948 was the first day of eight years in those two schools which were the center of my universe. When I close my eyes and look into those huge south windows, I hear once more the scratching chalk looping in perfect Palmer penmanship a nursery rhyme in German: *"Fuchs du hast die Gans gestohlen."* ("Fox, you stole the goose.") I smell that curiously purple sweeping compound

Everett C. Albers

The "little school" (left) and "big school" (right) at Hannover with the flag pole between them. Hannover children are now bussed to Center six miles away. The buildings were sold and removed after the parochial school closed in 1979. The parochial school opened in 1915, closed because of WWI in 1918, but held classes continuously from 1924 to closing — it became a public school temporarily during the Depression in 1932-33 and 1938-39. *(1981 photograph by Warren A. Henke)*

which came in huge cylinders which became the waste basket. I smell the lignite burning in the stove in the center of the little school and the unforgettable odor of the only-weekly completely washed bodies of the twenty to thirty first to fourth graders packed into that tiny room dominated by the teacher's desk. I hear again our voices pledging allegiance "to the flag of the United States of America and to the republic for which it stands, one nation" — not yet "under God" in 1948, a phrase that confused us all mightily when it was officially added in 1954. By then, I was in the "big school," where grades five to eight were taught. The big school was parochial, Missouri Synod Lutheran. In the big school, there was a separate room where we attended religion class each morning. We knew that the phrase "under God," had been added by Congress because of a campaign by the Knights of Columbus, the national Catholic laymen's organization. In Hannover Township in 1954, we were much more concerned about the influence of the Catholics who lived six miles to the east than we were of the Communists, although the daily news of the nuclear arms race with the Soviet Union and the possibility of the end of the world commanded no few of the conversations at noon over our Cloverdale baloney from the Hannover store on homemade bread sandwiches. But it remained a greater insult to call a schoolmate a Catholic than to suggest he was a Communist.

There were but four in the first grade that fall of 1948 in the little school — which was public. Three boys and a girl, and like those ahead in the seven grades which stretched before us in an eternity, if the world was not blown up before we made it through, we were all somewhat related. The Hannover community was settled in the 1880s by Plattdeutsch from Illinois and southern Minnesota who had come to America the generation before. They were related as well, so by the time we great-grandchildren of the founders started school, the Henkes, Bornemanns, Bargmans, Kitzmanns, Rabes, Bueligans, Meyers, Maiers, Oestrichs, Kochs, Reiners, Fleischers, Skubinnas, Beckers, Buchmanns, Klingensteins, Keuthers, Albers, and a few other

280

clans knew each other pretty well. At home, we spoke no German, but both my parents could understand the low German of their parents, and both had been schooled in high German, the German of Luther's Bible. When I was growing up, there were still two services every Sunday in the church next to the school: one in English and one in German. My mother was confirmed in German, my father in English — it was a matter of family choice by the early 1920s. Both German school and church were suspended for a time during World War I, but resumed shortly thereafter. But we all knew neighbors who spoke only German at home.

We four first graders — two Henkes, a Hintz and an Albers — didn't really have school in 1948-49. After fifty years, perhaps we can now tell the truth. Our teacher didn't want to bother with us, for the most part, so we played — outdoors in the fall and spring, in the basement in a sandbox throughout the winter, except for those long weeks when no one left home because of the deep snow. February and March 1949 was the year North Dakota's 5th Army had to come dig out Oliver County. There were weeks when no mail was delivered. It was just as well, for we were bored as stiff as our long johns frozen on our mothers' clothes lines in the winter with the new "Dick and Jane" books. We could see little point in seeing "Dick run" or "Spot jump." Contrary the raging defense of teaching phonetics fifty years later, we all read quite well; we learned at home by recognizing whole words in the Sears, Roebuck catalog, which also served as our major art source. From the photographs of models and things in that catalog we made up dramas which lasted for months.

The kid I met by the flagpole that first day of school was a total stranger. He lived more than ten miles away to the south, an enormous distance at a time when folks drained the crankcases of their cars, trucks and tractors in late October; removed the wheels and put the vehicles up on blocks. We used horses to get around until the following April. He told me about fishing, something I had never done. He stood there in his new bib overalls and told marvelous stories of dragging in huge Northern Pike until the teacher rang the bell and we entered the little school.

In March 1948 farms around Hannover plugged into electric power with the miracle of

A Country School Pupil Remembers — Hazel Bendix Schlanger

I was six years old when I started school in 1915. The school was 1 1/2 miles south of our Bendix homestead in Billings County. Sometimes it was called the Bendix School, sometimes the Little Knife Butte School. There was a butte about 1/4 mile from the school. The school yard included a little draw with trees in it, an ideal place for the pupils to play.

My first teacher was Charles Geesaman, a tall, thin man with a wife and two children. He lived about 4 miles west of the school and usually rode horseback to school. All the students were very fond of him; he was strict but just and had a sense of humor. We were never afraid of him but we respected him. He told us so many stories about the Spanish American War that it seemed like we were all in it. His lessons were full of stories and we learned so much better than just by reading the book. Many years later I used those same methods when I taught, I found them very satisfactory. There were usually about 25 pupils in school in all grades. We stood before him for classes. Sometimes when it was too warm in school we felt faint. One day Jennie Jagol did faint.

The other pupils that attended all the eight years I went to school were from the Tachenko, Jagol, Dodo, and Wallace families. From time to time other folk moved into the community and sent their children to school. We were not very kind to the newcomers.

My sister Ethel and I walked to Tachenko's farm, then joined the five boys and walked the rest of the way with them. If it was very cold Mrs. T, as we called her, stuck our feet in her kitchen-range oven and gave us something to eat before we went on. She didn't speak English but we understood each other.

Sometimes there was frost on the fence and we'd lick it off with our tongues. We learned, by having some skin taken off, not to lick too close to the wire. Once a pint of milk froze and broke in Ethel's pocket. One morning our dad was hitching up the team to the sled to take us to school. The horses started shivering from the cold, it was 40 degrees below zero. Our dad said, "To hell with going to school today." That was a pleasant decision for us.

We enjoyed our walks home with the Tachenko boys. Part of the way other students walked with us. We took notice of Mother Nature: spring and fall flowers, birds, the first crows and cranes and geese in the spring and

continued on next page

281

fall. We learned so many things. Those experiences helped us in later life.

We had such fun recesses and noons. We didn't always play organized games. Sometimes the boys would snare or drown out gophers but we never killed them. We hitched them together with string and drove them like horses. We were taught, both at school and at home, not to be cruel. Mostly we did things we made up. We slid down Little Knife Butte at least twice before the bell rang at noon. (How little we knew then that Little Knife would be the heart of oil country in later years.) In spring we ran down a slope, jumped the running little creek, ran up the other side and back across the creek again. Sometimes we slipped and fell into the water. Then we ran to school to dry or got dry by sun and wind. Mr. Geesaman never told us we couldn't play there. (Years later when I taught there I let the pupils do the same thing.) We climbed trees, played Hide and Seek in the brush, and played Cowboys and Indians. Sometimes we played Annie Over, Pom Pom Pull Away, Stealing Sticks, and Prisoners Base. Our favorite was Kick the Can. Mr. Geesaman always played that with us, he was such fun and so fast.

At Tachenko's there was a creek we had to cross. In spring it was a raging stream. Nick, the oldest boy, took the small ones across on a gentle horse, two or three at a time.

We girls usually wore dresses. If we wore pants to school we usually took them off when we got there. Mostly the girls wore black sateen bloomers under their dresses. How much more sensibly we would have been dressed had we worn overalls all the time. In the cold winter weather we had long underwear which to this day I can remember hating.

Our school was painted white. There was a belfry but no bell. It only proved a good place for balls to lodge. The older boys had to climb up on the barn, then onto the school, scoot across its length and get that misthrown ball down. There was a coal shed on the east side with a small one-horse barn tacked on. Later there was a larger barn built on the grounds to stable three or four horses.

There were two toilets out back, boys on the south, girls on the north.

We had no water except what we brought from home. We were allowed to hold chunks of snow against the heater's hot sides. Then we sucked the water out of the chunks. What a mess we made around that stove. Sometimes we brought corn to school and put it on the hot stove top to

continued on next page

REA (Rural Electrification Administration). Milking machines transformed the lives of that community of Holstein dairy farmers who sold their cream sweet to a cooperative they owned; with electric power, the time necessary to do chores was less than half. But no one I knew had indoor plumbing. We bathed on Saturday night next to the coal stove, and we changed our clothes once a week as well, usually. We talked a good deal about hygiene in those one-room schools.

Hannover was more than a church and two schools. There was the general store with the post office inside where candy bars were a nickel and pop a dime, the creamery across the road, a huge implement/hardware business, and my mother's parents, Grandma and Grandpa Henke who lived right in town in a little house with a much bigger barn. The "little" school teachers stayed at my Grandma Henke's place. Although the first four grades were public, the school board was very much Missouri Synod Lutheran, so they sought teachers trained by the church.

In the fall of 1949, I fell hopelessly in love with my second-grade teacher, a dark-haired beauty, who happened to share my left-handedness. The few times my first-grade teacher actually had us sitting in our desks, she had forced me to write with my right hand — something I found absolutely impossible to do. When told it was natural to write left-handed, I turned to scribbling with a vengeance. I'll never forget the day I discovered carbon paper. I slipped the blank sheet beneath the carbon and started to trace a drawing of the strange, incredibly clean Jane in the reader. Then, to my utter shame and total humiliation, I discovered that I had placed the carbon wrong-side-up and traced the image in the book. I carried my shame in secret for a week before I finally confessed — and immediately wet my bib overalls in relief. She never told, not even when asked rather pointed questions about my deportment by my grandmother at Sunday dinner the same week. She also found books, ordered books from the State Library in Bismarck to supplement the thirty catechisms, old encyclopedia, and old text books which were our total library. I'll never forget her for introducing me to Daniel Defoe's *The Life and Strange Surprizing Adventures of Robinson Crusoe, of York, Mariner: Who lived Eight and Twenty Years, all alone in an uninhabited Island on the Coast of America, near the Mouth of the Great River of Oroonoque; Having been cast on Shore by Shipwreck, wherein all the Men perished but himself. With An Account how he was at last as strangely deliver'd by Pyrates.* What a boon that book was, for the snow came again, and there was no mail for more than a week in March 1950.

But most weeks, new books would arrive from the State Library, and I learned that I could order them myself, in the summer as well (in 1950, there was no spring, for it snowed through most of May, and farmers didn't get into the fields until June). Miss Roegge taught me how to write letters to a woman at the State Library to ask for books — and even let me do it left-handed. I could return them in three weeks for a mere three cents a pound — "Library Rate." The return label was packed inside with the total postage necessary marked. Years later — the sixth grade, I think, about the time "under God" was added to the Pledge — I actually went to the library and met the woman who sent all those books. She took me through the stacks — room after room of books on every conceivable subject.

parch. That was our recess lunch, it held us till noon.

We did lots of board work. We wrote spelling words, did our arithmetic and drew maps on the blackboard. We worked in pairs or threes at the board. One would pronounce the words in a whisper and the others wrote them. The chalk and erasers flew, and chatter flew back and forth, too, but Mr. Geesaman never cared as long as we learned to spell. Some of our later teachers made us be quiet and learn by ourselves. Somehow that was an end of an era. We were not happy with the new system of quiet and studying alone and I don't think we ever learned as well after that.

I think we have a more practical approach to problems and living because we were brought up in a country school. We all worked for ourselves and didn't depend on others to keep us fed, housed, and clothed.

When I look back on my country school days I believe they were eight of the happiest years of my life. Youth is so joyous, we had ideals in school and home and goals we wanted to reach. There was no conflict between home and school. Things were not as permissive as they are today.

✎✎

Carol Roegge left when the snow and ice finally melted in June 1950. She was far from the typical country school teacher in Oliver County, for she had been to college for several years. That spring at the Log Cabin in Center, next to the monument to Hazel Miner, anyone eighteen-years-old with a high school diploma could take a test and become a teacher if they brought their "own pen, ink, and blotters. Fee is $2.00," reported *The Center Republican*.

The students of the Hannover "little" school (public) in 1949-50 with teacher Carol Roegge *(author second row, second from right [photo from author's collection])* The public school closed in 1973, the parochial school in 1979.

The big school was taught by Theodore Kaelberer, who grew up on a farm near New Salem some twenty miles away. He too had gone off to college. He taught for more than thirty years, from 1929 to 1963 with but one year off, and retired in the community he served as organist in the church, choir director, and piano teacher only after his health failed. Whether or not they could afford the fifty cents for piano lessons, every child who went to St. Peter's Lutheran School at Hannover learned to play the piano unless they absolutely willed themselves not to. They also learned to read music, to play ball (boys and girls together), to sing "Silent Night" in German, and to consider the possibility of other people in other places being as human as we, including Catholics, Indians, Tibetans, and even the devil-possessed Communists. Almost single-handedly, Ted Kalberer insidiously taught tolerance and a love of learning about the other to his students from two generations of families who lived in a community built upon an unquestioned faith in the rightness of their church's reading of the Bible.

Teacher
Theodore
Kaelberer
*(author's
collection)*

We learned not to judge too quickly, not to presume too much. Behind the creamery where our fathers gathered each morning after dropping us off at school lived Schuster Fritz, a bachelor who made and repaired harnesses, shoes, and worked with all things leather. Schuster Fritz didn't go to church. Surely, we thought, he was destined to go to the worst of places when he died, for people who didn't go to church were not even buried in the consecrated ground of the cemetery into which one could hit a home run batting left-handed when the wind was from the south.

One day Mr. Kaelberer addressed our conclusion summed up in the rhyme,

One, two, three, four, five, six, seven,
All the good people go to heaven;
When they get there, they will yell,
"Schuster Fritz, Schuster Fritz, went to hell!"

Mr. Kaelberer began by asking us whether Fritz had ever harmed us. "Never." Did we like going to his shop? "Of course." Did we need Schuster Fritz in Hannover? "Dumb question (although we would never have said such to Mr. Kaelberer)." He strongly suggested that we look to our own relationship with God instead of worrying about Schuster Fritz's. He also had us sing our standard closing song, even though it was the middle of morning:

If I have wounded any soul today,
If I have caused one foot to go astray,
If I have walked in my own willful way,
Dear Lord, forgive.

Forgive the sins I have confessed to thee,
Forgive the secret sins I do not see,
O guide me, love me, and my keeper be,
Dear Lord, forgive.

I'm not sure that some of those in the community who were the self-appointed guardians of our morality would have forgiven Mr. Kaelberer for letting us know about such as evolution and a universe possibly billions of years old. More than forty years

later, I recall his leading us through a book commissioned by the church which offered a pseudo-scientific defense of a universe created less than six thousand years ago, about 4,000 B.C., which in the early 1950s meant "Before Christ" with capital letters, not "before the common era." As we considered the possibility that the Great Flood survived by Noah and his family and two of every kind was solely responsible for the oil and coal desposits, Mr. Kalberer had other possibilities in that one-room school in books from the State Library, and, I suspect, from his private collection. Moreover, he was there to talk about alternatives to the official line with students who found the literal interpretation of the Bible too limiting.

Among the most memorable windows to a greater world beyond that township were the movies brought in for very special occasions, such as Halloween. The big windows would be covered with black, a decrepit 16mm projector plugged in, and the entire community would join us for an evening of a cartoon or two followed by a film feature from the 1920s or 1930s. We became actors and actresses ourselves in productions of vignettes from American history — the first Thanksgiving was among the favorites. I carried the message from Miles Standish to Patricia Mullens in an adaptation of Longfellow's "The Courtship of Miles Standish" and stood there speechless when told, "Speak for yourself, John."

We played ball in the fall and the spring — and occasionally played baseball with just the boys while the girls did something else, but more often kitten ball which all could play. We went outside in all but the bitterest of winter days to play "Fox and Geese" or have snowball fights from elaborate fortifications. Each spring we loaded into cars and traveled to a real park in a town where there was a lot more equipment than our six swings and two teeter-totters and a stream where we could fish before and after enjoying a feast of fried chicken, hot dogs, every conceivable hot dish and dessert, and ice cream. We exchanged valentines and those little hearts printed with such as "Be mine!" We raised a bit of money for equipment and books by selling Christmas cards published by the Missouri Synod and spent weeks preparing for the program held Christmas Eve at the church.

We great-grandchildren of the German-Americans of the Lutheran persuasion did not join the Young Citizens League or the Boy Scouts because the Lutheran Church Missouri Synod did not condone our joining with those not of our faith in anything which could even remotely be considered a religious exercise. We did have 4-H, because our leaders came from our church.

Theodore Kaelberer (back right) with his seventeen fifth to eighth graders at St. Peter's Lutheran School in Hannover in 1954-55 (author third boy to the left of teacher [from the author's collection])

A Country School Teacher Remembers — Clara Grubb

The most memorable event in my country school teaching career happened in the spring of 1929 while we were preparing for a school program. One of my sixth grade boys had gotten a team of horses and a wagon, without the wagon box, to haul lumber for a stage we were building. The lumber was borrowed from the local yard that was located in town, two miles away. As the boys were unloading the last plank, my first grade boy sat down on the wagon frame between the two front wheels. It was his dad's horse and wagon so he felt secure. A dog began to bark and the horses started running across the school yard, over a ditch, and up the road in the opposite direction of their home. The reins were dragging on the ground. When my pupils and I saw what was happening we all gave chase, first the older pupils, then the teacher, and last the smaller children who were crying. I thought as I ran, "We'll never have our program tomorrow night!" But it ended happily. The horses ran about a mile to a neighbor's barn and stopped. The little first grader was rescued unhurt by the farmer. Our program was held as scheduled.

We did what our parents and even some of our grandparents had done at that country school. But Mr. Kalberer was a visionary, for he anticipated the changes, the revolution which would come to Hannover Township with the paved roads, television, and high school for a generation less than half of whom would follow their parents into farming. He knew that many of us would leave home and a way of life which had not changed since the six square miles were settled seventy years before. We faced changes as great as the Missouri River dammed to the north in the early 1950s. The horse barn stood empty by the time I took the state exams in geography, arithmetic, English and social studies in May 1956, and my Dad winterized the car and drove it all winter. There were two bathrooms in the basement of the big school (in the little school as well), indoor plumbing in our farmhouse, and we talked about what we had seen on Milton Berle over our lunch from the black buckets — Cloverdale baloney on homemade bread sandwiches.

The questions we drew from the cigar box on Friday afternoons in our weekly half-hour treat, a Jeopardy like version of baseball, began to change as well. We divided into teams, fifth-graders through eighth-graders, and drew questions marked "single," "double," "triple," and "home run." The double for correctly naming the book of the Bible between Nahum and Zephaniah was still there — a give-away groaner for any kid from St. Peter's Lutheran. But there were fewer questions which identified the major breeds of hogs or hybrids of wheat, which we still memorized for our seventh-grade state exams in agriculture — every girl and boy at St. Peter's knew a Duroc Jersey from a Chester White and which resulted in the leaner bacon, and we knew that cows other than the black and white Holstein could be milked — even though only the most eccentric among us actually put a Jersey into a milking stanchion. Knowing that the Brooklyn Dodgers finally beat the New York Yankees in the 1955 World Series was only a single, but it was a double to know that the minimum wage was now an astonishing full one dollar (except for agricultural workers, of course, including Mr. Kalberer who donned bib overalls himself and drove a tractor as a hired hand in the summer). We could hit a home run by identifying Rosa Parks as the woman who refused to give up her seat on the bus to a white man, something we could learn by reading the *Time* magazine Mr. Kalberer brought to the classroom.

We knew more than facts, and we had learned to question even the ready answers to nearly every question provided in the religion workbooks we kept in that separate room where we gathered every morning for about forty-five minutes. We had learned by teaching others, for Mr. Kalberer expected everyone of us to teach those in the grades below, including the fifth graders who went back to the little school to help out from time to time.

The rooms of two schools in Hannover Township could have been a Black Hole, had it not been for the extraordinary teachers, Miss Roegge and Mr. Kalberer. In

A Country School Teacher Remembers —Gladys Thoe Brash

During my 47 years of teaching my most challenging and satisfying years were the 17 years I spent in rural schools. I was thrilled and excited the first day of school in the fall of 1924 in South Minnewaukan District School No. 3 in Ramsey County.

No other preparation was required at that time beyond high school where a course in Rural School Methods was offered. I knew all the pupils since they were all neighbors of my family. I had 12 pupils, 7 boys and 5 girls, in grades 1 to 8. A memorable incident was the first visit of County Superintendent of Schools Hazel McKay. During the recess period while she was in conference with me in the schoolhouse, the boys tied a rope all around her car. I was mortified and scared, but, of course, no harm was done and they removed it when I asked them to. Miss McKay wrote me a wonderful letter when she got back to her office that gave me more confidence, and her constructive criticism was helpful.

Two "fun" things we had at the schools I taught were to receive big boxes of library books from the State Library at Bismarck and listening to a half hour story program on the radio on Friday afternoon. The country school provided a good foundation in the basics before high school. The main defect was the lack of cultural development. Music and art were sadly neglected; many teachers lacked training, didn't have musical abilities, or didn't have enough time.

a community intellectually inbred with dour dogmatism, they alone invited such questions as "Why?" and "What if?" It was a time when excellence was measured by the ability to memorize dates, hard-to-spell words, pages of patriotic poems, varieties of wheat and breeds of hogs; when being able to diagram a complex sentence was much more important than being able to write one anyone would want to read; when memorization of the multiplication tables was mandatory and memorizing *Luther's Small Catechism* in its totality was the mark of the extraordinary scholar. It was a time when many men who found themselves teaching country school were of the ilk which gave rise to the turn-of-the-century saying, "A man who had failed at everything bought himself a birch rod and became a teacher."

Many parents believed in strong discipline, including corporal punishment. There was in fact a leather shaving strap which hung next to Mr. Kalberer's desk, but I don't remember him ever using it. He didn't even use it the day one among us confessed to putting the giant dill pickle in the drain in the new basement floor and caused a flood of the new coal furnace and the bathrooms. He didn't take down the strap when he discovered the peep hole cut between the boys' and girls' restrooms in the basement. But I will never forget the day he picked it up and stood over me because I refused to tell him how many pounds were in a ton. "You know," he said. "Why won't you answer?"

"Because it's here in the beginning of the dictionary," I said.

He put the strap away and said, "Stay here after lunch."

"Two thousand," I said quickly.

"Stay here after the rest go out to play ball anyway," he said with a laugh. We went on to recite the number of acres in a section, rods in a mile, and pounds in a bushel of wheat.

Our discussion after lunch was short. "You're teaching fifth-grade arithmetic for the next two weeks," he said. "Every day, I expect you to come in with a word problem that depends upon knowing how many pounds there are in a ton."

"What do I do if they ask me how many pounds there are?" I asked.

"They'll all remember two thousand," he said, "but if they don't, tell them to look at the beginning of the dictionary."

He taught what he was supposed to teach, of course. The course of study mandated by the Department of Public Instruction stressed the fundamentals. We were tested on the facts in exams of true and false, fill in the blanks, and multiple choice in the state-sanctioned finals. As a called and ordained teacher of the Lutheran Church, Missouri Synod, St. Peter's congregation, he taught us the dogma as well.

Yet, somehow, he found a way to encourage independent thought, creative writing, and an appreciation for music. He knew his students and found a way to develop each one in a special way — some of the boys learned how to throw a curve ball because of hours of after-school sessions with Ted Kaelberer, for example. He did more, much more. For many of us, he was our only hope for escape from a life by the numbers and values by rote. He alone, except for Miss Roegge in 1949 and my folks at home, invited me to ask "Why?" and "How?" instead of the "When and where, how many and how much — exactly?" which was the stuff of learning as usual in country schools.

He wrote me a letter in a special newspaper the entire school prepared when I was sick at home in the winter of 1953-54 — "Moments of this kind come to all people, even to young folks, but like all things, these moments have their purpose too. . . . We can be sure that Joseph at times felt very discouraged. But didn't it all work out for good?"

It did, Mr. Kaelberer, it did. I appreciated not only your letter, but also the drawing you sent of the flower with all the parts carefully labeled which helped me get a great grade on the seventh-grade state exams when I got back to school, I wish I had told you just how much you gave me, but even as I begin to regret, I remember how you ended every day of school with all mistakes forgiven. That things in my life worked out is in no small part thanks to you. Thank you.

Playing ball in
at a rural
school in
Grand Forks
County in
1937-38
(SHSND)

About the Editors

Warren A. Henke

A NATIVE NORTH DAKOTAN WHO GREW UP IN THE SMALL TOWN of New Salem, Warren A. Henke taught schools in his home state his entire academic career, including twenty-seven years teaching history at Bismarck State College. Also active outside the classroom, Henke was involved in 1972-73 in establishing the state partner of the National Endowment for the Humanities, the North Dakota Humanities Council, which he served as Chair, committee member for six years, and participant in many of its programs.

Henke, who holds a Ph.D. from the University of New Mexico, edited two previous works: *Prairie Politics: Parties and Platforms in North Dakota, 1889-1914*, and *Our Towns*, brief histories of 125 North Dakota communities. He also contributed chapters to the seminal work on North Dakota's ethnic history, *Plains Folk*, and to *The Centennial Anthology of North Dakota History*. He continues his profession as an active book reviewer and participant in regional historical conferences as well as research into North Dakota topics. Henke lives with his wife Rose Marie in Bismarck. A retired fourth-grade teacher, she continues to be active in community affairs. Called *Babushka* ("grandmother") by Ukrainian refugee families, she was named a *Bismarck Tribune* Award winner in 1992 for her work with them.

Everett C. Albers

ALBERS HAS SERVED AS THE EXECUTIVE DIRECTOR of the North Dakota Humanities Council since it began in 1973. He is one of the founders of the modern Chautauqua movement which features first-person characterizations of historical writers and thinkers presented in tents during summer tours of the Great Plains. He grew up on a family farm in Oliver County. Albers and his wife Leslie live in Bismarck. They have two children, Albert and Gretchen. Albers has edited two collections of memories by North Dakota seniors, *Aging: Winds of Change* and *Mostly Amusing, Always Amazingly True Memories*. He also co-edits the series *The Way It Was: The North Dakota Frontier Experience*. He operates Otto Design, a desktop publishing concern, as an avocation.

Index

Names

— — — — Names Index Continued — — — —

Counties

Towns & Cities

School Districts

Schools Attended by Teachers (*Listed by Present Name*)

Religious Denominations Mentioned

Ethnic Groups Mentioned

Miscellaneous Index

Contributors

Students play fox and geese during recess at a rural Morton County school in the 1930s *(Farm Security Administration photograph)*